BEARING WITNESS

BEARING WITNESS

Memories of Arkansas Slavery
Narratives from the 1930s WPA Collections

Edited by George E. Lankford

THE UNIVERSITY OF ARKANSAS PRESS
FAYETTEVILLE
2003

Copyright © 2003 by The University of Arkansas Press

07 06 05 04 03   5 4 3 2 1

Designer: John Coghlan

⊖ The paper used in this publication meets the minimum requirements of
the American National Standard for Permanence of Paper for Printed Library
Materials Z39.48-1984.

Library of Congress Cataloging-in-Publication Data
Bearing witness : memories of Arkansas slavery : narratives from the 1930s
WPA collections / edited by George E. Lankford.
    p. cm.
Includes bibliographical references and index.
    ISBN 1-55728-747-3 (pbk. : alk. paper)
    1. Slaves—Arkansas—Biography. 2. African Americans—Arkansas—
Interviews. 3. Arkansas—Biography. 4. African Americans—Arkansas—
History—Sources. I. Lankford, George E., 1938–
II. Federal Writers' Project.
    E445.A8 B43 2003
    976.7004'96'07300922—dc21

                   2002156541

Contents

Introduction

In the relatively brief history of the United States some dark clouds hang over the paths to the present. One of the largest and darkest of them is African American slavery. In attempting to penetrate the darkness, scholars have produced a great deal of words and ink, but the academic insights have had only limited influence, for their consumers are a small percentage of the population. Yet it remains important for each generation and each individual, not just the limited group of historians, to confront that dark period as directly as possible, if for no other reason than to appreciate the sheer alienness of it. For most people, the ideal experience would be to converse with the actual participants in the American phenomenon of slavery, especially ancestors on the land where the new generations now live.

In 1977, as a folklorist and local historian in north Arkansas, I thought I was finally able to do that. I held the four Arkansas volumes of ex-slave narratives in my hand for the first time. As I read, I realized with chagrin that I was not reading *Arkansas* testimony, but the stories of men and women from other states who had moved to Arkansas in postwar years. As they were at that time, the volumes of testimony were virtually unusable for my local historical interests. Unknown to me then, the editor of the published volumes already recognized my problem; he knew the publication's organization did not serve the needs of the local historians (Rawick 1977, 1:xl). I sadly set the books aside, vowing that I would return to them some day to reorganize them as the narratives of *Arkansas* slaves, if no other researcher did the task in the intervening years. Twenty-five years have passed, and no one has done so. This book is the result. My hope is that Arkansas historians and family researchers will find it helpful in understanding slavery in this state.

For American slavery in general, of course, there are some much used sources, such as public documents and the writings of slave owners, as well as the writings of white people who opposed the "peculiar institution." There are also voices from the other side of the racial divide, in particular the writings of African Americans who emerged from slavery as articulate chroniclers and interpreters and who recorded their memories and their thoughts. These literary slave narratives have also been much used by both literary and historical scholars. For more than a half century another body of evidence has existed, but it has been much less utilized than the other sources. In a brief period of time—largely between 1936 and 1938—a great many interviews were conducted with elderly African American men and women who had lived as slaves. This extraordinary project documented the testimony of people who otherwise would have gone to their graves without leaving behind a record of their experiences. These interviews, when added to the literary slave narratives, comprise an impressive corpus of personal testimony. In 1985 a team of historians was led to conclude that "the written and oral accounts of slavery known collectively as 'Afro-American Slave Narratives' have no parallel in the Western tradition in terms of sheer scope of testimony" (Davis and Gates 1985, 35). That same year, however, another historian pointed out that despite decades of the existence and availability of the interview collection, "historians have almost completely neglected these materials" (Woodward 1985, 48f).

There are several reasons for this neglect. One is the general distrust of oral testimony in historical research. The oral history movement in the historical fraternity only began a decade after the slave narrative project was conducted, and historians who are willing to work their way through the thickets of evidentiary problems in oral testimony are still in the minority today. Another reason for the neglect of these slave testimonies lies in the peculiarities in the way in which these materials were collected. These difficulties will be surveyed in a later section of this introduction, but it is fair to say that they are daunting for anyone seeking to establish reliability of evidence. Then, too, the materials have been difficult to use. The slave interviews were not published until the 1970s, and then they were printed only as state collections (Rawick 1972, 1977, 1979). Those state collections, moreover, were put forth in three separate published series, due to the difficulties of locating the materials, which had been scattered through many repositories. An index to the collection, as editor George Rawick promised, was published at the end of the Greenwood Press sequence of forty-one volumes, but it is only of limited use. It is symptomatic of the historical neglect that the Arkansas Writers' Project and the collection it produced have only been mentioned in the *Arkansas Historical Quarterly* in the form of references in a single brief article and an even shorter note signaling the publication of the index to *The American Slave* (Van Deburg 1976; *Arkansas Historical Quarterly* 41, no. 4 (1982): 361–62).

This new publication of the Arkansas materials is an attempt to make the testimony of those who experienced slavery in antebellum Arkansas more readily available, in order that the narratives can be examined at firsthand by a greater number of readers. Before the Arkansas narratives are introduced, however, it is important to become familiar with the details of the extraordinary project which produced the collection.

The Federal Writers' Project

As the Great Depression deepened in the 1930s, the New Deal programs expanded to include segments of the population which had not earlier been targeted for relief. Among them were artists and writers, whose talents were to be put to use in accomplishing cultural tasks. The Works Progress Administration (WPA) set up a program under its umbrella to oversee the new initiative. In 1935 the Federal Writers' Project (FWP) was created and given various assignments, including the writing of state guidebooks, histories, and folklore collections. It was determined that a state focus was more appropriate for that kind of localized work, and state offices of the FWP were set up across the country. As the FWP began to produce collections of information and writing from the states, it became clear that there was a need for an administrative emphasis on the hiring of Negro writers. In 1936 Sterling Brown, English professor at Howard University, was appointed national editor of Negro affairs, and he began to push for collecting and writing in the Negro communities in states where they existed in strength.

The FWP inherited the idea of such projects from earlier pioneers at Fisk University, whose collections were subsequently included in *The American Slave* as volumes 18 and 19. The immediate ancestor of the FWP endeavor was the Federal Emergency Relief Administration's work. One historian of the New Deal summarized it this way:

> The Writers' Project also helped to promote the first Negro studies to be conducted in the United States on an extensive scale. The most significant, gathering ex-slave narratives, began a year before the Project came into being, in 1934, under the auspices of the Federal Emergency Relief Administration, and chiefly at the instigation of Lawrence D. Reddick, a Negro history professor at Kentucky State Industrial College.... By the time the Writers' Project inherited the undertaking, it had been extended to eighteen states and involved the services of a number of Negro researchers. (Mangione 1972, 257)

When the FWP took over the task of collecting the narratives of former slaves in 1936, the state offices were already far along in their other tasks, such as preparing state guidebooks and collecting historical lore. Since some of their

collected materials fell in the realm of folklore, which was also the major discipline which specialized in interviewing, it must have seemed natural for the
FWP's national folklore editor, John A. Lomax, to take the slave narrative
project under his wing. Thus it was Lomax who "issued to Project field workers a set of 'detailed and homely questions' designed to 'get the Negro thinking and talking about the days of slavery'" (Mangione 1972, 263).

Henry Alsberg, the national director of the FWP, actively took part in the
direction of the slave narrative project, writing the state directors frequently
to ask about their progress and to suggest approaches and techniques. He also
urged the state directors to hire Negro writers and researchers, but, as
Mangione noted, a number of them, "swayed by local prejudices, showed no
inclination to comply with his directives" (Mangione 1972, 257).

The new initiative—the collecting of narratives from ex-slaves—had a
short life span, from 1936 to 1939. In the latter year Alsberg was fired as director of the Federal Writers' Project. When Sterling Brown resigned from the
FWP the next year, the Negro emphasis came to an end (Mangione 1972, 262).

From 1939 to 1941 Benjamin Botkin, who had replaced Lomax, "served
as chief editor of the Library of Congress Writers' Unit which sifted through
thousands of folklore and ex-slave manuscripts prepared by the Project
throughout the nation, and organized them for deposit in the library"
(Mangione 1972, 275). The result was that the almost twenty-two hundred
ex-slave narratives, typed, were put together into seventeen volumes and
placed in the Library of Congress, where they were available to the few
researchers who sought them out. Botkin himself was the first major scholar
to publish the materials. In 1945, having read all ten thousand pages of the
collection, he was able to publish his classic study of slave folklore, *Lay My
Burden Down*, based upon the FWP materials.

In the Library of Congress the collection languished for years, consulted
by only a few historians, such as Norman Yetman, whose 1970 study of the
FWP narratives is a classic still in print (2000). The collection was difficult to
use and forbidding in size. Moreover, the collection was not even in a single
location. Mangione warned in 1972, before Rawick had begun the arduous
task of tracking down all the scattered typescripts of the FWP interviews, that
"not all of the ex-slave narratives recorded by the Federal Writers' Project are
in the Library of Congress collection. Many additional narratives came in
after 1939 and were relegated to the WPA storage collection of the Library of
Congress. Some of the states involved in the Project retained the narratives
(Louisiana and Virginia among them) in specially designated depositories"
(1972, 263).

It was George P. Rawick, historian at Washington University in St. Louis, who undertook to ameliorate the situation, beginning in 1963. With the support of grants and an agreement with the Greenwood Press, Rawick put together a team who gathered the materials in the Library of Congress and prepared them for publication. The first publication (herein designated the *Main Series*) was in nineteen volumes (Rawick 1972). The opening volume, *From Sundown to Sunup*, was a study of slavery by Rawick and served as an introduction to the collection. The next sixteen volumes were the FWP narratives, published as they were found, as originally typed and with editorial notes included (Rawick 1977, 1:ix). The organization was by the states which had submitted the materials. The final two volumes in the series were, as already noted, the earlier ex-slave narratives collected by researchers at Fisk University.

Aware of the caveat mentioned by Mangione, Rawick then began the task of locating and preparing for publication the remainder of the FWP materials. Narratives from the Archive of American Folksong and WPA storage of the Library of Congress were published in another twelve-volume set, the *Supplement, Series 1,* by Rawick and the Greenwood Press in 1977. Rawick's task was still not complete, however, because there were likely to be other materials still in the hands of various state archives, because it appeared that not all the interview texts had been sent to Washington. Rawick had his suspicions early on: "I noted that there were only 174 pages of narratives for Mississippi, a total of twenty-six interviews. . . . I surmised either that the project had been deliberately curtailed by those who did not want such material in existence or that the bulk of the collection had never been sent to the national offices of the Federal Writers' Project in Washington, as they should have been, and might still be somewhere in Mississippi. Both guesses turned out to be correct" (1977, 1:xi). Rawick and his team sought out the materials retained by Mississippi and other states at the closing of the local FWP offices, and in 1979 they were able to publish the final collection, which consisted of both duplicate or alternate typescripts and new material. Greenwood Press published the final ten volumes as *Supplement, Series 2* (Rawick 1979). Shortly thereafter was issued the long awaited index to the entire published collection, which made the forty-one volumes a little easier to use. Rawick's sense of relief was evident in his comment in the introduction to the *Supplement, Series 2:* "There may be more ex-slave narratives somewhere from the Federal Writers' Project, but at this point I have no reason to believe any more exist. . . . [It] appears that this collection completes a body of work begun in 1963" (1979, xii).

Thanks to the work of Rawick and his colleagues, the ex-slave narratives were published and were generally available four decades after the close of the original collection project, at a time when it was unlikely that any of the original informants were still alive. The Rawick publications thus gave new life to voices which had been forever stilled or hidden in archival obscurity. The importance of the publication of the materials was indicated by the fact that the *Main Series* was reprinted by the Scholarly Press only five years after the original publication, and many libraries possess that edition rather than the out-of-print original. (Note: Those who use the Scholarly Press edition should be aware that the omission of Rawick's opening volume in the reprint has led to a change in the numbering of the volumes. Thus, for example, Rawick's volume 8 became volume 7 in the Scholarly Press edition. This is unfortunate, for it means that readers must be wary as they make or use source notations for the *Main Series*.)

Despite problems with the transcripts, problems which will be surveyed below, the fact remains that some two thousand former slaves were interviewed, with a written report of the information gathered. As sheer information, albeit information which must be judiciously sifted by historians in much the same way that documents must be assessed, the collection has no equal in the history of the study of slavery. The marvel of the collection is that it was done in such a brief period of time by hundreds of researchers at the instigation of the federal government. It was quite literally a massive recovery effort at the last possible moment. It produced a volume of material so great that it has still not been thoroughly utilized by historians and remains virtually unknown to the general public.

The Arkansas Project

The goal of this newly organized volume of the narratives of former slaves in Arkansas is to make it easier for researchers to use the materials to shed more light on the slavery era in Arkansas. This collection is not simply a reprint of the Rawick volumes, because there were several peculiarities of the Arkansas FWP ex-slave narratives which needed to be addressed in pulling together this material.

One peculiarity was noticeable right from the beginning. In Rawick's *Main Series,* the Arkansas collection comprised three and a half of the sixteen volumes of testimony. The simple fact was that the Arkansas FWP office produced a prodigious amount of interviews and written reports. The very success of the Arkansas team skewed the collection. Escott noted in 1979, "One of the oddities of the Federal Writers' Project was that the most extensive state project was in Arkansas, a state which had a small population and relatively few slaves in 1860. Nevertheless, because local officials proved ambitious and industrious, almost seven hundred interviews originated in that state" (1979, 12). Woodward made the same observation, with statistics: "The states included are very disproportionately represented. Arkansas, which never had more than 3.5 per cent of the slave population, furnished about 33 per cent of the ex-slaves interviewed, while Mississippi, which in 1860 contained more than 10 per cent of the slaves, is represented by little more than 1 per cent of those interviewed" (1985, 50; see also Blassingame 1985, 89). For researchers attempting to achieve a general understanding of slavery, this is a problem, for the Arkansas collection, by its sheer size, takes on more importance than it deserves statistically.

As if to balance the statistical misrepresentation, however, the Arkansas testimonies are not really from Arkansas slaves. Fewer than half of the interviews conducted in Arkansas in the original project were with people who had been slaves in the state. "The vast majority of former slaves who were interviewed in 'the land of opportunity' had moved there after the Civil War," Escott pointed out (1979, 12). His explanation was simple: there was a postbellum population shift which was not accounted for in the state organization of the FWP interviews. "The former slaves had continued to migrate away from the upper South, border states, and cotton areas just east of the Mississippi River and had headed west, primarily to Arkansas, Texas, or Oklahoma" (Escott 1979, 163). The Arkansas collection, therefore, was more a reflection of *Southern* slavery than slavery in antebellum Arkansas itself.

Rawick himself had made the same point, which he found to be a positive aspect of the Arkansas collection. "[B]ecause most of the black people in Arkansas in 1937, when the interviews were written, had moved to that state from all the other southern states after the end of the Civil War, this collection offers a particularly rich sample of slave experience from throughout the south. Scholars interested in slavery in any southern state would do well to consult the Arkansas collection" (Rawick 1979, 1:Part 3: I). For anyone attempting to find the testimony of Arkansas slaves, of course, this is not so positive a situation. This new volume is addressed to that particular need, for all of the narratives included here are those which were given by people who had been slaves in Arkansas, regardless of where they lived when they were interviewed. All available narratives have been examined for indications of an Arkansas origin of the informant, and those which appeared to meet the criterion have been included in this Arkansas volume.

Most of the narratives, it should be noted, are still from the Arkansas Writers' Project collection, but they have been augmented by those from other states. More importantly, those Arkansas interviews which were not with former Arkansas slaves have been omitted. One thing seems clear—the interviewers of the Arkansas Writers' Project were not particular about the origins of their informants. If they seemed to be good informants, were ex-slaves, and were available, the eager Arkansas team interviewed them. The result was an outstanding collection of narratives.

The details of how the Arkansas Writers' Project group of workers did it make an interesting tale. A lot of the credit goes to the director. The person hired as director of the Arkansas Writers' Project was Bernie Babcock, a sixty-seven-year-old writer in Little Rock who had some twenty books to her credit by 1931. As one of the most prolific published writers in Arkansas, she was a logical choice for the job. In 1935 she applied for the position of director of the Arkansas office of the Federal Writers' Project and was hired. She proved to be an efficient administrator and a hard worker.

Starting in November of 1935, Babcock followed the directives of the national FWP office and hired a small team of researchers who were set to work gathering information about the history of the state. The national emphasis on folklore was also part of the Arkansas project, and interviewers began to collect oral traditions about the state. The budget apparently never permitted a large staff at any one time, but there was a serial total of nineteen, both full- and part-time, through the three years of Babcock's directorship. She was replaced as director in December 1938, although she continued as a writer for the project for a time after that. Her full-time workers from the beginning were Irene Robertson, Samuel S. Taylor, and Bernice Bowden, while the others appear to have been part-time workers hired for limited periods to do interviewing in their areas of the state. Pernella Andrews, for example, was an African American woman in El Dorado who did interviews in the southern part of the state for a few months; Babcock noted in 1938 that Andrews was still interested in doing more work for the project (AHC, Babcock letters, Nov. 21, 1938).

In 1937, after months of interviewing of ex-slaves, Henry Alsberg, the national FWP director, began to push the state directors to focus more attention on the collection of the narratives of former slaves, even to the neglect of the other projects. One memo to all the state directors, written July 30, included these instructions: "We suggest that each state choose one or two of their most successful ex-slave interviewers and have them take down some stories *word* for *word*. Some Negro informants are marvellous in their ability to participate in this type of interview. *All stories should be as nearly word-for-word as is possible*" (AHC, FWP correspondence file).

It is not clear to what extent the Arkansas FWP office attempted to comply with this directive. As already noted, this collecting project was accomplished by a very small team of workers, with Bernie Babcock at the center of the group in the Little Rock office. Although an official list of the workers has not been located, the names which have been gleaned from the narrative type-scripts are as follows: Miss Pernella M. Anderson, Mrs. Bernice Bowden, Mrs. Carol Graham, Mrs. Beulah Hagg, Miss Mary Hudgins, T. Elmore Lucy, Watt McKinney, Mrs. Zillah Cross Peel, Miss Irene Robertson, and Samuel S. Taylor. (See interviewer index in this volume.) There is no indication in the texts as to which of these might have attempted to do verbatim transcripts.

Most of the Arkansas materials were sent to Washington as requested, with carbon copies being retained in Little Rock. As mentioned above, the materials resided in the Library of Congress, and on microfilm, with rela-tively little use for three decades. Apparently the FWP materials retained in Arkansas were not of much use, for they seem not to have been available. Folklorist Vance Randolph wrote in 1948 that he had tried to locate the Arkansas FWP folklore collections but had been unsuccessful. Bernie Babcock wrote him that "the ballads and other materials collected were in some way disposed of when the Project came to an end," but she did not know where. Randolph wrote the Library of Congress in 1946 but was told that the material was "not yet available for general use." In frustration he noted, "If a carbon of the Writers' Project collection still exists it should be somewhere in Little Rock, but I have so far been unable to locate it" (Randolph 1948, 7–8).

Two decades later, however, Rawick and the Greenwood Press publish-ing venture found the Arkansas interviews in the Library of Congress with-out any difficulty and published them in the *Main Series* in 1972. When the *Supplement, Series 1* was gathered for its 1977 printing, there was only a small amount of new Arkansas material which had shown up in the Archive of American Folksong in the Library of Congress. As Rawick looked for the hid-den material for the final supplement, he turned particularly to state archives where additional material never sent to Washington might still reside in obscurity. He found some in Arkansas.

Following a lead from Orson Cook, whom he thanked in his introduc-tion to the *Supplement, Series 2,* Rawick located a mass of materials in the Arkansas State Library. Although he quickly was able to identify most of it as copies of material which had been sent to Washington, and thus had been pub-lished already, Rawick did find "several hundred pages of material not con-tained in the RBR [Rare Book Room] collection or in the Archive of American Folksong material. These are published in this collection" (Rawick 1979, 1:xiii). Rawick was pleased with the assistance he received in Arkansas, and said so in his introduction. He thanked LeRoy T. Williams of the Department of History at the University of Arkansas at Little Rock (UALR) and John LeMay of UALR's Multi-Media Department for their help in identifying and microfilming the appropriate pages for publication. Their assistance "was another fine example of the kind of scholarly cooperation I have received throughout the years of working on this project," Rawick wrote (1979, 1:xii).

With the publication of the final series, the FWP ex-slave narrative corpus was in print and, along with it, the Arkansas collection. The greatest percentage of the narratives of ex-slaves from Arkansas was contained in the Arkansas state collection, since so many of the former Arkansas slaves had stayed in their home state. Some of those who had migrated, however, had been interviewed in their new homes, and their narratives were contained in the new state's collection. Because of this, for this new volume, the entire collection has been combed for narratives from Arkansans who were slaves, regardless of where they were located in the 1930s. This search has included a recent publication from Oklahoma, *The Oklahoma Slave Narratives*, which is a more thorough presentation of the Oklahoma narratives than is found in the Library of Congress or in Rawick's volumes (Baker and Baker 1996). This book has therefore been used as the source for narratives of Arkansas ex-slaves in that state.

The organization of this new Arkansas book is by county in Arkansas, in the hope that the localized views of former slaves from a small area may help shed light on antebellum historical circumstances. This collection contains narratives of former slaves from forty-one of the fifty-five Arkansas counties which existed in 1860. For those who seek particular individuals, however, there is an alphabetical name index which will quickly take readers to the pages they seek.

All of this material has been retyped by the editor. This has proved to be a more difficult task than originally envisioned. Most of the interviewers chose to create a written dialect form of English, presumably to give the reader the flavor of the conversation. Unfortunately, they did not manage to produce a commonly agreed upon form of spelling, and the result is, for the typist and the reader, a phantasmagoria of unique words. While there are higher level questions to be raised about this whole procedure in writing down interviews, the immediate consequence is that it is almost impossible to guarantee that the original spelling of the typescripts has been faithfully reproduced. That, however, is the goal. The only changes in the original typescripts are corrections of obvious typographical errors. All else—spelling, grammar, blunders—remains as written. For any reader for whom the issue is important, the original should be consulted in Rawick. Each narrative is provided with the bibliographic reference in a shorthand which is easily learned. (See the list of abbreviations.)

Bias Problems in the Narratives

There are yet other problems which should be mentioned concerning the narratives, if only to make the reader aware of how thorny is the task of reading this testimony. First are some insights into the processes of collecting and writing the interviews. It is tempting in this modern day of tape-recording devices to assume that the interviews are verbatim transcripts, but that would be a mistake. Other than a limited use of early recording devices for folk music, there was no mechanical recording employed in the FWP endeavor (Rawick 1977, 1:xxviii). Some of the interviewers may have been able to use stenography, but it seems that most of them simply took notes and wrote the interviews from their notes and from memory when they returned to their typewriters. At the very least, that means that the interviews are the work of the interviewer, and the correlation of the typescript with what the informant actually said can only be conjectured.

A second problem is that there is ample evidence in the Greenwood Press volumes that editors have also been at work. It is hard to identify the hand, but there are handwritten notes, corrections, and insertions in the typescripts, which are published as preserved in the Library of Congress. Moreover, there are some informants for whom two or even three typescripts exist. Some are the result of further interviews, but some are clearly different versions of a single interview. The reader is left to interpret the editorial process and wonder at the identity of the editor(s).

Third, since the typescript is not a verbatim transcript, it is hard to reconstruct the interview technique. The style of the written reports ranges from a fluent monologue purportedly by the informant to a literary account of the interviewer's visit to the home of the informant, together with descriptions and personal observations. Only rarely can the reader discern a sequence of questions which were asked by the interviewer, but when they do appear, they seem to be a somewhat standardized list of questions, perhaps reflecting a single list given to all interviewers. There is some hint of that possibility in that Henry Alsberg sent questions to the state directors for their use (Escott 1979, 5).

A fourth problem lies in the dialect renderings done by the interviewers. How to represent the language used by the informant was apparently the choice of the interviewer. Sterling Brown sent out a memo to all FWP workers, making suggestions for how they ought to handle dialect, such as his rule that "truth to idiom be paramount and exact truth to pronunciation secondary" (Mangione 1972, 263). Despite the fact that his recommendations seem reasonable, the diversity of dialect rendition in the typescripts argues that few interviewers took his counsel to heart. (Brown's memo is reprinted in Davis and Gates 1985, 37–39.) It is a thought-provoking fact that Samuel Taylor, the major African American interviewer in Arkansas, recorded his interviews in standard English, whereas some of the other texts are barely readable, so idiosyncratic is the dialectal spelling. In the twenty-first century, the attempts to record dialect in these narratives inevitably appear pejorative and hint at racism on the interviewer's part, regardless of the intention of the writer. Even so, the narratives are presented in this volume as close to the original as possible. The reader is thus left to make the judgments as to the trustworthiness of the dialect rendition.

Problems of bias go far beyond questions of technique and rules of standardization, for the racial identity of the interviewer was an important factor. Judging by the names of the interviewers given on the narrative typescripts, the most productive of the workers, probably because they worked full time, were Irene Robertson, Bernice Bowden, and Samuel Taylor. The first two received excellent reviews in 1941 from Henry Bennett, a literary evaluator in the Washington office. His comments gave high praise only to the two women (Rawick 1977, 1:liv). Not all critics were so kind. In 1976 the *Arkansas Historical Quarterly* published a study of the nature of the Negro slave "driver," who exercised oversight over his fellow slaves on behalf of their master. In the course of the study, the author, William L. Van Deberg, using the recently published *Main Series,* raised the issue of whether white interviewers were able to elicit honest responses from African American informants. He mentioned Irene Robertson as an example of a white interviewer who unconsciously manifested "white supremacy doctrine and Jim Crow etiquette" (Van Deburg 1976, 237).

Aware of the issue, Rawick, in his 1977 introduction to the Arkansas additional material in the *Supplement, Series 1,* listed the black interviewers and commented on their work. His characterization of Arkansas focused on Samuel S. Taylor, "whose many interviews are generally among the best in the collection, out of nineteen" (Rawick 1977, 1:xli). Two years later he spoke directly to the problem of white interviewers, defending the Arkansas workers:

> Babcock directed the slave narrative project and obviously chose the main interviewers with great care. Samuel S. Taylor, a black writer and scholar who worked for the Little Rock Urban League and who wrote a history of the black community of Little Rock, published by the Urban League, was responsible for 20 percent of all the interviews. Two other people, Irene Robertson and Bernice Bowden, two white women who were chosen by Babcock and who worked under her direction, collected between them 60 percent of the entire Arkansas narrative collection. They were careful, were

clearly seen by blacks as friends, and displayed interests very similar to Babcock's. An interest in spiritualism, for instance, is pervasive in the narratives Bowden took. Another 5 percent of the narratives were taken by Parnella Anderson, a young black woman who had worked for the Urban League. Thus, 85 percent of the Arkansas narratives were taken by outstanding interviewers who, it is clear, were accepted by blacks and were either black or thought to be sympathetic in an almost radical way with blacks. (Rawick 1979, 1:Part 3: ii-iii)

Readers, of course, will have to make their own judgments about the effect of the race of the interviewer on the informant. It is an important issue, and it leads this brief discussion into a deeper topic—the problem of informant candor in the racial climate of the 1930s. It may be argued that the enduring racism of the Jim Crow era, coupled with the poverty of the Great Depression, made it unlikely that the former slave would say anything which might be risky to his or her immediate circumstances. As Blassingame put it, "Many of the black informants lived in areas where labor contracts were negotiated in jails, debt was perpetual, travel was restricted, and the threat of violence made peonage a living hell. . . . Since many of the former slaves still resided in the same areas as their masters' descendants and were dependent on whites to help them obtain their old-age pensions, they were naturally guarded (and often misleading) in their responses to certain questions" (1985, 85).

This reluctance to be honest about certain issues, especially cruel punishment and sexual depredations by former masters, was surely exacerbated when the interviewers were white. Rawick himself raised the worst-case situation: "The white interviewers were frequently related to the local elite, a relationship that was known by the old black men and women being interviewed" (Rawick 1977, 1:xxxii). The result was that black informants "were not free to speak their minds to whites, and some former slaves admitted that they did not tell the 'white folks nuthin' 'case [they were] skeer'd to make enemies'" (Escott 1985, 42). Even to an African American interviewer, however, the informant may have been wary, for it would have been impossible to know who would be reading the narrative and what the consequences might be. It is certainly fair to say that in the 1930s there were good reasons for an elderly, impoverished black person to be circumspect in reporting the details of the experience of slavery.

On the other hand, such a situation suggests that the bias would have been only in one direction—toward suppression of dangerous details—which would strengthen the likelihood that when negative information is present in an interview, it is an honest statement, or one which hints at even worse experience than the former slave wishes to share. In this strange way, the probability of a lack of candor on the part of an ex-slave actually argues for trustworthiness of the narrative as received. When the additional bias of a white interviewer or editor, who was able to lessen the power of the testimony, is factored in, what remains in the narratives is likely to be a trustworthy indicator of the former slaves' more negative experiences.

These issues must inevitably be in the mind of the reader as the narratives are perused. Readers who wish to consider them in greater depth will find more discussion in the writings of Woodward, Escott, and Blassingame, beginning with their articles in a 1985 anthology (Davis and Gates 1985).

Beyond all these necessary reflections on the problems of reading the narratives, however, lies the power of the narratives themselves. Despite all the analytical concerns, the narratives represent an extraordinary historical circumstance—in the twilight of their lives, a large number of men and women who had been American slaves were given an opportunity to have their testimony recorded. For better or for worse, these pages are their voices and their legacy.

Reference List

Arkansas History Commission (AHC). Manuscript Collection, Book 12, Archives
Section. Federal Writers' Project (WPA) Ex-Slave Interviews (1,200 items): Acc.
#956. Little Rock, State Capitol Complex, Arkansas.

Baker, T. Lindsey, and Julie P. Baker, eds. 1996. *The Oklahoma Slave Narratives.* Norman:
University of Oklahoma Press.

Blassingame, John W. 1972. *The Slave Community.* New York: Oxford University Press.

————. 1977. *Slave Testimony: Two Centuries of Letters, Speeches, Interviews, and
Autobiographies.* Baton Rouge: Louisiana State University Press.

————. 1985. Using the Testimony of Ex-Slaves: Approaches and Problems. In *The
Slave's Narrative,* ed. Charles T. Davis and Henry Louis Gates Jr., 473–92. Oxford:
Oxford University Press.

Botkin, Benjamin A., ed. 1945. *Lay My Burden Down: A Folk History of American
Slavery.* Chicago: University of Chicago Press.

Brown, Sterling A. 1985. On Dialect Usage. In *The Slave's Narrative,* ed. Charles T. Davis
and Henry Louis Gates Jr., 37–39. Oxford: Oxford University Press.

Davis, Charles T., and Henry Louis Gates Jr., eds. 1985. *The Slave's Narrative.* Oxford:
Oxford University Press.

Escott, Paul D. 1979. *Slavery Remembered: A Record of Twentieth-Century Slave
Narratives.* Chapel Hill: University of North Carolina Press.

————. 1985. The Art and Science of Reading WPA Slave Narratives. In *The Slave's
Narrative,* ed. Charles T. Davis and Henry Louis Gates Jr., 40–48. Oxford: Oxford
University Press.

Federal Writers' Project. 1941. *Slave Narratives: A Folk History of Slavery in the United
States from Interviews with Former Slaves.* Typewritten records prepared by the
Federal Writers' Project, Washington, DC.

Mangione, Jerre. 1972. *The Dream and the Deal: The Federal Writers' Project, 1935–1943.*
Boston: Little, Brown and Co.

Perdue, Charles L., Jr., Thomas E. Barden, and Robert K. Phillps. 1976. *Weevils in the
Wheat: Interviews with Virginia Ex-Slaves.* Charlottesville: University of Virginia
Press.

Randolph, Vance. 1948. Ballad Hunters in North Arkansas. *Arkansas Historical Quarterly*
7, no. 1: 1–10.

Rawick, George P., ed. 1972. *The American Slave: A Composite Autobiography.* 19 vols.

Westport, CT: Greenwood Press. Reprinted in 1979, in 16 volumes, by Scholarly Press.

———. 1977. *The American Slave: A Composite Autobiography. Supplement, Series 1.* 12 vols. Westport, CT: Greenwood Press.

———. 1979. *The American Slave: A Composite Autobiography. Supplement, Series 2.* 10 vols. Westport, CT: Greenwood Press.

Van Deburg, William L. 1976. The Slave Drivers of Arkansas: A New View from the Narratives. *Arkansas Historical Quarterly* 35, no. 3: 231–46.

Woodward, C. Vann. 1985. History from Slave Sources. In *The Slave's Narrative,* ed. Charles T. Davis and Henry Louis Gates Jr., 48–59. Oxford: Oxford University Press.

Writers' Program of WPA (Virginia). 1941. *The Negro in Virginia.* Winston Salem, NC: John F. Blair, Publisher. Reprinted in 1973 with an introduction by Charles L. Perdue Jr.

Yetman, Norman R., ed. 1967. The Background of the Slave Narrative Collection. *American Quarterly* 19: 534–53.

———. 2000. *Voices from Slavery.* New York: Dover Publications. Reprint of *Life under the "Peculiar Institution": Selections from the Slave Narrative Collection* (New York: Holt, Rinehart, and Winston, 1970) and *Voices from Slavery* (New York: Holt, Rinehart, and Winston, 1972).

Abbreviations

Each narrative is supplied with a published source which may be checked by the reader. In some cases, there were two texts which were left in the records—some duplicates, some re-writes, some alternative interviews. Where they have been published, the references to both have been given.

M   *Main Series* (Rawick 1972)

S1   *Supplement, Series 1* (Rawick 1977)

S2   *Supplement, Series 2* (Rawick 1979)

OK *Oklahoma Slave Narratives* (Baker and Baker 1996)

The Rawick publications are in multiple volumes, so the volume number is given. Many of the volumes, moreover, are composed of several different parts which often have their own pagination, so the part number is supplied as needed. The final numbers are the pages on which the published narrative may be found. For example, [M:9: pt. 3: 195–201] is interpretable as pages 195 to 201 in part 3 of volume 9 in the *Main Series* (Rawick 1972).

Arkansas Counties

1860

50 miles

2003

50 miles

Arkansas—General

Briles, Frank
Age: 82 or 83
817 Cross Street
Little Rock, Arkansas
Interviewer: Samuel S. Taylor
[M:8: pt. 1: 251–52]

"I was born right here in Arkansas. My father's name was Moses Briles. My mother's name was Judy Briles. Her name before she was married I don't know. They belonged to the Briles. I don't know their first name either.

"My father was under slavery. He chopped cotton and plowed and scraped cotton. That is where I got my part from. He would carry two rows along at once. I was little and couldn't take care of a row by myself. I was born down there along the time of the War, and my father didn't live long afterwards. He died when they was settin' them all free. He was a choppin' for the boss man and they would set them up on blocks and sell them. I don't know who the man was that did the selling, but they tell me they would sell them and buy them.

"I am sick now. My head looks like it's goin' to bust open.

"I have heard them tell about the pateroles. I didn't know them but I heard about them. Them and the Ku Klux was about the same thing. Neither one of them never did bother my folks. It was just like we now, nobody was 'round us and there wasn't no one to bother you at all at Briles' plantation. Briles' plantation I can't remember exactly where it was. It was way down in the west part of Arkansas. Yes, I was born way back south—east—way back. I don't know what the name of the place was but it was in Arkansas. I know that. I don't know nothing about that. My father and mother came from Virginia, they said. My father used to drive cattle there, my mother said. I don't know nothin' except what they told me.

"I learnt a little something from my folks. I think of more things every time I talk to somebody. I know one thing. The woman that bossed me, she died. That was about—Lord I was a little bitty of a fellow, didn't know nothin' then. She made clothes for me. She kept me in the house all the time. She was a white woman. I know when they was setting them free. I was goin' down to get a drink of water. My father said, 'Stop, you'll be drowned.' And I said, 'What must I do?' And he said, 'Go back and set down till I come back.' I don't know what my father was doing or where he was going. There was a man—I don't know who—he come 'round and said, 'You're all free.' My mama said, 'Thank God for that. Thank God for that.' That is all I know about that.

"When I got old enough to work they put me in the woods splitting rails and plowing. When I grew up I scraped cotton and worked on the farm. That is where my father would come and say, 'Now, son, if anybody asks you how you feel, tell them the truth.'

"I went to school one session and then the man give down. He got sick and couldn't carry it no longer. His pupils were catching up with him I reckon. It was time to get sick or somethin'.

"I never did marry. I was promised to marry a woman and she died. So I said, 'Well, I will give up the ghost. I won't marry at all.'

"I ain't able to do no work now 'cept a little pittling here and there. I get a pension. It's been cut a whole lot."

[The Briles plantation may have been in Van Buren County. There was an 1860 census listing for John F. Briles in that county.—Ed.]

Coleman, Betty Robertson
Age: ca. 85
Austin, Texas
Interviewer: Alfred E. Menn
16 September 1937
[S2:3 (TX, pt. 2): 837–42]

As a girl, my name was Betty Robertson, and I was bawn about 85 years ago, in Arkansas. I don' know whut county——all that I kin tell yo' is Arkansas.

My mothaw was Violet Robertson, but she died a Milam. My fathaw was John Robertson, and he died two years after emancipation.

My fathaw was a great big man, with a mustache, and he looked lak a preachah, but he wasn't. I had the sweetest daddy that ever broke bread. My mothaw was a small woman, but later in life she fleshened up. She died about ten years ago.

We stayed on the Will Robertson plantation in Arkansas until five years befo' emancipation. Then Mawster Robertson brought us to Texas.

I was too small to do much field work. Mawster Robertson was a good man, and he allowed no overseer on his place. Mawster Robertson was jes' lak a brothaw to us. He even allowed us to go everywhere without a pass, and he let the other folks know that nobody was to bother "Robertson's fue niggers," and that he knowed they was out.

Mawster Robertson brought us to Texas jus' befo' the wah. We had a big plantation on the San Antonio Post Road, about seben miles south of Austin.

At this place, I had to help in the house. I had to do house work and pittle aroun'. We always called Mawster Robertson "Pa"; but we didn't call ole Mistress "Mama." Nawsuh! We called her Mistress Dellie. She sure would use a cowhide on us. There was times when Mis Dellie was cowhidin' me, and I'd make a big noise, and Mawster would come in and say:

"Say, Dellie, whut in the world are yo' doin' with my niggers? Why don' yo' leave 'em alone?"

When Mis Dellie would cowhide me, she wouldn't whoop hard, but Id cut up somethin' awful, and that woman was hardly beatin' me. I was so full of mischief. There was little Victoria, Mawster Robertson's baby girl. She learned me how to "snuff," and I was so full of mischief, that I had to keep her box of snuff until she got back f'um school. Her folks didn't know that she used snuff.

I remembah how three white slave-drivers once come by on the Post Road in a wagon. They had two slaves drivin' the hosses. The slave-drivers was out buyin' up slaves, and they was on their way to San Antonio. One of the slave boys had been whooped so much, that my mothaw, grandmothaw and grand-fathaw had to soak his shirt off'n his back.

Those slave-drivers stayed on the plantation that night, and when Mawster Robertson learned nex' mawnin' how the slave boy had been whooped, he stahted to chewin' and spittin' his tobakker, and said:

"By golly!"

And he sure was mad. "By golly" was his high cu'sin', and was as far as he would go.

We had good houses to live in. They might of been logs, but I remembah they was boa'ded up nice. We had good food.

Mothaw was a cook on the place. The white folks had their dinin' room, and the slaves had theirs. Sometimes there was okra on the table, and fathaw would say:

"Git this slop off'n the table!"

But I liked okra. Grandfathaw would say:

"John, yo' don' know whuts good."

But, of co'se, they wouldn't take it off'n the table jes' 'cause fathaw said to.

My fathaw was jes' a fahmer on the place. He was a gay ole feller. I remembah how he wore shoes that had wooden soles. One night the patrol chased him, and I could hear him runnin' up that 'dobe hill. I said:

"Mama, I hear fathaw runnin' with his ole wooden shoes!"
Mothaw said:
"You go on to sleep, 'cause yo' ain't heard nothin'."
But about that time fathaw come in. Mothaw asked:
"John , whut's wrong with yo'?"
He said: "Whew! the patrols was after me. But, I give 'em a wahm reception, and then I give 'em plenty of heel-dust."

This plantation had plenty of cotton. I didn't have to pick cotton, but I helped move the baskets down the rows. I would say, "I'll be glad when yo'-all staht pullin' cawn—don' have to lift baskets."

Fathaw tol' me: "Aw, go and sit down over there in the shade. You never was no-account, anyhow." But, I was the smartes' youngster that he had. I was sich a little woman.

I remembah how my fat sistah Mary had the tizziks—we call it asthma now—and she would keep us awake at night, 'cause she groaned so, and we had to rub her. We had to rub hot tallow and snuff on her chest. That would loosen the stuff, so it would come out.

I kin remembah that I was sich a little woman, that I ruled Mary, who was older than me. I would be at the wash-pot and say:
"Nigger, put some wood under that pot!"
Mary would jes' keep pittlin' aroun' until I slapped her one. She'd run and tell mothaw. Befo' long, mothaw'd come down and ask:
"Whut'd yo' hit Mary fo'?"
I said: "Mama, I hit her jes' one lick." Then I pointed to the pot, and said: "Look at that pot. That soap should of been melted already, and that clothes should of been boiled."
She'd look at the pot and see that I was right. So, as I said:
"Mama, take sistah Mary with yo'."
But sistah Mary was made to come back to the pot. Mama soon found out that I had the blood of my fathaw. Folks used to say: "Don' git John's blood stahted!"

One early mawnin', Mawster Robertson come to our cabin door, and said with much sadness:
"John and Uncle Jeff, I've come to tell you all somethin'. Yo'-all is as free today as I am."
Then he broke down and cried. My folks also broke down. Fathaw tol' Mawster Robertson:
"Well, I don' know whut we're a-goin' to do."
When he was able to talk, Mawster Robertson said: "Well, John, I'll give yo'-all half of all the food we got, till yo'-all git a job; and, now, when yo'-all

go out and work fo' somebody, don' work fo' nothin', 'cause yo'-all is as free as anybody. Yo'-all kin stay here until yo' find a job."

About this time, Mrs. Dellie come up. Mothaw said: "Mrs. Dellie, whut yo' goin to do fo' a cook?"

Mrs. Dellie fell on Mama and cried. It was somethin' pitiful. She said: "Violet, I don' know whut I'm goin' to do."

I didn't know whut had turned loose, but I knowed a key was loose somewhere.

We stayed with Mawster Robertson about a month and a half, befo' we got a job. Fathaw hired out to other fahmers.

I remembah how later I found out I was free, and whut it meant. I told mothaw: "Mrs. Dellie kain't whoop me no mo'e."

But, mama then took up the whoopin'! The folks always called me "Crazy Calico," 'cause I could never keep a good dress. When a dress had a hole in it, I would stick my fingah in it and rip it all the way down. Thats' why folks called me "Crazy Calico."

I never did learn to read and write, and kain't read and write to this day.

It was quite a numbah of years after slavery—I don' know when—that I married Joe Coleman. He was a preachah. We went to chu'ch, got married, and come on home. Joe had a home fo' me, when we got married. He had our home out in Decker.

We had twelve chillun—two sets of twins—six boys and six girls. There is three boys and three girls—exackly half—livin': Eliza, George, Melinda, Andrew, Lonnie, and Hattie. Andrew lives in Dallas; Hattie is in San Antonio; and the others live here in Austin.

Why, one of my boys got mo'e grey hair than I got. That makes me mad, 'cause I want white hair lak my mothaw had. Thats' her picture up there on the wall. She looks lak me, doesn't she? That one up there is my husband, who was a preachah. He was sich a good man, that all other men has seemed o'dinary to me. A lot of widowers has come aroun', but I tell 'em to git out! You tell the world fo' me that I've been married twice: Once to Joe Coleman, and now to Christ.

Harshaw, Plomer
Age: 86
Muskogee, Oklahoma
Interviewer: Ethel Wolfe Garrison
[OK: 188f]

I was born away down in Marshall County, Mississippi, on August 10,

1852, at Holly Springs. My father was Plomer Jo Vann, and my mother was Gradey Dowden. She died right after I was born and my mistress raised me like I was her own child. My mother was carried over here from Africa on a slave boat, but I don't know where my father come from.

Daniel Harshaw was my first master's name. He was a good master and the mistress was too. She told me I had a brother name of Oliver and a half brother name of Plumer. Maybe there was a sister, or another brother. Anyway she said either a sister or brother was born in 1837.

That Civil War was bad business. The master leave out of Mississippi and the white people took all the slaves to Arkansas. There was about eighty slaves and we all tried to settle at work but the war kept us running from place to place all the time.

We make several trips from Arkansas down to Wood County, Texas. We went to Texas in wagons and I reckon most of them was pulled with oxen.

In Arkansas the master fixed himself up a fine double frame house with lots of outbuildings. In them days he was wealthy. The furniture was good; high-post beds and plenty to eat. His stock was good stuff until the war broke him up.

The mistress wouldn't let any of the slaves sing about Yankee songs. They let us have church meetings but no singing about the Yankees. One slave girl got a whipping for sometimes singing about that John Brown. They tied her to a tree and the lashing bloodied up the tree all around.

There was lots of means things done in the slave days. Both the white people and the negroes was wrong part of the time. Like the time a white man Jim Standley, one of our neighbors, put one of his slaves in chains account of not doing something right. He sent the slave to work in the fields, chain and all. The evening when the work day was over that slave slipped up to where Jim Standley was rocking his baby on the porch of his own house. The master didn't know the slave was around and never did know, for the slave man chopped him with an axe while some negroes in the yard looked on. He was dead. The slave run away, and how he got rid of them chains nobody know, they never saw that negro again.

The patrollers took up the chase but even the bloodhounds couldn't track him. One slave man was killed by a hound.

It happened on our own place. Master had a hickory club and was going to lay it on but the negro grabbed that stick and took it away from master. Then he run, out toward some bushes. But that was far as he got. The dogs leap on him and tear him to pieces. I saw it with my own eyes.

There was an old slave woman on the place in Arkansas who scared the young folks with her haunts. Me too. One time the master had a thrashing machine in the field. The old woman said to us, "Look at that big haunt! That's the biggest ghost I ever knowed about."

The master had told me what it was and I wasn't scared. "That ghost done the master lots of good," I told her, "just about thrashed out all the oats!" That made her so mad she took off her leather belt and most smother me down with it.

Every New Year all the masters around the country have what they called a "nigger show." Just an auction for to get rid of the older slaves. The ones going to be sold was stripped down to show off the muscles. Like folks buy a horse, they look at the teeth.

Down in Texas I worked in what folks said was "government service." Same as slavery, I couldn't see no difference. Got whipped just the same. Worked in a loom house. Girls and men working hard all the day but nobody get any money for that. Part of the time I worked in a brickyard. The boss kept us trotting or running all the day. Nobody have time to just walk. That was work!

I didn't know what the white people meant when they said "Free." My young master was a lieutenant in the army under Col. Monroe. When the war was over my young master got me and took me back to Arkansas with him. I rode a mule out of Pine Bluff.

I been married three times and got so many grandchildren—must be nearly thirty-seven, and 15 great-grandchildren. They are all scattered, don't know where.

I belong to the Baptist Church in Muskogee.

That's all I remember of slavery.

Jeffries, Moses
Age: 81
1119 Izard Street
Little Rock, Arkansas
Interviewer: Samuel S. Taylor
[M:9: pt. 2: 38–42+]

"I was born in 1856. My age was kept with the cattle. As a rule, you know, slaves were chattels. There was a fire and the Bible in which the ages were kept was lost. The man who owned me couldn't remember what month I was born in. Out of thirteen children, my mother could only remember the age of one. I had twelve brothers and sisters—Bob Lacy, William Henry, Cain Cecil, Jessie, Charles, Harvey, Johnnie, Anna, Rose, Hannah, Lucy, and Thomas. I am the only one living now. My parents were both slaves. My father has been dead about fifty-nine years and my mother about sixty or sixty-one years. She died before I married and I have been married fifty years. I have them in my Bible.

I remember when Lincoln was elected president and they said there was going to be war. I remember when they had a slave market in New Orleans. I was living between Pine Bluff and New Orleans (living in Arkansas) and saw the slaves chained together as they were brought through my place and located somewhere on some of the big farms or plantations.

I never saw any of the fighting but I did see some of the Confederate armies when they were retreating near the end of the war. I was just about ten years old at the time and was in Marshall, Texas.

The man that owned me said to the old people that they were free, that they didn't belong to him any more, that Abraham Lincoln had set them free. Of course, I didn't know what freedom was. They brought the news to them one evening, and them Niggers danced nearly all night.

I remember also seeing a runaway slave. We saw the slaves first, and the dogs came behind chasing them. They passed through our field about half an hour ahead of the hounds, but the dogs would be trailing them. The hunters didn't bother to stop and question us because they knew the hounds were on the trail. I have known slaves to run away and stay three years at a time. Master would whip them and they would run away. They wouldn't have no place to go or stay so they would come back after a while. Then they would be punished again. They wouldn't punish them much, however, because they might run off again.

Marriage

If I went on a plantation and saw a girl I wanted to marry, I would ask my master to buy her for me. It wouldn't matter if she were somebody else's wife; she would become mine. The master would pay for her and bring her home and say, "John, there's your wife." That is all the marriage there would be. Yellow women used to be a novelty then. You wouldn't see one-tenth as many then as now. In some cases, however, a man would retain his wife even after she had been sold away from him and would have permission to visit her from time to time.

Inheritance of Slaves

If a man died, he often stated in his will which slaves should go to each child he had. Some men had more than a hundred slaves and they divided them up just as you would cattle. Some times there were certain slaves that certain children liked, and they were granted those slaves.

What the Freedmen Received

Nothing was given to my parents at freedom. None of the Niggers got anything. They didn't give them anything. The slaves were hired and allowed to work the farms on shares. That is where the system of share cropping came from. I was hired for fifty dollars a year, but was paid only five. The boss said he owed me fourteen dollars but five was all I got. I went down town and bought some candy. That was the first time I had had that much money.

I couldn't do anything about the pay. They didn't give me any land. They hired me to work around the house and I ate what the boss ate. But the general run of slaves got pickled pork, molasses, cornmeal and sometimes flour (about once a week for Sunday). The food came out of the share of the share cropper.

You can tell what they did by what they do now. It (share cropping) hasn't changed a particle since. About Christmas was the time they usually settled up. Nobody was forced to remain as a servant. I know one thing— Negroes did not go to jail and penitentiary like they do now.

Ku Klux Klan

The Ku Klux Klan to the best of my knowledge went into action about the time shortly after the war when the amendments to the Constitution gave the Negroes the right to vote. I have seen them at night dressed up in their uniform. They would visit every Negro's house in the community. Some they would take out and whip, some they would scare to death. They could ask for a drink of water and they had some way of drinking a whole bucketful to impress the Negroes that they were supernatural. Negroes were very superstitious then. Colonel Patterson who was a Republican and a colonel or general of the militia, white and colored, under the governorship of Powell Clayton, stopped the operation of the Klan in this state. After his work, they ceased terrorizing the people.

Political Officials

Many an ex-slave was elected sheriff, county clerk, probate clerk. Pinchback* was elected governor in Louisiana. The first Negro congressman was from Mississippi and a Methodist preacher, Hiram Revells.** We had a Nigger superintendent of schools of the state of Arkansas, J. C. Corbin***— I don't remember just when, but it was in the early seventies. He was also president of the state school in Pine Bluff—organized it.

Suffrage

The ex-slave voted like fire directly after the war. That was about all that did vote then. If the Niggers hadn't voted they would never have been able to elect Negroes to office.

I was elected Alderman once in Little Rock under the administration of Mayer Kemer. We had Nigger coroner, Chief of Police, Police Judge, Policemen. Ike Gillam's father was coroner. Sam Garrett was Chief of Police; Judge M. W. Gibbs was Police Judge. He was also a receiver of public lands. so was J. E. Bush, who founded the Mosaics (Modern Mosaic Templars of America). James W. Thompson, Bryant Luster, Marion H. Henderson, Acy L. Richardson, Chidress' father-in-law, were all aldermen. James P. Noyer Jones was County Clerk of Chicot County, S. H. Holland, a teacher of mine, a little black nigger about five feet high, as black as ink, but well educated was sheriff of Desha County. Augusta had a Negro who was sheriff. A Negro used to hold good offices in this state.

I charge the change to Grant. The Baxter-Brooks matter caused it. Baxter was a Southern Republican from the Northeastern part of the state, Batesville, a Southern man who took sides with the North in the war. Brooks was a Methodist preacher from the North somewheres. When Grant recognized the Baxter faction whom the old ex-slaveholders supported because he was a Southerner and sided with Baxter against Brooks. It put the present Democratic party in power, and they passed the Grandfather law barring Negroes from voting.

Negroes were intimidated by the Ku Klux. They were counted out. Ballot boxes were burned and ballots were destroyed. Finally, Negroes got discouraged and quit trying to vote."

* P.B.S. Pinchback, elected Lieutenant-Governor of La. Held office 43 days.

** Hiram Revells, elected to fill the unexpired term of Jefferson Davis.

*** J. C. Corbin, appointed state superintendent of public instruction in 1873—served until the end of 1875.

Johnson, Harry (Jim)
Age: 86
Pearsall, Texas
Interviewer: Mrs. Florence Angermiller
[M:4: pt. 2 (TX): 212–15]
[See also S2:6 (TX, pt. 5): 1994–2004]

Harry Johnson, 86, whose real name was Jim, was born in Missouri, where he was stolen by Harry Fugot, when about twelve years old, and taken to Arkansas. He was given the name of Harry and remained with Fugot until near the close of the Civil War. Fugot then sold him to Graham for 1,200 acres and he was brought to Coryell Co., Texas, and later to Caldwell Co. He worked in Texas two years before finding out the slaves were free. He later went to McMullen Co. to work cattle, but eventually spent most of his time rearing ten white children. He now lives in Pearsall, where he married at the age of 59.

"I come from Missouri to Arkansas and then to Texas, and I was owned by Massa Louis Barker and my name was Jim Johnson. But a white man name Harry Fugot stoled me and run me out to Arkansas and changed my name to Harry. He stoled me from Mississippi County in de southern part of Missouri, down close to de Arkansas line, and I was 'bout 12 year old then.

"My mama's name was Judie and her husband name Miller. When I wasn't big 'nough to pack a chip, old Massa Louis Barker wouldn't take $400 for me, 'cause he say he wants to make a overseer out of me. My daddy went off durin' de war. He carried off by sojers and he never did come back.

"Dey 'bout 30, 40 acres in Massa Barker's plantation in Missouri. He used to hire me out from place to place and de men what hires me puts me to doin' what he wanted. I was stole from my mammy when I's 'bout 10 or 12 and she never did know what become of me.

"O, my stars! I seed hun'erds and hun'erds of sojers 'fore I stole from Missouri. Dey what us call Yankees. I seed 'em strung out a half-mile long, goin' battle two and three deep. Dey never did destroy any homes. Dey took up a little stuff. I had five sacks of meal one day and was goin' to de mill and de sojers come along and taken me, meal and all. De maddes' woman I ever saw was dat day. De sojers come and druv off her cows. She told 'em not to, dat her husban' fightin' and she have to make de livin' off dem cows, but dey druv de cows to camp and kilt 'bout three of 'em. Dey done dat, I knows, 'cause I's with 'em.

"But down in Arkansas I seed de southern sojers and I's plowin' for a old lady call Williams, and some sojers come and goes in de house. I heered say dey was Green's men, and dey taken everything dat old woman have what dey wants, and dey robs lots of houses.

"It don't look reas'able to say it, but it's a fac'—durin' slavery iffen you lived one place and your mammy lived 'cross de street you couldn't go to see her without a pass. De paddlerollers would whip you if you did. Dere was one woman owns some slaves and one of 'em asks her for a pass and she give him de piece of paper sposed to be de pass, but she writes on it:

"'His shirt am rough and his back am tough,
    Do, pray, Mr. Paddleroller, give 'im 'nough.

"De paddlerollers beat him nearly to death, 'cause that's what's wrote on de paper he give 'em.

"I 'member a whippin' one slave got. It were 100 lashes. Dey's a big overseer right here on de San Marcos river, Clem Polk, him and he massa kilt 16 niggers in one day. Dat massa couldn't keep a overseer, 'cause de niggers wouldn't let 'em whip 'em, and dis Clem, he say, 'I'll stay dere,' and he finds he couldn't whip dem niggers either, so he jus' kilt 'em. One nigger nearly got him and would have kilt him. Dat nigger raise de ax to come down on Polk's head and de massa stopped him jus' in time, and den Polk shoots dat nigger in de breast with a shotgun.

"Dey had court days and when court met, dey passed a bill what say, 'Keep de niggers at home.' Some of 'em could go to church and some of 'em couldn't. Dey'd let de cullud people be baptized, but dey didn't many want it, dey didn't understan' it 'nough.

"After de war ends, Massa Fugot sells me to Massa Graham for 1,200 acres of land, and I lives in Caldwell County. He was purty good to he slaves and we live in a li'l old frame house, facin' west. I sleeps in de same house as massa and missus, to guard 'em. One night some men came and wake me up and tells me to put my clothes on. Missus was in de bed and she 'gin cryin' and tell 'em not to take me, but dey taken me anyway. We called 'em Guerrillas and dey thieves. Dey white men and one of 'em I had knowed a long time. I's with dem thieves and hears 'em talk 'bout killin' Yankees. Dey kep' me in de south part of Missouri a long time. I didn't do anything but sit 'round de house with dem.

"When I's sold to Massa Graham I didn't have to come to Texas, 'cause I's free, but I didn't know dat, and I's out here two years 'fore I knowed I's free. Down in Caldwell County is where de bondage was lifted offen me and I found out I's free. I jus' stays on and works and my massa give me he promise I's get a hoss and saddle and $100 in money when I's 21 year old, but he didn't do it. He give me a li'l pony and a saddle what I sold for $3.00 and 'bout eight or nine dollars in money. He had me blindfolded and I though I gwine git a good hoss and saddle and more money.

"I looks back sometimes and thinks times was better for eatin' in slavery dan what dey is now. My mammy was a reg'lar cook and she made me peach cobblers and apple dumplin's. In dem days, we'd take cornmeal and mix it with water and call 'em corn dodgers and dey awful nice with plenty butter. We had lots of hawg meat and when dey kilt a beef a man told all de neighbors to come git some of de meat.

"Right after de war, times is pretty hard and I's taken beans and parched 'em and got 'em right brown, and meal bran to make coffee out of. Times was purty hard, but I allus could find somethin' to work at in dem days.

"I lived all my life 'mong white folks and jus' worked in first one place and then 'nother. I raised ten white chillen, nine of de Lowe chillen, and dey'd mind me quicker dan dey own pappy and mammy. Dat in McMullin County.

"De day I's married I's 59 year old and my wife is 'bout 60 year old now. De last 20 years I's jus' piddled 'round and done no reg'lar work. I married right here in de church house. I nussed my wife when she a baby and used to court her mammy when she's a girl. We's been real happy together.

Jones, John
Age: 82
3109 W. 10th Avenue
Pine Bluff, Arkansas
Interviewer: Mrs. Bernice Bowden
[M:9: pt. 4: 149–50]

"I come here in 1856—you can figure it out for yourself. I was born in Arkansas, fifty miles below here.

"I remember the soldiers. I know I was a little boy drivin' the gin. Had to put me upon the lever. You see, all us little fellows had to work.

"I remember seein' the Indians goin' by to fight at Arkansas Post. They fought on the southern side. When I heard the cannons, I asked my mama what it was and she said 'twas war.

"John Dye—that was my young master—went to the War but Ruben had a kind of afflicted hand and he didn't go.

"Our plantation was on the river and I used to see the Yankee boats go down the river.

"My papa belonged to the Douglases and mama belonged to the Dyes. I was born on the Douglas place and I ain't been down there in over fifty years. They said I was born in March but I don't know any more bout it than a rabbit.

"Papa said he was raised up in the house. Said he didn't do much work—just tended to the gin.

"I remember one night the Ku Klux came to our house. I was so scared I run under the house and stayed till ma called me out. I was so scared I didn't know what they had on.

"I remember when some of the folks come back from Texas and they said peace was declared.

"I think my brother run off and jined the Yankees and come here when they took Pine Bluff. War is a bad thing. I think they goin' keep on till they hatch up another one.

"I didn't go to school much. I was the oldest boy at home and I had to plow. I went seven days all told and since then I learned ketch as ketch can. I can read and write pretty well. It's a consolation to be able to read. If you can't get all of it, you can get some of it.

"Been here in Jefferson County ever since 1867. I come here from Lincoln County.

"After freedom my papa moved my mama down on the Douglas place where he was and stayed one year, then moved on the Simpson place in Lincoln County, and then come up here in Jefferson County. I remember all the moves.

"I remember down here where Kientz Bros. place is was the gallows where they hung folks in slavery times. You know—when they had committed some crime.

"Yes'm, I voted but I never held any office.

"I know I don't look my age but I can tell you a heap of things happened before emancipation.

"I think the people are better off free—they got liberty."

Moore, Emma
Age: 80
3715 Short West Second
Pine Bluff, Arkansas
Interviewer: Mrs. Bernice Bowden
[M:10: pt. 5: 120–22]

"I'se born in slavery times. When my daddy come back from the War, he said I was gwine on seven or eight.

"He stayed in the War three years and six months. I know that's what he always told us. He went with his master, Joe Horton. Looks like I can see old Marse Joe now. Had long sandy whiskers. The las' time I seed him he come to my uncle's house. We was all livin' in a row of houses. Called em the quarters. I never will ferget it.

"I was born on Horton's Island here in Arkansas. That's what they told me.

"I know when my daddy went to war and when he come back, he put on his crudiments (accoutrements) to let us see how he looked.

"I seed the soldiers gwine to war and comin' back. Look like to me I was glad to see em till I seed too many of em.

"Yankees used to come down and take provisions. Yes, 'twas the Yankees!

"My granddaddy was the whippin' boss. Had a white boss too named Massa Fred.

"Massa Joe used to come down and play with us chillun. His name was Joe Horton. Ever'body can tell you that was his name. Old missie named Miss Mary. She didn't play with us much.

"Yes ma'am, they sure did take us to Texas durin' of the War—in a ox wagon. Stayed down there a long time.

"We didn't have plenty to eat but we had to eat what we did here. I member they wouldn't give us chillun no meat, jus' grease my mouf and make my mother think we had meat.

"Now my mother told me, at night some of the folks used to steal one of old massa's shoats and cook it at night. I know when that pot was on the rack but you better not say nothin' bout it.

"All us chillun stayed in a big long log house. Dar is where us chillun stayed in the daytime, right close to Miss Mary.

"I used to sit on the lever at the gin. You know that was glory to me to ride. I whipped the old mule. Ever' now and then I'd give him a tap.

"When they pressed the cotton, they wet the press and I member one time they wet it too much. I don't say they sont it back but I think they made em pay for it. And they used to put chunks in the bale to make it weigh heavy. Right there on that lake where I was born.

"Used to work in the field. These white folks can tell you I loved to work. I used to get as much as the men. My mammy was a worker and as the sayin' is, I was a chip off the old block.

"The first teacher I went to school to was named Mr. Cushman. Didn't go only on rainy days. That was the first school and you might say the las' one cause I had to nuss them chillun.

"You know old massa used to keep all our ages and my daddy said I was nineteen when I married, but I don't know what year 'twas—honest I don't.

"I been married three times.

"I member one time I was goin' to a buryin'. I was hurryin' to get dressed. I wanted to be ready when they come by for me cause they say it's bad luck to stop a corpse. If you don't know that I do—you know if they had done started from the house.

"My mama and daddy said they was born in Tennessee and was bought and brought here.

"I been goin' to one of these gov'ment schools and got my eyes so weak I can't hardly see to thread a needle. I'se crazy bout it I'm tellin' you. I sit up here till God knows how long. They give me a copy to practice and they'd brag on me and that turned me foolish. I jus' thought I was the teacher herself almos'. That's the truf now.

"I can't read much. I don't fool with no newspaper. I wish I could, woman—I sure do.

"I keep tellin' these young folks they better learn somethin'. I tell em they better take this chance. This young generation—I don't know much bout the whites—I'm tellin' you these colored is a sight.

"Well, I'm gwine away from here d'rectly—ain't gwine be here much longer. If I don't see you again I'll meet you in heaven."

Newton, George
Age: 71
Wichita Falls, Texas
Interviewer: Ethel C. Dulaney, P. W.
12 September 1938
[S2:7 (TX, pt. 6): 2909–10]

George Newton rooms and boards with a family living on Barwise Street. He is almost totally blind, but gets about by use of walking cane. George stutters when he talks. A typical negro.

"I wuz bo'n in Arkansas de secon' yeah aftah de surrendah. I nevah saw m' father. He wuz killed durin' th' wah. He had went t' th' wah wid Massa Newton. He wuzzen' shot. He wuz a makin' salt and fell in the vat an' got scalded t' death.

"My mother took me to Louisiana when I wuz a baby. We lived in Houma, near Shreveport, Claven Parish. Nevah went to school a day in m' life. Schools not plentiful den as dey is now. Lived in Louisiana tell I as big as I is now. I worked for white folks on de farm—raised up togedder wid white family name o' Smith.

"I married up wid Marthy Kilgore. We had two children. One boy an' one girl. don' know where dey is now. I done been sap'rated fr'm my wife 'bout forty yeahs. Lat' time I heared uv her she wuz in Denton.

"My mother wuz a house girl for de Newtons on her plantation. She say one time ol' massa had a cullud man whut wuz so lazy dat he wen' to de choppin' block and chop off his own han'. She say cullud folks could fiddle an' dance all dey please, but wa'n't 'lowed t' sing an' pray. She say sometimes dey go out an' turn de wash pot bottom up 'ards so de echo go under de pot an' de white folks couden' hear de songs. I've heared mother tell dat a hundred times.

"I come to Granbury, Texas, when I wuz 'bout thirty years ole. Come wid de Smiths, an' worked on a farm for 'em. It was called de Hasting farm. Hasting was de fur' man t' put up windmills.

"I lived in Spring town an' Fort Worth 'fore I come to Wichita Falls, when I could see good I worked at de 'Big Nigger Cafe' washin' dishes. Nevah wuz no han' t' lay 'roun' saloons much. I worked at one time, dough; it wuz de one wes' o' de ole frame deppo. I wuz here when dey went out (saloons).

"Firs' automobile I ever seen wuz run wid a chain. It had cogs lak de cotton planters an' cultivators down in Louisiana. You could hear it a comin' a long way off.

"I wuz raised in de sugah cane patch. Had m' fingers caught in de 'lasses mill many a time. I gets a pension fr'm de gov'ment. I gets 'long perty good, I guess."

Pollard, Melinda
Age: ?
Meridian, Texas
Interviewer: Mrs. Ada Davis, P. W.
Bosque County, Texas
7 August 1937
[S2:8: 3113–16]

"I don' know de zact time I wuz borned, but I does know dat I wuz born in de state of Mississippi back in slavery time. My owners wuz Tom Pollard an' Mealy Pollard. Dey moved to Atlanta, Georgia in my early life an' tuck me wid dem. I nebber libed in de slave quarters 'cause I wuz nussmaid for my mistiss two chillun, Jim an' Oscar. Dat caused me to lib in de big house wid de w'ite folks. Yes'um I felt big w'en I got 'roun' de uther niggers, 'cause I allus wore nice close an' wuz allus clean an' had my haid com'ed. My close wuz nuthin' fine but dey didn' have no holes in dem, dey wuz jes' home spun close but I wuz 'bout de bes' looking slave on de plantation. I don' know much 'bout what hap'ned in de quarters 'cause I didn' fool 'roun' de niggers no mor'en I had to.

"I 'members good de Wah, de Freedom Wah, 'specially w'en de fightin' got near de Pollard home in Georgia, an' us had to leave Georgia an' go to Arkansas. Dat trip frum Georgia to Arkansas wuz one more trip. Us had to keep out of de way of de 'Jay-hawkers' an' fer dat re'son us didn' go on de road, us jes' went thru de woods an' eny way us could to git 'cross de country. Us went in ox-waggins an' hit tuck a long time. It wuz a hard trip de way we had to go, us had to cook out in de open on dat trip, de cookin' wuz all over an' de fire put out befo' dark 'cause dat would be all de 'Jay-hawkers' needed to fin' us wuz a light or fire, each day when we left de place whar we camp'd de nite befo' all de place whar de fire had been wuz covered up so ef dey passed thru de woods dey would not know eny one had been dere de nite befo'. De ole marster didn' stay dere in Arkansas but one year, he didn' take time to gadder de crop but 'bout half way an' come to Texas. He come to Meridian an' wuz dere fer a w'ile an' den moved to Kimble Bend in Bosque County. I wuz set free June 19, 1865. I wuz told dat I wuz free befo' den, by some school teacher, atter I wuz gron' she tole me Mr. Abe Lincoln sot de niggers free long time befo' dat, an' de w'ite folks in Texas wanted to git dere crops done befo' de niggers wuz set free an' lef, guess dats why my c'usins in Georgia don' celebrate de June'teenth like us does. I wuz gron' an' Ko'tin w'en I wuz freed.

"I didn' git no more whupins den eny uther chile, my marster an' missus had to make me mind 'cause I wuz like all chillun I wanted to play w'en dere wuz wurk to be did. We played wid rag dolls an' dishes de w'ite chillun had chiney dolls; dey sho wuz pretty. I allus wurked 'roun' to git de w'ite chillun to let me play wid de chiney dolls, an' let dem hab my dolls made out ob rags. De way dem dolls wuz made, ole missus would cut out a piece of cloth de shape of a doll an' stuff hit wid cotton real tight an' den take a lead pencil an' make de eyes, nose an' mouth on one side of de haid an' dat wuz de face ob de doll. She would allus take an' make it a dress out of one of her pretty store bought dresses, an' dat would make me better satisfied to play wid it 'cause she knowed I didn' like dem rag dolls like I did de chiney dolls.

"I w'nt to church wid de w'ite marster an' missus an dem chillun, dey allus dressed me up on Sunday an' som'tims tied a pink or blue ribben on a piece of my hair. I nebber did keep my hair wrapped like lots ob de niggers, 'cause old missus made me comb it ebery day. De comb I used wuz one she bought from a peddler hit wuz made out ob a cow horn, hit sho did pull my nappie hair. I went mos' ebery whar wid ole missus. I mean when she tuck de chillun, 'cause, w'en she got all dressed up wid her finery on she didn' habe no time to be bothered wid dem chillun atter she got to whar she wuz goin', an' I had to see about dem.

"I didn' hab no need fer no money 'cause I had eberythin' de w'ite chillun had to eat, in de way ob candy an de sich, w'en us went eny place. At de house I had eberythin' de w'ite people had. My w'ite folks nebber did eat no possums or rabbits, us had fish som'tims.

"I nebber is seed no ghostes de w'ite folks allus tole us dere waz'nt any sich thing as ghostes. Dat dey wuz jes stories so as to make de bad chillun 'fraid so dey would be good. Dey use' to tell us 'bout de ghostes w'en us 'bout de fire at nite in de winter befo' us go to bed an' hit would hab me so 'fraid I would pull de kiver all ober my haid an sleep dat way all nite. I jes went to sleep so 'fraid I didn' move all nite an' w'en mornin' come an' hit wuz time to git up, I would be so tired I didn' want to git up. Ole missus would call me lots ob times an I didn' move. But one call from ole marse an' I would jump out ob dat bed an' go runnin'. De bed I had wuz a little bed dat rolled under de big one in de day an' at nite it wuz put in de hall or jes eny place dey wanted me to sleep I didn' hab no special place to sleep.

"I liked de slavery days 'cause I wuz treated good but I guess ef I had been treated like I has hearn 'bout some of dem wuz treated I would'n liked it. But dem days I had plenty to eat, a good place as eny body to stay an' plenty close to wear an' I didn' hab no worries like I had had since I been free, 'bout tryin' to find wurk an' hab a little somethin' to eat an wear. "Course I'ze ole now an' hab to depen' on somebody else fer w'at little I hab."

Thompson, Victoria Taylor
Age: 80
1618 Spruce Addition
Muskogee, Oklahoma
Interviewer: Ethel Wolfe Garrison
[OK: 422–25]

My mother, Judy Taylor, named for her mistress, told me that I was born 'bout three year before the war; that make me about 80 year old, so they say down at the Indian Agency where my name is on the Cherokee rolls since all the land was give to the Indian families a long time ago.

Father kept the name of "Doc" Hayes, and my brother Coose was a Hayes, too, but mother, Jude, Patsy, Bonaparte (Boney, we always called him), Lewis and me was always Taylors. Daddy was bought by the Taylors (Cherokee Indians); dey made a trade for him with some hilly land, but he kept the name of Hayes even then.

Like my mother, I was born on the Taylor place. Dey lived in Flint District, around the Caney settlement on Caney Creek. Lots of the Arkansas Cherokees settled around dere long times before the Cherokees come here from the east, my mother said.

The farm wasn't very big, we was the only slaves on the place, and it was just a little ways from a hill everybody called Sugar Mountain, because it was covered with maple sugar trees, and an old Indian lived on the hillside, making maple sugar candy to sell and trade.

Master Taylor's house had three big rooms and a room for the loom, all made of logs, with a long front porch high off the ground. The spring house set to the east, in the corner like. Spring water boiled up all the time, and the water run down the branch which we crossed on a log bridge.

On the north side of the front porch, under a window in the mistress' room, was the grave of her little boy who was found drowned in the spring. The mistress set a heap of sore by dat child; said she wanted him buried right where she could always see his grave. She was might good.

So was the master good, too. None of us was ever beat or whipped like I hear about other slaves. Dey fix up a log cabin for us close by the big house. The yard fenced high with five or six rails, and dere was an apple orchard that set off the place with its blooming in the spring days.

Mother worked in the fields and in the house. She would hoe and plow, milk and do the cooking. She was a good cook and made the best cornbread I ever eat. Cook it in a skillet in the fireplace—I likes a piece of it right now! Grub dese days don't taste the same. Sometimes after the war she cook for the prisoners in the jail at Tahlequah.

Dat was the first jail I ever saw; they had hangings there. Always on a Friday, but I never see one, for it scare me and I run and hide.

Well, mother leave us children in the cabin while she gets breakfast for the master. We'd be nearly starved before she get back to tend us. And we slept on the floor, but the big house had wood beds, with high boards on the head and foot.

Mother took me with her to weaving room, and the mistress learn me how to weave in the stripes and colors so's I could make up one hundred kind of colors and shades. She ask me the color and I never miss telling her. Dat's one thing my sister Patsy can't learn when she was a little girl. I try the knitting, but I drop the stitches and lay it down.

Some of the things mother made was cloth socks and fringe for the hunting shirt that daddy always wore. The mistress made long tail shirts for the boys; we wore cotton all the year, and the first shoes I ever see was brass toed brogans.

For sickness daddy give us tea and herbs. He was a herb doctor, dat's how come he have the name "Doc." He made us wear charms, made out of shiny buttons and Indian rock beads. Dey cured lots of things and the misery too.

I hear mother tell about the slaves running away from mean masters, and how she help hide them at night from the dogs that come trailing them. The high fence keep out the dogs from the yard, and soon's they leave the runoffs would break for the river (Illinois), cross over and get away from the dogs.

The master had a mill run by oxen, the same oxen used in the fields. Dey stepped on the pedals and turn the rollers, dat how it was done.

Dere was another mill in the hills run by a white man name of Uncle

Mosie. One day he stole me to live in a cabin with him. He branded a circle on my cheek, but in two days I got away and run back to the Taylors where I was safe.

When the war broke out my daddy went on the side of the South with Master Taylor. Dey was gone a long time and when they come back he told of fighting the Federals north of Fort Gibson (it may have been the battle of Locust Grove), and how the Federals drove dem off like dogs. He said most of the time the soldiers starved and suffered, some of them freezing to death.

After the war I was stole again. I was hired to Judge Wolfe, and his wife Mary took good care of me and I helped around the big two-story house. She didn't like my father and kept off the place. One day an Indian, John Prichett, told me my daddy wanted to see me down by the old barn, to follow him. He grabbed me when we got back of the barn and took me away to his place where my daddy was waiting for me. We worked for dat Indian to pay for him getting me away from Judge Wolfe. Dat was around Fort Gibson.

Dat's where I married William Thompson, an uncle of Johnson Thompson, who was born a slave and lives now on Four Mile Branch (near Hulbert, Okla.). Dere was seven boys; where dey is I don't know, except for my boy George Lewis Thompson, who lives in this four-room house he builds for us, and stays unmarried so's he can take care of his old mammy.

I been belonging to church ever since there was a colored church, and I thinks everybody should obey the Master. He died, and I wants to go where Jesus lives. Like the poor Indian I saw one time waiting to be hung. Dere he was, setting on his own coffin box, singing over and over the words I just said: "I wants to go where Jesus lives!"

Dere's one thing I wants to do before I go. My time is short and I wants to go back to the Taylor place, to my old mistress' place, and just see the ground where she use to walk—dat's what I most want, but time is short.

Wagoner, Sweetie Ivery
Age: 73
1602 N. Third
Muskogee, Oklahoma
Interviewer: Ethel Wolfe Garrison
[OK: 441–43]

If I was born the year of freedom or the year before my mammy didn't know. Her name was Bitty Ivery and pappy's name was Louis Ivery, belonging to old Newt Tittsworth who had a big plantation somewheres in Arkansas, but I don't know what the name of the town. Only thing I know that man had a big place—as far as the eye could see that man owned it. He had seven or eight slave families on the place; my mother was the house girl, done the spinning, the cooking, the cleaning and all such. The old master was good to the slaves my mammy always said; never whipped them, but if they got mean and worthless he would sell them.

My father was a slave, but he wasn't a Negro. He was a Creek Indian whom the Cherokee Indians stole long years ago and put in slavery just like he was a Negro, and he married with a slave woman (her mother, Betty) and raised a big family. There was King, Louis, Mary, Cindy, Lucy, Jane, Fannie, Martha, Emma, Adeline and myself. I don't know where any is now, we all get separated after the war and never find each other.

Master Titsworth's house was a pretty good frame place; the slave families sleep in their own cabins, but all their eating was done together in a long house made of rough brick, and the eatings was plentiful with fresh killed beef or pork, plenty of corn pone made of meal ground by the old rock mills, with potatoes and vegetables seasoned high with the meats.

The eatings wasn't so good after the war when the slaves have to reach out for themselves; mostly it was corn grits, then maybe it wouldn't be nothing like it is now when I gets hardly enough to live on, hungry most of the time and in the misery so deep I can do no work (she is an invalid and seems likely to die within a short time).

There was a white overseer on the plantation and he blowed the whistle which sent everybody out to their work. Mammy said he was a good man.

The slave owners was always wanting more young slaves and if there was a woman on the place that didn't have no man the old masters would send to another plantation and borrow a big husky slave man for the woman and when the woman was done with child they would send the man back to this own place.

Everybody get scared when the war come along; the master was afraid somebody steal his slaves so he ups and takes us to Texas and then we come back to Arkansas after a while and stay there until freedom.

We stay for a while with the old master after the war, then my pappy go to farming and making things like wooden tubs, oat straw hats, horse collars and most anything he could sell or trade to the neighbors.

My folks was part Indian alright; they wore blankets and breeches with fur around the bottoms. My father's own daddy was Randolph Get-a-bout, and when the Indian lands given out by the allotments I got me 160 acres right here in Muskogee just north of where I live now. I use to own all that, but no more.

Lots of the slaves never learn to read or write, but the mistress teach my own mammy after the day's work was done. They set in the house long after dark and the mistress teach her, and then on Sunday, every Sunday too, they would go to a little church for the preaching. My mammy would set back over on one side of the seat rows; never did she miss the Sabbath meeting.

I belong to the Methodist church, but since it been eight year that I been unable to get out, I just do all my praying at home. There's nothing else like religion for folks to enjoy.

Arkansas County

Finley, Molly
Age: 75?
Honey Creek, near Mesa, Arkansas
Interviewer: Irene Robertson
[M:8: pt. 2: 292–95]

"My master was Captain Baker Jones and his pa was John Jones. Miss Mariah was Baker Jones' wife. I believe the old man's wife was dead.

"My parents' name was Henry ("Clay") Harris and Harriett Harris. They had nine children. We lived close to the Post (Arkansas Post). Our nearest trading post was Pine Bluff. And the old man made trips to Memphis and had barrels sent out by ship. We lived around Hanniberry Creek. It was a pretty lake of water. Some folks called it Hanniberry Lake. We fished and waded and washed. We got our water out of two springs further up. I used to tote one bucket on my head and one in each hand. You never see that no more. Mama was a nurse and house woman and field woman if she was needed. I made fires around the pots and 'tended to mama's children.

"We lived on the Jones place years after freedom. I was born after freedom. We finally left. I cried and cried to let's go back. Only place ever seem like home to me yet. We went to the Cummings farm. They worked free labor then. Then we went to the hills. Then we seen hard times. We knowed we was free niggers pretty soon back in them poor hills.

"I was more educated than some white folks up in them hills. I went to school on the river. My teacher was a white man named Mr. Van Sang.

"Mama belong to the Garretts in Mississippi. She was sold when she was about four years old she tole me. There had been a death and old mistress bought her in. Master Garrett died. Then she give her to her daughter. She was her young mistress then. Old mistress didn't want her to bring her but she said she might well have her as any rest of the children. Mama never set eyes on none of her folks no more. Her father, she said, was light and part Enjun (Indian).

"John Prior owned papa in Kentucky. He sold him, brother and his mother to a nigger trader's gang. Captain Jones bought all three in Tennessee. He come brought them on to Arkansas. He was a field hand. He said they worked from daylight till after dark.

"They took their slaves to close to Houston, Texas to save them. Captain Jones said he didn't want the Yankees to scatter them and make soldiers of them. He brought them back on his place like he expected to do. Mama said they was out there three years. She had a baby three months old and the trip was hard on her and the baby but they stood it. I was her next baby after that. Freedom done been declared. Mama said they went in wagons and camped along the roadside at night.

"Before they left, the Yankees come. Old Master Jones treated them so nice, give them a big dinner, and opened up everything and offered some for them to take along that they didn't bother his stock nor meat. Then he had them (the slaves) set out with stock and supplies to Texas.

"Mama and papa said the Jones treated them pretty well. They wouldn't allow the overseers to beat up his slaves.

"The two Jones men put two barrels of money in a big iron chest. They said it weighed two hundred pounds. Four men took it out there in barrels and eight men lowered it. They took it to the family graveyard down past the orchard. They leveled it up like it was a grave. Yankees didn't get Jones money! Then he sent the slaves to Texas.

"Captain Jones had a home in Tennessee and one in Arkansas. Papa said he cleared out land along the river where there was panther, bears, and wild cats. They worked in huddles and the overseers had guns to shoot varmints. He said their breakfast and dinner was sent to the field, them that had wives had supper with their families once a day, on Sundays three times. The women left the fields to go fix supper and see after their cabins and children. They hauled their water in barrels and put it under the trees. They cooked wash-pots full of chicken and give them a big picnic dinner after they lay by crops and at Christmas. They had gourd banjos. Mama said they had good times.

"They had preaching one Sunday for white folks and one Sunday for black folks. They used the same preacher there but some colored preachers would come on the place at times and preach under the trees down at the quarters. They said the white preacher would say, 'You may get to the kitchen of heaben if you obey your master, if you don't steal, if you tell no stories, etc.'

"Captain Jones was good doctor. If a doctor was had you know somebody was right low. They seldom had a doctor. Mama said her coat tail froze and her working. But they wore warm clothes next to their bodies.

"Captain Jones said, 'You all can go back on my place that want to go back and stay. You will have to learn to look after your own selves now but I will advise you and help you best I can. You will have to work hard as us have done b'fore. But I will pay you.' My folks was ready to 'board the wagons back to Jones' farm then. That is the way mama tole me it was at freedom! It was a long time I kept wondering what is freedom? I took to noticing what they said it was in slavery times and I caught on. I found out times had changed just b'fore I got into this world.

"Some things seem all right and some don't. Times seem good now but wait till dis winter. Folks will go cold and hungry again. Some folks good and some worse than in times b'fore."

Interviewer's Comment
Gets a pension check.

Keaton, Sam
Age: 78
Brinkley, Arkansas
Interviewer: Irene Robertson
[M:9: pt. 4: 175–76]

"I was born close to Golden Hill down in Arkansas County. My parents names was Louana and Dennis Keaton. They had ten children. Their master was Mr. Jack Keaton and Miss Martha. They had four boys. They all come from Virginia in wagons the second year of the war—the Civil War. I heard 'em tell about walking. Some of em walked, some rode horse back and some in wagons. I don't know if they knowed bout slave uprisings or not. I know they wasn't in em because they come here wid Mr. Jack Keaton. It was worse in Virginia than it was down here wid them. Mr. Keaton didn't give em nothing at freedom. They stayed on long as they wanted to stay and then they went to work for Mr. Jack Keaton's brother, Mr. Ben Keaton. They worked on shares and picked cotton by the hundred. My parents staid on down there till they died. I been working for Mr. Floria for thirty years.

"My father did vote. He voted a Republican ticket. I haven't voted for fifty years. They that do vote in the General election know very little bout what they doing. If they could vote in the Primary they would know but a mighty little about it. The women ain't got no business voting. Their place is at home.

They cain't keep their houses tidied up and like they oughter be and go out and work regularly. That's the reason I think they oughter stay at home and train the children better than it being done.

"I think that the young generation is going to be lost. They killing and fighting. They do everything. No, they don't work much as I do. They don't save nothing! They don't save nothing! Times is harder than they used to be some. Nearly everybody wants to live in town. My age is making times heap harder for me. I live with my daughter. I am a widower. I owns 40 acres land, a house, a cow. I made three bales cotton, but I owe it bout all. I tried to get a little help so I could get out of debt but I never could get no 'sistance from the Welfare."

Miller, Matilda
Age: 79
Humphrey, Arkansas
Interviewer: Mrs. Annie L. LaCotts
[M:10: pt. 5: 90–92]

The day of the interview Matilda, a nice clean-looking Negro woman, was in bed, suffering from some kind of a pain in her head. She lives in a little two-room unpainted boxed house beside the highway in Humphrey. Her house is almost in the shadow of a big tank which was put up recently when the town acquired its water system.

When told that the visitor wanted to talk with her about her early life, Matilda said, "Well, honey, I'll tell you all I can, but you see, I was just a little girl when the war was, but I've heard my mother tell lots of things about then.

"I was born a slave; my mother and daddy both were owned by Judge Richard Gamble at Crockett's Bluff. I was born at Boone Hill—about twelve miles north of DeWitt—and how come it named Boone Hill, that farm was my young mistress's. Her papa give it to her, just like he give me to her when I was little, and after she married Mr. Oliver Boone and lived there the farm always went by the name of 'Boone Hill.' The house is right on top of a hill, you know, it shure was a pretty place when Miss Georgia lived there, with great big Magnolia trees all in the front yard. I belonged to Miss Georgia, my young mistress, and when the niggers were freed my mamma staid on with her. She was right there when both of his chillun were born, Mr. John Boone and Miss Mary, too. I nursed *both* of them chillun. You know who Miss Mary is now, don't you? Yes'um, she's Mr. Lester Black's wife and he's good, too.

"I was de oney child my mother had till twelve years after the surrender. You see, my papa went off with Yankees and didn't come back till twelve years after we was free, and then I had some brothers and sisters. Exactly nine months from the day my daddy come home, I had a baby brother born. My mother said she knew my daddy had been married or took up with some other woman, but she hadn't got a divorce and still counted him her husband. They lived for a long time with our white folks, for they were good to us, but you know after the boys and girls got grown and began to marry and lived in different places, my parents wanted to be with them and left the white folks.

"No mam, I didn't see any fighting, but we could hear the big guns booming away off in the distance. I was married when I was 21 to Henry Miller and lived with him 51 years and ten months; he died from old age and hard work. We had two chillun, both girls. One of them lives here with me in that other room. Mamma said the Yankees told the Negroes when they got em freed they'd give em a mule and a farm or maybe a part of the plantation they'd been working on for their white folks. She thought they just told em that to make them dissatisfied and to get more of them 'to join up with em' and they were dressed in pretty blue clothes and had nice horses and that made lots of the Negro men go with them. None of em ever got anything but what their white folks give em, and just lots and lots of em never come back after the war cause the Yankees put them in front where the shooting was and they was killed. My husband Henry Miller died four years ago. He followed public work and made plenty of money but he had lots of friends and his money went easy too. I don't spect I'll live long for this hurtin' in my head is awful bad sometime."

Mitchell, Moses
Age: 89
117 Worthen Street
Pine Bluff, Arkansas
Interviewer: Bernice Bowden
3 November 1938
[M:10: pt. 5: 114–16]

Description of room, house, surroundings, etc.—A frame house (rented), bare floors, no window shades; a bed and some boxes and three straight chairs. In an adjoining room were another bed, heating stove, two trunks, one straight chair, one rocking chair. A third room, the kitchen, contained cookstove and table and chairs.

"I was born down here on White River near Arkansas Post, August 1849.

I belonged to Thomas Mitchel and when they (Yankees) took Arkansas Post, our owners gathered us up and my young master took us to Texas and he sold me to an Irishman named John McInish in Marshall for $1500. $500 in gold and the rest in Confederate money. They called it the new issue.

"I was twelve years old then and I stayed in Texas till I was forty-eight. I was at Tyler, Texas when they freed us. When they took us to Texas they left my mother and baby sister here in Arkansas, down here on Oak Log Bayou. I never saw her again and when I came back here to Arkansas, they said she had been dead twenty-eight years. Never did hear of my father again.

"I'm supposed to be part Creek Indian. Don't know how much. We have one son, a farmer, lives across the river. Married this wife in 1873.

"My wife and I left Texas forty-one years ago and came back here to Arkansas and stayed till 1922. Then we went to Chicago and stayed till 1930, and then came back here. I'd like to go back up there, but I guess I'm gettin' too old. While I was there I preached and I worked all the time. I worked on the streets and the driveways in Lincoln Park. I was in the brick and block department. Then I went from there to the asphalt department. There's where I coined the money. Made $6.60 in the brick and block and $7.20 a day in the asphalt. Down here they don't know no more about asphalt than a pig does about a holiday. *A man that's from the South and never been nowhere, don't know nothin', a woman either.*

"Yes ma'm, I'm a preacher. Just a local preacher, wasn't ordained. The reason for that was, in Texas a man over forty-five couldn't join the traveling connection. I was licensed, but of course I couldn't perform marriage ceremonies. I was just within one step of that.

"I went to school two days in my life. I was privileged to go to the first free school in Texas. Had a teacher named Goldman. Don't know what year that was but they found out me and another fellow was too old so they wouldn't let us go no more. But I caught my alphabet in them two days. So I just caught what education I've got, here and there. I can read well—best on my Bible and Testament and I read the newspapers. I can sorta scribble my name.

"I've been a farmer most of my life and a preacher for fifty-five years. I can repair shoes and use to do common carpenter work. I can help build a house. I only preach occasionally now, here and there. I belong to the Allen Temple in Hoboken (East Pine Bluff).

"I think the young generation is gone to naught. They're a different cut to what they was in my comin' up."

Interviewer's Comment
This man and his wife live in the outskirts of West Pine Bluff. They receive

a small sum of money and commodities from the County Welfare Department. He has a very pleasant personality, a good memory and intelligence above the ordinary. Reads the Daily Graphic and Arkansas Gazette. Age 89. He said, *"Here's the idea, freedom is worth it all."*

Personal History of Informant
1.   Ancestry—Father, Lewis Mitchell; Mother, Rhoda Mitchell
2.   Place and date of birth—Oak Log Bayou, White River, near Arkansas Post, Ark.
3.   Family—Wife and one grown son
4.   Places lived in, with dates—Taken to Texas by his young master and sold in Marshall during the war. Lived in Tyler, Texas until forty-eight years of age; came back to Arkansas in 1897 and stayed until 1922; went to Chicago and lived until 1930; back to Jefferson County, Arkansas.
5.   Education, with dates—Two days after twenty-one years of age. No date.
6.   Occupations and accomplishments, with dates—Farmer, preacher, common carpenter, cobbler, public work on streets in Chicago. Farmed and preached until he went to Chicago in 1922. Then he worked in the maintenance department of city streets of Chicago and of Lincoln Park, Chicago.
7.   Special skills and interests—Asphalt worker
8.   Community and religious activities—Licensed Methodist Preacher. No assignment now.
9.   Description of informant—Five feet eight inches tall; weight, 165 pounds, nearly bald. Very prominent cheek bones. Keen intelligence. Neatly dressed.
10.   Other points gained in interview—Reads daily papers; knowledge of world affairs.

Payne, Harriett McFarlin
Age: 83
DeWitt, Arkansas
Interviewer: Mrs. Annie L. LaCotts
[M:10: pt. 5: 300–03]

"Aunt Harriett, were you born in slavery time?"

"Yes, mam! I was big enough to remember well, us coming back from Texas after we refugeed there when the fighting of the war was so bad at St. Charles. We stayed in Texas till the surrender, then we all come back in lots of wagons. I was sick but they put me on a little bed and me and all the little chillun rode in a 'Jersey' that one of the old Negro mammies drove, along behind the wagons, and our young master, Colonel Bob Chaney rode a great big black horse. Oh! he nice-looking on dat horse! Every once and awhile he'd ride back to the last wagon to see if everything was all right. I remember how scared us chillun was when we crossed the Red River. Aunt Mandy said, 'We crossin' you old Red River today, but we not going to cross you any more, cause we are going home now, back to Arkansas.' That day when we stopped to cook our dinner I picked up a lot little blackjack acorns and when my mammy saw them she said, 'Throw them things down, chile. They'll make you wormy.' I cried because I thought they were chinquapins. I begged my daddy to let's go back to Texas, but he said, 'No! No! We going with our white folks.' My mama and daddy belonged to Col. Jesse Chaney, much of a gentleman, and his wife Miss Sallie was the best mistress anybody ever had. She was a Christian. I can hear her praying yet! She wouldn't let one of her slaves hit a tap on Sunday. They must rest and go to church. They had preaching at the cabin of some one of the slaves, and in the Summertime sometimes they had it out in the shade under the trees. Yes, and the slaves on each plantation had their own church. They didn't go galavanting over the neighborhood or country like niggers do now. Col. Chaney had lots and lots of slaves and all their houses were in a row, all one-room cabins. Everything happened in that one room,—birth, sickness, death and everything, but in them days niggers kept their houses clean and their door yards too. These houses where they lived was called 'the Quarters.' I used to love to walk down by that row of houses. It looked like a town and late of an evening as you'd go by the doors you could smell meat a frying, coffee making and good things cooking. We were fed good and had plenty clothes to keep us dry and warm.

"Along about time for de surrender, Col. Jesse, our master, took sick and died with some kind of head trouble. Then Col. Bob, our young master, took care of his mama and the slaves. All the grown folks went to the field to work and the little chillun would be left at a big room called the nursing home. All us little ones would be nursed and fed by an old mammy, Aunt Mandy. She was too old to go to the field, you know. We wouldn't see our mammy and daddy from early in the morning till night when their work was done, then they'd go by Aunt Mandy's and get their chillun and go home till work time in the morning.

"Some of the slaves were house negroes. They didn't go to work in the fields, they each one had their own job around the house, barn, orchard, milk house, and things like that.

"When washday come, Lord, the pretty white clothes! It would take three or four women a washing all day.

"When two of de slaves wanted to get married, they'd dress up nice as they could and go up to the big house and the master would marry them. They'd stand up before him and he'd read out of a book called the 'discipline' and say, 'Thou shalt love the Lord thy god with all thy heart, all thy strength, with all thy might and thy neighbor as theyself.' Then he'd say they were man and wife and tell them to live right and be honest and kind to each other. All the slaves would be there too, seeing the 'wedden'.

"Our Miss Sallie was the sweetest best thing in the world! She was so good and kind to everybody and she loved her slaves, too. I can remember when Uncle Tony died how she cried! Uncle Tony Wadd was Miss Sallie's favorite servant. He stayed in a little house in the yard and made fires for her, brought in wood and water and just waited on the house. He was a little black man and white-headed as cotton, when he died. Miss Sally told the niggers when they come to take him to the grave yard, to let her know when they got him in his coffin, and when they sent and told her she come out with all the little white chillun, her little grandchillun, to see Uncle Tony. She just cried and stood for a long time looking at him, then she said, 'Tony, you have been a good and faithful servant.' Then the Negro men walked and carried him to the graveyard out in a big grove in de field. Every plantation had its own grave-yard and buried its own folks and slaves right on the place.

"If all slaves had belonged to white folks like ours, there wouldn't been any freedom wanted."

Word, Sam
Age: 79
1122 Missouri Street
Pine Bluff, Arkansas
Interviewer: Mrs. Bernice Bowden
[M:11: 7: 235–41]

"I'm a sure enough Arkansas man, born in Arkansas County near De Witt. Born February 14, 1859, and belonged to Bill Word. I know Marmaduke come down through Arkansas County and pressed Bill Word's son Tom into the service.

"I 'member one song they used to sing called the 'Bonnie Blue Flag.'

'Jeff Davis is our President
And Lincoln is a fool;
Jeff Davis rides a fine white horse
While Lincoln rides a mule.'

'Hurrah! Hurrah! for southern rights,
Hurrah!
Hurrah for the Bonnie Blue Flag
That bears a Single Star!'"

(The above verse was sung to the tune of "The Bonnie Blue Flag." From the Library of Southern Literature I find the following notation about the original song and its author, Harry McCarthy: "Like Dixie, this famous song originated in the theater and first became popular in New Orleans. The tune was borrowed from 'The Irish Jaunting Car', a popular Hibernian air. Harry McCarthy was an Irishman who enlisted in the Confederate army from Arkansas. The song was written in 1861. It was published by A. E. Blackmar who declared General Ben Butler 'made it very profitable by fining every man, woman, or child who sang, whistled or played it on any instrument twenty-five dollars.' Blackmar was arrested, his music destroyed, and a fine of five hundred dollars imposed upon him.")

"I stayed in Arkansas County till 1866. I was about seven years old and we moved here to Jefferson County. Then my mother married again and we went to Conway County and lived a few years, and then I come back to Jefferson County, so I've lived in Jefferson County sixty-eight years.

"In Conway County when I was a small boy livin' on the Milton Powell place, I 'member they sent me out in the field to get some peaches about a half mile from the slave quarters. It was about three o'clock, late summer, and I saw something in the tree—a black lookin' concern. Seem like it get bigger the closer I got, and then just disappeared all of a sudden and I didn't see it go. I know I went back without any peaches.

"And another thing I can tell you. In the spring of the year we was hoein' and when they quit at night they'd leave the hoes in the field, stickin' down in the ground. And next morning they wouldn't be where you left 'em. You'd have to look for 'em and they'd be lyin' on top of the ground and crossed just like sticks.

"I'll tell you what I do know. When us was livin' in Conway County old man Powell had about ten colored families he had emigrated from Jefferson County. Our folks was the only colored people in that neighborhood. And he had a white man that was a tenant on the place and he died. Now my mother and his wife used to visit one another. In them days the white folks wasn't like they are now. And so mother went there to sit up with his wife. And while he was sittin' up the house was full of people—white and colored. They begin to hear a noise about the coffin. So they begin to investigate the worse it got and moved around the room and it lasted till he was took out of the house.

Now I've heard white and colored say that was true. They never did see it but they heard it.

"I don't think there is any ghosts now but they was in the past generation.

"I know many times me and my stepfather would be pickin' cotton and my dog would be up at the far end of the row and just before dark he'd start barkin' and come towards us a barkin' and we never could see anything. He'd do that every day. It was a dog named Katch—an English bull terrier. He was give to me a puppy. He was a sure enough bulldog and he could whip any dog I ever saw. He was an imported dog.

"I remember a house up in Conway County made out of logs—a two-story one just this side of Cadron Creek on the Military Road. Then they called it the Wire Road because the telegraph wire run along it. The house was vacant after the people that owned it had died, and people comin' along late at night would stop to spend the night, and in the middle of the night they'd have to get out. Now I've heard that with my own ears. There was a spring not far from the house. It had been a fine house and was a beautiful place to stop. But in the night they'd hear chairs rattlin' and fall down. It's my belief they had spooks in them old days.

"Now I'll tell you another incident. This was in slave times. My mother was a great hand for nice quilts. There was a white lady had died and they were goin' to have a sale. Now this is true stuff. They had the sale and mother went and bought two quilts. And let me tell you, we couldn't sleep under 'em. What happened? Well, they'd pinch your toes till you couldn't stand it. I was just a boy and I was sleepin' with my mother when it happened. Now that's straight stuff. What do I think was the cause? Well, I think that white lady didn't want no nigger to have them quilts. I don't know what mother did with 'em, but that white lady just wouldn't let her have 'em.

"Now I'm puttin' the oil out of the can—I mean that what I say is true. People now will say they ain't nothin' to that story. At that time the races wasn't amalgamated. But people are different now—ain't like they was seventy-five years ago.

"Visions? Well, now I'm glad you asked me that. I'll take pleasure in tellin' you. Two years before I moved to this place I had a vision and I think I saw every colored person that was ever born in America, I believe. I was on the east side of my house and this multitude of people was about four feet from me and they was as thick as sardines in a box and they was from little tots up. Some had on derby hats and some was bareheaded. I talked with one woman—a brown skinned woman. They was sitting on seats just like circus seats just as far as my eyes could behold. Looked like they reached clear up in the sky. That was when I fust went blind. You've read about how John saw the multitude a hundred forty and four thousand and I think that was about one-fourth of what I saw. They was happy and talkin' and nothin' but colored people—no white people.

"Another vision I had. I dreamed that the day that I lived to be sixty-five, that day I would surely die. I thought the man that told me that was a little old dried-up white man up in the air and he had scales like the monkey and the cat weighed the cheese. I thought he said, 'That day you will surely die,' and one side of the scales tipped just a little and then I woke up. You know I believed this strong. That was in 1919 and I went out and bought a lot in Bellwood Cemetery. But I'm still livin'.

"Old Major Crawley who owned what they called the Reeder place on this side of the river, four miles east of Dexter, he was suposed to have money buried on his place. He owned it during slavery and after he died his relatives from Mississippi come here and hired a carriage driver named Jackson Jones. He married my second cousin. And he took 'em up there to dig for the money, but I don't know if they ever found it. Some people said the place was ha'nted. [Second Interview?]

"I was born February 14, 1859. My birthplace was Arkansas County. Born in Arkansas and lived in Arkansas seventy-eight years. I've kept up with my age—didn't raise it none, didn't lower it none.

"I can remember all about the war, my memory's been good. Old man Bill Word, that was my old master, had a son named Tom Word and long about in '63 a general come and pressed him into the Civil War. I saw the Blue and the Gray and the gray clothes had buttons that C.S., that meant secessioners. Yankees had U.S. on their buttons. Some of em come there so regular they got familiar with me. Yankees come and wanted to hang old master cause he wouldn't tell where the money was. They tied his hands behind him and had a rope around his neck. Now this is the straight goods. I was just a boy and I was cryin' cause I didn't want em to hang old master. A Yankee lieutenant come up and made em quit—they was just the privates you know.

"My old master drove a ox wagon to the gold fields in California in '49. That's what they told me—that was fore I was born.

"Good? Ben Word good? My God Amighty, I wish I had one-hundredth part of what I got then. I didn't exist—I lived.

"Ben Word bought my mother from Phil Ford up in Kentucky. She was the housekeeper after old mistress died. I'll tell you something that may be amusing. Mother had lots of nice things, quilts and things, and kept em in a chest in her little old shack. One day a Yankee soldier climbed in the back window and took some of the quilts. He rolled em up and was walking out of the yard when mother saw him and said, 'Why you nasty, stinkin' rascal. You say you come down here to fight for the niggers, and now you're stealin' from em.' He said, 'You're a G—D—liar, I'm fightin' for $14 a month and the Union.'

"I member there was a young man named Dan Brown and they called him Red Fox. He'd slip up on the Yankees and shoot em, so the Yankees was always lookin' for him. He used to go over to Dr. Allen's to get a shave and his wife would sit on the front porch and watch for the Yankees. One day the Yankees slipped up in the back and his wife said, 'Lord, Dan, there's the Yankees.' Course he run and they shot him. One of the Yankees was tryin' to help him up and he said, 'Don't you touch me, call Dr. Allen.' Yes ma'am, that was in Arkansas County.

"I never been anywhere 'cept Arkansas, Jefferson, and Conway counties. I was in Conway County when they went to the precinct to vote for or against the Fort Smith & Little Rock Railroad. The precinct where they went to vote was Springfield. It used to be the county seat of Conway County.

"While the war was goin' on and when young Tom Word would come home from school, he learned me and when the war ended, I could read in McGuffy's Third Reader. After that I went to school three months for about four years.

"Directly after Emancipation, the white men in the South had to take the Oath of Allegiance. Old master took it but he hated to do it. Now these are stubborn facts I'm givin' you but they's true.

"After freedom mother brought me here to Pine Bluff and put me in the field. I picked up corn stalks and brush and carried water to the hands. Children in them days worked. After they come from school, even the white children had work to do. Trouble with the colored folks now, to my way of thinkin', is they are top heavy with literary learning and feather light with common sense and domestic training.

"I remember a song they used to sing during the war:

'Jeff Davis is our President'
Lincoln is a fool;
Jeff Davis rides a fine white horse
While Lincoln rides a mule.'
"And here's another one:
'Hurrah for Southern rights, hurrah!
Hurrah for the Bonny Blue Flag
That bore the single star.'

"Yes, they was hants sixty years ago. The generation they was interested has bred em out. Ain't none now.

"I never did care much for politics, but I've always been for the South. I love the southland. Only thing I don't like is they don't give a square deal when it comes between the colored and the whites. Ten years ago, I was worth $15,000 and now I'm not worth fifteen cents. The real estate man got the best of me. I've been blind now for four years and all my wife and I have is what we get from the Welfare."

Ashley County

Densen, Nelson
Age: 90
Waco, Texas
Interview 1
Interviewer: ?
[M:4: pt. 1 (TX): 305–06]

Nelson Densen, 90, was born near Hambirg, Arkansas, a slave of Jim Nelson, who sold Nelsen and his family to Felix Grundy. Nelsen's memory is poor, but he managed to recall a few incidents. He now lives in Waco, Texas.

"I'll be ninety years old this December (1937). I was born in Arkansas, up in Ashley County, and it was the twenty-second day of December in 1847. My mammy was from Virginny and pappy was from old Kentucky, and I was one of eight chillen. Our owner, Marse Jim Densen, brung us to Texas and settled near Marlin, but got in debt and sold us all to Marse Felix Grundy, and he kep' us till freedom, and most of us worked for him after that.

"Marse Jim Densen had a easy livin' in Arkansas, but folks everywhere was comin' to Texas and he 'cides to throw in his fortunes. It wasn't so long after that war with Mexico and folks come in a crowd to 'tect theyselves 'gainst Indians and wild animals. The wolves was the worst to smell cookin' and sneak into camp, but Indians come up and makes the peace sign and has a pow wow with the white folks. Marse git beads or cloth and trade for leather breeches and things.

"I want to tell how we crosses the Red River on de Red River Raft. Back in them days the Red River was near closed up by dis timber raft and de big boats couldn't git up de river at all. We gits a li'l boat, and a Caddo Indian to guide us. Dis Red River raft dey say was centuries old. De driftwood floatin' down de river stops in de still waters and makes a bunch of trees and de dirt 'cumulates, and broomstraws and willows and brush grows out dis rich dirt what cover de driftwood. Dis raft growed 'bout a mile a year and de oldes' timber rots and breaks away, but dis not fast 'nough to keep de river clear. We found bee trees on de raft and had honey.

"It was long time after us come to Texas when the gov'ment opens up de channel. Dat am in 1873. 'Fore dat, a survey done been made and dey found de raft am a hundred and twenty-eight miles long. When we was on dat raft it am like a big swamp, with trees and thick brush and de driftwood and logs all wedge up tight 'tween everything.

"'Fore Texas secedes, Marse Jensen done sell us all to Marse Felix Grundy, and he goes to war in General Hardeman's Brigade and is with him for bodyguard. When de battle of Mansfield come I'm sixteen years old. We was camped on the Sabine River, on the Texas side, and the Yanks on the other side a li'l ways. I 'member the night 'fore the battle, how the campfires looked, and a quiet night and the whipporwills callin' in the weeds. We was 'spectin' a 'tack and sings to keep cheerful. The Yanks sings the 'Battle Cry of Freedom' when they charges us. They come on and on and, Lawd, how they fit! I stays clost to Marse Grundy and the rebels wins and take 'bout a thousand Yanks.

"Most the slaves was happy, the ones I knowed. They figgers the white men fightin' for some principal, but lots of them didn't care nothin' 'bout bein' free. I s'pose some was with bad white folks, but not round us. We had more to eat and now I'm so old I wouldn't feel bad if I had old marse to look after me 'gain.

Interview 2
Interviewer: Miss Effie Cowan, P.W.
18 September 1937
[S2:4: 1168–81]
[See also Interview 3, 4 December 1837, S2:4: 1182–92]

> "Strike the tent, the sun has risen,
> Not a vapor streakes the dawn,
> And the frosted prairies brightens,
> To the westward far and near.
>
> Prime afresh the trusty rifle,
> Sharpen well the hunting spear,
> For the frozen sod is trembling,
> And the noise of hoos I hear." (Bayard Taylor)

Nelson Taylor Densen was brought with his parents to Texas in 1854 by their owner Mr. Jim Densen, he saw the reaction of Texas from the Mexican War and served as body guard for his Master during the Civil War. His story follows:

"I wuz born near Hamburg, Arkansas, in Ashley County, on the twenty-second day of December, eighteen hundred and forty seven. I will be ninety years old this coming December. My mother wuz a Virginian, my father a Kentuckian. I wuz one of eight chillun, only four cum ter Texas with our parents. With their owner Mr. Jim Densen they settled about ten miles from Marlin in Falls County, Texas.

"We stayed with this owner Mr. Densen until he became involved in debt and sold us ter Mr. Felix Grundy whose body-guard I wuz during the Civil War. He kept us until freedom wuz declared and part of us stayed with him and part worked fer the near-by neighbors after freedom.

"I kin remember hearin' my parents tell of their life as slaves in their home state, and many incidents of their lives, they lived the average life of the plantation slaves, they were taught to read and write, hence my being able to be a minister of the Gospel.

"My first clear memory is playing as a child on the banks of the river near whar I lived in Arkansas, and the work on the plantation, they raised little patches of cotton and grain, and lots of strawberries, apples, dewberries and blackberries, as well as other fruit and vegetables. Also cowpeas which they fed to the stock.

"The timber made it a good place for cattle and hogs for at that time they run out in the woods free, and we did not have to buy our wood. The old Master had an easy livin' but the folks everywhar wuz a cumin ter Texcas, the land wuz very clean an they wuz bringin' in settlers and colonizing the new state, so our Master decided to throw in his fortunes with it too.

"Dis wuz right after the war with Mexico and dey wuz famblies dat would get together and all cum in the same crowd, in order ter help protect each other against the Indians and wild animals like bears and some panther's. Dey cum in de spring an' if de rivers would be up den dey would sometimes have ter camp an' wait until hit run down 'specially if dey has ter ford hit. Some rivers if dey wuz small an' had rock beds dey forded an if dey wuz big like de Red River dey crossed in er ferryboat.

"Sometimes dey had ter swim de horses an make several trips ter git dey things across, an den dey had de cattle ter git across too, an dey mos always swim de rivers if dey not too big.

"W'en dey made de camp de wagons wuz set in a circle and de camp fire in de center, dis wuz ter have a place ter keep a breastwork, in a way as protection from Indians, and de wild animals, de wolves wuz de worst ter smell de cookin an cum ter de camp. Sometime de camp guards would see two big eyes er lookin' out at dem from de trees an brush an' hit would be a wolf or bear, dey shoot de gun off an dat skeer dem away.

"Sometimes hit not an animal but an Indian an den dey goes an makes de peace sign and dey sit down an has a pow-wow wid dem, pretty soon de Master get up an cum an git some beans er some bright dress goods er beads er maybe little gunpowder, fer dey had learned ter shoot by den, an trade wid dem fer moccasens er leather breeches somethin dat dey make.

"De East Texas Indians wuz called de Timber Indians, but dey wuz known mostly as de Cherekee's an de Alabama Tribes, de settlers crowed de Indians out an lots of dem had gone furder west, dey had about dis time given dem a Reservation in Polk County, of about a thousand acres of land. Some of dem are still dar to dis day.

"De Plains Indians, among dem de Comanche, get so bold dat dey made raids in Texas, an de Texas Rangers wuz 'bout all dey wuz ter keep dem back, untill finally de Government built forts ter station de soljers an de Rangers ter live an be ready ter go after dem if dey made a raid, or watch fer dem, dey wuz not friendly like de Cherekees an de Alabama Tribes.

"W'en we cum ter Texas in 1854, dey had jes started de Reservation in Polk County. I understan' dat in 1928 de white people helped dem ter buy more land an now dey has 'bout four thousand acres, dey still make de bows an arrows, baskets, mats, rugs, flutes, spoons an other things. Dis dey sell ter de white folks an dey works for de white people too.

"I have learned too dat de Government had 'nuther Reservation at Ft. Belknap in Young County, an one on de Clear Fork ob de Brazos 'bout sixty miles from dis one, but hit did'nt work out bery well so dey moved dem ter de Indian territory dat we call Oklahoma now.

"I has some dates of things dat happened. I has kept all dose years an one is 'bout Cynthia Ann Parker, how she wuz captured at Parkers Fort on May de nineteenth 1836, near de town of Groesbeck, Texas. Five Americans wuz killed an' four wuz taken prisoner's. Of de twenty from de fort dat escaped dey wuz six days in the wilderness without food, ceptin' what dey find in de woods. A Mrs. Kellogg one of de prisoners wuz wid de Indians six months, Mrs. Plummer over a year an' her son 'bout six years, Cynthia Ann Parker twenty four years an her little brother if living is still wid dem at de time dis wuz written in 1878, in a Directory of Texas, Published at Austin.

"Dis wuz in May befo' Santa Anna wuz placed on de Texas war schooner ter be sent ter Vera Cruz. A Company of volunteers dat had jes arrived at

Belasco forcibly took him an brought him on shore. Dey gib him ter Gen Paaten of de army an dey taken him up de river ter a Dr. Phelps house whar dey kept him until a company of Bucheye Rangers cum an helped ter sneak him away ter de Mississippi river whar dey took de ship ter Washington an den President Jackson sent him ter Vera Cruz, Mexico.

"Yer ask me ter tell yer things dat happened in de early days dat we talked 'bout den, dis wuz w'en we first cum ter Texas, an dey not talkin' den 'bout de slavery question so much as de Mexican an de Indians, but dey did have some trouble wid de Mexicans befo' de Civil War 'bout de slaves, de Mexicans would try ter git dem ter run away an stay across de border wid dem an some ob dem did, however de nigger mos' afraid ob de Mexicans an so dey 'fraid ter do dis much.

"Dar wuz one Mexican name Jaun Cortena an his band dat robbed an stole from de Texas people until finally Gen Robert E. Lee of de United States Army run him back across de border. I hear dem talkin' bout dis in de war w'en Gen Lee wuz in command of de Confederate army.

"Dar is one more date dat I would like ter tell yer 'bout dat dey talk 'bout w'en we cum ter Texas, an dat wuz 'bout de Rangers under Gen. George Erath havin' a fight wid de Indians in Robertson County dat not far from whar we lived an how dey killed Frank Childress and Davie Clarke, dis wuz de folks dat de town of Childress wuz named fer an de Clarkes ar one ob de oldest famblies in Marlin.

"Den I could tell yer 'bout how dey talk 'bout de house of Mr. Morgan six miles above de falls ob de Brazos being attacked by dem, an five people killed. An' how Mr. Marlin, (fer whom de town ob Marlin named) on January 10, 1839 de Indians attacked Mr. Marlin's house, but dey drove de Indians back an den de white people followed under de command of Benjamin Bryant. Den on de twenty-first of April dey had another battle between de whites an de Indians on Brushy Creek, in de Marlin country between Waco an Marlin, an some white men by de name of Jacob Burlerson, James Gilleland, Edward Blakie, an John Waters were killed.

"Dis is 'bout all dat I have kept on de things dat happened near Marlin between de Indians an de white folks. But after dey quit being so much trouble de folks lived peacably an dey wuz more an' more settlers cumin in. Dey had an iron foundry at Rusk an Jefferson 'bout dis time, an at de penitentiary at Huntsville 'bout dis time dey had a mill dat dey make cotton an woolen goods fer de soljers, an de folks in Texas had ter wear some of de goods which helped dem ter have something widout havein ter spin de thread an weave de cloth like dey has ter do most places.

"In de spring de bluebonnets an de Indian blanket flowers wuz in bloom w'en we cum ter Texas an we never saw dem befo' dey looked like beds of red an blue blankets an dey wuz everywhar in April an May. I kin remember how we liked ter fish an de sweet smell ob de pine trees w'en dey build de campfire out ob de brush, an how we boys hunted fer de wild haw, de red haw, de pecans an de walnuts dat grew in de woods of East Texas as we cum thro' hit. Hit wuz all wonderful an beautiful ter us, jes ignorant little niggers, an if so ter us what must it have been ter de white settlers?

"We did not have de Buffalo in dis part ob de country like dey had further west, an de Indians more plentiful out dar. W'en de white men begun ter kill de buffalo, (dis wuz de Indians meat dey eat), den dey commence ter fight sure e'nuff, dey do like mos' folks would fight fer dey life, an widout de buffalo dey think dat dey can't live.

"Our ole Master stopped at Marshall, Texas first an decided dat he wants ter cum further south, so he cums ter Marlin or down near Marlin an lives dar de rest ob his life. De way dey all trabbel den wuz by wagon, de stage coach, an de boats on de rivers and de bayou's. In de northeast part ob Texas dey freighted dey cotton an grain ter Jefferson an den dey shipped by Cypress Bayou, an across Lake Caddo ter de Red River an from dar up North or maybe down ter New Orleans.

"In South Texas de shippin wuz in an out ob de bayou's an de rivers ter de coast, an on de Brazos River Richmon' wuz de head 'Ceptin' w'en de river wuz up and den dey ship ter de ole town ob Washington on de Brazos, dey called hit. De steambots made regular trips between Galveston an Houston up Buffalo Byou.

"Whar dey wasn't any rivers fer de boats, den dey trabbel by de stage coach an dey wuz heavy an drawn by six or eight horses, dey jes went eight or ten miles an hour an fresh teams wuz ready fer dem ter change along de way. Dey had a line down thro Marlin from North Texas, an we used ter watch hit cum in jes like de train or bus.

"Texas people wuz jes begginnin' ter git over de Mexican war w'en we cum ter de state, dey talk 'bout de Alamo an Gen. Sam Houston, Travis, who wuz killed at de Alamo an Bowie, an de battle ob San-Jacinto, w'en dey celebrated dey freedom from Mexico. De Mexicans had dey own Catholic schools an churches dat wuz established in de days ob de rule by Mexico an de Missions dat de Spaniards had built W'en dey first discovered Texas.

"De Baptist, Methodist an de Presbyrterians all had dey churches an some had started dey schools, but dey had not started de free schools until long time after dat. An' dey git ter know folks from other places at dem fer dey cum and camp two or three weeks. I has preached at dem an we felt dat de Lord wuz close ter us, w'en dey got religion dey git it ter de better an ter live right in dem days seem like we nearer ter God den we is now.

"Well, dis de way dat we livin' in Texas in de year we cum in 1854. Dey talk 'bout sending General Sam Houston ter Washington he voted against slavery up dar, so in 1857 he run fer Governor against Runnels he wuz beat, dey say, on account ob his vote against slavery, fer Texas wuz a slave holding state.

"W'en Runnels wuz Governor more an more immigrants cum ter Texas, but he wuz not popular an w'en he an General Houston run again in 1859 fer Governor General Houston beat Runnels.

"De people of Texas thought dat General Houston would keep Texas from getting into de war, an dat he could make peace wid de Indians an' dat wuz why he wuz elected. I kin 'member how he tells dem in his first message dat "if dey dont stan by the union dat de nation be destroyed by war." An w'en Lincoln wuz made de president, Houston stilled tried ter keep Texas from gittin in de war, an keep hit in de Union, but dey had a Convention at Austin an voted fer Texas to secede, dat wuz de twenty eighth day of January, 1861.

"Den w'en he refused ter take de oath ter de Confederacy dey removes him from de Governer's cheer an he went back ter his home at Huntsville, an never does take hit, but his son Sam went an fought fer de rebels.

"I wuz fourteen years old w'en Texas seceded, an w'en dey went ter de war my Master Mr. Felix Grundy went ter fight de Yankees. He wuz in General Hardemans Brigade an wuz in two or three battles den he cums back ter Texas on a fourlough an w'en dat is out an he goes back I goes with him as his body guard. De first firing he wuz in New Mexico, den he wuz transferred ter Louisiana an I wuz wid him.

"I was sixteen years old by dat time an I kin remember de way hit all wuz at de battle ob Mansfield, April 9, 1863. We wuz camped on de Sabine rivers, on de Texas side, an de Yankees on de other side up a little ways, I kin remember de night befo' how de camp fires looked, hit wuz a quiet night an de whipperwills er callin' in de weeds, we wuz expectin de attack an ter keep us cheerful we sing, "Tenting Ter Night on de Old Camp Groun'," an' den we sing,

> "Just befo' de battle, Mother,
> I am thinking most of you,
> While upon de fiel' we're watchin'
> Wid de enemy in view.
> Comrades brave are roun' me lying,
> Filled wid thoughts of home an' God,

For well they know dat on de morrow,
Some will sleep beneath de sod.

"We could see across de river de Yankees, an could hear dem, de night so still. In de hush befo' de battle every man wuz thinking of his mother, wife and fambly. W'en de bugle sounded taps, every head wuz bowed in prayer, I kin best describe de attack wid de last verse of song I has jes told yer dey sing.

"Hark, I hear de bugles soundin',
'Tis de signal fer de fight,
Now, may God protect you, Mother,
As he ever does de right,
Hear de "Battle Cry of Freeedom."
How hit swells upon de air,
Oh, Yes w'ell rally roun' de standard,
Or we'll perish nobly there.

De Yankees sung de Battle Cry of Freedom, as dey charged on us an we could hear de band er playin' hit as dey cum, but hit jes made our boys fight de hardest, den we sing dis song,

"Tramp, Tramp, Tramp, de boys are marchin'.
Cheer up comrades dey will cum,
And beneath de starry flag,
We shall breathe de air again,
In de freedom of our own beloved home.

"Dey come on an' on, and dey fights. Lord how dey fight's! I is a stayin' close ter my Master. I is jes as wild as any fer our boys ter win, yer can hear de clash of de bayonet w'en dey git gray uniforms as dey stood dey groun' and dey went down befo' dey would retreat,

"In de battle front dey stood,
W'en de fiercest charges wuz made,
An' dey swept us off a hundred men an more,
But befo' we reached dey lines,
Dey wuz beaten back dismayed,
An' we heard de cry of victory o'er an o'er.

"De rebels, our boys in de grey, win's an captures 'bout er thousan' Yankees, after dis de Yankees wuz mos' of dem taken ter help General Grand at Richmon' and General Sherman on his march ter de sea.

"De Captain of de company we wuz in at de battle of Pleasant Hill (near Mansfield), wuz John Dick Morris, dis company wuz organized near Marlin,

Texas, wuz called Company B. General J. G. Walker wuz de District Division Commander, dey wuz made up in dis company from de town of Marlin an de country, among dem Captain Carter of Cameron wuz wounded in de battle we wuz in.

"At Yellow Bayou de commanding officer of de brigade we wuz in wuz General Banks. Tom Green wuz killed at Blairs Landin' on Red River an General Hardeman took Tom Green's place.

"Bout de last of de war de Yankees commenced ter use de nigger's dat had run away ter dey lines fer soljers. I don't know much 'bout dat, but I does know dat de slaves dat wuz left at home ter look after de wimmen an chillun dat most of dem stayed an' kept de work on de place in de crops up and helped ter take keer of de ole men and de wimmen an chillun, dat dey wuz a whole lot more dat helped ter dis day dey wuz dat run away ter de Yankees.

"De most of de slaves wuz happy on de plantations, an dey looked on de war like dis, dat de white man wuz er fightin' fer his principles, at least de ones dat understood did. I has seen so much in my long life dat I feels dat God is more an more de Great Ruler, an dat hit all works out fer de best.

"I knows dat de old order has changed. Men now must be rich, it seems ter be powerful, once hit wuz not so. Once men held themselves more dearly dan dey held dey possessions. In de days of Ante-Bellum de attitude wuz fine an bright an glorious, folks believed in de virtues of truth, chastity, an' chivalry. Dey seem new ter be old fashioned words, whar is de chivalry dat dey lived in de days which yer is writin' about? Does dey help ter protect de wimmen like dey did in de days of old? No, dey worl' of finance will take away er womans home jes de same as er man's. Whar is de demand fer virtue? In de old days de ole time southern gentlemen demands dat his wife be virtues er he would not marry her, does dey do dis now? No, sad ter say hit looks as if de loose wimmen are de ones dat is preferred.

"Whar would dey grandmothers say ter dem smokin? Yes, de old fashion way is out ob date, de curtain of smoke swept away, hit seems, de beauty of de past, de sound of de spinning wheel wuz lost in de machinery of a later day, jes as de stately minuet wuz lost in de jass dances of dese day's.

"I hopes dat in de great windup dat in de words of de ole song hit will be dat "His truth will go Marchin' on."

"Mine eyes have seen de glory of de cumin' of de Lord,

He is tramplin' out de vintage whar de grapes of wrath are stored, He Hath loosed de fateful lightnin' of His terrible swift sword,

His truth is marchin' on.

Benton County

Myhand, Mary
Age: 85
Clarksville, Arkansas
Interviewer: Sallie C. Miller
[M:10: pt. 5: 177–78]

"My mammie died when I was a little girl. She had three children and our white folks took us in their house and raised us. Two of us had fever and would have died if they hadn't got us a good doctor. The doctor they had first was a quack and we were getting worse until they called the other doctor, then we commence to get well. I don't know how old I am. Our birthdays was down in the mistress' Bible and when the old war come up, the house was burned and lost everything but I know I am at least 83 or 84 years old. Our white folks was so good to us. They never whipped us, and we eat what they eat and when they eat. I was born in White County, Tennessee and moved to Missouri but the folks did not like it there so we come to Benton County, Arkansas. One side of the road was Benton County and the other side was Washington County but we always had to go to Bentonville, the county seat, to tend to business. I was a little tod of a girl when the war come up. One day word come that the 'Feds' were coming through and kill all of the old men and take all the boys with them, so master took my brother and a grandson of his and started South. I was so scared. I followed them about a half mile before they found me and I begged so hard they took me with them. We went to Texas and was there about one year when the Feds gave the women on our place orders to leave their home. Said they owned it now. They had just got to Texas where we was when the South surrendered and we all come back home.

"We stayed with our white folks for about twenty years after the war. They shore was good to me. I worked for them in the house but never worked in the field. I come across the mountain to Clarksville with a Methodist preacher and his family and married here. My husband worked in a livery stable until he died, then I worked for the white folks until I fell and hurt my knee and got too old. I draws my old age pension.

"I do not know about the young generation. I am old and crippled and don't go out none."

Bradley County

Coleman, Betty
Age: 80
1112 ½ Indiana Street
Pine Bluff, Arkansas
Interviewer: Mrs. Bernice Bowden
[M:8: pt. 2: 36–37]

"My father belonged to Mr. Ben Martin and my mother and me belonged to the Slaughters. I was small then and didn't know what the war was about, but I remember meetin' the Yankees and the Ku Klux.

"Old master had about fifteen or twenty hands but Mr. Martin had a plenty—he had bout a hundred head.

"I member when the war was goin' on we was livin' in Bradley County. We was goin' to Texas to keep the Yankees from gettin' us. I member Mr. Gil Martin was just a young lad of a boy. We got as far as Union County and I know we stopped there and stayed long enough to make two crops and then peace was declared so we come back to Warren.

"While the war was goin' on, I member when my mother took a note to some soldiers in Warren and asked em to come and play for Miss Mary. I know they stood under a sycamore and two catawba trees and played. There was a perty big bunch of em. Us chillun was glad to hear it. I member just as well as if 'twas yesterday.

"I member when the Yankees come and took all of Miss Mary's silver—took every piece of it. And another time they got three or four of the colored men and made em get a horse apiece and ride away with em bareback. Yankees was all ridin' iron gray horses, and lookin' just as mad. O Lord, yes, they rid right up to the gate. All the horses was just alike—iron gray. Sho was perty horses. Them Yankees took everything Miss Mary had.

"After the war ended we stayed on the place one year and made a crop and then my father bought fifty acres of Mr. Ben Martin. He paid some on it every year and when it was paid for Mr. Ben give him a deed to it.

"I'm the only child my mother had. She never had but me, one. I went to school after the war and I member at night I'd be studyin' my lesson and rooting potatoes and papa would tell us stories about the war. I used to love to hear him on long winter evenings.

"I stayed right there till I married. My father had cows and he'd kill hogs and had a peach orchard, so we got along fine. Our white folks was always good to us."

Green, O. W.
Age: 78
Del Rio, Texas
[M:4: pt. 2 (TX): 90–93]

"I was bo'ned in Arkansas. Frank Marks was my father and Mary Ann Marks my mother. She was bo'n on the plantation. I had two brothers.

"I don' 'member de quarters, but dey mus' of had plenty, 'cause dey was two, three thousand slaves on de plantation. All my kin people belonged to Massa Mobley. My grandfather was a millman and dey had one de bigges' grist mills in de country.

"Our massa was good and we had plenty for to eat. Dere was no jail for slaves on our place but not far from dere was a jail.

"De Ku Klux Klan made everything pretty squally, so dey taken de orphan chillen to Little Rock and kep' 'em two, three years. Dere was lots of slaves in dat country 'round Rob Roy and Free Nigger Bend. Old Churchill, who used to be governor, had a plantation in dere.

"When I was nine years ol' dey had de Bruce and Baxter revolution. 'Twas more runnin' dan fightin'. Bruce was 'lected for governor but Baxter said he'd be governor if he had to run Brooks into de sea.

"My young Massa, Jack Mobley, was killed in de war, is how I come to be one of de orphan chillen.

"While us orphan chillen was at Little Rock dere come a terrible soreness of de eyes. I heard tell 'twas caused from de cholera. Every little child had to take turns about sittin' by de babies or totin' them. I was so blind, my eyes was so sore, I couldn't see. The doctor's wife was working with us. She was tryin' to figure up a cure for our sore eyes, first using one remedy and den another. An old herb doctor told her about a herb he had used on the plantations to cure de slaves' sore eyes. Dey boiled de herb and put hit on our eyes, on a white cloth. De doctor's wife had a little boy about my age. He would lay with me, and thought I was about hit. He would lead me around, then he would run off and leave me and see if I could see. One day between 'leven and twelve o'clock—I never will fergit hit—he taken me down to de mess room. De lady was not quite ready to dress my eyes. She told me to go on and come back in a little while. When I got outside I tore dat old rag off of my eyes and throwed hit down. I told the little boy, 'O, I can see you!' He grabbed me by de arm and ran yellin' to his mammy, 'Mama, he can see! Mama, Owen can see!' I neva will fo'git dat word. Dey were all in so a rejoicin', excitable way. I was the first one had his eyes cured. Dey sent de lady to New York and she made plenty of money from her remedy.

"Things sure was turrible durin' de war. Dey just driv us in front of de soldiers. Dere was lots of cholera. We was just bedded together lak hogs. The Ku Klux Klan come behind de soldiers, killin' and robbin'.

"After two or three years in de camp with de orphans, my kin found me and took me home.

"My grandfather and uncle was in de fightin'. My grandfather was a wagon man. De las' trip he made, he come home bringin' a load of dead soldiers to be buried. My grandfather told de people all about de war. He said hit sure was terrible.

"When de war was over de people jus' shouted for joy. De men and women jus' shouted for joy. 'Twas only because of de cullud people, dey was freed, and de Lawd worked through Lincoln.

"My old masta was a doctor and a surgeon. He trained my grandmother; she worked under him thirty-seven years as a nurse. When old masta wanted grandmother to go on a special case he would whip her so she wouldn't tell none of his secrets. Grandmother used herbs fo' medicine—black snake root, sasparilla, blackberry briar roots—and nearly all de young'uns she fooled with she save from diarrhea.

"My old masta was good, but when he found you shoutin' he burnt your hand. My grandmother said he burnt her hand several times. Masta wouldn't let de cullud folks have meetin', but dey would go out in the woods in secret to pray and preach and shout.

"I jist picked up enough readin' to read my bible and scratch my name. I went to school one mo'ning and didn't git along wid de teacher so I didn't go no mo'.

"I 'member my folks had big times come Christmas. Dey never did work on Sundays, jist set around and rest. Dey never worked in bad weather. Dey never did go to de field till seven o'clock.

"I married in 1919. I have two step-daughters and one step-son. My step-son lives in San Antonio. I have six step-grandchillen. I was a member of de Baptist church befo' you was bo'n, lady.

Calhoun County

Ricks, Jim
Age: 79
517 E. 22nd Avenue
Pine Bluff, Arkansas
Interviewer: Mrs. Bernice Bowden
[M:10: pt. 6: 37–38]

"I was born in slavery times. I 'member runnin' from the Yankees when they wanted to carry me off. Just devilin' me, you know. You know how little chillun was 'bout white folks in them days.

"I went to school three weeks and my daddy stopped me and put me to work.

"Old master was named Jimmie Ricks. They named me after him, I think.

"My mother said he was a mighty good master. Didn't 'low his niggers whipped.

"Yes'm, I was born and raised in Arkansas, down here in Calhoun County.

"I had a chance to learn but I was a rowdy. I wanted to hunt. I was a mighty huntsman.

"I was a good worker too. White folks was all stuck on me 'cause I was a good worker.

"I did farm work and then did public work after the crops was laid by. But now I got too old to work.

"I seen the Ku Klux once or twice when they was Ku Klukin' around. Some of 'em would holler 'Kluk, kluk, kluk.' I was quite small, but I could remember 'em 'cause I was scared of 'em.

"I farmed all my life till year before last. I was a good farmer too.

"I used to vote years ago. I voted Republican. Yes ma'am.

"Younger generation ain't near like they was when I was young. I was well thought of. Couldn't be out after sundown or they'd bump my head. My stepfather would give me a flailin'. I thought he was mean to me but I see now he right by whippin' me.

"I know in slavery times they got plenty of somethin' to eat. Old master fed us well."

Robinson, Augustus
Age: 78
2500 W. Tenth Street
Little Rock, Arkansas
Interviewer: Samuel S. Taylor
[M:10: pt. 6: 55–59]

"I was born in Calhoun County, Arkansas in 1860, January 15th. I am going according to what my daddy told me and nothing else. That is all I could do.

How the Children Were Fed
"My grandmother on my mother's side said when I was a little fellow that she was a cook and that she would bring stuff up to the cabin where the little niggers were locked up and feed them through the crack. She would hide it underneath her apron. She wasn't supposed to do it. All the little niggers were kept in one house when the old folks were working in the field. There were six or seven of us.

Sold
"My daddy was a white man, my master. His wife was so mean to me that my master sold me to keep her from beating me and kicking me and knocking me 'round. She would have killed me if she could have got the chance. My daddy sold me to a preacher who raised me as though I were his own son. Whenever he sat down to the table to eat, I sat down. He made no difference at all. He raised me in El Dorado, Arkansas. His name was James Goodwin. He sent me to school too.

Visited by Father
"When Harrison and Cleveland ran for President, my father came to Little Rock. Some colored people had been killed in the campaign fights, and he had been summoned to Little Rock to make some statements in connection with the trouble. He stopped at a prominent hotel and had me to come to see him. When I went up to the hotel to meet him, there were a dozen or more white men at that place. When I shook hands with him, he said, 'Gentlemen, he's a little shady but he's my son.' His name was Captain I. T. Robinson. He lived in Lisbon, Arkansas.

Mother
"My mother's name was Frances Goodwin. She belonged to Captain Robinson. I don't know but I think that when they came to Arkansas, they

came from Georgia. They were refugees. When the War started, people that owned niggers ran from state to state to try to hold their niggers.

House

"I lived right in the yard. We had four houses in the yard and three of them was made of logs and one was made out of one-by-twelve planks. I lived in the one made out of planks. It had one big room. I reckon it was about twenty by fifteen, more than that, I reckon. It was a big room. There were two doors and no windows. We had old candlesticks for lights. We had old home-made tables. All food was kept in the smokehouse and the pantry. The food house and the smokehouse were two of the log cabins in the yard.

Schooling

"Goodwin schooled me. He had a teacher to come right on the place and stay there teaching. He raised me and brought me up just as though I was his own child.

"I remember getting one whipping. I didn't get it from Mr. Goodwin though. His brother gave it to me. His brother sent me to get a horse. An old hound was laying in the way on the saddle and the bridle. He wouldn't move so I picked up the bridle and hit him with it. He hollered and master's brother heard him and gave me a whipping. That is the only whipping I ever got when I was small.

Ku Klux

"I heard of the Ku Klux Klan but I don't know that I ever seen them. I never noticed what effect they had on the colored people. I just heard people talking about them.

Occupational Experiences

"The first work I did was farming—after the War. I farmed,—down close to El Dorado, about six miles away from there. I kept that up till I was about seventeen or eighteen years old or somewheres about there. That was on James Goodwin's place—my last master, the man who raised me. Then I left him and came to Little Rock. I don't remember in what year. I went to school here in Little Rock. I had already had some schooling. My grandmother sent me. The school I went to was called the Union School. It was down on Sixth Street. After I left there, I went to Capitol Hill School. I was going to school during the Brooks-Baxter War. The statehouse was on Markham Street and Center. My grandmother's name was Celie Robinson. She went by the name of her owner.

"After I had gone to school several years—I don't remember just how many—I worked down town about ten or eleven years. Then I went to railroading. First I was with the Iron Mountain and Southern. Later, it changed its name to the Missouri Pacific. I worked for them from 1891 to 1935. On August 29th I received my last pay check. I have tried ever since to get my railroad pension to which my years of service entitle me but have been unable to get it. The law concerning the pension seems to have passed on the same day I received my last check, and although I worked for forty-four years and gave entire satisfaction, there has been a disposition to keep me from the pension. While in service I had my jaw broken in two pieces and four front teeth knocked out by a piece of flying steel.

"Another man was handling the steam hammer. I was standing at my regular place doing my regular work. When that happened, I was cut down like a weed. There wasn't a man ever thought they would see me in that job again after that piece of steel cut me down.

"Also, I lost my right eye in the service when a hot cinder from the furnace flew in it while I was doing my regular work. Then I was ruptured because of the handling of heavy pieces of iron at my work. I still wear the truss. You can see the places where my jaw was broke and you can see where my teeth were knocked out.

"Out of all the ups and downs, I stuck to the company just the same until they retired me in 1935 because of old age. The retirement board wanted to know when I asked for a pension, why did I think I was entitled to a pension? I told them because I had been injured through service with the company and had honorably finished so long a period of service. It is now admitted that I am eligible to a railroad pension but there seems to still be a delay in paying it for some reason or other.

Support Now
"I get a little assistance from the Welfare, and I get some commodities. If it wasn't for that, I would be broke up."

Carroll County

Overton, Mary
Age: 100+
117 W. Heard St.
Cleburne, Texas
Interviewer: ?
[M:5: pt. 3 (TX): 162–64]
[See also S2:8 (TX, pt. 7): 3000–3005]

Mary Overton, 117 W. Heard St., Cleburne, Texas, was born in Tennessee, but moved when very young to Carroll Co., Arkansas, where her parents belonged to Mr. Kennard. Mary does not know her age.

"I'se born in Tennessee but I don' 'member where, and I don' know how ole I is. I don' 'member what de marster's name was dere. My mother's name was Liza and my father's named was Dick. When I was 'bout four year old, my marster and mistis give me to dere daughter, who married a Dr. James Cox and dey come to Texas and brought me with 'em. The marster in Arkansas, which give me to his daughter, was named Kennard. I never seed him but one time. Dat when he was sick and he had all his little niggers dressed up and brought in to see him.

"Dr. Cox and his wife and me come to Fort Graham, in Hill County, Texas, from Arkansas. We was 'bout two weeks comin'. Fort Graham wan' no reg'lar fort. Dere was jus' some soldiers campin' here and dere was a little town. Lots of Indians come in to trade. Den de doctor got a farm on Nolan river, not far from whar Cleburne is now, and we went there.

"While we was on de farm, I got married. My husban' was Isaac Wright. I had seven chillen by him. My second husban' was Sam Overton. Him and me had two chillen. I wasn't married to Isaac by a preacher. De slaves wasn' jin'rally married dat way. Dey jus' told dey marsters dey wanted to be husban' and wife and if dey agreed, dat was all dere was to it, dey was said to be married. I heered some white folks had weddin's for dere niggers, but I never did see none.

"My marster had 'bout four slaves. He sold and bought slaves sev'ral times, but he couldn' sell me, 'cause I belonged to de mistis, and she wouldn' let him sell me. I cooked and washed and ironed and looked after de chillen, mostly. Dey had three chillen, but de mistis died when the least one was 'bout six months old and I raised de two older ones. Dey was two boys, and dey was 'bout grown when I lef' after freedom.

"We slaves had good 'nuf houses to live in. We didn' have no garden. I wore cotton dresses in summer and linsey dresses and a shawl in de winter. I had shoes most of de time. My white folks was pretty good to keep me in clothes. I gen'rally went to church wid mistis.

"Didn' have no special clothes when I got married. I slep' in de kitchen gen'rally, and had a wooden bed, sometimes with a cotton mattress and sometimes it was a shuck mattress.

"My mistis teached me to read and write, but I wouldn' learn. I never went to school neither. She would read de Bible to us.

"I didn' know no songs when I was in slavery. I didn' know 'bout no baptizin'. I didn' play no certain games, jus' played roun' de yard.

"I wasn't at no sale of slaves, but saw some bein' tuk by in chains once, when we lived at Reutersville. Dey was said to be 'bout 50 in de bunch. Dey was chained together, a chain bein' run 'tween 'em somehow, and dey was all men and women, no chillen. Dey was on foot. Two white men was ridin' hosses and drivin' de niggers like dey was a herd of cattle.

"Lots of slaves run away, but I don' know how dey got word 'round 'mong de niggers.

"I don' 'member much 'bout de war. Dere wasn' no fightin' whar we was, on de farm on Nolan river. On de day we was made free, de marster come and called us out one at a time and tol' us we was free. He said to me, 'Mary, you is free by de law. You don' belong to me no more. You can go wherever you wan' to. I ain't got no more to say 'bout you.' He tol' us if we'd stay awhile he'd treat us good and maybe we'd better stay, as de people was pretty much worked up. De rest of 'em stayed 'bout a week, den dey went off, and never come back, 'cept Isaac. I didn' go, but I stayed a long time after we was made free. I didn' care nothin' 'bout bein' free. I didn' have no place to go and didn' know nothin' to do. Dere I had plenty to eat and a place to stay and dat was all I knowed 'bout.

"When I left I hired out as cook. I got ten dollars a month and all my food and clothes and a place to sleep. I didn' spend but one dime of my pay for eight months. I bought candy wid dat dime, like a walkin' stick.

"I sure wish I knew how old I is, but I ain' sure. I don' even know my birthday." (According to some white persons who have known Mary for a long time, calculated from information Mary had given them as to her younger days, when her memory was better than it is now, she is probably more than one hundred years old.)

Williams, Belle
Age: 87
Hutchinson, Kansas
17 May 1937
Interviewer: E. Jean Foote
[S2:1 (KS): 292–95]
[See also M:16: (KS): 14–17]

Belle Williams was born in slavery about the year 1850 or 1851. Her mother's name was Elizabeth Hulsie, being the slave of Sid Hulsie, her last name being the name of her master. The Hulsie plantation was located in Carroll County, Arkansas. Belle Williams, better known as "Auntie Belle," is most interesting. She lives in her own little home in the one hundred block on Harvey Street, Hutchinson, Kansas. She is too old and crippled to do hard work, so spends most of her time smoking her pipe and rocking in her old armchair on the little porch of her home. She is jolly, and most interesting.

"Yes, I was a slave," she said. "I was born a slave on a plantation in Carroll County, Arkansas and lived there 'till after the war. Law sakes, honey, I can see them 'Feds' yet, just as plain as if it was yesterday. We had a long lane—you know what a lane is—well, here they come! I run for mah mammy, and I'll never forget how she grabbed me and let out a yell, 'It's them Feds, them blue coats.'

"You see my massa was a good massa. He didn't believe in whipping niggers and he didn't believe in selling niggers, and so my mammy and me, we didn't want to leave our mistress and massa. We called them 'Mother Hulsie' and 'Massa Sid.' One officer told my mammy that she could take along with her, anything out of the cabin that she wanted. Mammy looked around and said, 'I don't want to take nothin' but my chillun,' so we all told Mother Hulsie 'goodbye' and when my mammy told her goodbye, why Mother Hulsie cried and cried, and said, 'I just can't let you go, Elizabeth, but go on peacefully, and maybe some day you can come back and see me.'"

As the story came word after word, big tears dropped on the thin black hands, and she reached for her tobacco can and pipe. The can was missing, so I offered to get it for her, for I was anxious for one long peep into "Auntie's" little house, but I couldn't find the can, so after moans and sighs, she got to her feet and found her favorite Granger Twist. After settling again in her chair and when her pipe was at its best, "Auntie" continued, "Oh, honey, it was awful! You see I never been nowhere and I was scairt so I hung onto my mammy. The soldiers took us to camp that night, and after staying there several days, we went on to Springfield, Missouri, and it was right at fifty-two years ago that I came here. I was married to Fuller, my first husband, and had seven chilluns. He helped me raise them that lived and, after he died, I married Williams and had two chilluns, but he didn't help me raise my chilluns. Why, honey, I raised my chilluns and my chilluns' chilluns, and even one great-grandchild now. Why, I always been a slave. I worked for all the early white families in this here town that needed help."

I asked "Auntie" if she were ever sold on the block, and she answered, "Law sakes, honey, I must tell you. No, I never was sold, but nuthin' but the Dear Blessed Lawd saved me. You see Massa Sid had gone away for a few days, and his boys was takin' care of things, when some nigger traders came and wanted to buy some niggers, and they picked on my grandmammy and me. How old was I? Well, I reckon I was about fourteen. You see, honey, I never could read or write, but I can count, and I can remember—Lawdy! how I can remember. Well, there I was on the block, just scairt and shivering—I was just cold all over—and them there nigger traders was jest a talkin' when down that long lane came Massa Sid, and I'm tellin' you, it was the Dear Lawd that sent him. He was a ridin' on his hoss, and he stopped right in front of me, standing there on the block. He looked at his boys, then he turned to them nigger traders and yelled out, 'What you all doin' here?' The boys told him there was just so many niggers on the place, and they wanted some money and when the nigger traders come along they thought they would sell a few niggers. Honey, I'm telling you, Massa Sid turned to them nigger traders and said, 'you nigger traders get out of here. These are my niggers and I don't sell niggers. I can feed them all, I don't want any help.' He grabbed me right off of the block and put me on the hoss in front of him and set me down in front of my cabin. Sceered, oh Lawdy I was sceered! No, suh, Massa Sid never sold no niggers."

"I must tell you about what happened one night while we were all there in the camp. One of the massa's boys that loved my uncle, came crawling on all fours, just like a pig, into camp. He passed the pickets, and when he found my uncle he laid there on the ground in my uncle's arms and cried like a baby. My uncle was old but he cried too and after a while he told the boy that he must go back—he was 'fraid that the pickets would see him and he would be shot, so he went with him, crawling on all fours just like a pig, till he got him past the pickets, and our young master never saw my uncle any more. Oh, honey, them was heart-breakin' times. The first night we was in camp, my mammy got to thinking about Mother Hulsie and how she was left all alone with all the work, and not a soul to help her. The blue coats had gone through the house and upset everything, so in the morning she asked the captain if she could ask just one thing of him, and that was that she and my uncle go back to Mother Hulsie just for the day, and help put everything away and do the washing. The captain said they could go, but they must be back by five o'clock and not one nigger child could go along, so they went back for the day and mammy did all the washing, every rag that she could find, and my uncle chopped and stacked outside the house, all the wood that he could chop that day, and then they came back to camp. My mammy said she'd never forget Mother Hulsie wringing her hands and crying, 'Oh Lawd, what will I do,' as they went down the lane."

Chicot County

Jones, Nannie
Age: 81
1601 Saracen Street
Pine Bluff, Arkansas
Interviewer: Mrs. Bernice Bowden
[M:9: pt. 4: 164–65]

"Good morning. Come in. I sure is proud to see you. Yes ma'am, I sure is.

"I was born in Chicot County. I heerd Dr. Gaines say I was four years old in slavery times. I know I ain't no baby. I feels my age, too—in my limbs.

"I heerd 'em talk about a war but I wasn't big enough to know about it. My father went to war on one side but he didn't stay very long. I don't know which side he was on. Them folks all dead now—I just can remember 'em.

"Dr. Gaines had a pretty big crew on the place. I'm gwine tell you what I know. I can't tell you nothin' else.

"Now I want to tell it like mama said. She said she was sold from Kentucky. She died when I was small.

"I remember when they said the people was free. I know they jumped up and down and carried on.

"Dr. Gaines was so nice to his people. I stayed in the house most of the time. I was the little pet around the house. They said I was so cute.

"Dr. Gaines give me my age but I lost it movin'. But I know I ain't no baby. I never had but two children and they both livin'—two girls.

"Honey, I worked in the field and anywhere. I worked like a man. I think that's what got me bowed down now. I keeps with a misery right across my back. Sometimes I can hardly get along.

"Honey, I just don't know 'bout this younger generation. I just don't have no thoughts for 'em, they so wild. I never was a rattlin' kind of a girl. I always was civilized. Old people in them days didn't 'low their children to do things. I know when mama called us, we'd better go. They is a heap wusser now. So many of 'em gettin' into trouble."

Clark County

Newton, Pete
Age: 83
Clarksville, Arkansas
Interviewer: Sallie C. Miller
[M:10: pt. 5: 216–18]

"My white folks was as good to me as they could be. I ain't got no kick to make about my white people. The boys was all brave. I was raised on the farm. I staid with my boss till I was nearly grown. When the war got so hot my boss was afraid the 'Feds' would get us. He sent my mammy to Texas and sent me in the army with Col. Bashom to take care of his horses. I was about eleven or twelve years old. Col. Bashom was always good to me. He always found a place for me to sleep and eat. Sometimes after the colonel left the folks would run me off and not let me stay but I never told the colonel. I went to Boston, Texas, with the colonel and his men and when he went on the big raid into Missouri he left me in Sevier County, Arkansas, with his horses 'Little Baldy' and 'Orphan Boy.' They was race horses. The colonel always had race horses. He was killed at Pilot Knob, Missouri. After the colonel was killed his son George (I shore did think a lot of George) come after me and the horses and brought us home.

"While I was in Arkadelphia with Col. Bashom's horses, I went down to the spring to water the horses. The artillery was there cleaning a big cannon they called 'Old Tom.' Of course I went up to watch them. One of the men saw me and hollered, 'Stick his head in the cannon.' It liked to scared me to death. I jumped on that race horse and run. I reconed I would have been killed but my uncle was there and saw me and stopped the horse.

"Another time we went to a place and me and another colored boy was taking care of the horses while our masters eat dinner. I saw some watermelons in the garden with a paling fence around it. I said if the other boy would pull a paling off I would crawl through and get us a watermelon. He did but the man who owned the place saw me just as I got the melon and whipped us and told us if we hollered he would kill us. We didn't holler and we never told Col. Bashom either.

"After the war my mammie come back from Texas and took me over to Dover to live but my old boss told her if she would let him have me he would raise and educate me like his own children. When I got back the old boss already had a boy so I went to live with one of his sons. He told me it was time for me to learn how to work. My boss was rough but he was good to me and taught me how to work. The old boss had five sons in the army and all was wounded except one. One of them was shot through and through in the battle of Oak Hill. He got a furlough and come back and died. I left my white folks in 1869 and went to farming for myself up in Hartman bottom. I married when I was about seventeen years old.

"They though' a house near us was hainted. Nobody wanted to live in it so they went to see what the noise was. They found a pet coon with a piece of chain around his neck. The coon would run across the floor and drag the chain.

"The children now are bad. No telling what will be in the next twenty or thirty years, everything is so changed now.

"I learnt to sing the hymns but never sang in the choir. We sang 'Dixie,' 'John Brown's Body Lies, etc.,' 'Juanita,' 'Just Before the Battle, Mother,' 'Old Black Joe.'"

Ross, Charley
Age: 87
Gibson Station, Oklahoma
Interviewer: Ethel Wolfe Garrison
[OK: 363–64]

I was born in the hill country around Arkadelphia, Arkansas, on May 13, 1851, a Friday it was, and Friday the 13th is my Lucky Day.

My father's name was Strotter Adams, the same as master's. The master was a preacher and a lawyer at Arkadelphia, and when his daughter married I went with her; her husband was Charley Ross. Then one of the master's sons took my father with him. He was John Adams. All the places was close together and we wasn't separated much.

The master had children named John, Billie, Christ, Walker, Miss Cornelia, Miss Liddie, and my sisters were Jane, Martha, and my brothers were Walter and Bob.

I was too young to work much, that's in the fields I mean. I use to help take care of the stock. One time I was sitting on top of rail fence, hold of a mule. I jest kept the rope light in my hands letting the mule graze, and then somehow I went to sleep. Right on top of the fence. The master saw me and slip up back of the mule. He hit the mule and when he jumped I went off the fence, right on the ground. Hard. And the master laughed when I sat there rubbing my eyes.

Then the young boys would ride the calves to make them gentle for driving, or what folks called "bridle wise." Most of the time we didn't ride only just long enough to get tossed off on the ground.

We had long-tailed cotton shirts in the summer and wool shirts and jackets in the winter. Once a white woman give some boys' shoes to the mistress and she gave them to me. It took time to get use to them but I was sure enough proud of them shoes. I was about nine years old before I ever had new shoes.

The master lived in a big up-to-date house like folks have now. There was three fireplaces in the house. He owned lots of slaves.

I didn't know anything about the Civil War. Except one day a smart negro told us that there was fighting and soon all the slaves would be free. And they was.

The master didn't allow dancing on the plantation but the slaves could get passes and go to dances on Saturday, but they had to get up Sunday and go to church.

The master never went to war. Maybe he was too old. Sometimes he would be gone three or four days. He said he as going to the war but he didn't go.

I've been married twice. My wife now is Rosy. She had two children when we married. Henry and Lutha Evans. My first wife had children named Bessie, Christine, and Jordan; and later on there was Norman, Winfred and Charley, Jr.

I am too sick to talk much and my time is about come.

Taylor, Anthony
Age: 78?
2424 W. Ninth Street
Little Rock, Arkansas
Interviewer: Samuel S. Taylor
[M:10: pt. 6: 259–65]

"I was born in Clark County adjoining Hot Spring County, between Malvern and Arkadelphia. Clark County was named after old man General Clark. He was worth four or five thousand acres of land.

"My father's name was Anthony McClellan. Why they called me Anthony Taylor was my stepfather was named Taylor. My mother's name was Lettie

Sunnaville. My mother has been dead thirty or forty years and my father died six months before I was born. He died a natural death. Sickness. He was exposed and died of pneumonia.

"Fayette Sunnaville was my grandfather on my mother's side. That was my mother's father. Rachel Sunnaville was my mother's mother's name. I don't know the names of my father's people. They was sold in slavery. But it is been so far back; I don't remember nothing, and I don't know whether they would or not if they was living.

"We stayed on the old plantation for seven or eight years before we had sense enough or knowed enough to get away from there and git something for ourselves. That is how I come to raise such big potatoes. I been raising them fifty years. These are hill potatoes. You have to know how to raise potatoes to grow 'em this big. (He showed me some potatotes, sweet, weighing about seven pounds—ed.)

"I have heard my mother and my grandfather tell lots of stories about slavery. I can't remember them.

"Old man Bullocks had about eight or ten families that I knew about. Those were the families that lived right near us in the quarters. I didn't say eight or ten hands—I said eight or ten families. Them was the ones that was right near us. We was awful small after freedom but them what was with him stayed with him quite a while—stayed with the old master. He could pay them so much after freedom come.

"Lawd, I could tell you things about slavery. But I'm forgitful and I can't do it all at once. He had the whole county from Arkadelphia clean down to Princeton and Tulip—our old mars did. Lonoke was between Princeton and Tulip. Princeton was the county-seat. He must have had a large number of slaves. Those ten families I knew was just those close 'round us. Most of the farm was fur pine country land. There would be thirty or forty acres over here of cultivation and then thirty or forty acres over there of woods and so on. He had more land than anybody else but it wasn't all under cultivation.

"He's been dead now twenty or thirty years. I don't know that he was mean to his slaves. If he had been, they wouldn't have gone on after freedom. They would have moved out. You see, they didn't care for nothing but a little something to eat and a fine dress and they would have gone on to somebody else and got that.

"Wasn't no law then. He was the law. I worked all day long for ten cents a day. They would allowance you so many pounds of meat, so much meal, so much molasses. I have worked all day for ten cents and then gone out at night to get a few potatoes. I have pulled potatoes all day for a peck of meal and I was happy at that. I never did know what the price of cotton was.

"Where we was, the Ku Klux never did bother anybody. All there was, every time we went out we had to have a pass.

"My grandfather and grandmother were both whipped sometimes. I don't know the man that whipped them. I don't know whether it was the agent or the owner or who, but they were whipped. Lots of times they had work to do and didn't do it. Naturally they whipped them for it. That was what they whipped my grandparents for. Sometimes too, they would go off and wouldn't let the white folks know where they was going. Sometimes they would neglect to feed the horses or to milk the cows—something like that. That was the only reason I ever heard of for punishing them.

"I heard that if the boss man wanted to be with women that they had, the women would be scared not to be with him for fear he would whip them. And when they started whipping them for that they kept on till they got what they wanted. They would take them 'way off and have dealings with them. That is where so much of that yellow and half-white comes from.

"There was some one going through telling the people that they was free and that they was their own boss. But yet and still, there's lots of them never did leave the man they was with and lots of them left. There was lots of white people that wouldn't let a nigger tell their niggers that they was free, because they wanted to keep them blind to that for years. Kept them for three or four years anyway. Them that Bullocks liked was crazy about him. He would give them a show—so much a month and their keeps. I don't remember exactly how much it was but it was neighborhood price. He was a pretty good man. Of course, you never seen a white man that wouldn't cheat a little.

"He'd cheat you out of a little cotton. He would have the cotton carried to the gin. He would take half the corn and give us five or six shoats. After he got the cotton all picked and sold, the cotton it would all go to him for what you owed him for furnishing you. You never saw how much cotton was ginned, nor how much he got for it, nor how much it was worth nor nothing. They would just tell you you wasn't due nothing. They did that to hold you for another year. You got nothing to move on so you stay there and take what he gives you.

"Of all the crying you ever heard, one morning we'd got up and the pigs and hogs in the lot that we had fattened to go on that winter, he was catching 'em. After we'd done fattened them with the corn that was our share, he took 'em and sold 'em. We didn't even know that we owed him anything. We thought the crops had done settled things. Nobody told us nothin'. All we children cried. The old man and the old woman didn't say nothing, because they was scared. My mother would get up and go down and milk the cows and what she'd get for the milking would maybe be a bucket of buttermilk.

"We'd have a spoonful of black molasses and corn bread and buttermilk for breakfast. We got flour bread once a week. We would work hard all the week talkin' 'bout what good biscuits we'd have Sunday morning. Sack of flour would last two or three months because we wouldn't cook flour bread only once a week—Saturday night or Sunday morning.

"We had no skillet at that time. We would rake the fireplace and push the ashes back and then you would put the cake down on the hearth or on a piece of paper or a leaf and then pull the ashes over the cake to cook it. Just like you roast a sweet potato. Then when it got done, you would rake the ashes back and wash the cake and you would eat it. Sometimes you would strike a little grit or gravel in it and break your teeth. But then I'm tellin' you the truth about it.

"When our hogs was taken that time, we didn't have nothing to go on that winter. They would compel us to stay. They would allowance us some meat and make us split rails and clear up land for it. It was a cinch if he didn't give it to you you couldn't get nothin'. Wasn't no way to get nothing. Then when crop time rolled 'round again they would take it all out of your crops. Make you split rails and wood to earn your meat and then charge it up to your crop anyhow. But you couldn't do nothin' 'bout it.

"Sometimes a barrel of molasses would set up in the smokehouse and turn to sugar. You goin' hungry and molasses wastin'. They was determined not to give you too much of it.

"I made my way by farming. After I got to be some size, I started at it. I farmed all my life. While I could work, things was pretty good. Wisht I was on a farm now. Even when I'm 'round here sick, I can git these potatoes raised with a little help from the neighbors.

"I don't belong to church. I oughter, but I don't. Then again, I figure that a man can be just as good out of it as he can in it. I've got good desires, but I never confessed to the public.

"I have had three hundred dollars worth of stuff stolen from me. Everything I produced is stolen from me because I have no way to protect myself. What I raise if I don't get shet of it right away, the people get shet of it for me. I had eighty head of chickens in the barn out there runnin' 'round. When I got sick and was in the bed and couldn't help myself, the chickens went. In the daytime, they would fix traps and jerk a strings and pull a board down on them and then go out in the weeds and get them. I never reported nothin' to the police. I wasn't able to report nothing. I was just batching, and now and then people would come in and report them to me. They would wait till they saw somebody come in and when they saw that I was talking and wouldn't notice them, they would steal anything they wanted. The police came by here and ran them once. But that didn't do no good.

"Once somebody stole an automatic shotgun. They stole a colt one time. They stole all my clothes and pawned them to a whiskey dealer. He got sent to the pen for selling whiskey, but I didn't get my clothes. They come in the yard and steal my potatoes, collards, turnips, ochre (okra?), and so on. I lay there in the bed and see them, but I can't stop them. All I can do is to holler, 'You better go on and let them things alone.' Ever since the last war, I haven't been able to work. I am barefooted and naked now on account of not bein' able to support myself.

"I just come out of the hospital. I been too sick even to work in my garden. After I come home I taken a backset but I am still staying here. I am just here on the mercies of the people. I don't get nothing but what the people give me. I don't get no moddities nor nothin' from the Government.

"I ain't never been able to get no help from the Government. Long time ago, I went down to the place and asked for help and they told me that since I was alone, I oughta be able to help myself. They gimme a ticket for twenty meals and told me by the time I ate them up, they might have something else they could do for me. I told them I couldn't go back and forth to git the meals. I have the ticket now. I couldn't git to the place to use it none, so I keep it for a keepsake. It 'round here somewheres or other. I was past the pension age. I ain't been able to do no steady work since the war. I was too old for the war—the World War."

Interviewer's Comment

The spelling of the name Summaville is phonetic. I don't recognize the name and he couldn't spell it of course.

When I called, he had potatoes that weighed at least seven pounds. They were laid out on the porch for sale. He had a small patch in his yard which he cultivated, and had gotten about ten bushels from it.

His account of slavery times is so vivid that you would consider his age nearer eighty than sixty-eight. A little questioning reveals that he has no idea of his age although he readily gives it as sixty-eight—a memorized figure.

Columbia County

Dockery, Railroad
Age: 81
1103 Short 13th
Pine Bluff, Arkansas
Interviewer: Mrs. Bernice Bowden
[M:7: pt. 2: 164–65]

"Railroad Dockery, that's my name. I belonged to John Dockery and we lived at Lamartine, Arkansas where I was born. My mother's name was Martha and I am one of quadruplets, three girls and one boy, that's me. Red River, Ouachita, Mississippi and Railroad were our names. (Mrs. Mary Browning, who is now ninety-eight years of age, told me that her father, John Dockery, was the president of the Mississippi, Red River, Ouachita Railroad, the first one to be surveyed in Arkansas, and that when the directors heard of the quadruplets' birth, they wanted to name them after the railroad, which was done—ed.)

"Yes ma'm, Red River and Ouachita died when they were tots and Mississippi and Railroad were raised. Now that's what my mother said. Mississippi died five or six years ago and I'm the onliest one left.

"I remember mighty little about the war. I never thought anything about the war. All I did then was a crowd of us little chaps would go to the woods and tote in the wood every day for the cook woman. That's what I followed. Never did nothing else but play till after the war.

"After surrender I went with my father and mother to work for General Tom Dockery. He was John Dockery's brother. I was big enough to plow then. I followed the plow all the time. My father and mother were paid for their work. We stayed there about five years and then moved to Falcon, Arkansas. Father died there.

"In the time of the war I heard the folks talkin' about freedom, and I heard my father talk about the Ku Klux but that was all I knowed, just what he said about it.

"I remember the presidents and I voted for some of them but oh Lord, I haven't voted in several years.

"I got along after freedom just as well as I ever did. I never had no trouble—never been in no trouble.

"About the world now—it looks like to me these days things are pretty tight. I could hardly tell you what I think of the younger generation. I think one thing—if the old heads would die all at once they would be out, because it's all you can do to keep em straight now.

"I went to school only three months in my life. I learned to read and write very well. I don't need glasses and I read principally the Bible. To my mind it is the best book in the world. Biggest part of the preachers now won't preach unless they are paid three-fourths more than they are worth.

"The biggest part of my work was farming. I never did delight in cooking. Now I can do any kind of housework, but don't put me to cooking.

"I just can't sing to do no good. Never could sing. Seems like when I try to sing something gets tangled in my throat.

"O Lord, I remember one old song they used to sing
'A charge to keep I have
A God to glorify.'

"I don't remember anything else but now if Mississippi was here, she could tell you lots of things."

Crawford County

Kye, George
Age: 110
Fort Gibson, Oklahoma
Interviewer: Ethel Wolfe Garrison
[OK: 241–44]

I was born in Arkansas under Mr. Abraham Stover, on a big farm about twenty miles north of Van Buren. I was plumb grown when the Civil War come along, but I can remember back when the Cherokee Indians was in all that part of the country.

Joe Kye was my pappy's name what he was born under back in Garrison County, Virginia, and I took that name when I was freed, but I don't know whether he took it or not because he was sold off by old Master Stover when I was a child. I never have seen him since. I think he wouldn't mind good, leastways that what my mammy say.

My mammy was named Jennie and I don't think I had any brothers or sisters, but they was a whole lot of children at the quarters that I played and lived with. I didn't live with mammy because she worked all the time, and us children all stayed in one house.

It was a little one room log cabin, chinked and daubed, and you couldn't stir us with a stick. When we went to eat we had a big pan and all ate out of it. One what ate the fastest got the most.

Us children wore homespun shirts and britches and little slips and nobody but the big boys wore any britches. I wore just a shirt until I was about 12 years old, but it had a long tail down to my calves. Four or five of us boys slept in one bed, and it was made of hewed logs with rope laced acrost it and a shuck mattress. We had stew made out of pork and potatoes, and sometimes greens and pot liquor, and we had ash cake mostly, but biscuits about once a month.

In the winter time I had brass toed shoes made on the place, and a cloth cap with ear flaps.

The work I done was hoeing and plowing, and I rid a horse a lot for old Master because I was a good rider. He would send me to run chores for him, like going to the mill. He never beat his negroes but he talked mighty cross and glared at us until he would nearly scare us to death sometimes.

He told us the rules and we lived by them and didn't make trouble, but they was a neighbor man that had some mean negroes and he nearly beat them to death. We could hear them hollering in the field sometimes. They would sleep in the cotton rows, and run off, and then they would catch the cat-o-nine tails sure nuff. He would chain them up, too, and keep them tied out to trees, and when they went to the field they would be chained together in bunches sometimes after they had been cutting up.

We didn't have no place to go to church, but old Master didn't care if we had singing and praying, and we would tie our shoes on our backs and go down the road close to the white church and all set down and put our shoes on and go up close and listen to the service.

Old Master was baptized almost every Sunday and cussed us all out on Monday. I didn't join the church until after freedom, and I always was a scoundrel for dancing. My favorite preacher was old Pete Conway. He was the only ordained colored preacher we had after freedom, and he married me.

Old Master wouldn't let us take herb medicine, and he got all our medicine in Van Buren when we was sick. But I wore a buckeye on my neck just the same.

When the war come along I was a grown man, and I went off to serve because old Master was too old to go, but he had to send somebody anyways. I served as George Stover, but every time the sergeant would call out "Abe Stover," I would answer "Here."

They had me driving a mule team wagon that Old Master furnished, and I went with the Sesesh soldiers from Van Buren to Texarkana and back a dozen times or more. I was in the War two years, right up to the day of freedom. We had a battle close to Texarkana and another big one near Van Buren, but I never left Arkansas and never got a scratch.

One time in the Texarkana battle I was behind some pine trees and the bullets cut the limbs down all over me. I dug a hole with my bare hands before I hardly knowed how I done it.

One time two white soldiers named Levy and Briggs come to the wagon train and said they was hunting slaves for some purpose. Some of us black boys got scared because we heard they was going to Squire Mack and get a reward for catching runaways, so me and two more lit out of there.

They took out after us and we got to a big mound in the woods and hid. Somebody shot at me and I rolled into some bushes. He rid up and got down to look for me but I was on t'other side of his horse and he never did see me. When they was gone we went back to the wagons just as the regiment was pulling out and the officer didn't say nothing.

They was eleven negro boys served in my regiment for their masters. The first year was mighty hard because we couldn't get enough to eat. Some ate poke greens without no grease and took down and died.

How I knowed I was free, we was bad licked, I reckon. Anyways, we quit fighting and a Federal soldier come up to my wagon and say: "Whose mules?" "Abe Stover's mules," I says, and he tells me then, "Let me tell you, black boy, you are as free now as old Abe Stover his own self!" When he said that I jumped on top of one of them mules' back before I knowed anything!

I married Sarah Richardson, February 10, 1870, and had only eleven children. One son is a deacon and one grandson is a preacher. I am a good Baptist. Before I was married I said to the gal's old man, "I'll go to the mourners' bench if you'll let me have Sal," and sure nuff I joined up just a month after I got her. I am head of the Sunday School and deacon in the St. Paul Baptist church in Muskogee now.

I lived about five miles from Van Buren until about twelve years ago when they found oil and then they run all the negroes out and leased up the land. They never did treat negroes good around there anyways.

I never had a hard time as a slave, but I'm glad we was set free. Sometimes we can't figger out the best thing to do, but anyways we can lead our own life now, and I'm glad the young ones can learn and get somewhere these days.

Crittenden County

Wells, John
Age: 82
Edmondson, Arkansas
Interviewer: Irene Robertson
[M:11: pt. 7: 85–88]

"I was born down here at Edmonson, Arkansas. My owner was a captain in the Rebel War [Civil War]. He run us off to Texas close to Greenville. He was keeping us from the Yankees. In fact my father had planned to go to the Yankees. My mother died on the way to Texas close to the Arkansas line. She was confined and the child died too. We went in a wagon. Uncle Tom and his wife and Uncle Granville went too. He left his wife. She lived on another white man's farm. My master was Captain R. Campbell Jones. He took us to Texas. He and my father come back in the same wagon we went to Texas in. My father [Joe Jones Wells] told Captain R. Campbell Jones if he didn't let him come back here that he would be here when he got here—beat him back. That's what he told him. Captain brought him on back with him.

"What didn't we do in Texas? Hooeee! I had five hundred head of sheep belonging to J. Gardner, a Texan, to herd every day—twice a day. Carry 'em off in the morning early and watch 'em and fetch 'em back b'fore dark. I was a shepherd boy is right. I liked the job till the snow cracked my feet open. No, I didn't have no shoes. Little round cactuses stuck in my feet.

"I had shoes to wear home. Captain Jones gave leather and everything needed to Uncle Granville. He was a shoemaker. He made us all shoes jus' before we was to start back. Captain Jones sent the wagon back for us. My father come back right here at Edmondson and farmed cotton and corn. Uncle Tom and Uncle Granville raised wheat out in Texas. They didn't have no overseer but they said they worked harder 'an ever they done in their lives, 'fore or since.

"My father went to war with his master. Captain Jones served 'bout three years I judge. My father went as his waiter. He got enough of war, he said.

"Captain R. Campbell Jones had a wife, Miss Anne, and no children. I seen mighty near enough war in Texas. They fit there. Yes ma'am, they did. I seen soldiers in Greenville, Texas. I seen the cavalry there. They looked so fine. Prettiest horses I ever seen.

"Freedom! Master Campbell Jones come to us and said, 'You free this morning. The war is over.' It been over then but travel was slow. 'You all can go back home, I'll take you, or you can go root hog or die.' We all get to gatherin' up our belongings to come back home. Tired of no wood neither, besides that hard work. We all share cropped with Captain R. Campbell Jones two years. I know that. We got plenty wood without going five or six miles like in Texas. After freedom folks got to changing 'bout to de better I reckon. I been farmin' right here all my life. We didn't have a lot to eat out in Texas neither. Mother was a farm woman too.

"I never seen a Ku Klux. Bad Ku Klux sound sorter like good Santa Claus. I heard 'em say it was real. I never seen neither one.

"I did own ten acres of land. I own a home now.

"My father drove a grub wagon from Memphis to Lost Swamp Bottom—near Edmondson—when they built this railroad through here.

"Father never voted. I have voted several times.

"Present times is tougher now than before it come on. Things not going like it might somehow. We wants more pension. Us old folks needs a good living 'cause we ain't got much more time down here.

"Present generation—they are slack—I means they slack on their parents, don't see after them. They can get farm work to do. They waste their money more than they ought. Some folks purty nigh hungry. That is for a fact the way it is going.

Edmondson, Arkansas

"Master Henry Edmondson owned all the land to the Chatfield place to Lehi, Arkansas. He owned four or five thousand acres of land. It was bottoms and not cleared. They had floods then, rode around in boats sometimes. Colored folks could get land through Andy Flemming [colored man]. Mr. Henry Edmondson and whole family died with the yellow fever. He had several children—Miss Erma, Henry, and Will I knowed. It is probably his father buried at far side of this town. A rattlesnake bit him. Lake Rest or Scantlin was a boat landing and that was where the nearest white folks lived to the Edmondsons. I worked for Mr. Henry Edmonson, the one died with yellow fever. He was easy to work for. Land wasn't cleared out much. He was here before the Civil War. Good many people, in fact all over there, died of yellow fever at Indian Mound. Me and my brother waited on white folks all through that yellow fever plague. Very few colored folks had it. None of 'em I heered tell of died with it. White folks died in piles. Now when the smallpox raged the colored folks had it seem like heap more and harder than white folks. Smallpox used to rage every few years. It break out and spread. That is the way so many colored folks come to own land and why it was named Edmondson. Named for Master Henry—Edmondson, Arkansas.

"Mrs. Cynthia Ann Earle wrote a diary during the Civil War. It was partly published in the Crittenden County Times—West Memphis paper—Fridays, November 27 and December 4, 1936. She tells interesting things happening. Mentions two books she is reading. She tells about a flood, etc. She tells about visiting and spending over a thousand dollars. Mrs. L. A. Stewart or Mrs. H. E. Weaver of Edmondson owns copies if they cannot be obtained at the printing office at West Memphis."

Cross County

Allison, Lucindy
Age: 61
Marked Tree, Arkansas
Interviewer: Irene Robertson
[M:8: pt. 1: 41–43

"Ma was a slave in Arkansas. She said she helped grade a hill and help pile up a road between Wicksburg and Wynne. They couldn't put the road over the hill, so they put all the slaves about to grade it down. They don't use the road but it's still there to show for itself.

"She was a tall rawbony woman. Ma was a Hillis and pa's name was Adam Hillis. He learned to trap in slavery and after freedom he followed that for a living. Ma was a sure 'nough field hand. Mama had three sets of children. I don't know how many she did have in all. I had eleven my own self. Grandma was named Tempy and I heard them tell about when she was sold. She and mama went together. They used to whoop the slaves when they didn't work up peart.

"When the 'Old War' come on the Yankees come they took everything and the black men folks too. They come by right often. They would drive up at mealtime and come in and rake up every blessed thing was cooked. Have to go work scrape about and find something else to eat. What they keer 'bout you being white or black? Thing they was after was filling theirselves up. They done white folks worse than that. They burned their cribs and fences up and their houses too about if they got mad. Things didn't suit them. If they wanted a colored man to go in camp with them and he didn't go, they would shoot you down like a dog. Ma told about some folks she knowd got shot in the yard of his own quarters.

"Us black folks don't want war. They are not war kind of folks. Slavery wasn't right and that 'Old War' wasn't right neither.

"When my children was all little I kept Aunt Mandy Buford till she died. She was a old slave woman. Me and my husband and the biggest children worked in the field. She would sit about and smoke. My boys made cob pipes and out came j'ints for 'er to draw through. Red cob pipes was the prettiest. Aunt Mandy said her master would be telling them what to do in the field and he say to her, 'I talking to you too.' She worked right among the men at the same kind of work. She was tall but not large. She carried children on her right hip when she was so young she dragged that foot when she walked. The reason she had to go with the men to the field like she did was 'cause she wasn't no multiplying woman. She never had a chile in all her lifetime. She said her mother nearly got in bad one time when her sister was carrying a baby. She didn't keep up. Said the riding boss got down, dug a hole with the hoe to lay her in it 'cause she was so big in front. Her mother told him if he put her daughter there in that hole she'd cop him up in pieces wid her hoe. He found he had two to conquer and he let her be. But he had to leave 'cause he couldn't whoop the niggers.

"If I could think of all she tole I'd soon have enough to fill up that book you're getting up. I can't recollect who she belong to, and her old talk comes back to me now and then. She talked so much we'd get up and go on off to keep from hearing her tell things over so many times.

"Folks like me what got children think the way they do is all right. I don't like some of my children's ways but none of us perfect. I tells 'em right far as I knows. Times what makes folks no 'count. Times gets still around Biscoe. Heap of folks has plenty. Some don't have much—not enough. Some don't have nothing.

"I don't believe in women voting. That ruined the country. We got along very well till they got to tinkering with the government."

Bond, Scott
Age: 84
[S2:1 (AR): 25–50]

[Eighty-four] years ago there was born near Canton, in Madison County, Mississippi, a slave child that was destined to show the possibilities of every American-born child of any race. It was a boy. His mother was subject to the unhallowed conditions of that time. That her son was to be numbered among the leaders of his generation was not to be thought of; that he should become the largest planter and land owner of his race and state seemed impossible;

that as a merchant and all-round business man, owning and operating the finest and one of the largest mercantile establishments in his state was not to be dreamed of; that at the advanced age of 61 he would erect and operate successfully the largest excavating plant of its kind in Arkansas and one of the only two in the entire southland was beyond conception. Yet, these things and many others equally remarkable have been accomplished by the little Mississippi-born slave boy whose history these pages recount.

At the age of eighteen months, little Scott removed with his mother to Collierville, Fayette County, Tennessee, and at the age of five years removed with his mother and step-father, William Bond, to the Bond farm, Cross County, Arkansas. The question of "States' Rights" was uppermost in the mind of the American people. Mighty things were to happen that would settle forever this vexatious question. The south was drawing farther and farther from the north. The north was declaring "Union forever."

Bleeding Kansas! Forensic battles in the Congress of the United States! John Brown's Raid! Then in April, 1861, the first shot of the civil war crashed against the solid granite walls of old Fort Sumpter. What has all this to do with some little obscure mulatto boy, born on an obscure plantation somewhere down in Dixie? Just this: Had these tremendous events not transpired and ended as they did, the country would have still kept in bondage a race of men who have in fifty years—years of oppression and repression—shown to the world what America was losing. Booker T. Washington would not have revolutionized the educational methods of the world. Granville T. Woods would not have invented wireless telegraphy. There would have been no Negro troops to save the rough riders on San Juan Hill. There would have been no Negro soldiers to pour out their life blood at Carrizal. There would be no black American troops to offer to bare their dusky bosoms in the firey hell beyond the seas today in the mighty struggle for world democracy. Scott Bond would have had no opportunity to prove to the world that if a man will he may.

Scott Bond's Mother

I have said little about my mother. She was a slave and as such was house maid. This brought her in close contact with the white people and gave her training not common to the masses of colored women of her day. Her duties were such however, that she could give but little attention to me. Still her sympathy and love for me was as great as any woman ever bore in her bosom for a son. I can remember on one occasion when I was quite small my heels were chapped. In those days, Negro boys were not allowed to wear shoes until 12 or 14 years of age. When I would walk early in the morning or late in the evening, blood that would ooze from the cracks in my feet would mark my tracks.

On one occasion when my mother had finished her task as maid in the house she came to me late at night and took me from my bed to look at my feet. In those days, tallow was the cure all. One of my heels was so chapped and cracked open that one could almost lay his finger in the opening. She got some tallow and warmed it in a spoon and having no idea how hot it was poured it into the crack in my heel. As I held my heel up and my toe on the floor, the hot tallow filled the crack and ran down over my foot to my toes. I cried because of the intense pain the hot grease caused. My mother quieted me as best she could and put me to bed. When she got up next morning she examined my foot and to her amazement the hot tallow had raised a blister full length of my foot as large as one's finger. When she saw this she cried as if her heart would break and said as the tears streamed down her cheeks: "I did not mean to burn my child. I did not dream the tallow was so hot."

As mentioned before, slave boys rarely wore shoes until they were 12 or 14 years of age. It was great fun to go 'possum and coon hunting in those days or rather nights. Young Scott would take long trips through the woods and swamps with the other slaves and would risk all the dangers of briers and of being bitten by poisonous reptiles because of bare feet.

On one occasion when the dogs had treed a 'possum little Scott was the one to climb the tree and shake him out. The 'possum was away out on the end of a limb. The boys and men on the ground assured him the limb would not break. He let go the body of the tree and started out on the limb, which broke under the added weight and there was a squirming mixture of limb, boy, 'possum and snapping dogs on the ground. Fortunately he was not bitten. Scott came out of the scrimmage victorious with a fall and a 'possum.

On these trips the hunt would continue until all were loaded down with game, then they would return home.

On another occasion his mother had secured a pair of old boot tops and had a pair of shoes made for him. The first time he went out his mother insisted that he wear the shoes. He put them on and started out. When he reached the wood pile he pulled off the shoes and hid them in the wood pile because their unfamiliar weight cumbered his progress.

It was on one of these hunting excursions that he so sprained his ankle that the next morning his foot was as large as two feet. An old slave woman advised him to hold his foot in cold water. He accordingly crawled to the well where the mules were watered and put his foot in the tub of water standing there. One of the hands rode up to water his mules and compelled the boy to take his foot out of the tub. The mules drank all the water and left the tub empty.

Scott put his foot back into the tub and shortly another man came along, drew water for his mules and then filled the tub for Scott's benefit. About this time the overseer came along and asked him what he was doing. Scott withdrew his foot from the water and showed him his swollen ankle. When asked about it he explained the cause of the accident. The overseer called one of the hands and had him empty the tub and fill it with fresh water for Scott and told him that was the best thing he could do.

Mr. Bond says that after all these years as he looks back upon that time, he wonders whether it was kindness in the overseer or the saving of a valuable Negro boy that prompted the action.

His mother was away above the average slave woman, in her training being a housemaid and seamstress in the days before the sewing machine. She came in daily contact with the most cultured and refined white women and was thereby immensely benefited. She had no time to give to her boy except late at night when her daily work was through and most other people were in bed. For this reason, Scott missed his mother's ministrations in the years when most needed.

Poultry wire was unknown, the poultry yards were fenced with rails to keep the hogs from devouring the young fowls. Imagine if you can, a rail fence built tight enough to keep the hogs out and little goslings, turkeys and chickens in. It was one of little Scott's principal duties to march around the poultry yard and look after the young fowls. In cold weather the frost would bite his bare feet. In rainy weather he acted as a brooder. Boys in those days wore single garments, a long sack-like slip with holes cut for head and arms. When it rains, goslings will stand with their heads up and drown in a short time if left to themselves. Little Scott would gather little goslings under his slip as the hen hovers her brood and thus protect them from the falling rain. It must have been a ticklish task to have a half hundred little geese under one's single garment scrounging and crowding for warmth.

After the war when his step father started out on his own hook, Scott's mother continued in the same line that she had been trained. It was Scott's duty to see after the fowls and at times to look out for the welfare of the sitting hens. His mother would mark the eggs which she would put under the hen ready to set. Scott would have to keep the nests in repair and keep fresh eggs from the sitters' nests. Upon one occasion, Scott in his round, found a nest out of repair. He removed the hen, took the eggs from the nest and put them on the ground. He repaired the nest, put the hen back on the nest and left the eggs on the ground. The next morning his mother discovered the eggs on the ground and took the boy to task for his absent mindedness. Drawing him across her lap, she took her slipper and was applying the treatment in the most approved way. That the operation was painful to Scott, goes without the saying. His mother told him she was not punishing him for the value of the eggs, but because of his forgetfulness; and seeing far into the future she told him further that his absent mindedness was the only thing that would ever "misput" him in life. Scott noticing the tone of her voice looked up and found her crying. He says, that from that moment, he felt no further pain from the slipper as his mother continued for some little time to wield it.

Scott Bond Hunts His Father

When the writer asked Mr. Bond what he knew of his father, he related this story of his hunt for his father:

"My mother died when I was quite small, and had never explained to me who was my father. She married my step-father, who is still living, when I was eighteen months old.

"As I grew older and found that he was only my step-father, I began to inquire who was my father, and where he lived. My Aunt Martha told me I was born in Madison County, Mississippi, twelve miles from Canton, the county seat, at a little town called Livingston. That my father was a man, Wesley Rutledge, the nephew of Wm. H. Goodlow.

"After I had gotten started out in life and had accumulated a little spare money, I thought I would like to visit the place of my birth and, if possible, find my father, and if he was in need, help him.

"In ante-bellum days Mr. Goodlow was a very rich man. He owned five hundred slaves and thousands of acres of land.

"My mother had a large chest, which, in those days, was used as a trunk. I had often seen her going through the things in that old chest. She would take out her calico dresses, which we people called "Sunday Clothes." She would hang them out to air on Sundays. Among the things she would take from the chest was a pair of little red shoes and a cap, and would say to me: 'These are the shoes your father gave you.' Being only a child, I thought she referred to my step-father.

"I was married and we had two children and had rented a large farm, and I thought it a good time for this trip.

"I purchased a nice suit of clothes, then paid a visit to the barber and got neatly shaved and trimmed up, and pulled out for Canton, Miss., where I arrived at night. The next day was a rainy, drizzly day. It was March, but the people were bringing into Canton onions, lettuce and other early vegetables. I was surprised to see this and thought they were being shipped in from farther south. I went to the livery stable the next day and introduced myself to the livery man as Bond from Arkansas. I told him I wanted to drive to

Livingston, sixteen miles away. The liveryman, thinking I was white, said, 'All right Mr. Bond, the horse and buggy and nigger to drive you will cost you three dollars.'

"I told him I would be ready in about thirty minutes; and at the appointed time I paid him the money and started out for Livingston.

"We drove about two and one half miles and opened a gate to the enclosed farm of Mr. Goodlow. The old colored man who was driving was as active as a boy, although his hair was as white as cotton. This old gentleman took me to be a white man, and as he had never asked me I did not make myself known to him. He used these words.

'White folks, I have been in the country since I was a boy, and since that time I saw the man you are going to visit, harness up a hundred and fifty mules to be used on this farm. In those days the water almost boiled in this country. When you went to bed at night you could hear the blood hounds, and in the morning when you would wake up, you could hear them running colored people. The white folks said the music they made was the sweetest music in the world. There was once a runaway slave who had been chased at different times for four years. At last a set of patrolers came in with their dogs and said they were determined to catch him. They ran him for two days. Once in a while he would mislead the dogs and make them double on their tracks and he would gain a little rest. Eventually they would again pick up the trail and you could hear the hounds as they ran; say, here he goes, sing-a-ding; there he goes, sing-a-ding. At last, finding that he could not escape, he ran deliberately into a blazing furnace and was burned to death rather than be caught and suffer the tortures that awaited him.'

"He regaled me with many other stories of slave life that he had witnessed.

"He told me that many a time he would be so tired from his day's work that he would not wake up in the morning until the horn blew for work. He would not have time to cook himself any bread, and that he would run to the meal bowl and put a handful or two of meal in his hat and run with his bridle and catch his mule and while the mule was drinking, he would take water and mix the meal. Then when he got to the field he would go to a burning log-heap, when the overseer was not looking, and rake a place in the ashes and hot embers, put his cake in and cover it. Later, when chance permitted, he would take out his ash cake and eat it as he plowed. Thus he would work until dinner time.

"This old man was more than an average man.

"After telling me many other stories of the hardships of the slave, he said that after all, the things that looked hardest to him, were really blessings in

disguise. These hardships had developed his self-reliance and resourceful-
ness, and now that he was a free man and a citizen, he could see a benefit,
even in the hardships he had undergone. He said that he knew he was a
Christian and that he was respected by all his neighbors, black and white.

"This instance is but one of ten thousand, showing that the Negro in his
long apprenticeship has gained in adverse circumstances, that he has wrung
victory from oppression.

"By this time we had reached an elevation. He stopped his horse and
pointed to a house in the distance that looked no larger than a cow. He told
me that was the house to which we were going.

"As the distance lessened, the house proved to be a great mansion with
beautiful lawns.

"He stopped in front. I got out, and as I passed up the walk, knowing this
to be my birth-place, I felt that I was at home. I rang the bell. It was answered
by a large gentleman, who had a perfect bay window of a stomach. He was so
large that he was unable to tie and untie his shoes.

"I said, 'I suppose this is Mr. Goodlow?'

"'Yes, this is Goodlow.'

"'Mr. Goodlow, this is Bond from Arkansas.'

"'Come in, Mr. Bond.'

"As I walked into the parlor over elegant brussels carpets, I could see
myself reflected from the mirrors on either side of the hall. The furniture was
rare and elegant, and was typical of the splendor of the old time southern
mansion. I was invited to sit down and for the next hour answered a rain of
questions about Arkansas.

"Mr. Goodlow was very much interested in the young state of Arkansas.

"At that time wild life in the state had not been much disturbed. Bears,
wolves and panthers were plentiful. Arkansas at that time bore the reputa-
tion of being a paradise for murderers and other criminals fleeing from justice. Hence, Mr. Goodlow was interested to learn from me all he could about
these things, as well as about the climate and country in general.

"After I had imparted to him all I knew, I was then able to ask him a few
questions, and began by saying:

"Mr. Goodlow, can you recollect hiring some slaves from the widow
Bond's estate in 1852?"

"To which he replied, 'Yes; I remember hiring some slaves from the
Maben estate. Mrs. Bond was a Miss Maben.'"

"I suppose you are right. Do you remember hiring a man named Alex, a
woman named Martha and also a bright mulatto girl named Ann? Ann was
said to be your house servant at that time."

"'Yes,' he said, 'I remember that very distinctly.'"

"I proceeded: 'Ann gave birth to a child while she was your servant. It is said that Mr. Rutledge, who was your nephew and manager of your farm at that time, was the father of this child. It is further said that Mrs. Goodlow dressed the child and called it Scott Winfield."

"'You are certainly right,' he said. 'All that is true.'"

"I then arose from my chair and, standing erect, said, 'I am the kid.'"

"I was at that time a young man, and from what I felt, and others said, I was a very good looking young man. I had not been married a great while, and I knew my wife was a judge of beauty.

Mr. Goodlow said, 'Wait a minute.' He stepped to the parlor door and called Mrs. Goodlow, telling her to come in, he wanted her to see some one.

According to custom it took Mrs. Goodlow sometime to dress and make her appearance.

As she entered Mr. Goodlow said to her, "Do you know this boy sitting here?"'

"I got up and put on my best looks.

"'No,' she replied. 'Mr. Goodlow, I have never seen him before.'"

"Mrs. Goodlow was a typical southern matron, and with her wealth of silvery hair, was the personification of womanly grace and dignity.

"'Yes you have,' remarked Mr. Goodlow. 'You put the first rag on him and named him 'Scott Winfield,' at the time our son James was a baby.'"

"'No, Mr. Goodlow. I do not remember.'"

"'Don't you remember Ann, our housemaid, at the time Wess was managing our business?'"

"'Yes! Yes!' she exclaimed. 'I remember now. You are Scott Winfield.'

"She grasped my hand and said: 'I certainly dressed you and named you Scott Winfield.'

"It would be impossible to describe the scene that followed this greeting. Tears were shed, words were spoken that came from deep down in our hearts. A more touching and sincere greeting rarely comes to one in a life time.

'I was most hospitably treated and was urged to stay all night. I accepted and was given a nice room. The next day I was shown the place where I was born.

"Mr. Goodlow accompanied me. He had a man go into the "plunder room" and get out an old chair they used to tie me in, when my mother was about the duties in the house.

"One who does not know the south, can form no conception of the extreme hardships some of the slaves had to undergo; the many peculiar situations that would arise, nor can he have the faintest idea of the deep regard, and at times, even real affection that existed between the master and the favored slave. It is a reflex for this regard that is the basis of all the helpful things the better class of southern white people are now doing to help the Negro better his condition to rise to higher planes of manhood.

The following day I found an opportunity to explain to Mr. Goodlow, privately, the cause of my visit, and to ask the whereabouts of my father.

"I told him that prior to the war, there were many people who were wealthy. Many of these were greatly impoverished by changed conditions. I had come to find my father, and if he was in need, to help him.

"I was informed by Mr. Goodlow that he was very sorry he would have to tell me that my father was dead. That he had moved to Texas twelve years before, and had died two years later. He also informed me that he had three children living and doing business in Canton, Miss.

"When I was ready to leave, Mr. Goodlow had me driven to Canton in his magnificent carriage. I called on the children in Canton and introduced myself as Bond from Arkansas. I congratulated them on their business but did not make myself known to them, so that all they ever knew of me was 'Bond from Arkansas.'"

This brings up a thought. It has been stated by some careful statisticians that there are about 10,000,000 _____-blooded Negroes in the United States. Without accepting or rejecting this estimate, we will say that there are enough of that part of our population mixed-blood to at least keep the pot from calling the kettle black, in point of moral rectitude.

Settling a Strike

I had a tenant on my place named Charley Dilahunty, who claimed that he knew how to lay foundations and set up engines. He agreed to work for me at $1.50 per day.

When the machinery arrived, Charley and I started with our square, level and plumb bob and erected a plant that answered our purpose and paid for itself in two years.

On one occasion Charley claimed on Monday morning to be sick. I went to the gin, fired up and attempted to run the engine myself. I had been watching Charley pretty closely in order to get an idea as to how to handle the engine.

I raised steam, put on two gauges of water, oiled up and opened the throttle to start. The engine failed to turn. I closed the throttle and examined the engine to the best of my ability. I could find nothing wrong. I then turned on the steam slowly until I had the throttle wide open, still the engine would not move. I closed the throttle and had the boys help me turn the fly-wheel over. Five men put on all their strength and yet they failed to move the fly-wheel.

By this time the steam gauge showed up one hundred pounds, and the boiler was popping off.

I threw open the exhaust, raised the flue door and put on the water. I was afraid to take the wrench and go to loosening bolts for fear of loosening the wrong one.

The ginner came down to the engine room and said, "Mr. Bond, I thnk Charley Dilahunty jammed that engine."

"Why do you think so?"

"Because he said Saturday night that he did not expect that engine to turn any more until he got $2.00 per day for his services."

"Did Charley tell you this?"

"He did!"

I was at a loss to know what to do. I walked off and sat down on a bench. The more I studied over it, the worse shape I found myself in. I called for my horse which was hitched to the fence, jumped into my saddle. I went half a mile past Charley's house and a half mile farther to my own house.

I grabbed my shotgun and returned to Charley's house. I called Mary, his wife, to the door. I told her to ask Charley to come out.

He came. I said to him, "Come here, Charley." I opened the gate. "Get on up the road to the gin house," I ordered. He wanted to go back and get his hat. I told him they did not bury men with their hats on.

Up the road he went for about three hundred yards. He then stopped and said: "I have not done anything to the engine."

"Get on up the road," I commanded.

When we arrived at the gin, I said to him: "Walk up to the door and stop."

I dismounted, advanced on him with my shotgun and told him to get the wrench and unjam that engine. If he did not do it in ten minutes, I would kill him if he was the last man on earth.

He picked up the wrench, made two turns on a certain nut. I asked him if the engine was ready for service.

He said, "Yes sir."

He opened the throttle. The engine moved off nicely.

I said to him, "I look for you to stay here and run this engine until night." It was about twelve o'clock. Charley said, "I have not had any dinner yet."

"You may not need any dinner after today."

Charley weighed about 190 pounds. I, a little insignificant Negro, weighed about 108 pounds, so I thought it a wise plan to keep close company with my shotgun.

He ginned six bales of cotton after dinner. I weighed the cotton. At seven o'clock I sent a boy into the engine room to tell Charley to blow the whistle for quitting time.

I locked up the gin and got on my horse. Charley had cooled down and was standing at the door of the engine room. He said, "Mr. Bond, I want you to forgive me for the wrong I have done."

"What have you done wrong, Charley?"

"I jammed the engine and caused you to lose half of the day's work with all the crew."

"What prompted you to do that?"

"I thought I should have more wages—$1.75 a day anyhow."

"Why did you not walk up to me like a man and say so?"

"All I can say is I did wrong and I want you to forgive me."

"This was your own contract—to help me set up the engine and run the gin for the season for a dollar and a half a day. Now, Charley, I am going to give you $2.00 per day and I want steam at five o'clock every morning from now on."

We were good friends after that. All went well.

Scott Bond Moves to Madison

Scott Bond moved to Madison, St. Francis County, Ark., with his step-father, who had bargained to buy a farm, in 1872, and remained with him until he was 21 years of age. He then undertook to vouch for himself. His step-father contracted with him to remain with him until he was 22 years of age. His pay was to be one bale of cotton, board, washing and patching. He thought the pay was small, but for the sake of his little brothers, that they might have a home paid for, he remained that year. The next year he walked eighteen miles to the Allen farm, having seen the possibilities in the fertile soil of that place in the two years he had worked on it with his step-father. He decided that would be the place to make money. He rented 12 acres of land at $6.50 per acre. He had no money, no corn, no horse, nothing to eat, no plows, no gears; but all the will-power that could be contained in one little hide. In 1876 he married Miss Magnolia Nash at Forrest City. The Allen farm, as stated else-where, contained 2,200 acres. The proprietor lived in Knoxville, Tenn. She sent her son over the next autumn, who insisted on Scott Bond renting the whole place. This he refused to do on the ground that he was unable to furnish the mules, feed, tools and other stock sufficient to cultivate it. Mr. Allen took a letter from his pocket that read: "Now, Scott, I have told Johnnie to be sure and do his uttermost to rent you this place, and as I am sure it would be quite a burden on you financially, you may draw on me for all the money that is required to buy mules, corn and tools." And at the bottom: "Scott, I think this will be one of the golden oportunities of your life." This lady was near kin to Scott Bond's former owner. He grasped the opportunity. There were all sorts of people living on the Allen farm. Some half-breed Indians, some few white families and some low, degraded colored people. The whites were no better than the others. The first thing Scott Bond had to do was to clean up the farm along those lines. He then secured axes, cross cut saws, and built a new fence around the entire farm—something that had not been done for 20 years. When the crops were gathered and disposed of, Scott paid Mrs. Allen and everyone else for the rent and all other obligations. He received from Mrs. Allen, the owner of the farm, who lived in Knoxville, Tenn., a fine letter of thanks and congratulations for the improvements on the farm. The net profits, all bills paid, were $2,500, in addition to the gains on cotton seed. This farm is situated right at the east base of Crowley's Ridge, 42 miles due west of the Mississippi river. There were no levees in this county at that time, and when the overflows came we had a sea of water spread out from the Mississippi to the ridge. Mr. Bond said the next winter there came the biggest overflow he had ever seen. He took his boat and moved all the people, mules, cattle, hogs and horses to Crowley's Ridge. He lived about a mile and a half from Crowley's Ridge and owing to a deep slough or bayou between him and the ridge he was compelled to use a boat. There was perhaps no more exciting time in Mr. Bond's life than when with his boat he would brave the dangers of the murky flood and with the help of his crew scout the country over hunting out and rescuing people and stock from the rising, rushing waters. It is said by those who know, that Scott Bond saved the lives of hundreds of people, white and black. In this particular overflow he had 7,000 bushels of corn and 10,000 pounds of meat that he had killed and cured. He saved all this by putting it in the lofts of the different buildings on the place. Having secured his own people and property, he spent his time looking out and helping his neighbors. He lived in the great house on the Allen farm. He took flour barrels, placed planks on them for a scaffold to put his cooking stove and bed on. The next day he ran his dugout into the house and tied it to his bed post. Three days later he was compelled to get another set of barrels to raise his scaffold a little higher. On the third evening he arrived at home between sundown and dark with all his boatmen in dugouts. It was impossible to get in the door on account of the water. They ran the boats in through the windows, each man to his sleeping place. Every one of them was as wet as rats. They would have to stand on the head end of their boats to change their wet clothing before getting into their beds. The cook and his helper, who looked after things in the absence of the boats, were brave to start in with and promised to stay with

Scott Bond as long as there was a button on his shirt, but when they saw the boats coming in through the top sash of the window their melts drew up. They said, "Mr. Bond, we like you and have always been willing to do anything you asked us to do, but this water is away beyond where we had any idea it would be. We are going to leave tomorrow morning."

They had all changed and put on dry clothing, and as a matter of course felt better. The next call was supper and dinner combined. A big tea kettle full of strong, hot coffee, spare ribs, back bones, hog heads, ears and noses. There was some shouting around that table. Mr. Bond says he did not attempt to pacify the cook and hostler until after all had finished supper, as the time to talk to an individual is when he has a full stomach.

"The next day when we started out," says Mr. Bond, "I instructed my men to 'do as you see me do.' If a cow jumps over board, follow her and grab her by the tail and stick to her until you come to some sapling or grape vine; grab it and hold to it until help arrives. Any man can hold a cow by the tail or horn in this way."

All Mr. Bond's people were comfortably housed on Crowley's Ridge. In those days people did not need the assistance of the government to take care of them. They had plenty of corn, meat and bread they produced at home. Six months later you could not tell that there ever had been an overflow from the looks of the corn and cotton.

"But to return to the boys who were getting frightened at the ever-increasing flood," said Mr. Bond, "we all loaded our pipes and you may know there was a smoke in the building. 'Twas then I said, 'Boys, all sit down and let's reason with one and another. The water will be at a standstill tomorrow evening. I really know what I am talking about, because the stage of the river at Cairo always governs the height of the water here. That is a thing I always keep posted on. While this, the great house, is two-thirds full of water, you must remember that this is the eddy right along here, and anyone of you take your spike pole and let it down to the floor and you will find from 8 to 10 inches of sand and sediment.'

"One man said, 'I know he is right, because whenever an overflow subsides I have to shovel out from ten to twelve inches of sand. This house is built out of hewn logs, 46 feet long and the biggest brick stack chimneys in the middle I ever saw. Now, boys, with all this meat and other things piled on this scaffold you are perfectly safe. I am feeding you boys and paying you well. I am only asking you to do what you see me do. This satisfied them and we stuck together."

Starting a Negro School

In 1886, a northern gentleman, Mr. Thorn, was renting the Bond farm. He was very kindly disposed toward the colored people. He wrote to Memphis for a teacher for a colored school. The parties to whom he wrote, referred him to Miss Celia Winchester. She accepted the school.

There were no railroads in this part of the country at that time. The only method of transportation was from Memphis, by steam boat, down the Mississippi and up the St. Francis rivers to Wittsburg.

When the boat arrived at Wittsburg, Mr. Thorn, not knowing the customs of the south, secured a room at the hotel for Miss Winchester, who was an Oberlin, Ohio, graduate. She had attended school with the whites at that famous seat of learning. She too, was ignorant of the customs prevailing in the south.

When the proprietor of the hotel learned that Miss Winchester was colored, he went out and bought a cowhide. He met Mr. Thorn on the street, held a pistol to him and cow-hided him.

Mr. Thorn stood and cried. He said that he was seventy years old and had never done any one any harm in his life. What he had done was not intended as a violation of custom.

We lived about sixteen miles out of Wittsburg. The next day a wagon met Mr. Thorn and Miss Winchester and took them to the farm.

Thus was opened the first school for Negroes in this part of the country and the first school I had ever seen. In the school my step-father and myself were classmates in the A B C class.

Sitting on a Snake

There was a woman named Julia Ann on our plantation, who, one day at dinner time, went to a tree where she had hung her dinner bucket. She reached up and got the bucket and backed up to the tree and sat down between its protruding roots to eat her dinner. When she got up, she found she had been sitting on a rattle snake. The snake was killed. He had fifteen rattlers and a button on his tail. Ann fainted when she saw the snake. She said that she had felt the snake move, but thought that it was the cane giving way beneath her.

Snakes of that size and variety were numerous in Arkansas in those times.

I heard of an instance where a man built a house on a flat, smooth rock on a piece of land that he had bought. It was in the autumn when he built his house. When the weather grew cold he made a fire on the rock. There had been a hole in the rock, but the man had stopped it up.

One night he had retired, and late in the night, his child, which was sleeping between him and his wife, became restless and awakened him. He reached for the child and found what he supposed was his wife's arm across the child. He undertook to remove it and to his consternation, found he had hold of a large snake. He started to get out of bed, to make a light, and the whole floor was covered with snakes. He got out of the house with his wife and child.

The next day the neighbors gathered, burned the house and (manuscript breaks off)

Brown, William
Age: 78
439 W. Twenty-fifth Street
North Little Rock, Arkansas
Interviewer: Samuel S. Taylor
[M:8: pt. 1: 317–23]

"I was born in Arkansas in Cross County at the foot of Crowley's Ridge on the east side of the Ridge and just about twelve miles from Old Wittsburg, on May 3, 1861. I got the date from my mother. She kept dates by the old family Bible. I don't know where she got her learning. She had a knowledge of reading. I am about her sixth child. She was the mother of thirteen.

"My mother's master was named Bill Neely. Her mistress was named Mag Neely.

"My mother was one of the leading plow hands on Bill Neely's farm. She had a old mule named Jane. When the Yankees would come down, Bill Neely and all his friends would leave home. They would leave when they would hear the cannon, because they said that meant the Yankees were coming. When Neely went away, he would carry my mother to do his cooking.

"She would leave the children there and carry just the baby when she went. Old Aunt Malinda—she wasn't our aunt; she was just an old lady we called Aunt Malinda who cooked for the kitchen—would cook for us while she was gone. When the Yankees had passed through, my mother and the master would all come back.

"My original name was not Brown. It was Pope. I became Brown after the War was over. I moved on the old Barnes' farm. When the soldiers were mustered out in the end of the War, a lot of soldiers worked on that place. Peter Brown, an old colored soldier mustered out from Memphis, met my mother, courted her, and married her. All the other children that were born to her were called Brown, and the people called her Brown, and just called all the other children Brown too, including me. And I just let it go that way. But my father was named Harrison Pope. He died in the Confederate army out there somewheres around Little Rock. He had violated some of the military laws, and they put him in that thing they had to punish them by, and when they taken him out, he contracted pneumonia and died. I don't know where he is buried. I would to God I did! You know when those Southern armies went along they carried colored stevedores to do the work for them.

Patrollers

"I was a little fellow in the time of the pateroles. If the slaves wanted to go out anywhere, they had to get a pass and they had to be back at a certain time. If they didn't get back, it would be some kind of punishment. The pateroles was a mighty bad thing. If they caught you when you were out without a pass, they would whip you unmercifully, and if you were out too late they would whip you. Wherever colored people had a gathering, them pateroles would be there looking on to see if they could find anybody without a pass. If they did find anybody that couldn't show a pass, they would take him right out and whip him then and there.

Ku Klux

"I know the Ku Klux must have been in use before the War because I remember the business when I was a little bit of a fellow. They had a place out there on Crowley's Ridge they used to meet at. They tried to make the impression that they would be old Confederate soldiers that had been killed in the battle of Shiloh, and they used to ride down from the Ridge hollering, 'Oh! Lordy, Lordy, Lordy!' They would have on those old uniforms and would call for water. And they would have some way of pouring the water down in a bag or something underneath their uniforms so that it would look like they could drink four or five gallons.

"One night when they come galloping down on their horses hollering 'Oh! Lordy, Lordy' like they used to, some Yankee soldiers stationed nearby tied ropes across the road and killed about twenty-five of the horses and broke legs and arms of about ten or fifteen. They never used the ridge any more after that.

Parents

"My father's master was Shep Pope and his wife was named Julia Pope. I can't remember where my father was born but my mother was born in Tuscaloosa County, Alabama. I don't know the names of my grandfather and grandmother on either side.

Slave Houses

"The old slave house was a log house built out of hewed logs. The logs were scalped on each side to give it the appearance of a box house. And they said the logs would fit together better, too. They would chink up the cracks with grass and dirt—what they called 'dob'. That is what they called chinking to keep the wind and rain out.

"I was born in a one-room hut with a clapboard room on one side for the kitchen and storeroom. They would go out in the woods and split out the clapboards. My mother had eight of we children in that room at one time.

Furniture

"As to furniture, well, we had benches for chairs. They were made out of punching four holes in a board and putting sticks in there for legs. That is what we sat on. Tables generally were nailed up with two legs out and with the wall to support the other side. The beds were made in a corner with one leg out and the two walls supporting the other sides. They called that bed the 'Georgia Horse'. We had an old cupboard made up in a corner.

Food

"Food was generally kept in the old cupboard my mother had. When she had too much for the cupboard, she put it in an old chest.

Right after the War

"My mother had eight children to feed. After the emancipation she had to hustle for all of them. She would go up to work—pick cotton, pull corn, or what not, and when she came home at night she had an old dog she called 'Coldy'. She would go out and say, 'Coldy, Coldy, put him up.' And a little later, we would hear Coldy bark and she would go out and Coldy would have something treed. And she would take whatever he had—'possum, coon, or what not—and she would cook it, and we would have it for breakfast the next morning.

"Mother used to go out on neighboring farms and they would give her the scraps when they killed hogs and so on. One night she was coming home with some meat when she was attacked by wolves. Old Coldy was along and a little yellow dog. The dogs fought the wolves and while they were fighting, she slipped home. Next morning old Coldy showed up cut almost in two where the wolves had bitten him. We bandaged him up and took care of him. And he lived for two or more years. The little yellow dog never did show up no more. Mother said that the wolves must have killed and eaten him.

Schooling

"I put in about one month schooling when I was a boy about six or seven years old. Then I moved into St. Francis County and went two weeks to a subscription school a few miles below Forrest City. Later I went back and took the examination in Cross County and passed it, and taught for a year. I got the bulk of my education by lamp light reading. I have done some studying in other places—three years in Shorter College where I got the degrees of B. D. and D. D. at the age of fifty-five. I have preached for fifty-seven years and actually pastored for forty-four years. I followed farming in my early days. When I first married my wife, we farmed there for ten or twelve years before I entered the ministry. I have been married fifty-seven years.

Marriage

"I was married January 15, 1888. I am now in the fifty-seventh year of marriage. My wife was named Mary Ellen Stubbs. She was from Baldwyn, Mississippi. They moved from Mississippi about the winter of 1880 and they made one crop in Arkansas before we married. They stopped in our county and attended our church. I met her in that way. The most remarkable thing was that during the time I was acquainted with her our pastor became incapacitate and I took charge of the church. I ran a revival and she was converted during the revival. But she joined the C. M. E. church. I belong to the A. M. E.

Slave Sales

"I remember my mother carrying the children from the Bill Neely place to the Pope place. That Saturday evening after we got there, there come along some slave traders. They had with them as I remember some ten or twelve boys and girls and some old folks that were able to work. They had them chained. I asked my mother what they were going to do with them and she said they were carrying them to Louisiana to work on a cane farm. One boy cried a lot. The next morning they put those slaves in the road and drove them down to Wittsburg the same as you would drive a drove of cattle. Wittsburg was where they caught the boat to go down to Louisiana. That was the best mode of travel in those days.

Opinions

"In a few words, my opinion of the present is that our existence as Democrats and Republicans is about played out.

"If Mr. Roosevelt is elected for a third term, I think we will go into a dictatorship just as Russia, Germany, and Italy have already done. I think we are nearer to that now than we have ever been before. I do not think that Mr.

Roosevelt will become a dictator, but I do believe that his being elected a third time will cause some one else to become dictator. My opinion is that he is neither Democrat nor Republican.

"Our young people are advancing from a literary point of view, but I claim that they are losing out along moral lines. I don't believe that we value morals as well as the people did years ago who didn't know so much. I believe that the whole nation, white and black, is losing moral stamina. They do not think it is bad to kill a man, take another man's wife or rob a bank, or anything else. They desecrate the churches by carrying anything into the church. There is no sacred place now. Carnivals and everything else are carried to the church.

"If Mr. Roosevelt is not reelected again, the country is going to have one of the bloodiest wars it has ever had because we have so many European doctrines coming into the United States. I have been living 78 years, and I never thought that I would live to see the day when the government would reach out and take hold of things like it has done—the WPA, the [illegible], and the [illegible], and other work going on today. We are headed for communism and we are going to get in a bloody war. There are hundreds of men going 'round who believe in communism but who don't want it to be known now."

Dallas County

Badgett, Joseph Samuel
Age: 72
1221 Wright Avenue
Little Rock, Arkansas
Interviewer: Samuel S. Taylor
[M:8: pt. 1: 78–83]

"My mother had Indian in her. She would fight. She was the pet of the people. When she was out, the pateroles would whip her because she didn't have a pass. She has showed me scars that were on her even till the day that she died. She was whipped because she was out without a pass. She could have had a pass any time for the asking, but she was too proud to ask. She never wanted to do things by permission.

Birth
"I was born in 1864. I was born right here in Dallas County. Some of the

most prominent people in this state came from there. I was born on Thursday, in the morning at three o'clock, May the twelfth. My mother has told me that so often, I have it memorized.

Persistence of Slave Customs

"While I was a slave and was born close to the end of the Civil War, I remember seeing many of the soldiers down here. I remember much of the treatment given to the slaves. I used to say 'master' myself in my day. We had to do that till after '69 or '70. I remember the time when I couldn't go nowhere without asking the 'white folks.' I wasn't a slave then but I couldn't go off without asking the white people. I didn't know no better.

"I have known the time in the southern part of this state when if you wanted to give an entertainment you would have to ask the white folks. Didn't know no better. For years and years, most of the niggers just stayed with the white folks. Didn't want to leave them. Just took what they give 'em and didn't ask for nothing different.

"If I had known forty years ago what I know now!

First Negro Doctor in Tulip, Arkansas

"The first Negro doctor we ever seen come from Little Rock down to Tulip, Arkansas. We were all excited. There were plenty of people who didn't have a doctor living with twenty miles of them. When I was fourteen years old, I was secretary of a conference.

Schooling

"What little I know, an old white woman taught me. I started to school under this old woman because there weren't any colored teachers. There wasn't any school at Tulip where I lived. This old lady just wanted to help. I went to her about seven years. She taught us a little every year—especially in the summer time. She was high class—a high class Christian woman—belonged to the Presbyterian church. Her name was Mrs. Gentry Wiley.

"I went to school to Scipio Jones once. Then they opened a public school at Tulip and J. C. Smith taught there two years in the summer time. Then Lula Baily taught there one year. She didn't know no more than I did. Then Scipio came. He was there for a while. I don't remember just how long.

"After that I went to Pine Bluff. The County Judge at that time had the right to name a student from each district. I was appointed and went up there in '82 and '83 from my district. It took about eight years to finish Branch Normal at that time. I stayed there two years. I roomed with old man John Young.

"You couldn't go to school without paying unless you were sent by the Board. We lived in the country and I would go home in the winter and study in the summer. Professor J. C. Corbin was principal of the Pine Bluff Branch Normal at that time. Dr. A. H. Hill, Professor Booker, and quite a number of the people we consider distinguished were in school then. They finished, but I didn't. I had to go to my mother because she was ill. I don't claim to have no schooling at all.

"Forty Acres and a Mule"

"My mother received forty acres of land when freedom came. Her master gave it to her. She was given forty acres of land and a colt. There is no more to tell about that. It was just that way—a gift of forty acres of land and a colt from her former master.

"My mother died. There is a woman living now that lost it (the home). Mother let Malinda live on it. Mother lived with the white folks meanwhile. She didn't need the property for herself. She kept it for us. She built a nice log house on it. Fifteen acres of it was under cultivation when it was given to her. My sister lived on it for a long time. She mortgaged it in some way I don't know how. I remember when the white people ran me down there some years back to get me to sign a title to it. I didn't have to sign the paper because the property had been deeded to Susan Badgett and HEIRS; lawyers advised me not to sign it. But I signed it for the sake of my sister.

Father and Master

"My mother's master was named Badgett—Captain John Badgett. He was a Methodist preacher. Some of the Badgetts still own property on Main Street. My mother's master's father was my daddy.

Marriage

"I was married July 12, 1889. Next year I will have been married fifty years. My wife's name was Elizabeth Owens. She was born in Batesville, Mississippi. I met her at Brinkley when she was visiting her aunt. We married in Brinkley. Very few people in this city have lived together longer than we have. July 12, 1938, will make forty-nine years. By July 1939, we will have reached our fiftieth anniversary.

Patrollers, Jayhawkers, Ku Klux, and Ku Klux Klan

"Pateroles, jayhawkers, and the Ku Klux came before the war. The Ku Klux in slavery times were men who would catch Negroes out and keep them if they did not collect from their masters. The pateroles would catch Negroes out and return them if they did not have a pass. They whipped them some-times if they did not have a pass. The jayhawkers were highway men or rob-bers who stole slaves among other things. At least, that is the way the people regarded them. The jayhawkers stole and pillaged, while the Ku Klux stole those Negroes they caught out. The word 'Klan' was never included in their name.

"The Ku Klux Klan was an organization which arose after the Civil War. It was composed of men who believed in white supremacy and who regu-lated the morals of the neighborhood. They were not only after Jews and Negroes, but they were sworn to protect the better class of people. They took the law in their own hands.

Slave Work

"I'm not so certain about the amount of work required of slaves. My mother says she picked four hundred pounds of cotton many a day. The slaves were tasked and given certain amounts to accomplish. I don't know the exact amount nor just how it was determined.

Opinions

"It is too bad that the young Negroes don't know what the old Negroes think and what they have done. The young folks could be helped if they would take advice."

Interviewer's Comment

Badgett's distinctions between jayhawkers, Ku Klux, patrollers, and Ku Klux Klan are most interesting.

I have been slow to catch it. All my life, I have heard persons with ex-slave background refer to the activities of the Ku Klux among slaves prior to 1865. I always thought that they had the Klux Klan and the patrollers confused.

Badgett's definite and clear-cut memories, however, lead me to believe that many of the Negroes who were slaves used the word Ku Klux to denote a type of persons who stole slaves. It was evidently in use before it was applied to the Ku Klux Klan.

The words "Ku Klux" and "Ku Klux Klan" are used indiscriminately in current conversation and literature. It is also true that many persons in the present do, and in the past did, refer to the Ku Klux Klan simply as "Ku Klux."

It is a matter of record that the organization did not at first bear the name "Ku Klux Klan" throughout the South. The name "Ku Klux" seems to have grown in application as the organization changed from a moral association of the best citizens of the South and gradually came under the control of lawless persons with lawless methods—whipping and murdering. It is antecedently reasonable that the change in names accompanying a change in policy would be due to a fitness in the prior use of the name. The recent use of the name seems mostly imitation and propaganda. Histories, encyclopedias, and dictionaries, in general, do not record a meaning of the term Ku Klux as prior to the Reconstruction period.

Dortch, Charles Green
Age: 81
804 Victory Street
Little Rock, Arkansas
Interviewer: Samuel S. Taylor
[M:8: pt. 2: 169–79]

"I was born June 18, 1857. The reason I don't show my age is because I got Scotch-Irish, Indian, and Negro mixed up in me. I was born in Princeton—that is, near Princeton—in Dallas County. Princeton is near Fordyce. I was born on Hays' farm. Hays was my second master—Archie Hays. Dortch was my first master. He brought my parents from Richmond, Virginia, and he settled right in Princeton.

"My father's name was Reuben Rainey Dortch. He was an octoroon I guess. He looked more like a Cuban than a Negro. He had beautiful wavy hair, naturally wavy. He was tall, way over six feet, closer to seven. His father was Dortch. Some say Rainey. But he must have been a Dortch; he called himself Dortch, and we go in the name of Dortch. Rainey was a white man employed on Dortch's plantation. Rainey's name was Wilson Rainey. My name has always been Dortch.

"My mother was named Martha Dortch. I am trying to think what her maiden name was. My sister can tell you all the details of it. She is five years older than I am. She can tell you all the old man's folks and my mother's too more easily than I can.

"My father had, as nearly as I can remember—lemme see—Cordelia, Adrianna, Mary, Jennie, Emma, and Dortch. Emma and Dortch were children by a first wife. Cordelia was his stepdaughter. My brothers were Alex and Gabe. There is probably some I have overlooked.

"The Indian blood in me came through my mother's father. He was a full-blooded red Indian. I can't think of his name now. Her mother was a dark woman.

"My father was a carpenter, chair maker, and a farmer too. all the work he did after peace was declared was carpentry and chair and basket making.

He made coffins too just after peace was declared. They didn't have no under-takers then. He made the bottoms to chairs too. He could put a roof on a house beautifully and better than any one I know. Nobody could beat him putting shingles on a house.

"My mother was reared to work in the house. She was cook, housekeeper. She was a weaver too. She worked the loom and the spinning wheel. She gar-dened a little. But her work was mostly in the house as cook and weaver. She never went out in the field as a hand. My father didn't either.

Kind Masters

"My father seemed to have been more of a pet than a slave. He was a kind of boss more than anything else. He had his way. Nobody was allowed to mis-treat him in any way. My mother was the same way. I don't think she was ever mistreated in any way by the white folks—not that I ever saw.

Attitude of Slaves toward Father

"There wasn't any unfriendliness of the other slaves toward my father. My oldest sister can tell you with clearness, but I don't think he ever had any trouble with the other slaves any more than he had with the white folks. He was well liked, and then too he was able to take care of himself. Then again, he had a good master. Hays was a good man. We made a trip down there just a short while ago. We hadn't been there since the Civil War. They made it so pleasant for us! We all set down to the same table and ate together. Frank was down there. He was my young master.

Thirty Acres—Not Forty

"They gave us thirty acres of land when we came out of slavery. They didn't give it to us right then, but they did later. I am going down there again sometime. My young master is the postmaster down there now. He thinks the world and all of me and my oldest sister.

"I don't mind telling people anything about myself. I was born in June. They ain't nothing slipping up on me. I understand when to talk. There are two of us, Adrianna Kern—that's her married name. She and I are the ones Mr. Frank gave the thirty acres to. I have a younger sister.

Slave Work

"I don't know how much cotton a slave was expected to pick in a day. The least I ever heard of was one hundred fifty pounds. Some would pick as high as three and four hundred pounds.

"My father was not a field hand. He was what they called the first man 'round there. He was a regular leader on the plantation—boss of the tool room. He was next to the master of them, you might say. He was a kind of boss.

"I never heard of his working for other men besides his master. I believe he drove the stage for a time from Arkadelphia to Camden or Princeton. I don't know just how that come about. My sister though has a more exact remembrance than I have, and she can probably tell you the details of it.

Boyhood Experiences

"My father used to take me to the mill with him when I was a kid. That was in slavery time. He went in a wagon and took me with him.

"The biggest thing I did was to play with the other kids. They had me do such work as pick berries, hunt up the stock, drive the sheep home from the pasture. And as near as I can remember it seems like they had me more picking berries or gathering peaches or something like that.

Food, Houses, Clothes

"Cornbread, buttermilk and bacon and all such as that and game—that was the principal food. The people on our place were fed pretty well. We lived off of ash cakes and biscuits.

"The slaves lived in old log houses. I can almost see them now.

Let's see—they usually had just one window. The slaves slept on pallets mostly and wore long cotton shirts.

Patrollers

"I have heard a great deal of talk about the pateroles—how they tied ropes across the road and trapped them. Sometimes they would be knocked off their horses and crippled up so that they had to be carried off from there. Of course, that was sometimes. They was always halting the slaves and questioning them and whipping them if they didn't have passes.

How Freedom Came

"The way I understand it there came a rumor all at once that the Negroes were free. It seems that they throwed up their hands. They had a great fight at Pine Bluff and Helena and De Valls Bluff. Then came peace. The rumor came from Helena. Meade and Thomas winded the thing up some way. Sherman made his march somewhere. The colored soldiers and the white soldiers came pouring in from Little Rock. They come in a rush and said, 'Tell them niggers they're free.' They run into the masters and notified them they were going to take all the Negroes to Little Rock. It wasn't no time afterwards before here come the teams and the wagons to take us to Little Rock.

"When they brought us here, they put us in soldiers' camps in a row of houses up just west of where the Arch street graveyard is now. They put us all there in the soldiers' buildings. They called them camps. They seemed to be getting us ready for freedom. It wasn't long before they had us in school and in church. The Freedmen's Bureau visited us and gave us rations just like the Government has been doing these last years. They gave us food and clothes and books and put us in school. That was all done right here in Little Rock.

Schooling

"My first teacher was Miss Sarah Henley. I could show you the home she used to live in. It's right up the street. It's on Third Street between Izard and State right in the middle of the block—next to the building on the corner of Izard on the south side of Third street. There is a brick building there on the corner and her house is a very pretty one right next to it. She was a white woman and was my first teacher. She taught me, as near as I can remember, one session. My next teacher was Mrs. Hunt. She was from Ohio. My first teacher was from Ohio too. Mrs. Hunt taught me about two sessions. Lemme see, Mrs. Clapp came after her. She was from Pennsylvania. Mrs. Clapp taught me one session. I am trying to think of that other teacher. We went over to Union School then. Charlotte Andrews taught us there for a while. That was her maiden name. Her married name is Stephens. She was the first colored teacher in the city. Mrs. Hubbard teached us a while, too. Mrs. Scull taught us right here on Gaines and Seventh Streets where this church is now. They moved us a long time ago down to the Mess House at the Rock Island for a while but we didn't stay there long. We came back to the Methodist church— the one on Eighth and Broadway, not the Bethel Church on Ninth and Broadway. There was a colored church on Eighth and Broadway then. They kept sweeping us 'round because the schools were all crowded. Woods, a colored man, was one of the teachers at Capitol Hill Public School. We were there when it first opened. That was the last school I went to. I finished eight grades. Me and Scipio Jones went to school together and were in the same class. I left him in school and went to work to take care of my folks.

Occupational Experiences

"Right after the Civil War, I went to school. I did no work except to sell papers and black boots on the corner of Main and Markham on Sunday. After I stopped school I went to work as assistant porter in the railroad office at the Union Station for the St. Louis, Iron Mountain, Southern Railway and Cairo and Fulton. That was one road or system. I stayed with them from 1873 till 1882 in the office as office porter. From that I went train porter till 1892. Then right back from 1892 I went in the general superintendent's private car. Then from there I went to the shop here in North Little Rock—the Missouri Pacific Shops—as a straw boss of the storeroom gang. That was in 1893. I stayed in the shop until 1894. Then I was transferred back on this side as coach cleaner. That was in 1895. I stayed as coach cleaner till 1913. From that I went to the State Capitol and stayed there as janitor of the Supreme Court for three years. In 1917, I went back to the coach cleaning department. That was during the war. I stayed there till 1922. I come out on the strike and have been out ever since. Since then I have done house cleaning all over the city. That brings me up to about two years ago. Now I pick up something here and something there. I have been knocking around sick most of the time and supported by the Relief and the Welfare principally.

Ku Klux Klan

"I don't remember much about the Ku Klux Klan. They never bothered me, and never bothered any one connected with me.

Powell Clayton

"I have stood at the bar and drank with Powell Clayton. He had been 'round here ever since we had. He was a very particular friend of my boss'— the bosses of my work after the war and freedom. They were all Yankees together. They would all meet at the office. That was while I was workng my way through school and afterwards too. He was strictly a 'Negroes' Friend'. He was a straight out and out Yankee.

A Broken Thumb in a Political Fight

"I got this thumb broken beating a white man up. No, I'll tell the truth. He was beating me up and I thought he was going to kill me. It was when Benjamin Harrison had been elected President. I was in Sol Joe's saloon and I said, 'Hurrah for Harrison.' A white man standing at the bar there said to me, 'What do you mean, nigger, insulting the guests here?' And before I knew what he was going to do—bop!—he knocked me up on the side of the head and put me flat on the floor. He started to stamp me. My head was roaring, but I grabbed his legs and held them tight against me and then we was both on the floor fighting it out. I butted him in the face with my head and beat him in the face with my fists until he yelled for some one to come and stop me. There was plenty of white people 'round but none of them interfered. A great commotion set up and I slipped out the back door and went home during the excitement.

"When I went back to the saloon again after about a week or so, the fellow had left two dollars for me to drink up. Sol Joe told me that he showed the man he was wrong, that I was one of his best customers. To make Sol and me feel better, he left the two dollars. When I got there and found the money waiting for me, I just called everybody in the house up to the bar and treated it out.

"They claimed I had hit him with brass knucks, but when I showed them my hand—it was swollen double—and then showed them how the thumb was broken, they agreed on what caused the damage. That thumb never did set properly. You see, it's out of shape right now.

Domestic Life

"I met my wife going home. I was a train porter between here and Memphis. She was put in my care to see that she took her train all right out of Memphis, Tennessee, going on farther. I fell in love with her and commenced courting her right from there. She was so white in color that you couldn't tell she was colored by looking at her. After I married her, I was bringing her home, and three white men from another town got on the train and followed us, thinking she was white. Every once in a while they would come back and peep in the Negro coach. Sometimes they would come in and sit down and smoke and watch us. My sister notice it and called my attention to it. I went to the conductor and complained. He called their hand.

"It seems that they were just buying mileage from time to time and staying on the train to be able to get off where I got off. The conductor told them that if they went into Little Rock with the train there would be a delegation of white people there to meet them and that the reception wouldn't be a pleasant one, that I worked on the road, and that all the officials knew me and knew my wife, and that if I just sent a wire ahead they'd find themselves in deep. They got off the train at the next stop, but they gave me plenty of eye, and it looked like they didn't believe what had been told them.

"We were married only three and a half years when she died. Her name was Lillie Love Douglass before she married me. She was a perfect angel. White folks tried to say that she was white. We had two children. Both of them are dead. One died while giving birth to a child and the other died at the age of thirty-three.

"I married the second time. I met my second wife the same way I met the first. I was working on the railroad and she was traveling. I was a coach cleaner. We lived together three years and were separated over foolishness. She had long beautiful hair and an old friend of hers stopped by once and said that he ought to have a lock of her hair to braid into a watch chain. She said, 'I'll give you a lock.' I said, 'You and your hair both belong to me; how are you going to give it away without asking me?' She might have been joking, and I was not altogether serious. But it went on from there in to a deep quarrel. One day, I had been drinking heavily, and we had an argument over the matter. I don't remember what it was all about. Anyway, she called me a liar and I slapped her before I thought.

"For two or three weeks after that we stayed together just as though nothing had happened, except that she never had anything more to say to me. She would lie beside me at night but wouldn't say a word. One day I gave her a hundred dollars to buy some supplies for the store. She was a wonderful hat maker, and we had put up a store which she operated while I was out on the road working. When I came back that evening, the store was wide open and she was gone. She had slipped off and gone home from the station across the river. I didn't find that out till the next day. She hid during part of the night at the home of one of my friends. And another of my friends carried her across the river and put her on the train. I was out with a shotgun watching. I am glad I did not meet them. She is living in Chicago now, married to the man she wanted to give the lock of hair to and doing well the last I heard from her. She was a good woman, just marked with a high temper. There was no reason why we should not have lived together and gotten along well. We loved each other and were making money hand over fist when we separated.

Opinions

"The young people are too much for me. Women are awful now. The young ones are too wild for me. The old ones allow them too much freedom. They are not given proper instruction and training by their elders."

Interviewer's Comment

Dortch's grandfather on the father's side was a white man and either his master or someone closely connected with his master—his first master. His last master was the father of his half-sister, Cordelia, born before any of the other members of his family. These facts account largely for the good treatment accorded his mother and father in slave time and for the friendly attitude toward them subsequent to slavery.

Dortch's whole sister, Adrianna, is living next door to him, and is eighty-five years old going on eighty-six. She has a clearer memory than Dortch, and has also a clear vigorous mentality. She never went to school but uses excellent English and thinks straight. I have not made Dortch's interview any longer because I am spending the rest of this period on his sister's, and there was no need of taking some material which would be common to both and more clearly stated by her. I have already finished ten pages of her story.

Kerns, Adrianna W.
Age: 85
800 Victory Street
Little Rock, Arkansas
Interviewer: Samuel S. Taylor
[M:9: pt. 4: 191–95]

"When they first put me in the field, they put me and Viney to pick up brush and pile it, to pick up stumps, and when we got through with that, she worked on her mother's row and I worked on my aunt's row until we got large enough to have a row to ourselves. Me and Viney were the smallest children in the field and we had one row each. Some of the older people had two rows and picked on each row.

"My birthday is on the fourth of November, and I am eighty-five years old. You can count back and see what year I was born in.

Relatives
"My mother's first child was her master's child. I was the second child but my father was Reuben Dortch. He belonged to Colonel Dortch. Colonel Dortch died in Princeton, Arkansas, Dallas County, about eighty-six miles from here. He died before the War. I never saw him. But he was my father's first master. He used to go and get goods, and he caught this fever they had then—I think it was cholera—and died. After Colonel Dortch died, his son-in-law, Archie Hays, became my father's second master. Were all with Hays when we were freed.

"My father's father was a white man. He was named Wilson Rainey. I never did see him. My mother has said to me many a time that he was the meanest man in Dallas County. My father's mother was named Viney. That was her first name. I forget the last name. My mother's name was Martha Hays, and my grandmother's name on my mother's side was Sallie Hays. My maiden name was Adrianna Dortch.

A Devoted Slave Husband
"I have heard my mother tell many a time that there was a slave man who used to take his own dinner and carry it three or four miles to his wife. His wife belonged to a mean white man who wouldn't give them what they needed to eat. He done without his dinner in order that she might have enough. Where would you find a man to do that now? Nowadays they are

taking the bread away from their wives and children and carrying it to some other woman.

Patrollers

"A Negro couldn't leave his master's place unless he had a pass from his master. If he didn't have a pass, they would whip him. My father was out once and was stopped by them. They struck him. When my father got back home, he told Colonel Dortch and Colonel Dortch went after them pateroles and laid the law down to them—told them that he was ready to kill [remainder of sentence is missing]

"The pateroles got after a slave named Ben Holmes once and run him clean to our place. He got under the bed and hid. But they found him and dragged him out and beat him.

Work

"I had three aunts in the field. They could handle a plow and roll logs as well as any man. Trees would blow down and trees would have to be carried to a heap and burned.

"I been whipped many a time by my mistress and overseer. I'd get behind with my work and he would come by and give me a lick with the bull whip he carried with him.

"At first when the old folks cut wood, me and Viney would pick up chips and burn up brush. We had to pick dry peas in the fall after the crops had been gathered. We picked two large basketsful a day.

"When we got larger we worked in the field picking cotton and pulling corn as high as we could reach. You had to pull the fodder first before you could pull the corn. When we had to come out of the field on account of rain, we would go to the corn crib and shuck corn if we didn't have some weaving to do. We got so we could weave and spin. When master caught us playing, he would set us to cutting jackets. He would give us each two or three switches and we would stand up and whip each other. I would go easy on Viney but she would try to cut me to pieces. She hit me so hard I would say, 'Yes suh, massa.' And she would say, 'Why you sayin' "Yes suh, massa," to me? I ain't doing nothin' to you.'

"My mother used to say that Lincoln went through the South as a beggar and found out everything. When he got back, he told the North how slavery was ruining the nation. He put different things before the South but they wouldn't listen to him. I heard that the South was the first one to fire a shot.

"Lemme tell you how freedom came. Our master came out where we was grubbing the ground in front of the house. My father was already in Little

Rock where they were trying to make a soldier out of him. Master came out and said to mother, 'Martha, they are saying you are free but that ain't goin' to las' long. You better stay here. Reuben is dead.'

"Mother then commenced to fix up a plan to leave. She got the oxen yoked up twice, but when she went to hunt the yoke, she couldn't find it. Negroes were all going through every which way then. Peace was declared before she could get another chance. Word came then that the government would carry all the slaves where they wanted to go. Mother came to Little Rock in a government wagon.

"She left Cordelia. Cordelia was her daughter by Archie Hays. Cordelia was supposed to join us when the government wagon came along but she went to sleep. One colored woman was coming to get in the wagon and her white folks caught her and made her go back. Them Yankees got off their horses and went over there and made them turn the woman loose and let her come on. They were rough and they took her on to Little Rock in the wagon.

"The Yankees used to come looking for horses. One time Master Archie had sent the horses off by one of the colored slaves who was to stay at his wife's house and hide them in the thicket. During the night, mother heard Archie Hays hollering. She went out to see what was the matter. The Yankees had old Archie Hays out and had guns poked at his breast. He was hollering, 'No sir, I don't.' and mother came and said, 'Reuben, get up and go tell them he don't know where the horses is.' Father got up and did a bold thing. He went out and said, 'Wait, gentlemen, he don't know where the horses is, but if you'll wait till tomorrow morning, he'll send a man to bring them in.' I don't know how they got word to him but he brought them in the next morning and the Yankees taken them off.

"Once a Rebel fired a shot at a Yankee and in a few minutes, our place was alive with them. They were working like ants in a heap all over the place. They took chickens and everything on the place. Master Archie didn't have no sons large enough for the army. If he had, they would have killed him because they would have thought that he was harboring spies."

Interviewer's Comment

Mrs. A. (Adrianna) W. Kerns is a sister to Charles Green Dortch. Cross reference; see his story.

Pattillo, Solomon P.
Age: 76
1502 Martin Street
Little Rock, Arkansas

Interviewer: Samuel S. Taylor
[M:10: pt. 5: 292–96]

"I was born November 1862. I was three years old at the time of the surrender. I was born right here in Arkansas—right down here in Tulip, Dallas County, Arkansas. I have never been out of the state but twice.

Refugeeing

"My daddy carried me out once when they took him to Texas during the war to keep the Yanks from setting him free.

"Then I went out once long after slavery to get a load of sand. On the way back, my boat nearly sank. Those are the only two times I ever left the state.

Parents

"My father's name was Thomas Smith, but the Pattillos bought him and he took the name of Pattillo. I don't know how much he sold for. That was the only time he was ever sold. I believe that my father was born in North Carolina. It seems like to me I recollect that is where he said he was born.

"My mother was born in Virginia. I don't know how she got here unless she was sold like my father was. I don't know her name before she got married. Yes, I do; her name was Fannie Smith, I believe.

Houses

"We lived in old log cabins. We had bedsteads nailed to the wall. Then we had them old fashioned cordboard springs. They had ropes made into springs. That was a high class bed. People who had those cord springs felt themselves. They made good sleeping. My father had one. Ropes were woven back and forth across the bed frame.

"We had those old spinning wheels. Three cuts was a day's work. A cut was so many threads. It was quite a day to make them. They had hanks too. The threads were all linked together.

"My mother was a spinner. My father was a farmer. Both of them worked for their master,—old Massa, they called him, or Massa, Mass Tom, Mass John or Massta.

War Recollections

"I remember during the war when I was in Texas with a family of Moody's how old Mistiss had me packing rocks out of the yard in a basket and cleaning the yard. I didn't know it then, but my daddy told me later that that was when I was in Texas,—during the war. I remember that I used to work in my shirt tail.

"The soldiers used to come in the house somewhere and take anything they could get or wanted to take.

Pateroles
"When I was a boy they had a song, 'Run, Nigger, run! The Pateroles will get you.' They would run you in and I have been told they would whip you. If you overstayed your time when your master had let you go out, he would notify the pateroles and they would hunt you up and turn you over to him.

Church Meetings
"Way long then, my father and mother used to say that man doesn't serve the Lord—the true and living God and let it be known. A bunch of them got together and resolved to serve Him any way. First they sang in a whisper, 'Come ye that love the Lord.' Finally they get bold and began to sing in tones that could be heard everywhere, 'Oh for a thousand tongues to sing my Great Redeemer's praise.'

After the War
"After the war my father farmed—made share crops. I remember once how some one took his horse and left an old tired horse in the stable. She looked like a nag. When she got rested up she was better than the one that was took.

"His first farm was down here in Dallas County. He made a share crop with his former master, Pattillo. He never had no trouble with him.

Ku Klux
"I heard a good deal of talk about the Ku Klux Klan, but I don't know anything much about it. They never bothered my father and mother. My father was given the name of being an obedient servant—among the best help they had.

"My father farmed all his life. He died at the age of seventy-two in Tulip, near the years 1885, just before Cleveland's inauguration. He died of Typhoid Pneumonia. My mother was ninety-six years old when she died in 1909.

Little Rock
"I came to Little Rock in 1894. I came up here to teach in Fourche Dam. Then I moved here. I taught my first school in this county at Cato. I quit teaching because my salary was so poor and then I went into the butcher's business, and in the wood business. I farmed all the while.

"I taught school for twenty-one years. I always was a successful teacher.

I did my best. If you contract to do a job for ten dollars, do as much as though you were getting a hundred. That will always help you to get a better job.

"I have farmed all my life in connection with my teaching. I went into other businesses like I said a moment ago. I was a caretaker at the Haven of Rest Cemetery for sometime.

"I was postmaster from 1904 to 1911 at Sweet Home. At one time I was employed on the United States Census.

"I get a little blind pension now. I have no other means of support.

Loss of Eyes
"The doctor says I lost my eyesight on account of cataracts. I had an operation and when I came home, I got to stirring around and it caused me to have a hemorrhage of the eye. You see I couldn't stay at the hospital because it was costing me $5 a day and I didn't have it. They had to take one eye clean out. Nothing can be done for them, but somehow I feel that the Lord's going to let me see again. That's the way I feel about it.

"I have lived here in this world this long and never had a fight in my life. I have never been mistreated by a white man in my life. I always knew my place. Some fellows get mistreated because they get out of their place.

"I was told I couldn't stay in Benton because that was a white man's town. I went there and they treated me white. I tried to stay with a colored family way out. They were scared to take me. I had gone there to attend to some business. Then I went to the sheriff and he told me that if they were scared to have me stay at their home, I could stay at the hotel and put my horse in the livery stable. I stayed out in the wagon yard. But I was invited into the hotel. They took care of my horse and fed it and they brought me my meals. The next morning, they cleaned and curried and hitched my horse for me.

"I have voted all my life. I never had any trouble about it.

"The Ku Klux never bothered me. Nobody else ever did. If we live so that everybody will respect us, the better class will always try to help us."

Sloan, Peggy
Age: 80+
2450 Howard Street
Little Rock, Arkansas
Interviewer: Samuel S. Taylor
[M:10: pt. 6: 167–69]

"I was born in Arkansas in Tulip, in Dallas County I think it is, isn't it?

"Charlotte Evans was mother's name and my father's name was Lige Evans. Gran'daddy David was my mother's father, and Cheyney was my mother's mother.

"Mr. Johnnie Sumner was the name of my young master, and the old man was Mr. Judge Sumner. The old people are all dead now. Mr. Judge Sumner was Johnnie Sumner's father. Me and Mr. Johnnie suckled together. Mr. Johnnie came to Fordyce they say looking for the old slaves. I didn't know about it then. I never would know him now. That is been so long ago. I sure would like to see 'im.

"My mother ain't told me much about herself in slave times. She was a nurse. She lived in a log cabin. You know they had cabins for all of them. The colored lived in log houses. The white people had good houses. Them houses was warmer than these what they got now.

"My grandma could cut a man's frock-tail coat. These young people don't know nothin' 'bout that. Grandma was a milliner. She could make anything you used a needle to make.

"Lige Evans was the name my father took after the surrender. He wasn't named that before the surrender—in the olden times. My mother had fifteen children. She was the largest woman you ever seen. She weighed four hundred pounds. She was young Master Johnnie's nurse. Mr. Johnnie said he wanted to come and see me. I heard he lives way on the other side of Argenta somewheres.

"I was my mama's seventh girl, and I got a seventh girl living. I had fifteen children. My mother's children were all born before the surrender.

"Mr. Judge Sumner and his son were both good men. They never whipped their slaves.

"They didn't feed like they do now. I et corn bread then, and I eat it now. Some people say they don't. They would give them biscuits on Sundays. They had a cook to cook for the hands. She got all their meals for them.

"They had a woman to look after the little colored children, and they had one to look after the white children. My mother was a nurse for the white children. My mother didn't have nothing to do with the colored children.

"I didn't never have no trouble with the pateroles. Sometimes they would come down the lane running the horses. When I would hear them, I would run and git under the bed. I was the scaredest soul you ever seen. I think that's about all I can remember.

"I was the mother of fifteen children. I had one set of twins, a boy and a girl. The doctor told me you never raise a boy and a girl twin. My boy is dead. All of my children are dead but two.

"I was raised on the farm. I want a few acres of ground now so bad.

"I never was married but once. My husband's name was David Sloan. I don't know exactly how long he and me were married. It was way over twenty years. My license got burnt up.

"You know I couldn't be nothin' but a Christian."

Interviewer's Comment

Peggy Sloan's memory is going. She is not certain of the number of children her mother had although she knows there were more than seven because she was the seventh.

She remembers nothing about her age, but she knows definitely that all of her mother's children were born before the War—that is before the end of the War. Since the War ended seventy-three years ago and she was the seventh child with possibly seven behind her, I feel that she could not be younger than eighty. She remembers definitely running at the approach of men she calls pateroles during "slavery time."

Her mind may be fading, but it is a long way from gone. She questioned me closely about my reason for getting statements from her. She had to be definitely satisfied before the story could be gotten.

Warrior, Evans
Age: 80
609 E. 23rd Avenue
Pine Bluff, Arkansas
Interviewer: Mrs. Bernice Bowden
[M:11: pt. 7: 44–45]

"I was born here in Arkansas in Dallas County. I don't know zackly what year but I was bout five when they drove us to Texas. Stayed there three years till the war ceasted.

"Old master's name was Nat Smith. He was good to me. I was big enough to plow same year the war ceasted.

"Yankees come through Texas after peace was 'clared. They'd come by and ask my mother for bread. She was the cook.

"We left Arkansas 'fore the war got busy. Everything was pretty ragged after we got back. White folks was here but colored folks was scattered. My folks come back and went to their native home in Dallas County.

"Never did nothin' but farm work. Worked on the shares till I got able to rent. Paid five or six dollars a acre. Made some money.

"I heered of the Ku Klux. Some of em come through the Clemmons place and put notice on the doors. Say VACATE. All the women folks got in one house. Then the boss man come down and say there wasn't nothin' to it. Boss man didn't want em there.

"I went to school a little. Kep' me in the field all the time. Didn't get fur enuf to read and write.

"Yes'm, I voted. Voted the Republican ticket. That's what they give me to vote. I couldn't read so I'd tell em who I wanted to vote for and they'd put it down. Some of my friends was justice of the peace and constables.

"I been in Pine Bluff bout four years—till I got disabled to work.

"I been married five times. All dead but two. Don't know how many chillun we had—have to go back and study over it.

"Some of the younger generation is out of reason. Ain't strict on chillun now like the old folks was."

Weathers, Cora
Age: 79
818 Chester Street
Little Rock, Arkansas
Interviewer: Samuel S. Taylor
[M:11: pt. 7: 73–75]

"I have been right on this spot for sixty-three years. I married when I was sixteen and he brought me here and put me down and I have been here ever since. No, I don't mean he deserted me; I mean he put me on this spot of ground. Of course, I have been away on a visit but I haven't been nowheres else to live.

"When I came here, there was only three houses—George Winstead lived on Chester and Eighth Street; Dave Davis lived on Ninth and Ringo; and George Gray lived on Chester and Eighth. Rena Lee lived next to where old man Paterson stays now, 906 Chester. Rena Thompson lived on Chester and Tenth. The old people that used to live here is mostly dead or moved up North.

"On Seventh and Ringo there was a little store. It was the only store this side of Main Street. There was a little old house where Coffin's Drug Store is now. The branch ran across there. Old man John Peyton had a nursery in a little log house. You couldn't see it for the trees. He kept a nursery for flowers. On the next corner, old man Sinclair lived. That is the southeast corner of Ninth and Broadway. Next to him was the Hall of the Sons of Ham.

"That was the first place I went to school. Lottie Stephens, Robert Lacy, and Gus Richmond were the teacher. Hollins was the principal. That was in the Sons of Ham's Hall.

"I was born in Dallas County, Arkansas. It must have been 'long 'bout in eighty-fifty-nine, 'cause I was sixteen years old when I come here and I been here sixty-three years.

"During the War, I was quite small. My mother brought me here after the War and I went to school for a while. Mother had a large family. So I never got to go to school but three months at a time and only got one dollar and twenty-five cents a week wages when I was working. My father drove a wagon and hoed cotton. Mother kept house. She had—lemme see—one, two, three, four—eight of us, but the youngest brother was born here.

"My mother's name was Millie Stokes. My mother's name before she was married was—I don't know what. My father's name was William Stokes. My father said he was born in Maryland. I met Richard Weathers here and married him sixty-three years ago. I had six children, three girls and three boys. Children make you smart and industrious—make you think and make you get about.

"I've heard talk of the pateroles; they used to whip the slaves that was out without passes, but none of them never bothered us. I don't remember anything myself, because I was too small. I heard of the Ku Klux too; they never bothered my people none. They scared the niggers at night. I never saw none of them. I can't remember how freedom came. First I knowed, I was free.

"People in them days didn't know as much as the young people do now. But they thought more. Young people nowadays don't think. Some of them will do pretty well, but some of them ain't goin' to do nothin'. They are gittin' worse and worser. I don't know what is goin' to become of them. They been dependin' on the white folks all along, but the white folks ain't sayin' much now. My people don't seem to want nothin'. The majority of them just want to dress and run up and down the streets and play cards and policy and drink and dance. It is nice to have a good time but there is something else to be thought of. But if one tries to do somethin', the rest tries to pull him down. The more education they get, the worse they are—that is, some of them."

Desha County

Tillman, Joe
Age: 79
W. 10th and Highway No. 79
Pine Bluff, Arkansas
Interviewer: Mrs. Bernice Bowden
[M:10: pt. 6: 334–35]

"I was born in 1859 down here at Walnut Lake. The man what owned us was Crum Holmes.

"All I can remember was the patrollers and the Ku Klux. I reckon I ought to, I seed 'em. I got skeered and run. I heered 'em talk about how they'd do the folks and we chillun thought they'd do us the same way.

"I 'member hearin' 'em talk 'bout the Yankees—how they'd come through there and how they used to do.

"I guess we had plenty to eat. All I know was when I got ready to eat, I could eat.

"My parents were brought from Tennessee but all the place I know anything about is Walnut Lake.

"I know my mother said I was the cause of her gettin' a lot of whippin's. I'd run off and the boss man whipped her cause she wasn't keepin' me at home. If he didn't whip her, he'd pull her ears.

"When we was comin' up they didn't 'low the chillun to sit around where the old folks was talkin', and at night when company come in, we chillun had to go to bed out the way. Sometimes I'm glad of it. See so many chillun now gettin' into trouble.

"I never been arrested in my life. Been a witness once or twice—that's the only way I ever been in court. If I'd a been like a lot of 'em, I might a been dead or in the pen.

"In them days, if we did something wrong, anybody could whip us and if we'd go tell our folks we get another whippin'.

"After freedom my parents stayed there and worked by the day. They started me bustin' out the middles till I learnt how and then they put the plowin' in my hands.

"White people been pretty good to me 'cause I done what they told me.

"I went to school a little 'long about '70. I learnt how to read and kept on till I could write a little.

"I used to vote 'til they stopped us. I used to vote right along, but I stopped foolin' with it. 'Course we can vote in the president election but I got so I couldn't see what ticket I was votin', so I stopped foolin' with it.

"I farmed till 'bout '94, then I worked at the compress and brick work."

Winston, Sarah
Age: 83
2728 Ave. M
Galveston, Texas
Interviewer: Mary E. Liberato, P.W.
6 December 1937
[S2:10 (TX, pt. 9): 4258–59]

Sarah Winston, 2728 Ave. M, was born a slave of the Ford family near Arkansas (probably Arkansas City), Arkansas, about 1854. In 1864 when slavery was abolished in Arkansas, she and her family were brought to Montgomery, Texas, to the Yvoch Plantation. After the war she helped her father farm a small section of land on the former Yvoch Plantation until her marriage at the age of 19. She then helped her husband farm his section of land near Montgomery, Texas, until his death at the age of 104 years in 1932. Since that time she has been living in Galveston, Texas, with her daughter.

"I 'clare I hate to ask anybody to come in de house in de fix it's in, but dese chillun jes' tear it up faster'n I can keep it clean. Look at 'em now in de middle of de room I jes' got finish sweeping jes' 'fore you come! Pick up dat paper, you Sammy! Ain' I tol' you to go out on de front porch when you tear up any paper? Ain' I? Ain' you 'shamed of yourself? What de white lady going to think 'bout your house all tore up like dis? Chillun is shore dif'runt den dey use to be. When I was little I had to work, I ain' had no time to mess up de house. Git out of here now an' chase up a chair for de lady. An', Sammy, if I catch you on dat fence again en de new pants you Ma jes' got you, I'm going to beat you. I done warn you now an' you needn' say I ain'. Go 'way now an' let me talk to de lady.

"I don' know how much I 'member 'bout slavery now. My daughter use to git me to talk 'bout it all de time to her. She like to hear me tell 'bout how we use to live 'way back yonder.

"I don' know for sure when I was born. De white lady for de pension figgered up I was born 'bout 1854 'cause I was 'bout ten years old when we was freed. I know I was born in Ar-kansas, Arkansas, though 'cause Mr. Ford own us an' he live dere. 'Course he own a lot more slaves 'sides us, 'bout a couple hundred counting de young'uns. Dere was lots of chillun an' dey all mind. You tell 'em to do something an' dey go right 'long an' does it. Dey don' give you no back talk like dey do now. Dey ain' spoil by dere Ma giving in to 'em all de time. Now I forgit what I was talking 'bout.

"I 'clare dese young'uns make me so mad some times I ain' got good sense. All time studying up what dey can do next. Now I 'member what I was talking 'bout.

"De marster an' de ol' Mistress an' dere chillun live in de big white house right smack-a-dab on de road dat goes to Ar-kansas. Me an' my grandma an' my father an' my brothers an' sisters lived down in de quarters, 'cross de field from de big house. De cabins was all set. (Eds. Note: Manuscript breaks off here.)

Drew County

Bailey, Jeff
Age: 77
713 W. Ninth Street
Little Rock, Arkansas
Interviewer: Samuel S. Taylor
December 1938
[M:8: pt. 1: 84–90]

"I was born in Monticello. I was raised there. Then I came up to Pine Bluff and stayed there thirty-two years. Then I came up here and been here thirty-two years. That is the reason the white folks so good to me now. I been here so long. I been a hostler all my life. I am the best hostler in this State. I go down to the post office they give me money. These white folks here is good to me.

"What you writing' down? Yes, that's what I said. These white folks like me and they good to me. They give me anything I want. You want a drink? That's the best bonded whiskey money can buy. They gives it to me. Well, if you don't want it now, come in when you do.

"I lost my wife right there in that corner. I was married just once. Lived with her forty-three years. She died here five months ago. Josie Bailey! The white folks thought the world and all of her. That is another reason they give me so much. She was one of the best women I ever seen.

"I gits ten dollars a month. The check comes right up to the house. I used to work with all them money men. Used to handle all them horses at the post office. They ought to give me sixty-five dollars but they don't. But I gits along. God is likely to lemme live ten years longer. I worked at the post office twenty-two years and don't git but ten dollars a month. They ought to gimme more.

"My father's name was Jeff Wells. My mother's name was Tilda Bailey. She was married twice. I took her master's name. Jeff Wells was my father's name. Governor Bailey ought to give me somethin'. I got the same name he has. I know him.

"My father's master was Stanley—Jeff Stanley. That was in slavery time. That was my slave time people. I was just a little bit of a boy. I am glad you are gittin' that to help the colored people out. Are they goin' to give the old slaves a pension? What they want to ask all these questions for then? Well, I guess there's somethin' else beside money that's worth while.

"My father's master was a good man. He was good to him. Yes Baby! Jeff Wells, that my father's name. I was a little baby settin' in the basket 'round in the yard and they would put the cotton all 'round me. They carried me out where they worked and put me in the basket. I couldn't pick no cotton because I was too young. When they got through they would put me in that big old wagon and carry me home. There wasn't no trucks then. Jeff Wells (that was my father), when they got through pickin' the cotton, he would say, 'Put them children in the wagon; pick 'em up and put 'em in the wagon.' I was a little bitty old boy. I couldn't pick no cotton then. But I used to pick it after the surrender.

"I remember what they said when they freed my father. They said, 'You're free. You children are free. Go on back there and work and let your children work. Don't work them children too long. You'll git pay for your work.' That was in the Monticello courthouse yard. They said, 'You're free! Free!'

"My mistress said to me when I got back home, 'You're free. Go on out in the orchard and git yoself some peaches.' They had a yard full of peaches. Baby did I git me some peaches. I pulled a bushel of 'em.

Ku Klux Klan

"The Ku Klux run my father out of the fields once. And the white people went and got them 'bout it. They said, 'Times is hard, and we can't have these people losin' time out of the fields. You let them people work.' A week after that, they didn't do no mo. The Ku Klux didn't. Somebody laid them out. I used to go out to the fields and they would ask me, 'Jeff Bailey, what you doin' out here?' I was a little boy and you jus' ought to seen me gittin 'way frum there. Whooo-eeee!

"I used to pick cotton back yonder in Monticello. I can't pick no cotton now. Naw Lawd! I'm too old. I can't do that kind of work now. I need help.

Carl Bailey knows me. He'll help me. I'm a hostler. I handle horses. I used to pick cotton forty years ago. My mother washed clothes right after the War to git us children somethin' to eat. Sometimes somebody would give us somethin' to help us out.

"Tilda Bailey, that was my mother. She and my father belonged to different masters. Bailey was her master's name. She always called herself Bailey and I call myself Bailey. If I die, I'll be Bailey. My insurance is in the name of Bailey. My father and mother had about eight children. They raised all their children in Monticello. You ever been to Monticello? I had a good time in Monticello. I was a baby when peace was declared. Just toddling 'round.

"My father drank too much. I used to tell him about it. I used to say to him, 'I wouldn't drink so much whiskey.' But he drank it right on. He drank hisself to death.

"I believe Roosevelt's goin' to be President again. I believe he's goin' to run for a third term. He's goin' to be dictator. He's goin' to be king. He's goin' to be a good dictator. We don't want no more Republic. The people are too hard on the poor people. President Roosevelt lets everybody git somethin'. I hope he'll git it. I hope he'll be dictator. I hope he'll be king. Yuh git hold ub some money with him.

"You couldn't ever have a chance if Cook got to be governor. I believe Carl Bailey's goin' to be a good governor. I believe he'll do better. They put Miz Carraway back; I believe she'll do good too."

Extra Comment

Jeff Bailey talked like a man of ninety instead of a man of seventy-six or seven. It was hard to get him to stick to any kind of a story. He had two or three things on his mind and he repeated those things over and over again— Governor Bailey, Hostler, Post Office. He had to be pried loose from them. And he always returned the next sentence.

Darrow, Mary Allen
Age: 74
Forrest City, Arkansas
Interviewer: Irene Robertson
[M:8: pt. 2: 95–96]

"I was born at Monticello, Arkansas at the last of the Cibil (Civil) War. My parents' names was Richard and Ann Allen. They had thirteen children. Mother was a house girl and papa a blacksmith and farmer.

"My great-grandma and grandpa was killed in Indian Nation (Alabama) by Sam and Will Allen. They was coming west long 'fo'e the war from one of the Carolinas. I disremembers which they told me. Great-grandpa was a chief. They was shot and all the children run but they caught my Grandma Evaline and put her in the wagon and brought her to Monticello, Arkansas. They fixed her so she couldn't get loose from them. She was a little full-blood Indian girl then. They got her fer my great-grandpa a wife. He seen her and thought she was so pretty.

"She was wild. She wouldn't eat much else but meat and raw at that. She had a child 'fo'e ever she'd eat bread. They tamed her. Grandpa's pa that wanted the Indian wife was full-blood African. Mama was little lighter than 'gingercake' color.

"My Indian grandma was mean. I was feard of 'er. She run us down and ketch us and whoop us. She was tall slender woman. She was mean as she could be. She'd cut a cat's head off fer no cause er tall. Grandpa was kind. He'd bring me candy back if he went off. I cried after him. I played with his girl. We was about the same size. Her name was Annie Mathis. He was a Mathis. He was a blacksmith too at Monticello and later he bought a farm three and one-half miles out. I was raised on a farm. Papa died there. I washed and done field work all my life. Grandma married Bob Mathis.

"Our owner was Sam and Lizzie Allen. William Allen was his brother. I think Sam had eight children. There was a Claude Allen in Monticello and some grandchildren, Eva Allen and Len Allen. Eva married Robert Lawson. I lived away from them Allen's and Mathis' and Gill's so long and 'bout forgot 'em. They wasn't none too good to nobody—selfish. They'd make trouble, then crap out of it. Pack it on anybody. They wasn't none too good to do nothing. Some of 'em lazy as ever was white men and women. Some of 'em I know wasn't rich—poor as 'Jobe's stucky.' I don't know nothing 'bout 'em now. They wasn't good.

"I was a baby at freedom and I don't know about that nor the Ku Klux. Grandpa started a blacksmith shop at Monticello after freedom.

"My pa was a white man. Richard Allen was mama's husband.

"Me and my husband gets ten dollars from the Old Age Pension. He is ninety-six years old. He do a little about. I had a stroke and ain't been no 'count since. He can tell you about the Cibil War."

Interviewer's Comment
    I missed her husband twice. It was a long ways out there but I will see him another time.

Haynes, Tom
Age: ?
1110 W. Second Street
Pine Bluff, Arkansas
Interviewer: Mrs. Bernice Bowden
[M:9: pt. 3: 227–28]

"I was six years old when the war ended—the day we was set free. My old mistress, Miss Becky Franks, come in and say to my mother "Addie, you is free this morning" and commenced cryin'. She give my mother some jerked beef for us.

"I know I run out in the yard where there was eighty Yankee soldiers and I pulled out my shirt tail and ran down the road kickin' up the dust and sayin', "I'm free, I'm free!' My mother said, "You'd better come back here!"

"I never knew my mother to get but one whippin'. She put out her mouth against old mistress and she took her out and give her a breshin'.

"I can remember away back. I can remember when I was three years old. One day I was out in yard eatin' dirt and had dirt all over my face. Young master Henry come out and say "Stick out your tongue, I'm goin' to cut it off." I was scared to death. He said "Now you think you can quit eatin' that dirt?" I said "Yes" so he let me go.

"One time the Yankee soldiers took young Master Henry and hung him up by the thumbs and tried to make him tell where the money was. Master Henry's little brother Jim and me run and hid. We thought they was goin' to hang us too. We crawled under the house just like two frogs lookin' out.

"Old master had about thirty-five hands but some of em run away to war. My father run away too, but the war ended before he could get into it.

"I went to school a little while, but my father died and my mother bound me out to a white man.

"When we was first freed I know those eighty soldiers took us colored folks to the county band in Monticello. There was forty soldiers in the back and forty in front and we was in the swing.

"I learned to read after I was grown. I worked for the railroad in the freight office fifteen years and learned to check baggage.

"I was a house mover when I was able, but I'm not able to work now. I own this house here and I'm livin' on the relief.

"My father was a blacksmith and shoemaker—made all our shoes. I've lived in town all my life.

"The people are better off free if they had any sense. They need a leader.

When they had a chance if they had bought property, but no—they wanted to get in office and when they got in they didn't know how to act. And the young people don't use their education to help themselves."

Jones, Cyntha
Age: 88
3006 W. Tenth Avenue
Pine Bluff, Arkansas
Interviewer: Mrs. Bernice Bowden
[M:9: pt. 4: 138–40]

"Well, here's one of em. Born down in Drew County.

"Simpson Dabney was old master and his wife named Miss Adeline.

"I reckon I do remember bout the War. Yes ma'am, the Yankees come and they had me scared. I wouldn't know when they got in the yard till they was all around me. Had me holdin' the bridles.

"My young missis' husband was in the War and when they fought the last battle at Princeton, she had me drive the carriage. When I heard them guns I said we better go back, so I turned round and made them horses step so fast my dress tail stood out straight. I thought they was goin' to kill us all. And when we got home all the windows was broke. Miss Nancy say, 'Cyntha, somebody come and broke all my windows,' but it was them guns broke em.

"Old master was a doctor but my young missis' husband wasn't nothin' but a hunter till they carried him to war. He was so skeered they had to most drag him.

"I seen two wars and heered tell of another.

"I member when the Yankees come and took things I just fussed at em. I thought what was my white folks' things was mine too. But when they got my old master's horse my daddy went amongst em and got it back cause he had charge of the stock. I don't know whether he got em at night or not but I know he went in the daytime and come back in the daytime.

"Old master's children and my father's children worked in the field just alike. He wouldn't low a overseer on the place, or a patroller either.

"Dr. Dabney and his sister raised my mother. They brought her from some furrin' country to Arkansas. And when he married, my mother suckled every one of his children.

"I just worked in the house and nussed. Never worked in the field till I was grown and married. I was nineteen when I married the fust time. I stayed right there in that settlement till the second year of surrender.

"When I was twenty-one they had me fixed up for a midwife. Old Dr.

Clark was the one started me. I never went to school a minute in my life but the doctors would read to me out of their doctor books till I could get a license. I got so I could read print till my eyes got so bad. Old Dr. Clark was the one learned me most and since he died I ain't never had a doctor mess with me.

"In fifteen years I had 299 babies on record right there in Rison. That's where I was fixed up at—under five doctors. And anybody don't believe it, they can go down there and look up the record.

"We had plenty to eat in slave times. Didn't have to go to the store and buy it by the dribble like they does now. Just go to the smokehouse and get it.

"I got such a big mind and will I wants to get about and raise something to eat now so we wouldn 't have to buy everything, but I ain't able now. I've had twenty-one children but if I had em now they'd starve to death.

"I been married four times but they all dead—every one of em.

"When freedom come my old master give my mother $500 cause she saved his money for him when the Yankees come. She put it in the bed and slept on it. He had four farms and he told her she could have any one of em and any of the stock, but my father had done spoke for a place in Cleveland County—he had done bought him a place.

"And old master on his dying bed, he asked my mother to take his two youngest children and raise em cause their mother was sickly, but she didn't do it.

"I don't know hardly what to think of this younger generation. Used to be they'd go to Sunday school barefooted but now'days, time they is born they got shoes and stockin's on em.

"I used to spin, knit and weave. I even spun thread to make these ropes they use to plow. I could spin a thread you could sew with, and weave cloth with stripes and flowers. Have to know how to dye the thread. That's all done in the warp. Call the other the filler.

"Now let me tell you, when that was goin' on and you raised your meat and corn and potatoes, that was livin'!"

Meeks, Jesse
Age: 76
707 Elm Street
Pine Bluff, Arkansas
Interviewer: Mrs. Bernice Bowden
[M:10: pt. 5: 70–71]

"I am seventy-six. 'Course I was young in slavery times, but I can remember some things. I remember how they used to feed us. Put milk and bread or poke salad and corn-meal dumplin's in a trough and give you a wooden spoon and all the children eat together.

"We stayed with our old master fourteen years. They were good folks and treated us right. My old master's name was Sam Meeks—in Longview, Drew County, Arkansas, down here below Monticello.

"I got a letter here about a month ago from the daughter of my young mistress. I wrote to my young mistress and she was dead, so her daughter got the letter. She answered it and sent me a dollar and asked me was I on the Old Age Pension list.

"As far as I know, I am the onliest one of the old darkies living that belonged to Sam Meeks.

"I remember when the Ku Klux run in on my old master. That was after the War. He was at the breakfast table with his wife. You know in them days they didn't have locks and keys. Had a hole bored through a board and put a peg in it, and I know the Ku Klux come up and stuck a gun through the auger hole and shot at old master but missed him. He run to the door and shot at the Ku Klux. I know us children found one of 'em down at the spring bathin' his leg where old master had shot him.

"Oh! they were good folks and treated us right."

Superstitions

"I remember there was an old man called Billy Mann lived down here at Noble Lake. He said he could 'give you a hand.' If you and your wife wasn't gettin' along very well and you wanted to get somebody else, he said he could 'give you a hand' and that would enable you to get anybody you wanted. That's what he said.

"And I've heard 'em say they could make a ring around you and you couldn't get out.

"I don't believe in that though 'cause I'm in the ministerial work and it don't pay me to believe in things like that. That is the work of the devil."

Parker, Fannie
Age: 90?
1908 W. Sixth Street
Pine Bluff, Arkansas
Interviewer: Mrs. Bernice Bowden
[M:10: pt. 5: 240–41]

"Yes, honey, this is old Fannie. I'se just a poor old nigger waitin' for Jesus to come and take me to Heaven.

"I was just a young strip of a girl when the war come. Dr. M. G. Comer was my owner. His wife was Elizabeth Comer. I said Marse and Mistis in them days and when old mistress called me I went runnin' like a turkey. They called her Miss Betsy. Yes Lord, I was in slavery days. Master and mistress was bossin' me then. We all come under the rules. We lived in Monticello—right in the city of Monticello.

"All I can tell you is just what I remember. I seed the Yankees. I remember a whole host of 'em come to our house and wanted something to eat. They got it too! They cooked it them selves and then they burned everything they could get their hands on. They said plenty to me. They said so much I don't know what they said. I know one thing they said I belonged to the Yankees. Yes Lord, they wanted me to tell 'em if I was free. I told 'em I was free indeed and that I belonged to Miss Betsy. I didn't know what else to say. We had plenty to eat, plenty of hog meat and buttermilk and cornbread. Yes ma'm—don't talk about that now.

"Don't tell me 'bout old Jeff Davis—he oughta been killed. Abraham Lincoln thought what was right was right and what was wrong was wrong. Abraham was a great man cause he was the President. When the rebels ceded from the Union he made 'em fight the North. Abraham Lincoln studied that and he had it all in his mind. He wasn't no fighter but he carried his own and the North give 'em the devil. Grant was a good man too. They tried to kill him but he was just wrapped up in silver and gold.

"I remember when the stars fell. Yes, honey, I know I was ironin' and it got so dark I had to light the lamp. Yes, I did!

"It's been a long time and my mind's not so good now but I remember old Comer put us through. Good-bye and God bless you!"

Sexton, Sarah
Age: 79
Route 4, Box 685
Pine Bluff, Arkansas
Interviewer: Bernice Bowden
3 November 1938
[M:10: pt. 6: 136–39]

Description of room, house, surroundings, etc.—Frame house, front porch with two swings. Fence around yard. Chinaberry tree and Tree of Paradise, Coxcomb in yard. Southeast of Norton-Wheeler Stave Mill just off Highway 65.

Text of Interview

"Prewitt Tiller bought my mother and I belonged to young master. In slavery I was a good-sized-young girl, mama said. Big enough to put the table cloths on the best I could. After freedom I did all the cookin' and milkin' and washin'.

"Now listen, this young master was Prewitt's son.

"Grandpa's name was Ned Peeples and grandma was Sally Peeples. My mother was Dorcas. Well, my papa, I ain't never seed him but his name was Josh Allen. You see, they just sold 'em around. That's what I'm talkin' about—they went by the name of their owners.

"I'm seventy-eight or seventy-nine or eighty. That's what the insurance man got me up.

"I been in a car wreck and I had high blood pressure and a stroke all at once. And that wreck, the doctor said it cracked my skull. Till now, I ain't got no remembrance.

"You know how long I went to school? Three days. No ma'm I had to work, darlin'.

"I was born down here on Saline River at Selma. I done forgot what month."

"What kinda work have I done? Oh, honey, I done farmed myself to death, darlin'. You know Buck Couch down here at Noble Lake? Well, I hoped pick out eight bales of cotton for him.

"I wish I had the dollars I had workin' for R. A. Pickens down here at Walnut Lake. Yes, honey, I farmed for him bout fifteen or twenty years steady. And he sure was nice and he was mischievous. He called all of us his chillun. He use to say, 'Now you must mind your papa! And we'd say 'Now Mr. Pickens, you know you ain't got no nigger chillun'. He use to say to me 'Sallie, you is a good woman but you ain't got no sense'. Them was fine white folks.

"Honey, these white folks round here what knows me, knows they ain't a lazy bone in my body.

"I'se cooked and washed and ironed and I'se housecleaned. Yes'm, I certainly was a good cook.

"I belongs to the Palestine Baptist Church. Yes ma'm, I don't know what I'd do if twasn't for the good Master. I talks to Him all the time.

"I goes to this here government school. A man teaches it. I don't know what his name is, we just calls him Professor.

"Well, chile, I'll tell you the truf. These young folks is done gone. And some o' these white headed women goes up here truckin'. It's a sin and a shame. I don't know what's gwine come of 'em.

Interviewer's Comment

This woman lives with her daughter Angeline Moore who owns her home.

Mother and daughter both attend government school. Both were neatly dressed. The day was warm so we sat on the front porch during the interview.

Personal History of Informant

1. Ancestry—Grandfather, Ned Peeples; grandmother, Sally Peeples; mother, Dorcas Peeples; Father, Josh allen.
2. Place and date of birth—On Saline River, Selma, Arkansas. No date.
3. Family—Two daughters and granddaughter.
4. Places lived in, with dates—Desha County, Walnut Lake, Noble Lake (Arkansas), Poplar Bluff, Missouri. No dates.
5. Education with dates: Three days, "after freedom." Attends government school now.
6. Occupations and accomplishments, with dates—Farmwork, cooking, laundry work until 1936.
7. Special skills and interests—Cooking.
8. Community and religious activities—Member of Palestine Baptist Church.
9. Description of informant—Medium height, plump, light complexion and gray hair.
10. Other points gained in interview—Injured in auto wreck seven years ago.

Shelton, Laura
Age: 60
1518 Pulaski Street
Little Rock, Arkansas
Interviewer: Samuel S. Taylor
[M:10: pt. 6: 148–53]

Text of Interview

"My mother used to sit down and talk to us and tell us about slavery. If she had died when I was young I wouldn't have known much. But by her living till I was old, I learned a lot.

"My mother's old master was Tom Barnett, so she said. No, not 'so she said' because I have seed him. He give her her age and all at that time. I have it in my Bible. He said that she was twelve years old the Christmas before the surrender. The surrender was in May, wasn't it?

"My mother's name was Susan Bearden. She married Ben Bearden. She worked in Tom Barnett's house. She milked and churned and 'tended to the children and all such as that. He never allowed her to go to the field. Neither her mother, my grandmother. She was the cook. My mother's name before she married was Susan Barnett.

"An old colored lady that they had there seed after the colored children. She looked after my mother too. She was so old she couldn't do nothin' so they had her to look after the children. My grandmother was kept busy because she had the white folks to cook for and she had all the colored folks to cook for too.

"There is an old lady down on Spring Street that can give you a lot of information about slavery time.

"A boy was telling her that somebody was going 'round asking questions about slavery and she said she wished he would come and see her.

"My mother never had any chance to go to school before freedom and she never had any chance to go afterwards because she didn't have any money. When they turned them loose the white folks didn't give 'em anything, so they had to work. They didn't allow them to pick up a piece of paper in slave time for fear they would learn.

"My mother remembered the pateroles. She said they used to catch and whip the colored men and women when they would get out.

"My mother's old master was the one that told mama she was free. He told her she was free as he was. After they learned that they were free, they stayed on till Christmas.

"After Christmas, they went to another plantation. My gran'pa, he come and got them all to come. My gran'pa's name was Harvey Barnett. His old master's son had married and he had been staying with him. That made him be on another place. There was a good many of the children in my grandmother's family. Mama had a sister named Lucy, one named Lethe, one named Caroline, one named Annie, and one named Jane. She had two boys—one named Jack, and one named Barnett. She had another sister named—I don't remember her name.

"After freedom, we sharecropped for a number of years up until my father died. He died about twenty-four years ago.

"After that mama washed and ironed for about ten or twelve years. That she got too old to work and we took care of her. My mother died last March on the ninth day. She always had good health for an old lady. Never got so she couldn't get up and do her light work such as dress herself, cooking, sweeping, and so on. She would even do her own washing and ironing if we would let her. She would hide from us and pick cotton till we stopped her.

"She was sick only one week and the doctor said she died of old age. He said it was just her time. She didn't have nothin' the matter with her but jus' old age he said so far as he could find. Dr. Fletcher was our doctor. She died in Jerome, Arkansas about sixteen miles from the Louisiana line. She always told us that she had her business fixed with the Lord and that when she taken sick, it wouldn't be long. And sure 'nough, it wasn't.

"I farmed until my mother and brother died. Then I came up here with my sister as I had no children living. I jus' wash and iron now whenever I can get somethin' to do.

"I have been married once. I had three children. All of them are dead. My children are dead and my husband is dead.

"I belong to the Baptist church down on Spring Street. I always unite with the church whenever I go to a place. I don't care whether I stay there or not.

"My mama's master was good as far as white folks generally be in slavery times. He never whipped my grandmother nor my mother. He was good to the field hands too. He never whipped them. He would feed them too. He had right smart of field hands but I don't know just how many. I don't think he ever sold any of his slaves. I think he come by them from his father because I have heard them say that his father told him before he died never to 'part with Black Mammy. That was what he called her. And he kept them altogether jus' like his father told him to. His father said, 'I want you to keep all my Negroes together and Black Mammy I don't want you to let her be whipped because she nursed all of you.' She said she never was whipped 'cept once when she got a cockle berry up her nose and he got it out and gave her a little brushing—not as much as grandma would have given her.

"He kept them all in good shoes and warm clothes and give them plenty to eat. So many of the slaves on other plantations didn't have half enough to eat and were half naked and barefooted all the time."

Personal History of Informant

1.   Ancestry—mother, Susan Barnett; father, Ben Bearden; grandfather, Harvey Barnett.
2.   Place and date of birth—Arkansas, 1878
3.   Family—Three children . . .
5.   Places lived in with dates—Jerome, Arkansas and Little Rock. No dates.
6.   Occupations—Farmed, wash and iron . . .
8.   Community and religious activities—Belongs to Baptist Church . . .

Young, John
Age: 92
923 N. 15th Avenue
Pine Bluff, Arkansas
Interviewer: Mrs. Bernice Bowden
[M:11: pt. 7: 255–57]

"Well, I don't know how old I is. I was born in Virginia, but my mother was sold. She was bought by a speculator and brought here to Arkansas. She brought me with her and her old master's name was Ridgell. We lived down around Monticello. I was big enough to plow and chop cotton and drive a yoke of oxen and haul ten-foot rails.

"Oh Lord, I don't know how many acres old master had. He had a territory—he had a heap a land. I remember he had a big old carriage and the carriage man was Little Alfred. The reason they called him that was because there was another man on the place called Big Alfred. They won't no relation—just happen to be the same name.

"I remember when the Yankees come and killed old master's hogs and chickens and cooked 'em. There was a good big bunch of Yankees. They said they was fightin' to free the niggers. After that I runned away and come up here to Pine Bluff and stayed awhile and then I went to Little Rock and jined the 57th colored infantry. I was the kittle drummer. We marched right in the center of the army. We went from Little Rock to Fort Smith. I never was in a big battle, just one little scrummage. I was at Fort Smith when they surrendered and I was mustered out at Leavenworth, Kansas.

"My grandfather went to war as bodyguard for his master, but I was with the Yankees.

"I remember when the Ku Klux come to my grandmother's house. They nearly scared us to death. I run and hid under the bed. They didn't do nothin', just the looks of 'em scared us. I know they had the old folks totin' water for 'em. Seemed like they couldn't get enough.

"After the war I come home and went to farmin'. Then I steamboated for four years. I was on the Kate Adams, but I quit just 'fore it burned, 'bout two or three weeks.

"I never went to school a minute in my life. I had a chance to go but I just didn't.

"No'm I can't remember nothin' else. It's been so long it done slipped my memory."

"I know I was born in Arkansas. The first place I recollect I was in Arkansas.

"I was a drummer in the Civil War. I played the little drum. The bass drummer was Rheuben Turner.

"I run off from home in Drew County. Five or six of us run off here to Pine Bluff. We heard if we could get with the Yankees we'd be free, so we run off here to Pine Bluff and got with some Yankee soldiers—the twenty-eighth Wisconsin.

"Then we went to Little Rock and I j'ined the fifty-seventh colored infantry. I thought I was good and safe then.

"We went to Fort Smith from Little Rock and freedom come on us while we was between New Mexico and Fort Smith.

"They mustered us out at Fort Leavenworth and I went right back to my folks in Drew County, Monticello.

"I've been a farmer all my life till I got too old."

Faulkner County

Rye, Katie
Age: 82
Clarksville, Arkansas
Interviewer: Sallie C. Miller
[M:10: pt. 6: 111–12]

"We lived in Greenbrier, Faulkner County, Arkansas. All staid at home and got along very well. We had enough to eat and wear. Mistress was awful mean to us but we staid with them until after the war. After the war master moved us off to another place he had and my father farmed for his self, master and his pa and ma, and mistress' pa and ma. They awful good to us, but mistress was so high tempered she would get mad and whip some of the slaves but she never whipped any of us. She worried so over the loss of her slaves after the war she went crazy. We had two white grand pas and grand mas. We colored children called them grandpa and ma and uncle and aunt like the white children did and we didn't know the difference. The slaves was only allowed biscuit on Christmas and sometimes on Sundays but we had beef and plenty of honey and everything after we moved from the big house. Mistress used to come down to see us an' my mother would cook dinner for her and master. He was such a good man and the best doctor in the State. He

128

would come in and take the babies up (mother had nine children) and get them to sleep for my mother. His mother would come to the kitchen and ask for a good cup of coffee and mother would make it for her. The master and his family were Northern people and my mother was given to the mistress by her father and mother when she married.

"After my father bought his own farm about ten miles from the big house, father would put us all in an ox wagon and take us back to see our white folks.

"The mistress claimed to be a christian and church member but I don't see how she could have been she was so mean.

"I think the present day generation mighty wicked. Seems like they get worse instead of better, even the members of the church are not as good as they used to be. They don't raise the children like they used to. They used to go to Sunday School and church and take the children, now the children do as they please, roam the streets. It is sad to see how the parents are raising the children, just feed them and let them go. The children rule the parents now.

"We sang the old hymns and 'Dixie', 'Carry Me Back to Old Virginia', 'When You and I Were Young, Maggie.'"

Greene County

Brown, Betty
Age: ?
Cape Girardeau, Missouri
[M:11: pt. 8: 52–55]

"In de ole' days we live in Arkansaw, in Greene County. My mammy wuz Mary-Ann Millan, an' we belong to 'Massa' John Nutt, an' 'Miss' Nancy.'

"Our white folks live in a big double house, wid a open hall between. It wuz built of hewed logs an' had a big po'ch on de wes' side. De house stood on Cash rivuh, at the crossroads of three roads; one road go tuh Pocahontas, one tuh Jonesburg, an' one tuh Pie-Hatten, (Powhatan).

"Now whut fo' you wanna' know all dem things? Air ye tryin' to raise de daid? Some o' 'em, ah don' wanna see no mo', an' some o' 'em ah wants to stay whar dey is. Pore mammy! Ah shore had one sweet muthuh, an' ah wants huh to stay at rest.

"De wuz jus' us one family o' cullud folks on de place. You see, 'Miss' Nancy' hired us fum her fathuh, 'Ole Massa Hanover. Jes' mah mammy an' huh chillern. She had five, 'fore de war wuz ovuh. Our daddy; he wuz an Irishman, name Millan, an' he had de bigges' still in all Arkansas. Yes'm, he had a white wife, an' five chillern at home, but mah mammy say he like huh an' she like him. You say ah don' look half white? Maybe I's fadin'.

"We live in a little ole' log house, it wuz so low a big feller had to stoop to git in. Our folks wus mighty good tuh us, an' we stayed dar wid 'em after we's freed.

"Ah don' rightly know how old ah is, but de priest writ' it all down fo' me, when ah's gittin' mah pension. Sho' ahs a Catholic. Is they anything else? Fo' fifteen year ah tended de Catholic church, swept an' dusted, an' cleaned, but ah's too ole' fo' dat now, an' ah's po'ly in mah back, cain't git 'round' like dat no mo'.

"We lived de ole'-time way of livin', mammy done de cookin an' we had plenty good things to eat. Mammy made all de clothes, spinnin', an' weavin' an' sewin'. Ah larned to spin when ah wuz too little tuh reach de broach, an' ah could hep her thread de loom. An' mammy wuz a shoe-maker, she'd make moccasins for all o' us.

"Two o' the Nutt boys made shoes too, heavy, big ones dey wuz; but dey kep' our feet [illegible]. An' de had a ten hand. Ah uste wade barefooted in dem pit's an' work wid dem hides, but ah wouldn't wanna do it now.

"Dey wuz a grove o' post-oak timber, 'bout five, or six acres, all cleaned out; an' in der, dey raised bear cubs. Why, dey raised 'em tuh eat. Lawd! dat's good eatin'. Jes' gimme a' bear meat an' den let me go tuh sleep! M-m-m!

"They wuz fruit trees planted all 'long de road, planted jes' like fence-posts for 'bout a mile, an' all de fruit dat fell in de road de hogs got, we'ens could go get any of it, any time, an' travelers, 'long de road, was a'ways welcome ter hep dey selves. 'Massa' nevuh planted no shade trees. Iffen trees wuz planted dey had to be fruit trees. 'Ceptin' de holly bush, he like dat 'cause its green in winter.

"They wus some flowers 'round de house. Snow-balls, batchelor-buttons, old-maids; jes' such old-fashion ones, no roses, n'er nothin' like dat.

"Masse' raise some cotton, but 'Ole Massa' Hanover had sech a big cotton patch yuh couldn't look across it. An' dey all kinda fowls yu'd find any where's, guinie's Ducks, n' geese, n' turkey's, n' peafowl's, an' lotsa chicken's a' 'cose.

"My mamma could hunt good ez any man. Us'tuh be a coup'la pedluh men come 'round' wuth they packs. My mammy'd a'ways have a pile o' hides tuh trade with 'em fer calico prints n' trinkets, n' sech-like, but mos'ly fo' calico prints. She'd have coon hides a' deer n' mink, n' beavers, lawd! I kin still hear dem beavers slashin' 'round' dat dam. Dis time 'er marning' dey's a'way's shore busy. An' folks in cities goes tuh pawks now to see sech animal. Huh! Ah seen all 'em things ah wants tuh see.

"Good Lawd! We didden' know whut church wuz n'er school nuther, an' the whites nevuh nutthur. Dey wuz a couple o' men us'ta come by, an' hole a camp-meetin'. Dey'd build a big arbuh, with branches o' leaves over de top, an' build benches; dey's come aftuh crops wuz laid by, an' preach 'til cotton wuz openin'. Ah never knowed whut sect dey belong to, n'er whar dey go, n'er what dey come fum 'nuther.

"Yes'm, we seed sojers, an' we seed lot's o' 'em. Dah wuz de 'blue-coats'; some o' de folks call 'em 'Bluebelly Yank's, dey had fine blue coats an' the brass buttons all ovuh the front 'o 'em shinin' like stahs. Dey call us little cullud folks', 'cubs', an'; dey burn down Jonesburg. Yes'm we seed Jonesburg down in ashes. Dem 'Blue-coat's' wuz devils, but de 'gray-coats uz wusser. Dey turn over our bee-gums an' dey kill our steers, an' carry off our provisions, an' whut dey couldn't carry off dey ruint. Den 'dey go roun' killin' all de cullud men an' bayanettin' de chillern.

"No, dat wuzzen' de 'gray-coats' doin' de killin', dat wuz 'bushwackers' an' 'Ku Klux'ers', dey sho' wuz bad. Dey shot my little sistuh in back o' her neck an' dey shot me in de leig. See dat scar, dat whar dey shoot me. An' dey kill my gran'fathuh; dey sho' did.

"Gran'fathuh's name wuz 'Jim Hanover'. 'Ole Massa Hanover', he wuz a lawyer, an' he educated ma gran'fathuh tuh be a overseuh. He lived wid' 'Massa Hanover for long time. He wuz a good man, mah gran'fathuh wuz, an' he wuz smart too, an' when de war surrenduh, dey make him Mayor of Pie-hatten, an' he made a good mayer too; people all said so, an' dey wuz gonna' 'lect him fo' foe mo' year, an' de 'Ku Klux'ers said dey wuz en' gonna have no 'nigguh' mayor. So dey tuk him out an' killed him. Dey wuz awful times. Now you know dat wuzzen right an' who's de curse fo' such things gonna rest on?

"Ah disamembuh jes' when we come tuh Missouri, but it wuz when 'Hayes,' an 'Wheeler' wuz 'lected President. (Rutherford B. Hayes, 19th president, 1877–81.) Down in Arkansas dey say dey gonna make us all vote Democrat. My step-daddy say he die 'fore he vote Democrat.

"Der wuz two white men say dey'd get us to Cape Girda. Dey had two covered wagons, an' dey wuz forty-eight o' us cullud folks. We put our belongin's in de wagon. Dey wuz a coupl'a ole' gramma's rode in de wagons, an' some little feller's, but de rest of us walk ever step o' de way. An' it rained on us ever' step o' de way. At night we'd lay down to sleep unduh de wagon so tired we nevuh even know'd it wuz rainin'.

"When we got to St. Francis Rivuh dey ferried us across on a big flat, an' had a rope tied across der rivuh to pull us ovuh. But we had to ford White Watuh, an Castuh rivuh, an' Niggerwool swamp. When we'd come to de rivuh de white man 'ud say: 'Ack like sojers'. De hosses 'ud swim across, pullin' de wagon, some o' de big folks 'ud grab hole' de feed box an' de rest 'ud each grab roun' de one in front an' dat way we fords de rivuhs, wid stings a' folk hangin' out behin' de wagons.

"Hoo-doos', ghosts's er signs? No mam! Ah don' believe in none of dat. Now you is tryin' to call up de devil. But wait! Ah kin tell you one sign dat ah knows is true. If de dog jes' lays outside de do' sleepin' an' has his haid inside de do', you's gonna' git a new member in de family befo' de year is out. An' jes' de othuh way roun'. Ef de dog lays sleepin' inside de do' an' has his haid hangin' out, you's gwine a lose a 'membuh o' yuh family fo' de end a' de yeah.

"Dey wuz sumpin' funny happen when ma little girl die sometime ago. She wuz a sweet chile. She wuz stayin' wuth Miss' English on Henderson Ave., an' she lost her mind. Ah don' know whut's a matter wuth her, but ah brung her home to take keer o' her, but she don' get no bettuh. One day she's standin', lookin' out de front do' an' she holler: 'Heah dey's comin' aftuh me'. Ah don' know whut she see, but she run to de back room an' stan' right dere.

Her daddy an' me look at huh an' dar wuz a big ball o' fire hangin' ovuh her haid. We picked huh up, an' put huh to bed. We sent fo' de doctah an' fo' de priest, an' we got de nurse we had when she fust took sick. I nevuh knowed whut wuz de mattuh with her. De priest wouldn't tell me, de doctuh wouldn't tell me, an' ah guess de nurse was ez green about it ez ah wuz. Some folks tell me she wuz conjured. Mah po' little girl".

Brown, Casie Jones
Age: 91
Paragould, Arkansas
Interviewer: Velma Sample
[M:8: pt. 1: 267–71]

Casie Jones Brown was a dearly loved Negro servant. He was known for his loving kindness toward children, both black and white. Lots of the white children would say, "Casie sure is smart" because Casie was a funny and witty old darkie. Casie has a log house close to his master, Mr. Brown. They live on what is called the Brown Plantation. The yard had large old cedars planted all around it. They were planted almost a century ago. The plantation is about six miles from Paragould, Arkansas, where the hills are almost mountains. There have been four generations living in the old house. They have the big sand stone fireplaces. Casie has a spiritual power that makes him see and hear things. He says that sometimes he can hear sweet voices somewhere in his fireplace. In the winter time he does all of his cooking in a big black kettle with three legs on it, or a big iron skillet. And when he first settled there he did not have a stove to cook on except the fireplace. He says the singing that comes from somewhere about the fireplace is God having his angels entertain him in his lonely hours. Casie is 91 years old and has been in that settlement as long as he can remember.

The little white boys and girls like to be entertained by Casie. He tells them stories about the bear and peter rabbit. Also he has subjects for them to ask questions about and he answers them in a clever way. He was kind enough to let me see the list and the answers. He cannot write but he has little kids to write them for him. He cannot read, but they appoint one to read for him, and he has looked at the list so much that he has it memorized.

Casie, what does hat mean or use hat for a subject.

"De price ob your hat ain't de medjer ob your brain."

Coat—"If your coat tail catch afire don't wait till you kin see de blaze 'fo' you put it out."

Graveyard—"De graveyard is de cheapes' boardin' house."

Mules—"Dar's a fam'ly coolness 'twix' de mule an' de single-tree.

Mad—"It pesters a man dreadful when he git mad an' don' know who to cuss."

Crop—"Buyin' on credit is robbin next 'er's crop."

Christmas—"Christmas without holiday is like a candle without a wick."

Crawfish—"De crawfish in a hurry look like he tryin' to git dar yastiddy."

Lean houn'—"Lean houn' lead de pack when de rabbit in sight."

Snow Flakes—"Little flakes make de deepes' snow."

Whitewash—"Knot in de plank will show free de whitewash."

Yardstick—"A short yardstick is a po' thing to fight de debbul wid."

Cotton—"Dirt sho de quickes' on the cleanes' cotton."

Candy—"De candy-pullin' din call louder dan de long-rollin'."

Apple—"De bes' apple float on de top o' 'ligion heaps de half-bushel."

Hoe—"De steel hoe dat laughs at de iron one is like de man dat is shamed o' his grand-daddy."

Mule—"A mule kin tote so much goodness in his face dat he don't hab none lef' for his hind legs."

Walks—"Some grabble walks may lead to de jail."

Cow bell—"De cow bell can't keep a secret."

Tree—"Ripe apples made de tree look taller."

Rose—"De red rose don't brag in de dark."

Billy-goat—"De billy-goat gits in his hardes' licks when he looks like he gwine to back out o' de fight."

Good luck—"Tis hard for de bes' an' smartes' fokes in de wul' to git 'long widout a little tech o' good luck."

Blind horse—"Blind horse knows when de trough empty."

Wagon—"De noise of de wheels don't medjer de load in de wagon."

Hot—"Las' 'ear's hot spell cools off mighty fast."

Hole—"Little hole in your pocket is wusser'n a big one at de knee."

Time o' day—"Appetite don't regerlate de time o' day."

Quagmire—"De quagmire don't hand out no sign."

Needle—"One pusson kin th'ead a needle better than two."

Pen—"De pint o' de pin is de easier in' to find."

Turnip—"De green top don't medjer de price o' de turnip."

Dog—"Muzzle on de yard dog unlocks de smokehouse."

Equal to the Emergency

Hebe: "Unc Isrul, mammy says, hoccume de milk so watery on top in de mornin'."

Patriarch: Tell you' mammy dat's de bes' sort o' milk, dat's de dew on it, de cows been layin' in de dew."

Hebe: "An' she tell me to ax you what meck it so blue."

Patriarch: "You ax your mammy what meck she so black."

Here are some of Casie's little rhymes that he entertained the neighbor children with:

Look at dat possum in dat hollar log. He hidin' he know dis nigger eat possum laik a hog.

Hear dat hoot owl in dat tree. Dat old hoot owl gwine hoot right out at yew.

Rabbit, rabbit, do you know; I can track you in de snow.

One young man lingered at the gate after a long visit, but a lots ob sweethearts do dat. His lady love started to cry. He said, "Dear, don't cry; I will come to see you again." But she cried on. "Oh, darling don't cry so; I will come back again, I sure will." Still she cried. At last he said: "Love, did I not tell you that I would soon come again to see you?" And through her tears she replied: "Yes, but I am afraid you will never go; that is what is the matter with me. We must all go."

Uncle Joshua was once asked a great question. It was: "If you had to be blown up which would you choose, to be blown up on the railroad or the steamboat?" "Well," said Uncle Joshua, "I don't want to be blowed up no way; but if I had to be blowed up I would rather be blowed up on de railroad, because you see, if you is blowed up on de railroad, dar you is, but if you is blowed up on de steamboat, whar is you?"

Casie tells me of some of his superstitions:

If you are the first person a cat looks at after he has licked hisself, you are going to be married.

If you put a kitten under the cover of your bed and leave it until it crawls out by itself, it will never leave home.

If you walk through a place where a horse wallows, you will have a headache.

If a woodpecker raps on the house, someone is going to die.

If an owl screeches, turn the pocket of your apron inside out, tie a knot in your apron string, and he will stop.

If a rabbit runs across the road in front of you, to the left, it is a sign of bad luck; if it goes to the right, it is a sign of good luck.

If you cut a child's finger nails before it is a year old, it will steal when it grows up.

If you put your hand on the head of a dead man, you will never worry about him; he will never haunt you, and you will never fear death.

If the pictures are not turned toward the wall after a death, some other member of the family will die.

If you see a dead man in the mirror, you will be unlucky the rest of your life.

Hempstead County

Crane, Sallie
Age: 90+
Pulaski County, Arkansas
Interviewer: Samuel S. Taylor
[M:8: pt. 2: 50–56]

"I was born in Hempstead County, between Nashville and Greenville, in Arkansas, on the Military Road. Never been outside the state in my life. I was born ninety years ago. I been here in Pulaski County nearly fifty-seven years.

"I was born in a old double log house chinked and dobbed. Nary a window and one door. I had a bedstead made with saw and ax. Chairs were made with saw, ax, and draw knife. My brother Orange made the furniture. We kept the food in boxes.

"My mother's name was Mandy Bishop, and my father's name was Jerry Bishop. I don't know who my grand folks were. They was all Virginia folks—that is all I know. They come from Virginia, so they told me. My old master was Harmon Bishop and when they divided the property I fell to Miss Evelyn Bishop.

Age

"The first man that came through here writing us up for the Red Cross, I give him my age as near as I could. And they kept that. You know peace was declared in 1865. They told me I was free. I got scared and thought that the speculators were going to put me in them big droves and sell me down in Louisiana. My old mistress said, 'You fool, you are free. We are going to take you to your mammy.' I cried because I thought they was carrying me to see my mother before they would send me to be sold in Louisiana. My old mistress said she would whip me. But she didn't. When we got to my mother's, I said, 'How old is I?' She said, 'You are sixteen.' She didn't say months, she didn't say years, she didn't say weeks, she didn't say days; she just said, 'You are sixteen.' And my case worker told me that made me ninety years old.

"I was in Hempstead County on Harmon Bishop's plantation. It was Miss Polly, Harmon's wife, that told me I was free, and give me my age.

"I know freedom come before 1865, because my brothers would tell me to come home from Nashville where I would be sent to do nursing by my old mistress and master too to nurse for my young mistress.

"When my old master's property was divided, I don't know why—he wasn't dead nor nothin'—I fell to Miss Evelyn, but I stayed in Nashville working for Miss Jennie Nelson, one of Harmon's daughters. Miss Jennie was my young mistress. My brothers were already free. I don't know how Miss Polly came to tell me I was free. But my brothers would see me and tell me to run away and come on home and they would protect me, but I was afraid to try it. Finally Miss Polly found that she couldn't keep me any longer and she come and told me I was free. But I thought that she was fooling me and just wanted to sell me to the speculators.

Family

"My mother was the mother of twenty children and I am the mother of eighteen. My youngest is forty-five. I don't know whether any of my mother's children is living now or not. I left them that didn't join the militia in Hempstead County fifty-seven years ago. Them that joined the milita went off. I don't know nothin' about them. I have two girls living that I know about. I had two boys went to France and I never heard nothin' 'bout what happened to them. Nothing—not a word. Red Cross has hunted 'em. Police Mitchell hunted 'em—police Mitchell in Little Rock. But I ain't heard nothin' 'bout 'em.

Work

"The first work I did was nursing and after that I was water toter. I reckon I was about seven or eight years old when I first began to nurse. I could barely lift the baby. I would have to drag them 'round. Then I toted water to the field. Then when I was put to plowing, and chopping cotton, I don't know exactly how old I was. But I know I was a young girl and it was a good while before the War. I had to do anything that come up—thrashing wheat, sawing logs, with a wristband on, lifting logs, splitting rails. Women in them days wasn't tender like they is now. They would call on you to work like men and you better work too. My mother and father were both field hands.

Soldiers

"Oo-oo-oo-oo-oo-oo!! Man, the soldiers would pass our house at day-light, two deep or four deep, and be passing it at sundown still marching making it to the next stockade. Those were Yankees. They didn't set no slaves free. When I knowed anything about freedom, it was the Bureaus. We didn't know nothing like young folks do now.

"We hardly knowed our names. We was cussed for so many bitches and sons of bitches and bloody bitches, and blood of bitches. We never heard our names scarcely at all. First young man I went with wanted to know my initials! What did I know 'bout initials? You ask 'em ten years old now, and they'll tell you. That was after the War. Initials!!!

Slave Sales

"Have I seen slaves sold! Good God, man! I have seed them sold in droves. I have worn a buck and gag in my mouth for three days for trying to run away. I couldn't eat nor drink—couldn't even catch the slobber that fell from my mouth and run down my chest till the flies settled on it and blowed it. 'Scuse me but jus' look at these places. (She pulled open her waist and showed scars where the maggots had eaten in—ed.)

Whippings

"I had been whipped from sunup till sundown. Off and on, you know. They whip me till they got tired and then they go and res' and come out and start again. They kept a bowl filled with vinegar and salt and pepper settin' nearby, and when they had whipped me till the blood come, they would take the mop and sponge the cuts with this stuff so that they would hurt more. They would whip me with the cowhide part of the time and with birch sprouts the other part. There were splinters long as my finger left in my back. A girl named Betty Jones come over and soaped the splinters so that they would be softer and pulled them out. They didn't whip me with a bull whip; they whipped me with a cowhide. They jus' whipped me 'cause they could—'cause they had the privilege. It wasn't nothin' I done; they jus' whipped me. My married young master, Joe, and his wife, Jennie, they was the ones that did the whipping. But I belonged to Miss Evelyn.

"They had so many babies 'round there I couldn't keep up with all of them. I was jus' a young girl and I couldn't keep track of all them chilen. While I was turned to one, the other would get off. When I looked for that one, another would be gone. Then they would whip me all day for it. They would whip you for anything and wouldn't give you a bite of meat to eat to save your life, but they'd grease your mouth when company come.

Food

"We et out of a trough with a wooden spoon. Mush and milk. Cedar trough and long-handled cedar spoons. Didn't know what meat was. Never got a taste of egg. Oo-ee! Weren't allowed to look at a biscuit. They used to make citrons. They were good too. When the little white chilen would be comin' home from school, we'd run to meet them. They would say, 'Whose nigger are you?' And we would say, 'Yor'n!' And they would say, 'No, you ain't.' They would open those lunch baskets and show us all that good stuff they'd brought back. Hold it out and snatch it back! Finally, they'd give it to us, after they got tired of playing.

Health

"They're burying old Brother Jim Mullen over here today. He was an old man. They buried one here last Sunday—eighty some odd. Brother Mullen had been sick for thirty years. Died settin' up—settin' up in a chair. The old folks is dyin' fas'. Brother Smith, the husband of the old lady that brought you down here, he's in feeble health too. Ain't been well for a long time.

"Look at that place on my head. (There was a knot as big as a hen egg—smooth and shiny—ed.) When it first appeared, it was no bigger than a pea. I scratched it and then the hair commenced to fall out. I went to three doctors, and been to the clinic too. One doctor said it was a busted vein. Another said it was a tumor. Another said it was a wen. I know one thing. It don't hurt me. I can scratch it; I can rub it. (She scratched and rubbed it while I flinched and my flesh crawled—ed.) But it's got me so I can't see and hear good. Dr. Junkins, the best doctor in the community, told me not to let anybody cut on it. Dr. Hicks wanted to take it off for fifty dollars. I told him he'd let it stay on for nothin'. I never was sick in my life till a year ago. I used to weigh two hundred ten pounds; now I weigh one hundred forty. I can lap up enough skin on my legs to go 'round 'em twice.

"Since I was sick a year ago, I haven't been able to get 'round any. I never been well since. The first Sunday in January this year, I got worse settin' in the church. I can't hardly get 'round enough to wait on myself. But with what I do and the neighbors' help, I gets along somehow.

Present Condition
"If it weren't for the mercy of the people through here, I would suffer for a drink of water. Somebody ran in on old lady Chairs and killed her for her money. But they didn't get it, and we know who it was too. Somebody born and raised right here 'mongst us. Since then I have been 'fraid to stay at home even.

"I had a fine five-room house and while I was down sick, my daughter sold it and I didn't get but twenty-nine dollars out of it. She got the money, but I never seed it. I jus' lives here in these rags and this dirt and those old broken-down pieces of furniture. I've got fine furniture that she keeps in her house.

"I get some help from the Welfare. They give me eight dollars. They give me commodities too. They give me six at first, and they increased it. My case worker said she would try to git me some more. God knows I need it. I have to pay for everything I get. Have to pay a boy to go get water for me. There's people that gits more 'n they need and have plenty time to go fishin' but don't have no time to work. You see those boys there goin' fishin'; but that's not their fault. One of the merchants in town had them cut off from work because they didn't trade with him.

"You gets 'round lots, son, don't you? Well, if you see anybody that has some old shoes they don't want, git 'em to give 'em to me. I don't care whether they are men's shoes or women's shoes. Men's shoes are more comfortable. I wear number sevens. I don't know what last. Can't you tell? (I suppose that her shoes would be seven E—ed.) I can't live off eight dollar. I have to eat, git help with my washing, pay a child to go for my water, 'n everything. I got these dresses give to me. They too small, and I got 'em laid out to be let out.

"You just come in any time; I can't talk to you like I would a woman; but I guess you can understand me."

Interviewer's Comment
Sallie Crane lives near the highway between Sweet Home and Wrightsville. Wrightsville post office, Lucinda Hays' box. McLain Birch, 1711 Wolfe Street, Little Rock, knows the way to her house.

Her age is not less than ninety, because she hoed cotton and plowed before the War. If anything, it is more than the ninety which she claims. Those who know her well say she must be at least ninety-five.

She has a good memory although she complains of her health. She seems to be pretty well dependent on herself and the Welfare and is asking for old clothes and shoes as you will note by the story.

Fergusson, Mrs. Lou
Age: 91
Wade Street
Hot Springs, Arkansas
Interviewer: Mary D. Hudgins
[M:8: pt. 2: 276–81]

Zig-zaging across better than a mile of increasingly less thickly settled territory went the interviewer. The terrain was rolling—to put it mildly. During most of the walk her feet met·the soft resistance of winter-packed earth. Sidewalks were the exception rather than the rule.

Wade Street, she had been told was "somewhere over in the Boulevard". Holding to a general direction she kept her course. "The Boulevard", known on the tax books of Hot Springs as Boulevard Addition, sprawls over a wide area. Houses vary in size and construction with startling frequency. Few of them are pretentious. Many appear well planned, are in excellent state of repair and front on yards, scrupulously neat, sometimes patterned with flower beds. Occasionally a building leans with age, roof caving and windows and doors yawning voids—long since abandoned by owners to wind and weather.

Up one hill, down another went the interviewer. Given a proper steer here and there by colored men and women—even children along the way, she finally found herself in front of "that green house" belonging to Peach Sinclair.

Two colored women, middle aged, sat basking in the mild January sunlight on a back porch. "I beg your pardon," said the interviewer, approaching the step, "is this the home of Peach Sinclair, and will I find Mrs. Lou Fergusson here?"

"It sure is," the voice was cheerful. "My mother is in the house. Come around to the front," (the interviewer couldn't have reached the back steps, even if she had wanted to—the back yard was fenced from the front) "she's in the parlor."

Mrs. Lou turned out to be an incredibly black, unbelievably plump-cheeked, wide smiling "motherly" person. She seemed an Aunt Jemima grown suddenly old, and even more mellow. "Mamma, this young lady's come to see you. She wants to talk to you and ask you some questions, about when—about before the war." (The situation is always delicate when an ex-slave is asked for details. Somehow both interviewer and interviewee avoid the ugly word whenever possible. The skillful interviewer can generally manage to pass it by completely, as well as any variant of the word negro. The informant is usually less squeamish. "Black folks", "colored folks", "black people", "Master's people", "us" are all encountered frequently.

Five minutes of pleasant chatter preceeded the formal interview. Both Mrs. Sinclair and her guest (unintroduced) sat in on the conference and made comments frequently. "Law, child, we bought this place from your father. He was a mighty fine man." Mrs. Sinclair was delighted to find her guest to be "Jack Hudgins daughter." And later in the chat, "You done lost everything? Even your home—that's going? Too bad. But then I guess at that you're better off than we are. I've been trying for nearly a year to get my mother on the old age pension. They say she has passed. That was way along last March. Here it is January and she hasn't got a penny. No, I know you can't help. Yes, I see what you're doing. But if ever you does get on the pensions work—I'm going to 'hant' you." (a wide grin)

[Note at bottom of page: "Hant" was an intentional barbarism.]

The old woman rocked and smiled. "Yes, ma'am. I'm her oldest, alive. She had 17 and 15 of them lived to grow up. But I'm about as old as she is, looks like. She never did have glasses—and today she can thread the finest needle. She can make as pretty a quilt as you'd hope to see. Makes fine stitches too. Seems like they made them stronger in her day." A nod of delighted approval from Mrs. Fergusson.

"I was born in Hempstead County, right here in this state. The town we were nearest was Columbus. I lived around there all of my life until I come here to be with my daughter. That was 15 years ago. Yes, I was born on a farm. From what I know, I'm over ninety. I was around 20 when the war ceaseted.

The man what owned us was named Ed Johnson. Yes ma'am he had lots of folks. Was he good to us? Well, he was and he wasn't. He was good himself, wouldn't never have whipped us—but he had a mean wife. She'd dog him, and dog him until he'd tie us down and whip us for the least little thing. Then they put overseers over us. They was most generally mean. They'd run us out way fore day—even in the sleet—run us out to the field.

Was the life hard—well it was and it wasn't. No ma'am, I didn't get much learning. Some folks wouldn't let their black folks learn at all. Then there was some which would let their children teach the colored children what they learned at school. We never learned very much.

You see, Master didn't live on the place. He lived bout as far as from here to town" (fully two miles) "The overseer looked after us mostly. No, ma'am I don't remember much about the war. You see, they was afraid that the fighting was going to get down there so they run us off to Texas. We settled down and made a crop there. How'd we get the land? Master rented it.

We made a crop down there and later we come back. No, ma'am we didn't stay with Mr. Johnson more than a month after there was peace. We come on in to Washington. No, ma'am, I never heard tell that Washington had been the Capitol of Arkansas for a while during the War. No, I never did hear that. Guess it was when we was in Texas. Then we folks didn't hear so much anyway.

We stayed in Washington most a year. Was I with my Mother? No, ma'am I was married—married before the war was thru. Married—does you know how we folks married in them days? Well the man asked your mother. Then you both asked your master. He built you a house. You moved in and there you was. You was married. I did some washing and cooking when I was in Washington. Then we moved onto a farm. I sort of liked Washington, but I was born on a farm and I sort of liked farm life.

We didn't move around very much—just two or three places. We raised cotton, corn, vegetables, peas, watermelons and lots of those sort of things. No ma'am, didn't nobody think of raising watermelons to ship way off like they does in Hempstead county now. Cotton was our cash crop. We rented thirds and fourths. Didn't move but three times. One place I stayed 15 years.

I been a widow 40 years. Yes, ma'am. I farmed myself, and my children helped me. Me and the owners got along well. Made good crops, me and the children. I managed to take good care of them. Made out to raise 15 out of the 17 to be grown. There's only 5 of them alive now.

Hard on a woman to run a farm by herself. Well now, I don't know. I made out. I raised my children and raised them healthy. I got along well with the farm owner. You might know when I was let to stay on one place for 15 years. You know I must have treated the land right and worked it fair.

Yes ma'am I remembers lots. Seems like women folks remembers better than men. I've got a good daughter. I'm still strong and can get about good. Guess the Lord has been good to me."

Ray, Joe
Age: 83
Muskogee, Oklahoma
Interviewer: Ethel Wolfe Garrison
[OK: 343–45]

My folks was shipped from Africa across the waters and fetched a good price on the slave market at New Orleans where my pappy stayed for a long time helping with the fresh Negroes that come over on the slave boats.

His name was John and my Mammy's name was Rhoda. She belonged to Jim Hawkins who had a plantation at Fulton, Arkansas, down in Hempstead County. When she met my pappy old master Hawkins sold her to pappy's master, name of Ray, so's dey could stay together.

Dere at Fulton I was born in 1855. I was eight year old when Vicksburg give up to the Yankees and an old slave man dere looked at the lines on my hand and said I was eight year old. My twin sister, Josephine, is still living down in Shreveport, La., and a brother Charles lives in Tampico, Mexico. Dat's where I want to go for I is afraid the Japs is coming over here and I is too feeble to dodge stray cannon balls!

Some of the slaves was moved around all over the south during the War. Me and pappy was at Vicksburg when the Rebels stuck their swords in the ground to give up. But dem Yanks had a terrible time whipping us. The Yank soldiers dug holes in the ground and put in kegs of powder. Den dey blowed up the land down by the river and almost turned the river (Mississippi) around! When the powder blasts go off lots of Rebels was killed and dere wasn't many left to give up when General Grant took the town.

I remember General Grant talking and laughing about the war. He was a fighter, dat man! I eat two-three meals at the General's place; he took me in one terrible cold night, I was almost froze.

Master Ray sold mammy, me and my twin sister and two brothers to Enoch Smith, and he was the last master we had. Some of my folks stayed with him a long time after they was free—doing washings, ironings and cooking. The boys tend to his horses and work in the fields.

The Smith plantation was called "Seven Mile Square"—it was that size and had about 350 slaves most of the time. He was a big trader. His house was made of sawed cedar logs from a close by mill, and the beds had round logs made of cedar posts, with rope slats made diamond fashion. When the ropes was drawn up it made the bottom tight as a dollar bill.

The slaves lived in log huts, mostly one room, with a tar roof. Dere was no beds like the master had. Just a kind of bunk with corn shuckings stuck in a cotton bag for to lay on. After working in the fields all day, sometimes without anything to eat for dinner, the slaves come to the cabins at night, cook their supper of white salt meat and talk awhile before going to sleep. Dey had to get sleep early and get up early; nobody sleep late, even on Sunday.

Dere was two overseers on the place and dey carried a bull whip all the time. Dey didn't whip the girls; the old master pinch their ears if dey get mean and not mind. But I saw a slave man whipped until his shirt was cut to pieces! Dey whipped dem like horses, but the master didn't want dem beat to death. If dey whip dem too hard the old master shake his head and say, "Dat's too much money to kill!"

My pappy killed an overseer who tried to lash him; they sent him off to another plantation for a while. Dat's all the punishment he got.

The auction sales brought the master lots of money. One man sold for $1,500. The slaves stand bare to the waist, men and women alike, for buyers feeling of dem to see if dey was solid and looking for scars to see if dey had been mean enough for whippings.

The old master kept his money hidden in two kegs under the stairway. I seen him putting money dere one day and he chased me out of the house. But another Negro found out about it and he stole some of it and run off to Texas. Dey said he bout a farm dere; anyway, dey never got the slave nor the money back, dat's what I know.

Alma Cinda was the mistress' name. Dere was boy name of Joe and a girl name of Athlene. Dat boy was a terror; folks said he was a cattle stealer. One year he come home and died of pneumonia.

The master give each slave family about 4-pounds of fat meats every week, with a quart of molasses, a peck of corn meal and some bran for flour. When dat run out you was just out until Saturday night come around again.

The clothes was all home spun, made of cotton, and when I was a little boy the master give me a pair of red shoes. In dem days I wore a charm for sharp luck. It was a needle with a blue velvet string through the eye, but when I do something mean that charm didn't keep the master's whip off my back!

After freedom one time I worked at the old Peabody hotel in Memphis. Lots of gamblers around dere den; dey come down the river and have some big gambling games. I done some gambling too, but not like dem white folks who paid me a dollar for a cigar after dey have a streak of big winnings.

Dem old south slave girls I love, but not dem northern girls—dere is a difference! I lived with one of them south girls name of Jennie Harris from Mississippi. She leave me for a nappy headed preacher. Den I married Mandy Drew, another Mississippi girl, who leave me for a man with two kinky heads (children). A long time later I see dat man on a river boat and I was fixing to shoot him but dere was too many laws at the boat landing so he got away.

That black-as-a-skillet Mandy give me a boy, Dick Ray, and a girl Jabo who full grown weighted about 400-pounds. Dere was four other wives, but dey're all gone now and I ain't studying nobody now, I is dat old.

Lincoln was a great man, but dis country needs a king.

Folks call me a prophet, because I tell dem things dat comes true. Now I been telling dem dat slavery is coming back and it ain't far away. Maybe dey won't believe it—but slavery is coming soon.

Rowe, Katie
Age: 88
1004 N. Lansing
Tulsa, Oklahoma
Interviewer: Robert Vinson Lackey
[OK: 364–71]

I can set on de gallery, whar de sunlight shine bright, and sew a power-ful fine seam when my grandchillun wants a special purty dress for de school doings, but I ain't worth much for nothing else I reckon.

These same old eyes seen powerful lot of tribulations in my time, and when I shets 'em now I can see lots of li'l chillun just lak my grandchillun, toting hoes bigger dan dey is, and dey poor little black hands and legs bleeding whar dey scratched by de brambledy weeds, and whar dey got whuppings 'cause dey didn't git out all de work de overseer set out for 'em.

I was one dem little slave gals my own self, and I never seen nothing but work and tribulations till I was a grown up woman, jest about.

De niggers had hard traveling on de plantation whar I was born and raised, 'cause old Master live in town and jest had de overseer on the place, but iffen he had lived out dar hisself I speck it been as bad, 'cause he was a hard driver his own self.

He get biling mad when de Yankees have dat big battle at Pea Ridge and scatter de 'Federates all down through our country all bleeding and tired up and hungry, and he jest mount on his hoss and ride out to de plantation whar we all hoeing corn.

He ride up and tell old man Saunders—dat de overseer—to bunch us all up round the lead row man—dat my own uncle Sandy—and den he tell us de law!

"You niggers been seeing de 'Federate soldiers coming by here looking purty raggedy and hurt and wore out," he say, "but dat no sign dey licked!

"Dem Yankees ain't gwine git dis fur, but iffen dey do you all ain't gwine git free by 'em, 'cause I gwine free you befo' dat. When dey git here dey going find you already free, 'cause I gwine line you up on the bank of Bois d'Arc Creek and free you wid my shotgun! Anybody miss jest one lick wid de hoe, or one step in de line, or one clap of dat bell, or one toot of de horn, and he gwine be free and talking to de debil long befo' he ever see a pair of blue britches!"

Dat de way he talk to us, and dat de way he act wid us all de time.

We live in the log quarters on de plantation, not far from Washington, Arkansas, close to Bois d'Arc Creek, in de edge of the Little River bottom.

Old Master's name was Dr. Isaac Jones, and he live in de town, whar he keep four, five house niggers, but he have about 200 on de plantation, big and little, and old man Saunders oversee 'em at the time of de War. Old Mistress' name was Betty, and she had a daughter name Betty about grown, and then they was three boys, Tom, Bryan, and Bob, and they was too young to go to de War. I never did see 'em but once or twice till after de War.

Old Master didn't go to de War, 'cause he was a doctor and de onliest one left in Washington, and purty soon he was dead anyhow.

Next fall after he ride out and tell us dat he gwine shoot us befo' he let us free he come out to see how his stream gin doing. De gin box was a little old thing 'bout as big as a bedstead, wid a long belt running through de side of de gin house out to de engine and boiler in de yard. De boiler burn cord wood, and it have a little crack in it whar de nigger ginner been trying to fix it.

Old master come out, hopping mad 'cause de gin shet down, and ast de ginner, old Brown, what de matter. Old Brown say de boiler weak and it liable to bust, but old Master jump down off'n his hoss and go 'round to de boiler and say, "Cuss fire to you black heart! Dat boiler all right! Throw on some cordwood, cuss fire to your heart!"

Old Brown start to de wood pile grumbling to hisself and old Master stoop down to look at de boiler again, and it blow right up and him standing right dar!

Old Master was blowed all to pieces, and dey jest find little bitsy chunks of his clothes and parts of him to bury.

De wood pile blow over, and old Brown land way off in de woods, but he wasn't killed.

Two wagons of cotton blowed over, and de mules run away, and all de niggers was scared nearly to death 'cause we knowed de overseer gwine be a lot worse, now dat old Master gone.

Before de War when Master was a young man de slaves didn't have it so hard, my mammy tell me. Her name was Fanny and her old mammy name was Nanny. Grandma Nanny was alive during the War yet.

How she come in de Jones family was dis way: old Mistress was jest a little girl, and her older brother bought Nanny and give her to her. I think his name was Little John, anyways we called him Master Little John. He drawed up a paper what say dat Nanny allus belong to Miss Betty and all de chillun Nanny ever have belong to her, too, and nobody can't take 'em for a debt and things like dat. When Miss Betty marry, old Master he can't sell Nanny or any of her chillun neither.

Dat paper hold good, too, and grandmammy tell me about one time it hold good and keep my own mammy on de place.

Grandmammy say mammy was jest a little gal and was playing out in de road wid three, four other little chillun when a white man and old Master rid up. The white man had a paper about some kind of a debt, and old Master say take his pick of de nigger chillun and give him back de paper.

Jest as Grandmammy go to de cabin door and hear him say dat the man git off his hoss and pick up my mammy and put her up in front of him and start to ride off down de road.

Pretty soon Mr. Little John come riding up and say something to old Master, and see grandmammy standing in de yard screaming and crying. He jest job de spur in his hoss and go kiting off down the road after dat white man.

Mammy say he ketch up wid him jest as he git to Bois d'Arc Creek and start to wade de hoss across. Mr. Little John holler to him to come back wid dat little nigger 'cause de paper don't kiver dat child, 'cause she old Mistress' own child, and when de man jest ride on, Mr. Little John throw his big old long hoss-pistol down on him and make him come back.

De man hoppin mad, but he have to give over my mammy and take one de other chillun on de debt paper.

Old Master allus kind of techy 'bout old Mistress having niggers he can't trade or sell, and one day he have his whole family and some more white folks out at de plantation. He showing 'em all de quarters when we all come in from de field in de evening, and he call all de niggers up to let de folks see 'em.

He make grandmammy and mammy and me stand to one side and den he say to the other niggers, "Dese niggers belong to my wife but you belong to me, and I'm de only one you is to call Master."

"Dis is Tom, and Bryan, and Bob, and Miss Betty, and you is to call 'em dat, and don't you ever call one of 'em Young Master or Young Mistress, cuss fire to your black hearts!" All de other white folks look kind of funny, and old Mistress look 'shamed of old Master.

My own pappy was in dat bunch, too. His name was Frank, and after de War he took de name of Frank Henderson, 'cause he was born under dat name, but I allus went by Jones, de name I was born under.

Long about de middle of de war, after old Master was killed, de soldiers begin coming 'round de place and camping. Dey was Southern soldiers and dey say dey have to take de mules and most de corn to get along on. Jest go in de barns and cribs and take anything dey want, and us niggers didn't have no sweet 'taters nor Irish 'taters to eat on when dey gone neither.

One bunch come and stay in de woods across de road from de overseer's house, and dey was all on hosses. Dey lead de hosses down to Bois d'Arc Creek every morning at daylight and late every evening to git water. When we going to de field and when we coming in we allus see dem leading big bunches of hosses.

Dey bugle do jest 'bout de time our old horn blow in de morning and when we come in dey eating supper, and we smell it and sho' git hungry!

Before old Master died he sold off a whole lot of hosses and cattle, and some niggers too. He had de sales on de plantation, and white men from around dar come to bid, and some traders come. He had a big stump whar he made de niggers stand while dey was being sold, and dem men and boys had to strip off to de waist to show dey muscle and iffen dey had any scars or hurt places, but de women and gals didn't have to strip to de waist.

De white men come up and look in de slave's mouth jest lak he was a mule or a hoss.

After old Master go, de overseer hold one sale, but mostly he jest trade wid de traders what come by. He make de niggers git on de stump, though. De traders all had big bunches of slaves and dey have 'em all strung out in a line going down de road. Some had wagons and de chillun could ride, but not many. Dey didn't chain or tie 'em 'cause dey didn't have no place dey could run to anyway.

I seen chillun sold off and de mammy not sold, and sometimes de mammy sold and a little baby kept on de place and give to another woman to raise. Dem white folks didn't care nothing 'bout how de slaves grieved when dey tore up a family.

Old man Saunders was de hardest overseer of anybody. He would git mad and give a whipping some time and de slave wouldn't even know what it was about.

My uncle Sandy was de lead row nigger, and he was a good nigger and never would tech a drap of likker. One night some de niggers get hold of some likker somehow, and dey leave de jug half full on de step of Sandy's cabin. Next morning old man Saunders come out in de field so mad he was pale.

He jest go to de lead row and tell Sandy to go wid him, and start toward de woods along Bois d'Arc Creek wid Sandy follering behind. De overseer always carry a big heavy stick, but we didn't know he was so mad, and dey jest went off in de woods.

Purty soon we hear Sandy hollering and we know old overseer pouring it on, den de overseer come back by his self and go on up to de house.

Come late evening he come and see what we done in de day's work, and go back to de quarters wid us all. When he git to mammy's cabin, whar grand-mammy live too, he say to grandmammy, "I sent Sandy down in de woods to hunt a hoss, he gwine come in hungry purty soon. You better make him an extra hoe cake," and he kind of laugh and go on to his house.

Jest soon as he gone we all tell grandmammy we think he got a whipping, and sho' nuff he didn't come in.

De next day some white boys find uncle Sandy what dat overseer done killed him and throwed him in a little pond, and dey never done nothing to old man Saunders at all!

When he go to whip a nigger he make him strip to de waist, and he take a cat-o-nine tails and bring de blisters, and den bust the blisters wid a wide strap of leather fastened to a stick handle. I seen de blood running out'n many a back, all de way from de neck to de waist!

Many de time a nigger git blistered and cut up so dat we have to git a sheet and grease it wid lard and wrap 'em up in it, and dey have to wear a greasy cloth wrapped around dey body under de shirt for three-four days after dey git a big whipping!

Later on in de War de Yankees come in all around us and camp, and de overseer git sweet as honey in de comb! Nobody git a whipping all de time de Yankees dar!

Dey come and took all de meat and corn and 'taters dey want too, and dey tell us, "Why don't you poor darkeys take all de meat and molasses you want? You made it and it's your'n as much as anybody's!" But we know dey soon be gone, and den we git a whipping iffen we do. Some niggers run off and went wid de Yankees, but dey had to work jest as hard for dem, and dey didn't eat so good and often wid de soldiers.

I never forget de day we was set free!

Dat morning we all go to the cotton field early, and den a house nigger come out from old Mistress on a hoss and say she want de overseer to come into town, and he leave and go in. After while de old horn blow up at the over-seer's house, and we all stop and listen, 'cause it de wrong time of day for de horn.

We start chopping again, and dar go de horn again.

De lead row nigger holler "Hold up!" And we all stop again. "We better go on in. Dat our horn," he holler at the head nigger, and de head nigger think so too, but he say he afraid we catch de devil from the overseer iffen we quit widout him dar, and de lead row man say maybe he back from town and blowing de horn hisself, so we line up and go in.

When we git to de quarters we see all de old ones and de chillun up in de overseer's yard, so we go on up dar. De overseer setting on de end of de gallery wid a paper in his hand, and when we all come up he say come and stand close to de gallery. Den he call off everybody's name and see we all dar.

Setting on de gallery in a hide-bottom chair was a man we never see before. He had on a big broad black hat lak de Yankees wore but it didn't have no yaller string on it lak most de Yankees had, and he was in store clothes dat wasn't homespun or jeans, and dey was black. His hair was plumb gray and so was his beard, and it come way down here on his chest, but he didn't look lak he was very old, 'cause his face was kind of fleshy and healthy looking. I think we all been sold off in a bunch, and I notice some kind of smiling, and I think they sho' glad of it.

De man say, "You darkies know what day dis is?" He talk kind, and smile.

We all don't know of course, and we jest stand dar and grin. Pretty soon he ask again and de head man say, "No, we don't know."

"Well dis the fourth day of June, and dis is 1865, and I want you all to 'member de date, 'cause you allus going 'member de day. Today you is free, jest lak I is, and Mr. Saunders and your Mistress and all us white people," de man say.

"I come to tell you," he say, "and I wants to be sho' you all understand, 'cause you don't have to git up and go by de horn no more. You is your own bosses now, and you don't have to have no passes to go and come."

We never did have no passes, nohow, but we knowed lots of other niggers on other plantations got 'em.

"I wants to bless you and hope you always is happy, and tell you got all de right and life dat any white people got," de man say, and den he git on his hoss and ride off.

We all jest watch him go on down de road, and den we go up to Mr. Saunders and ask him what he want us to do. He jest grunt and say do lak we dam please, he reckon, but git off dat place to do it, less'n any of us wants to stay and make de crop for half of what we make.

None of us know whar to go, so we all stay, and he split up de fields and show us which part we got to work in, and we go on lak we was, and make de crop and git it in, but dey ain't no more horn after dat day. Some de niggers lazy and don't git in the field early, and dey git it took away from 'em, but dey plead around and git it back and work better de rest of dat year.

But we all gits fooled on dat first go-out! When de crop all in we don't git half! Old Mistress sick in town, and de overseer was still on the place and he charge us half de crop for de quarters and de mules and tools and grub.

Den he leave, and we gits another white man, and he sets up a book, and give us half de next year, and take out for what we use up, but we all got something left over after dat first go-out.

Old Mistress never git well after she lose all her niggers, and one day de white boss tell us she jest drap over dead setting in her chair, and we know her heart jest broke.

Next year de chillun sell off most de place and we scatter off, and I and mammy go into Little Rock and do work in de town. Grandmammy done dead.

I git married to John White in Little Rock, but he died and we didn't have no chillun. Den in four, five years I marry Billy Rowe. He was a Cherokee citizen and he had belonged to a Cherokee name Dave Rowe, and lived east of Tahlequah before de War. We married in Little Rock, but he had land in de Cherokee Nation, and we come to east of Tahlequah and lived till he died, and den I come to Tulsa to live wid my youngest daughter.

Billy Rowe and me had three chillun, Ellie, John, and Lula. Lula married a Thomas, and it's her I lives with.

Lots of old people lak me say dat dey was happy in slavery, and dat dey had the worst tribulations after freedom, but I knows dey didn't have no white master and overseer lak we all had on our place. Dey both dead now I reckon, and dey no use talking 'bout de dead, but I know I been gone long ago iffen dat white man Saunders didn't lose his hold on me.

It was de fourth day of June in 1865 I begins to live, and I gwine take de picture of dat old man in the big black hat and long whiskers, setting on de gallery and talking kind to us, clean into my grave wid me.

No, bless God, I ain't never seen no more black boys bleeding all up and down de back under a cat o' nine tails, and I never go by no cabin and hear no poor nigger groaning, all wrapped up in a lardy sheet no more!

I hear my chillun read about General Lee, and I know he was a good man. I didn't know nothing about him den, but I know now he wasn't fighting for dat kind of white folks.

Maybe dey dat kind still yet, but dey don't show it up no more, and I got lots of white friends too. All my chillun and grandchillun been to school, and dey git along good, and I know we living in a better world, whar dey ain't nobody "cussing fire to my black heart!"

I sho' thank de good Lawd I got to see it.

Winn, Willis
Age: 116
Marshall, Texas
Interviewer: Alex Hampton
3 May 1937
[S2:10 (TX, pt. 9): 4249–57]

Willis Winn, now of Marshall, claims to be 116 years of age. He was born in Homer, Louisiana as a slave of Bob Winn, who, Willis claims, taught him from youth that his birthday was March 10, 1822. (This age is shown also on Harrison County relief roll records.) Willis worked as a farmhand for the Winns until 1865, when he moved with his father to Hope, Arkansas. After residing in Arkansas about sixteen years, he moved to Texarkana, where he resided until his removal to Marshall fourteen years ago. Since 1865, he has always earned a livlihood from public work, until his health failed about four years ago. He now lives alone in a one-room log house in the rear of the Howard Vestal home on the Powder Mill Road, 3–½ miles north of Marshall. He is presently supported by Howard Vestal, an employee of the Marshall Fire Department, and a $11.00 per month Government pension.

The onliest statement I can make 'bout my age is that my ole Master, Bob Winn, allus told me if anyone ask me how ole I is to say I was bo'n March 10, 1822. I'se knowed my birthday since I was a shirt-tail boy, but can't tells how ole I is by figures. I can read some and write my name, but can't figure in my head.

Me Daddy was Daniel Winn and come from Alabama. I 'members he allus was saying he like to go back to Alabama and get some chestnuts. My mother was named Patsy Winn, but I don't know where she was bo'n. In Louisiana, I suppose. They was nine of us chil'ren. I'se the oldest and onliest one living. The five boys was me, Willie, Hosea and two Georges. One of my brudders named his-self for Master Bob, what was named George. The girls was named Carolina, Dora, Anna, and Ada. All of us lived to be grown, married and have chil'ren.

Master Bob's house faced the "qua'ters" where he could hear us holler when he blowed his big horn for us to rise. All the houses of the slaves and Master's too was made of logs. They didn't use lumber till after surrender. We slep on shuck and grass mattress what was allus full of chinches. I still sleep on grass mattresses cause I can't rest on cotton and feather beds.

We et yaller (yellow) bread, peas, greens, hog-jowl, potlicker and sopped lasses (molassses). The Niggers and white fo'ks all cooked on fire places. A big iron pot hung out in the yard for to bile (boil) greens, hog-jowl and sich like. We didn't know nothing 'bout baking powder and made our soda from burn cobs. That's jest as good soda as this Arm and Hammer you get in the store. We et flour bread on Sunday, but you darsn't be caught with flour dough 'cept on the day they giv' it to you. My mammy stole lots of flour dough. She rolled it up, put it round her head and kivered (covered) it with her head-rag. Wild game was all over the country; buffalo, bears, panther, deer, possum, coon and squirrels most run over you in the woods. We et at a long wooden trough. It was clean and allus full of plenty of grub. We used buffalo and fish bones for spoons. The Niggers on some of the places et with their hands. The grub I liked best was 'jest whatever I could git'.

Slaves didn't wear nothing but white lowell cloth. They giv' us pants for Sunday what had a black strip down the leg. The Chil'ren wore wool clothes in the winter, but big fo'ks wore the same outfit the year round. They didn't care if you froze.

I can show you right where I was when the stars fell. Some say that they kivered (covered) the ground like snow, but nary one ever hit the ground. They fell in 'bout twelve feet of the ground. The chil'ren jumped up and try to catch them. They whipped them for grabbing at them when they first started falling, but finally paid no attention to them. I don't 'member how long they fell, but they was shooting through the air like sky-rockets for quite a spell.

My Mistress Callie had one girl, June, and two boys, Johnnie and Ruben. Master Bob had three overseers. He didn't have "Nigger-drivers" but had his pets. We called them "Pimps" cause they was allus tattling when we done anything. His place was jest as far as you could let your eye see, 'bout 1800 or 1900 acres. He owned more than 500 Niggers.

I still got the bugle he woke us with at four in the morning. When the bugle blowed you'd better go to hollering so the overseer could hear your. If he had to call you, it was too bad. The first thing in the morning we go to the lot and feed, then go to the wood pile till breakfast. They put our grub in the trough and giv' us so long to eat. Master hollered, if we was slow eating, "Swallow that grub now and chaw it tonight. Better be in that fiel' by daybreak." We worked from "see to can't", from the time you could see the furrow till you can't see it.

I'se seed many Niggers whipped on a "buck and gag" bench. You don't know what that is, do you? They buckle you down hard and fast to a long bench, gag your mouth with cotton, and when Master got through laying on that cowhide the blood was running off on the ground. Next morning after he whip you, he come around to the quarters when you get up and say, "Boy, how is you feeling'. No matter how sore you is, you'd better jump and kick your heels and show how lively you is. Master hated me to his dying day cause I told Mistress 'bout him whipping a girl scandously in the fiel' cause she wanted to go to the house to her sick baby. Mistress Callie didn't whip us, but she twist our nose and ears nearly off. Them fingers felt like a pair of pinchers (plyers). She stropped on her guns and rode a big bay horse to the fiel'. She wouldn't let Master whip us.

Master had a gin on the place and I wo'ked in the fiel' and haul cotton to Port Caddo. That was a big port on Caddo Lake and is older than Jefferson. I drove eight mules and hauled eight bales of cotton. Master followed me with two mules and two bales of cotton. I usually had a good start on him. The Pattyrollers has cotched me and unhitched my mules and drive them off leaving me in the middle of the road. They'd start back home, but when they overtook Master they stopped cause he drove the lead mules. He fotched them back and say, "Willis, what happened". I tell him the Pattyrollers cotched me and run my mules off. He sho' cussed them Pattyrollers and say he'll get even yet.

They was selling slaves all the time, putting them on the block and selling them 'cording to how much work they could do in a day and how strong they was. I'se seed lots of slaves in chains like cows and mules. If a owner had more slaves than he needed, he jest hit the road with them and sell them off to jining farms. No slaves ever run off to the North. They couldn't get away, I'se seed too many try it. If the Pattyrollers didn't cotch you, some of the white fo'ks put you up and send for your Master. They had a "greement" to be on the watch for run-a-way Niggers. The young boys run off cause Master was so hard on them. They'd go to a neighbors house and ask for something to eat. The Master of the house would say, "Boy, who you belong to?" You tell him why you leave, and he say, "That's a shame; he ought to be whipped hisself; you is going to stay right here with us; and if you be good and work we'll take care of you and treat you right". Then he feed you and send you off to do some task. That evening you see the Master leave and 'bout night when he come back your Master was with him. When he got you back home and got through with you, you'd sho' stay home.

In slavery time the Niggers warn't lowed to look at a book. I learned to read and write after surrender in the Hot Springs, Arkansas jail. The white fo'ks giv' us cake at Christmas, and egg-nogg and "Silly-bug" from the "yallers" (yellows). You have to churn the yallers and whiskey to make "Silly-bug".

Master had a big place there close to his house for the chil'ren to play. We played "seven-up" with marbles, running base and sich like. We didn't know nothing 'bout baseball and games they have now. The white fo'ks liked to gang on Master's porch and watch the darkies play.

Co'n shuckings was the things them days. I liked to see them come. They cooked up guineas, ducks, chickens, and sometimes roast a pig. Master keep twenty or thirty barrels of whiskey round over the place all the time, with tin cups hanging on the barrels. You could drink when you wanta but sho better not get drunk. Master had to watch his corners when the co'n shucking was over or the Niggers grab him and walk him round in the air on their hands.

When some of the white fo'ks died every Nigger on the place had to go to the grave and walk round and drap in some dirt on him. They buried the Niggers anyway. Jest dig a ditch and civer them up. I can show you right now down in Louisiana where I was raised, forty acres where nothing but Niggers is buried. Haunts and ghosts was the go in them days, but I never seed any in all my life. I don't believe in sich like. I stayed all night in a cemetery one night jest to see if I could see one. The black man that was with me saw something jump out of a tree, he say and left. I didn't see nothing and lay down and slep' till morning right there in the cemetery.

I 'members lots 'bout the War, but can't tell all of it cause every War has its secrets. That war had four salutes, and when you meet the Captain you'd better give the right salute. Jeff Davis was agin (against) freeing the slaves. I'se heard the Niggers in Louisiana sing "Gonna hang Jeff Davis to a sour apple tree". Grant was for freeing them. The last battle of the War was fought at Mansfield, Louisiana. My Daddy fought in it with Master Bob, and was shot. Master Bob warn't touched by a bullet. I stayed at home and took care of Mistress and help tend to the things.

When the 'Federates come in sight of Mansfield they was carrying a red flag, and kep' it raised till surrender. When the Yankees come in sight of Mansfield they raised a white flag and wanted the 'Federates to surrender, but they wouldn't answer them. It warn't long till the whole world 'round there smelt like powder. Them guns don't shoot like the guns they have now. Guns now-days just goes "Pop-pop", but them guns sounded like thunder. I don't know how long they fought. After surrender, Master freed the men and Mistress freed the wimmen, but he didn't let us loose when he ought. There warn't no places divided with the Niggers as I heard of. Niggers in Louisiana say that Queen Elizabeth sent a boat-load of gold to America to give the free men, but we never seed any of it. Master giv' all his Niggers a barrel of meal, a barrel of flour, a side of meat and ten gallons of lasses and tell them they can work for who they please. Daddy bought two cows, a horse, eight hogs and a goat from Master on credit and we moved to our place, and made three craps (crops).

Master say when we was freed, "Some of you is going to get lynched". 'Fore three years was gone I saw a Nigger lynched close to Hainsville for 'saulting a white girl. They tied him to a tree, piled rich pine round him, poured on ten gallons of coal oil and set him fire.

The Yankees stayed round Louisiana a long time after surrender. They come to the white fo'ks house that hadn't freed the slaves and bust their meal and flour barrels and burn their meat and say, "If we have to face you again, we will sweep you from the cradle up".

I'se been cotched by the Ku Kluxers several times. They couldn't hurt you, but have lots of fun out of you making you cut capers. They pulled my clothes off once and made me run 'bout 400 yards and then stand on my head in the middle of the road. If you was hauling cotton they made your team run away. They'd take grub or anything you had they wanted away from you, but didn't hurt you.

There is plenty Niggers in Louisiana that is still slaves. A spell back I made a trip where I was raised to see my old Mistress 'fore she died, and there was Niggers in twelve or fourteen miles of that place that didn't know they is free. There's plenty Niggers round Marshall that is same as slaves. They is worked for white fo'ks twenty and twenty-five years and ain't drawed a 5¢, jest some old clothes and something to eat. That's the way we was in slavery.

'Bout four years after surrender Daddy say that he hear folks say that gold was kivering (covering) the ground at Hope, Arkansas. We pulled up and moved there. We found lots of munney there where they was a big camp, but there warn't no gold. We lived in Arkansas 'bout sixteen years then I come to Texarkana, and worked twelve years for G. W. George Fawcett's sawmill. I never married till I was old. I was married in little Washington, Arkansas and live with my wife thirty-six years 'fore she died. We raised eighteen children to be grown, and nary one of them was ever arrested. Two of the girls is still living. One is in Shreveport and one is in Texarkana. I was allus wild and played for dances. My wife was religious and knelt and prayed three times a day. After I married I quieted down cause she was religious. When I jined the church, I burned my fiddle up. I'se allus made a living from the public road work since I left Texarkana till I got no count for work.

I never took no thought how come they stopped the Niggers from voting. It never done no good when I voted. The onliest time I voted was in Hope, Arkansas. I voted the Republican ticket and all my fo'ks got mad.

I don't hardly know what to think of the young set of Niggers. I know they won't help us old Niggers. If it warn't for the good white fo'ks, I'd starve to death. 'Fore I come to Vestals, I was living in a shack over on the T. & P. Tracks. It belonged to one of them young Niggers in town. I was sick and couldn't pay no rent, and the woman it belonged to made me get out. Master Vestal [Typescript ends here in Rawick 1979].

Hot Spring County

Baker, James
Age: 81
Interviewer: Mary D. Hudgins
941 Wade Street
Hot Springs, Arkansas
[M:8: pt. 1: 91–96]

The outskirts of eastern Hot Springs resemble a vast checkerboard—patterned in Black and White. Within two blocks of a house made of log-faced siding—painted a spotless white and provided with blue shutters will be a shack which appears to have been made from the discard of a dozen generations of houses.

Some of the yards are thick with rusting cans, old tires and miscelaneous rubbish. Some of them are so gutted by gully wash that any attempt at beautification would be worse than useless. Some are swept—farm fashion—free from surface dust and twigs. Some attempt—others achieve grass and flowers. Vegetable gardens are far less frequent than they should be, considering space left bare.

The interviewer frankly lost her way several times. One improper direction took her fully half a mile beyond her destination. From a hilltop she could look down on less elevated hills and into narrow valleys. The impression was that of a cheaply painted back-drop designed for a "stock" presentation of "Mrs. Wiggs of the Cabbage Patch."

Moving along streets, alleys and paths backward "toward town" the interviewer reached another hill. Almost a quarter of a mile away she spied an old colored man sunning himself on the front porch of a well kept cottage. Something about his white hair and erectly-slumped bearing screamed "Ex-slave" even at that distance. A negro youth was passing.

"I beg your pardon, can you tell me where to find Wade Street and James Baker?" "Ya—ya—ya—s ma'am. Dat—dat—dat's de house over da—da—da—da—r. He—he—he lives at his daughter's." "Could that be he on the porch?" Ya—ya—yas ma'am. Dat—dat—dat's right."

"Yes, ma'am I'm James Baker. Yes ma'am I remembers about the war. You want to talk to me about it. Let me get you a chair. You'd rather sit right there on the step? All right ma'am.

I was born in Hot Spring county, below Malvern it was. I was borned on the farm of a man named Hammonds. But I was pretty little when he sold me to some folks named Fenton. Wasn't with them so very long. You know how it goes—back in them days. When a girl or a boy would marry, why they'd give them as many black folks as they could spare. I was give to one of the daughters when she marrried. She was Mrs. Samuel Gentry.

I wasn't so very big before the war. So I didn't have to work in the fields. Just sort of played around. Can't remember very much about what happened then. We never did see no fighting about. They was men what passed through. They was soldiers. They come backwards and forewards. I was about as big as that boy you see there"—pointing to a lad about 8 years old—"some of them they was dressed in blue—sort of blue. We was told that they was Federals. Then some of them was in grey—them was the Southerners.

No, we wasn't scared of them—either of them. They didn't never bother none of us. Didn't have anything to be scared of not at all. It wasn't really Malvern we was at—that was sort of before Malvern come to be. Malvern didn't grow up until after the railroad come through. The town was across the river, sort of this side. It was called Rockport. Ma'am—you know about Rockport"—a delighted chuckle. "Yes, ma'am. don't many folks now-a-days know about Rockport. Yes ma'am the river is pretty shoaly right there. Pretty shoaly. Yes ma'am there was lots of doings around Rockport. Yes ma'am. Dat's right. Before Garland county was made, Rockport was the capitol—I mean de county seat of Hot Spring County. Hot Springs was in that county at that time. There was big doings in town when they held court. Real big doings.

No, ma'am I didn't do nothing much when the war was over. No, I didn't go to be with my daddy. I moved over to live with a man I called Uncle Billy—Uncle Billy Bryant he was. He had all his family with him. I stayed with him and did what he told me to—'til I grew up. He was always good to me —treated me like his own children.

Uncle Billy lived at Rockport. I liked living with him. I remember the court house burned down—or blowed down—seems like to me it burned down. Uncle Billy got the job of cleaning bricks. I helped him. That was when they moved over to Malvern—the court house I mean. No—no they didn't. Not then, that was later—they didn't build the railroad until later. They built it back—sort of simple like—built it down by Judge Kieth's.

No ma'am. I don't remember nothing about when they built the railroad. You see we lived across the river—and I guess—well I just didn't know nothing about it. But Rockport wasn't no good after the railroad come in. They moved the court house and most of the folks moved away. There wasn't nothing much left.

I started farming around there some. I moved about quite a bit. I lived down sort of by Benton too for quite a spell. I worked around at most any kind of farming.

'Course most of the time we was working at cotton and corn. I's spent most of my life farming. I like it. Moved around pretty considerable. Sometimes I hired out—sometimes I share cropped—sometimes I worked thirds and fourths. What does I mean by hired out—I means worked for wages. Which way did I like best—I'll take share-cropping. I sort of like share-cropping.

I been in Hot Springs for 7 years. Come to be with my daughter." (An interruption by a small negro girl—neatly dressed and bright-eyed. Not content with watching from the sidelines she had edged closer and squatted comfortably within a couple of feet of the interviewer. A wide, pearly grin, a wee pointing forefinger and, "Granddaddy, that ladys got a tablet just like Aunt Ellen. See, Grandddaddy.") "You mustn't bother the lady. Didn't your mother tell you not to stop folks when they is talking."—the voice was kindly and there was paternal pride in it. A nickle—tendered the youngster by the interviewer—and guaranteed to produce a similar tablet won a smile and childish silence.

Yes, ma'am, I lives with my daughter—her name is Lulu Mitchell. She owns her house—yes ma'am it helps. But it's sure hard to get along. Seems like it's lots harder now than it used to be when I was gitting started. Lulu works—she irons. Another daughter lives right over there. Her name's Ellen. She works too—at what she can get to do. She owns her house too.

Three of my daughters is living. Been married twice—I has. Didn't stay with the last one long. Yes ma'am I been coming backwards and forewards to Hot Springs all my life—you might say. 'Twasn't far over and I kept a'coming back. Been living all around here. It's pretty nice being with my daughter. She's good to me. I loves my granddaughter. We has a pretty hard time—harder dan what I had when I was young—but then it do seem like it's harder to earn money dan what it was when I was young."

Golden, Joe
Age: 86
722 Gulpha Street
Hot Springs, Arkansas
Interviewer: Mary D. Hudgins
[M:9: pt. 3: 47–52]

"Yes, ma'am to be sure I remembers you. I knew your father and all his brothers. I knew your mother's father and your grandmother, and all the

Denglers. Your grandpappy was mighty good to me. Your grandmother was too. Many's the day your uncle Fred followed me about while I was hunting. I was the only one what your grandpappy would let hunt in his garden. Yes, ma'am! If your grandmother would hear a shot across the hill in the garden, she'd say, "Go over and see who it is." And your grandfather would come. He'd chase them away. But if it was me, he'd go back home and he'd tell her, "It's just Joe. He's not going to carry away more than he can eat. Joe'll be all right."

Yes, ma'am. I was born down at Magnet Cove. I belonged to Mr. Andy Mitchell. He was a great old man, he was. Did he have a big farm and lot of black folks? Law, miss, he didn't have nothing but children, just lots of little children. He rented me and my pappy and my mother to the Sumpters right here in Hot Springs.

I can remember Hot Springs when there wasn't more than three houses here. Folks used to come thru and lots of folks used to stay. But there wasn't more than three families lived here part of the time.

Yes, ma'am we worked. But we had lots of fun too. Them was exciting times. I can remember when folks got to shooting at each other right in the street. I run off and taken to the woods when that happened. No, miss, we didn't live in Hot Springs all thru the war. When the Federals taken Little Rock they taken us to Texas. We stayed there until '68. Then we come back to Hot Springs.

Yes, miss, Hot Springs was a good place to make money. Lots of rich folks was coming to the hotels. Yes, ma'am, I made money. How'd I make it? Well, lots of ways. I used to run. I was the fastest runner what was. Folks would bet on us, and I'd always win. Then I used to shine shoes. Made money at it too. Lots of days I made as much as $4 or $5. Sometimes I didn't even stop to eat. But I was making money, and I didn't care.

Then there was a feller, a doctor he was. He give me a gun. I used to like to hunt. Hunted all over these mountains (units of Hot Springs National Park), hunted quail and hunted squirrel and a few times I killed deers. The man what gave me the gun he promised me twenty five cents apiece for all the quail I could bring him. Lots of times I came in with them by the dozen.

I tried to save my money. Didn't spend much. I'd bring it home to my mother. She'd put it away for me. But if my pappy knowed I got money he'd take it away from me and buy whiskey. You might know why, miss. He was part Creek—yes ma'am, part Creek Indian.

Does you remember chinquepins? They used to be all over the hill up yonder. I used to get lots of them. Sell them too. One time I chased a deer up there. Got him with a knife, didn't have a gun. The dogs cornered him for me. Best dog I ever had, his name was Abraham Lincoln. He was extra good for a possum dog. Once I got a white possum in the same place I got a deer. It was way out yonder—that place there ain't nothing but rocks. Yes, ma'am, Hell's Half Acre (spot without soil or vegetation—broken talus rock).

Yes, miss, I has made lots of money in my time. Can't work none now. Wish you had got to me three years ago. That was before I had my stroke. Can't think of what I want to say, and can't make my mouth say it. You being patient with me. I got to take time to think.

Me and my wife we gets along pretty well. We have our home, and then I got other property. (Home clean, well painted and cared for, two story, large lot. Rental cottage, good condition, negro neighborhood.) We was real well off. I had $1200 in the bank—Webb's Bank when it failed. (Bank owned and operated for and by negroes—affiliated with headquarters of large national negro lodge.) Never got but part of my money back.

When I sold out my bootblack stand I bought a butcher shop. I made a lot of money there. I had good meat, and folks, black folks and white folks came to buy from me. So you remembers my barbecue, do you? Yes, miss, I always tried to make it good. Yes, I remembers your pappy used to always buy from me.

Your grandmother was a good woman. I remember when your Uncle Freddy had been following me around all day while I was hunting—it was in your grandpappy's garden—his vinyard too—it was mighty big. I told Freddy he could have a squirrel or a quail. He took the squirrel and I gave him a couple of quail too. Went home with him and showed your grandmother how they ought to be fixed.

I can remember before your father lived in Hot Springs. He and his brothers used to come thru from Polk County. They'd bring a lot of cotton to sell. Yes, ma'am lots of folks came thru. They'd either sell them here or go on to Little Rock. Lots of Indians—along with cotton and skins they'd bring loadstone. Then when your pappy and his brothers had a hardware store I bought lots of things from them. Used to be some pretty bad men in Hot Springs— folks was mean in them days. I remember when your father kept two men from killing each other. Wish, I wish I could remember better. This stroke has about got me.

Yes, miss, that was the garden. I used to sell garden truck too. Had a bush fence around it long before a wire one. Folks used to pass up others folks to buy truck from me. Your mother did.

Life's been pretty good to me. I've lived a long time. And I've done a lot. Made a lot of money, and didn't get beyond the third grade (no public schools in Hot Springs until the late 1870s). Can't cultivate the garden now. My wife does well enough to take care of the yard. She's a good woman, my wife is.

So you're going to Fayetteville to see Miss Adeline? I remember Miss Adeline (the Adeline Blakely of another Arkansas interview with slaves). She worked for your pappy's brother didn't she. Yes, I knowed her well. I liked her.

Yes miss, I'm sort of tired. It's hard to think. And I can't move about much. But I got my home and I got my wife and we're comfortable. Thank you."

Interviewer's note:
I left him sitting and rocking gently in a home-made hickory stationary swing eyes half closed looking out across his yard and basking in the warm sunshine of late afternoon.

Howard County

Claridy, George Washington
Age: 84
Oklahoma City, Oklahoma
Interviewer: Willie Allen
2 July 1937
[OK: 76–78]

I was bo'n in Centerpoint, Howard County, Arkansas, October 5, 1853, so dey tell me; dat's all I know'd 'cep' what dey tell me for the truth.

Well, it's kinda surprise for someone to come around to talk to me. I never gits to talk to anybody much; folks don't care nothing bout me; dey all calls me de drunkard, gambler, horse thief and murderer. I'se been practically all dem things too. I'se been a wicked man ever since my first wife died. I confessed religion in 1863 and lived like a gentleman until de death of my wife; den I felt lak everything I had was gone so I jes started getting drunk, gambling and raising hell. I'se never fooled with any woman to mount to nothin since my wife died; I jes get drunk, gambled and forgot about de women. I've made lots o' money gambling and selling whiskey. I've seed de time when I would write a check for five thousand dollars any day. Cose I ain't got nothin' now. Jes lak I made it I let it get away from me, jes dat quick. I got in jail once bout some whiskey. I had a fellow to build me a barn right dere on dat corner, (1st and Central) and underneath dat barn I had him to build a place for me to hide my whiskey. I done good business for a long time den I decided to have me a house build so got dis same fellow dat built de barn to figger wid me on de house. Well, he knew I had plenty money so he tried to skin me, so I got a nudder fellow and he figured de house three hundred dollars cheaper. Well, I let him build it for me. Now here's what happened: dat other low down rat, jes cause I wouldn't let him skin me out o' my money he went to the sheriff's office and told him about dis place he built fo me to keep my whiskey. Well, de sheriff come out dere and began to look around fo de stuff and when he found de place, it was locked in. He told me to unlock it and he would tare de place up, pore out de whiskey, and let me go. Cose you know I was lak most Niggers would be wid a little money; I cussed him out, told him dat was my place and he better not put his damn hand on it. He didn't say a word; he jes went back got some mo fellows and dey come dere, broke dat place open and carried away seven hundred and seventy-five dollars worth of whiskey for me. Well dey put me in jail and I stayed dere one hundred and fifteen days. It cost me a lot o' money to keep from going to the peniteniary. I gave old Norman Pruitt nigh five thousand dollars to get me out of it.

Ah! kid, I tell yo I am George Washington Claridy; I'se been into a little o' everything; I know de ropes. Cose dey call me a murderer, but I ain't never killed nobody. Dey jes put dat on to it case I'se such a wicked fellow. I ain't no count now. I'se such a wicked fellow. I ain't no count now. I jes drag around; I don't ask nobody fo nothin'. I ain't never asked anybody for a dime in my life. I gits a little $21.50 check from de pension folks each month and I makes dat last me.

Now you want me to tell you somethin' about slavery times: sorry I got away from you in de beginning, but I jes lak to tell folks de kind o' life I've lived. Well, my father and mother was named Cats and Clarenda Claridy. Dey came from South Carolina, I don't know what place; all I know is jes South Carolina. I have two brothers and two sisters; cose one brother and one sister is jes half brother and sister to me, case after my pa went to de war and never did come back, my mother had dese two kids by another man. Now James and Ann Claridy was my whole brother and sister, and John and Arena was my half brother and sister. I don't know what their las name is case I never did know what the fellow's name was my mother married the second time.

We were good livers on plantation, ole Master laked us a lot. He let us live in de best house on de plantation. It was as good as a lot o' dese little shacks you see over here now. De beds was alright, cose we slept on straw mattresses but that didn't make no diffunce to us; dey slept mighty fine.

Well, I don't recollect nothin bout my grandmother, only a little dat my grandfather told me. Now, I know a lots bout him cose we stayed on with old Master for six months after freedom, den we started to workin on halves for a nudder fellow down there in Arkansas. We started out hoping dat we would soon be able to buy us a farm of our own, so we began saving every dime we could git our hands on, and we did dat for eight years, den my grandpa got down wid de rheumatism. Dere was a old lady in dat contry dat was a good doctor fo dat kind a stuff; so we sent for her. She came over dere and doctored on my grandpa and it seemed to have done lots o' good; so after dat, we would send for her every two or three days, and he kept on getting better and better. Now we jes kept our money in a sack hanging on de wall and every time she came, I would git de sack off of de wall, pay her and put it back. So finally, one day after Pa had got up enough to walk and thought he could make it alright from then on, we decided we would go out and git the old lady some vegetables to take home wid her. While we were gone, I be-dog-gone if that old lady didn't git that sack and we haven't seen or heard from her since. We had purty near a thousand dollars in that sack too.

Well, I'll tell you how I feel about religion. Now I jined that church once, but I soon found out dat most o' de folks in dere didn't have religion, even de preacher. De biggest thing they want is money. Since I'se found dat out de only thing I do is read my Bible every day and try to treat my fellow man right; cose I tell you I don't believe in dis here singing and shouting on Sunday and raising de devil wid yo neighbor on Monday.

I neber did no nothing bout Abraham Lincoln, Jeff Davis and dem fellows. I jes heard bout 'em. Cose dey was mighty big men from what I could hear.

Well, I'll tell we lived mighty good in slavery time days, dat is, our family did, but even at dat price, I would hate to have to go over it again; yes sir I sho' would.

Jameson, Hannah
Age: 86?
Bright Star, Arkansas
Interviewer: Alex Hampton, P.W.
Marshall, Texas
[S2:6 (TX, pt. 5): 1933–38]

Hannah Jameson, an aged Negress of Marshall, was born in Bright Star, Arkansas, about 1850, as a slave of Henry Larry. During her childhood Hannah's father was sold off the place and her mother was given another husband, Cole Copeland. During the war, 1863, Hannah's Master brought his family and a large number of slaves to Texas and settled a plantation near Hughes Springs. Hannah's mother and step-father and family remained on their owner's place for about five years. Hannah married John Jameson, moving to Jefferson and later to Marshall. She has been married twice and raised

four step-children. Since her separation from her second husband, five years
ago, she has been supported by her step-children and Government relief. She
now lives with a widowed sister on the Carters Ferry Road, in southwest sub-
urbs of Marshall and receives a $12.00 per month old age pension.

My name is Hannah Jameson. I 'members coming to Texas in 1863, when
I was 'bout thirteen years old. I can read and write and tell you lots 'bout
slavery times.

I 'members where I was bo'n back in Arkansas, close to Bright Star. There
was no towns much dem days. Bright Star was jest a village. There was a store
and postoffice and a man rid (rode) a mule and carried mail on a ten mile
route.

My father come from North Carolina with Henry Larry and my mother
come from Mississippi with John Paterson. The Patersons and Larrys settled
on a jinning places there in Arkansas. John Paterson sold my father to Henry
Larry and Larry give him to my mother for her man. There warn't no wedding by law and preachers dem days. My mother was named Fannie. She
raised three slavery children, me and my brothers, Nelson and Solomon. Den
Larry sold my father and my mother took Cole Copeland for her man. She
had of the free-bo'n children, William, Jim, Cole, Susie and Mariah. I never
seed my father no mo' after he was sold off the place.

I 'members coming to Texas. My mother say it was in '63. When we left
Arkansas, I was big enuff to milk and churn and tote wood. I 'members dat
like it was yesterday ca'se when we got to Texas they put us out in the woods
in a pen to protect us from the wolves and varmits till them could fix us a
place to live in. Varmits was as thick as they could be and they darsn't let us
out after sundown. Henry Larry built his place right there at Hughes Spring
on the big road to Linden. He fixed a regular place for the Niggers. You never
seed beds like we had them days. They had jest one leg, you couldn't put them
no where but in the corner. They had pole rails and board slats, and dere
warn't no a-falling down to 'em. Den we pulled grass and fix the mattress.

In my owners family there was four boys, Jim, Jeff, John and Shuck. They
done the bossing. My Mistress was Nancy. She had two girls, Caldonia and
Miss Ella. Our white folks warn't cruel to us. My Master had 'bout fifty
Niggers, he didn't own big droves like some of the owners. All the white folks
warn't alike. There was good and bad like today. Some wouldn't give you no
chance, I'se seed them on jinning places tie Niggers hand with a rope and
whip them till all they could say was, "Pray, Master". At night they cooked a
little supper, did their task and go to bed. Every Saturday the owners give
them rations. If it didn't last—do the best you could to Saturday agin. They

got what the white folks say to get out of the garden. There was no chance to have their own gardens. The good folks give the Niggers parties, but the bad ones didn't give them a chance to get over the fence. Lots of them had to wash at night and on Sunday, down by the spring by a pine knot torch, ca'se they had to come out clean Monday morning. Most of the owners worked the Niggers all day Saturday. At night the wimmen had to spin three or four curts of cloth. The men had a task and if they didn't done it, there was where a whipping scrape come in.

I never seen any Niggers sold, but seed them driv' down the road to the sale block. The owners went to sell off their Niggers the first of January.

We liked our white folks ca'se they warn't cruel to us and teached us to read and write. I tell you how that was. Ole Mistress girls and boys all had them a little Nigger. Miss Ella was my young Mistress. She divide her bread and meat with me and take her book and give me my A B Cs. The white boy and the Nigger et bread and meat together, played together and if old Master or Mistress started to whip him, he would say, "This is my Nigger, don't thrash him".

I sho' members them corn shuckings. Dey was sumpin. After the corn was all husked and all the white folks was gone to bed they danced the rabbit dance and sing alike this:

> Early one morning, on my Massa's farm
>   Cut that pigeon wing, Lizy Jane
> I heard dem chickens a-givin the alarm
>   shake yo feet, Miss Lizy Jane
> Shake yo feet, Niggers, It'll soon be day,
>   Skoot along lively, Miss Lizy Jane;
> Massa ketch us dancin', there'll be — to pay,
> We got taters to dig and hoe dat corn
>   Hit dat duffle-shiffle, Lizy Jane
> You'd bettter be a-humpin, coz it'll soon be morn,
> Shake dat balmoral, Lizy Jane.

Lordy me, dem was the times. De best days of dis ole Niggers life am gone, but when I think of the good times before the war, dese bones of mine get to live agin like dey was at dem parties when de niggers knocked off dat:

> Rooster in de chicken coop, crowing for day
> Horses in the stable go nay, nay, nay
> Ducks in the yard go quack, quack, quack,
> And de geese go filley-I-fee,
> Pigs in the pen squealing for slop,

> Big dogs barking like they never will stop,
> Guines in de tree go pat-a-rack, pat-a-rack
> And de goose go filley-I-fee.

When we was coming to Texas I seed the soldiers and heard 'em say, "Them is Yankees going to fight". My Master's boy, Shuck, he fit (fight) in the war but warn't shot. I waited on my Mistress and fetched her things when we was a-coming to Texas, and in Arkansas. The first work I done in slavery was waiting on Mistress and toting water to the field. I don't 'members much of de war 'cept dem soldiers going to fit (fight).

Master told us we was free. At first he wouldn't, den he had to. He told all the Niggers, "You is free; you got no more Master and Mistress; you can go or stay". When surrender broke, you could tie all a Nigger family had in a bed sheet. They had nothing 'cept a house full of Niggers and no where to go. Most of the old ones stayed with old Master, but the young ones separated.

I married five years after surrender to John Jameson and we come to Jefferson. We stayed there 'bout five years and come on to Marshall and here I still is and don't know zactly how old I is.

Me and Jameson lived together twenty years and he died. I married a Nigger, Creer, but he was so no account I quit him and took back on Jameson's name.

I sho do 'members the Ku Klux raging and beating folks. That's the reason ma and my step-pa stayed with old Master. He protect them.

I don't take no stock in politics. I leave that to the men folks. If'n they can't tend to it, I don't see dat de wimmen would help things any.

I don't know 'bout these young ones that is a-coming up. I worked for the white folks as long as I was able to work and didn't take no stock in their doings.

Me and my sister, Mariah, bo'n the second year of surrender, live by ourself. The relief folks helped us on. I gets $12.00 a month pension and dat man at de courthouse say Mariah is going to get hers.

Stewart, Minnie Johnson
Age: 60?
3210 W. Sixteenth Street
Little Rock, Arkansas
Interviewer: Samuel S. Taylor
[M:10: pt. 6: 236–37]

"My mother's name was Mahala McElroy. Her master's name was Wiley McElroy. She was living in Howard County, Arkansas near Nashville. She worked in the field, and sewed in the house for her mistress. One time she said she never would forget about slavery was a time when she was thirteen years old, and the overseer beat her.

"My mother was a real bright woman with great long black hair. Her master was her father. She told me that the overseer grabbed her by her hair and wound it 'round his arm and then grabbed her by the roots of it and jerked her down to the ground and beat her till the blood ran out of her nose and mouth. She was 'fraid to holler.

"Mother married when she was fourteen. I can't remember the name of her husband. The preacher was an old man, a faith doctor, who read the ceremony. His name was Lewis Hill.

"I heard mother say they beat my brother-in-law (his name was Dave Denver) till he was bloody as a hog. Then they washed him down in salt and water. Then they beat him again because he hollered.

"She told us how the slaves used to try to pray. They were so scared that the overseer would see them that early in the morning while they were going to their work in the field at daybreak that they would fall down on one knee and pray. They were so 'fraid that the overseer would catch them that they would be watching for him with one eye and looking for God with the other. But the Lord understood.

"My mother was seventy years old when she died. She has been dead thirty years."

Thompson, Ellen Briggs
Age: 83
3704 W. Twelfth Street
Little Rock, Arkansas
Interviewer: Samuel S. Taylor
[M:10: pt. 6: 309–14]

Birth and Relatives
"I was born in October 1844 in Nashville, Arkansas. I don't remember the exact day. I have went through thick and thin. I was a small girl when my mother died. I got the rheumatism so bad I can't hardly walk. It hurts me now. My oldest brother, Henry Briggs, was five years older than me, and my youngest brother, Isaac Briggs, was five years younger than me. I was born October, but he was born at Christmas Eve just after surrender. My oldest brother died last year. My youngest brother is in Galveston, Texas. If he is living, he is there. My name was Briggs before I married. I was just studying about my sister-in-law when you come up. If I could get the money, I would

go to see her. She was my oldest brother's wife. Her name was Frances Briggs after she marrried. She lives in Emmet, Arkansas, where he married her. I just had two brothers, no sisters.

"My husband's name was Henry Thompson. He has been dead about twelve or thirteen years. I have had so much sickness I can't remember exactly. I married him a long time ago. I got it put down in the Bible. I married yonder in Emmet, Arkanasas. I ain't got the Bible nor nothing. My brother had it and he is dead.

"My father's name was Daniel Briggs. He died in Hot Springs. We were small children when he and my mother was separated. He was in one place and we were in another. He tried to get us children when he died, but we was little and couldn't get to him. My mother was dead then.

"My mother's name was Susanna Briggs. Her father's name was Isaac Metz. The children left him in South Carolina. The white folks sold them away from him. My mother just had three children: me, and my two brothers. I don't know how many my grandfather had. There were four sisters that I know besides my mother and two boys: Aunt Melissa, and Aunt Jane, and Aunt Annie, and Aunt Sarah, and Uncle Albert Mitchell, and Uncle Ben. My grandmother's name was Betsy. I never got to see her but they told me about her.

Good Masters

"I have heard them say that their white folks didn't whip them. My master was a good man. My young master, when it come to the surrender, slipped back home and told them they was going to be free as ever he was. His name was Joe Mitchell. I never seed my white folks whip anybody in my life. They just never whipped anybody. They never whipped me. I have seen the white folks next to us whip their Negroes and I asked grandma about it. She said that those were their Negroes and she would explain what they was being whipped for. They was on another farm. I don't remember what they was being whipped for.

"My young master told the slaves when he notified them they was free that if they didn't want to stay with him, he would give them enough to go on till they could make it, you know, to keep them from starving. He was a good man.

"The old man, Joe's father, was named Thomas Mitchell. He died before I was born. I never seed him, just knowed his name. Joe's mother was named Isabel Mitchell. I came to be named Briggs because her husband's name was Briggs. He belonged to a Briggs. I don't know what his name was also. They didn't belong to the same master. They used to let them marry. They would fix great big tables. Sometimes they would marry in the home; that was in the winter. Then sometimes they would marry outdoors. Then they would set a long table for all their associates to eat just like you would fix a table for your friends. Looked like they would be so glad to see their boys and girls marry. They would have regular preacher and marry just like they do now.

"There wasn't no breeders on our place. But I have heard of people who did keep a woman just for that purpose. They never whipped her nor nothing. They just let her have children. As soon as she had one, they would take it away from her so that she could have another one right away.

Jayhawkers

"When my young master was gone to the War and the jayhawkers would come around, my young master's mother would take all the colored women and children and lock them up and she would take a big heavy gun and go out to meet them. The jayhawkers were white people who would steal corn and horses and even slaves if they could get them. But colored folks was sharp. They would do things to break their horses' legs and they would run and hide. My uncle was a young boy. He saw the jayhawkers coming once. And he ran and pressed himself under the crib. The space was so small he nearly broke his ribs. His mistress had to get him out and take him to the house.

"My grandmother used to take me with her after dark when she'd go out to pray. She wouldn't go anywhere without me. One time when she was out praying, I touched her and said to her that I heard something in the corn crib. She cut her prayer off right now and went and told it to her old mistress, and to the young master, who was in the house just then telling the Negroes they were all going to be free. The jayhawkers spied us and they got out and went on their way. My young master crawled out and went back to the Confederate army. He had to crawl out because he wanted to keep anybody from seeing him and capturing him.

Soldiers

"I never seed but one or two soldiers. That was after the surrender. I suppose they were Union soldiers. They had on their blue jackets. There never was any fighting in Nashville, while I was living there.

"About all that I knew about the War was that the men went off to fight. None of the colored men went—just the white men. The colored men stayed back and worked in the field. Isabel Mitchell and her boys were bosses. What they said goed.

Slave Houses

"The slaves lived in old log houses. Some of them were plank houses.

Some of the slaves chinked 'em up with dirt. They had these big wooden windows in the houses. Sometimes they would be two, sometimes they would be three windows—one to each room. There would be two or three or four rooms to the house. That would be according to the family. My mother had three girls besides her own children. She had a four-room house. Her house was built right in the white folks' yard. My grandmother didn't work in the field. She tended to the children. She worked in the big house. My mother was boss of the whole thing. She would go and work in the field but grandmother would see after the children. She wouldn't let me go from there to the gate without her. I just had to follow her everywhere she went.

"Grandmother besides taking care of us used to make clothes. She cooked for the white folks. But she sure had to see after us children. I seed after myself. I was all the girl-child there and I just did what I wanted to.

"The country was kind of wild in those days. The deer used to come loping down and we would be scared and run and hide. Some people would set the dogs on them and some people would kill them no matter who they belonged. You see, some people had them as pets.

Amusements

"I never seed nothing in the way of amusements except people going to church and going to parties and all such as that. They believed in going to church. They would have parties at night. The white folks didn't care what they had. They would help prepare for it. They would let 'em have anything they wanted to have and let 'em go to church whenever they wanted to go. And if they took a notion they would have a supper. When they would have a party they would do just like they do now. They would have dancing. I never seen any playing cards. When they danced, somebody would play the fiddle for them. When they had a supper, they would usually sell the things. Then the white folks would come and buy from them. There would be nice looking things on the table.

Church

"They had meetings at Center Point, and at Arkadelphia. And they would let us go to them or anywhere else we wanted. We had to have passes, of course. They had colored preachers. Sometimes the slaves would go to the white people's church. They wouldn't go often, just every once in awhile. White ladies would get after the colored to come and go with them sometimes. Sometimes, too, when they would have a dinner or something, they would take Aunt Sue or mother to cook for them. They wouldn't let nobody meddle with them or bother them—none of the other white folks. And they would let them fix a table for their own friends that they would want to have along.

Personal Occupations

"I used to work in the field or in the house or anything I could get to do. I would even go out and saw these big rails when my husband would have a job and wouldn't get a chance to do it. It has been a good while since I have been able to do any good work. My husband has been dead fifteen years and I had to quit work long before he died.

Right after the War

"Right after the War my folks worked in the field, washed, cooked, or anything they could do. They left the old place and came down about Washington, Arkansas. I don't know just how long they stayed in Washington. From Washington, my mother went to Prescott and settled there at a little place they called Sweet Home, just outside of Prescott. That is where my daughter was born and that is where my mother died. I came here about nine years ago.

Present Support

"I came here to stay with my daughter. But now she doesn't have any help herself. She had three small children and she's their only support now. She's not working either. She just come in from the Urban League looking for a job. They say that they don't have a thing and that the people don't want any women now. They just want these young girls because they make them work cheaper. We have both applied for help from the Welfare but neither of us has gotten anything yet."

Independence County

Osborne, Harve
Age: 101
9 October 1926
[S2:1 (AR): 115–16]

A remarkable character seen daily on the streets of Batesville is Uncle Harve Osborne, negroe ex-slave, who is 101 years old, he has the distinction of being the oldest inhabitant of Independence County.

"Uncle Harve" is a valued employee of the street cleaning department of the city, and despite his age has not missed a day at work this year. He is liked by whites & negroes alike. T. R. Osborne of Ft. Smith (a son of Uncle Harve's old master) gives the year of his birth as 1825. He was born on the Osborne farm on the pigeon river near Ashville, N. Carolina. His first owner was Morgan Osborne. His mind is clear on important incidents of his early days especially before the Civil War. He delights to tell of playing with the picaninnies & dancing to the music of the banjo.

His first duties were driving his master's cows to the pasture in the morning and back again in the evening, working in the field between times.

Tales of the West caused Harve's old master to leave his plantation to a brother and start out for Arkansas, in 1850—at which time Harve was separated from his parents and never saw them again. The trip took over a month, the entire party halting at Batesville. Osborne homesteaded a large tract of land on White River about 10 miles from Batesville, known to this day as the Osborne place. Harve tells of being leased for a year to another plantation and while hoeing cotton he broke a hoe handle. The overseer ordered that he be whipped, but somehow this was delayed because of other duties. In the meantime Harve broke and ran away finally reaching his own masters place and told the story in full. The overseer at once came after him but Osborne refused to turn him over, breaking the contract for the lease.

The outbreak of the Civil War made many changes, Harve was taken to the front by Jonathan and Arch Osborne, nephews of his master, as their bodyguard and servant. Jonathan was killed in battle. Arch was taken prisoner by the Yankees at Helena and never heard of again. After the war ended Harve had many varied experiences. Finally he got back to the old Osborne farm remaining there as hired man till the place was sold. Moving to Batesville 15 years ago, he has been a city employe for the last 5 years & loves the memories of his old master and his slave days. He says he was whipped but 3 times while in slavery and then only with a light switch, his master doing so with reluctance.

[Editor's note: This is a newspaper article, from Clara B. Eno's Scrapbook, Arkansas History Commission.]

Scroggins, Cora

Age: 50
Clarendon, Arkansas
Interviewer: Irene Robertson
[M:10: pt. 6: 134–35]

"My mother was born in Spring Hill, Tennessee and brought to Arkansas by her master. Her name was Margaret. Dr. and Mrs. Porter brought my mother to Batesville, Arkansas when she was eight years old and raised her. She was very light. She had long straight hair but was mixed with white. She never knew much about her parents or people.

"Mr. William Brook (white) came to De Valls Bluff from Tennessee and brought her sister soon after the War. She was a very black woman.

"Dr. Porter had a family. One of their daughters was Mrs. Mattie Long, another Mrs. Willie Bowens. There were others. They were all fine to my mother. She married in Dr. Porter's home. Mrs. Porter had learnt her to sew. My father was a mechanic. My mother sewed for both black and white. She was a fine dressmaker. She had eight children and raised six of us up grown.

"My father was a tall rawbony brown man. His mother was an Indian squaw. She lived to be one hundred seven years old. She lived about with her children. The white folks all called her 'Aunt Matildy' Tucker. She was a small woman, long hair and high cheek bones. She wore a shawl big as a sheet purty nigh all time and smoked a pipe. I was born in Batesville.

"My mother spoke of her one long journey on the steamboat and stage-coach. That was when she was brought to Arkansas. It made a memorable picture in her mind.

"Dr. and Mrs. Porter told her she was free and she could go or stay. And she had nowheres to go and she had always lived with them white folks. She never did like black folks' ways and she raised us near like she was raised as she could.

"She used to tell us how funny they dressed and how they rode at night all through the country. She seen them and she could name men acted as Ku Kluxes but they never bothered her and she wasn't afraid of them.

"I cooked all my life till I got disabled. I never had a child. I wish I had a girl. I've been considered a fine cook all of my life."

Simpson, Burke
Age: 86
Mart, Texas
Interviewer: Miss Effie Cowan, P.W.
8 March 1938
[S2:9: 3556–57]

"I wuz born in de year 1852 in Batesville, Arkansas. My daddy's name wuz Isaac Simpson, an' he took his name from his first Master, a man by de name of Simpson, who sold my folks to de nigger traders, dey wuz my daddy an' mammy an' five chillun in de bunch an' I wuz one of de chillun.

"De way de nigger traders did, dey took de slaves dey trade for in wagons an' travel 'bout from one state to another an' sell dem. Dey would stop at de houses an' ask de owner if he wuz in de market for slaves or mules, if he had any mules. (Dey wuz begginin' to sell de mules den.) W'en dey make de places in de country dey den go to de towns an' den sometimes dey auction dem off, but mostly dey jes traded dem.

"Well de trader who bought my folks cum down into Texas an' at de town of Fairfield he sold us to Rod Oliver de father of Frank Oliver who has a son at Grosbeck now. At dis time dey lived eight miles south of Fairfield, Texas, dis wuz befo' de Civil War. Our new Master Mr. Oliver had a plantation of cotton, corn, an' stock, we lived in de quarters, an' de Massa lived in de big house. I wuz jes a boy w'en we wuz brought to Texas, but I kin 'member how de little town of Fairfield looked whar we went to town on a Saturday. Hit had two or three stores an' a court house, on de court days de crowds would cum from all over de country to do dey tradin' an' to court.

"W'en de Massa send his cotton to de market he sends hit by wagon train driven wid oxen, usually three or four yokes of steers to a wagon, an' he sent hit to San Antonio to sell an' buy de provisions dat could not be gotton at Fairfield, dey would be gone 'bout eight or ten weeks an' dey would haul 'bout eight or ten bales of cotton to a wagon. W'en dey camp at night dey would have bells on de oxen to know how to find dem de next morning.

"De time I am tellin' you 'bout jes before an' right after de Civil War, during de war dey would ship de cotton from San Antonio to Europe thro' Mexico an' hit would bring from fifty cents to a dollar a pound. On account of de Texas ports being blockaded hit wuz hard to ship hit to Europe an' de best way wuz thro' Mexico.

"At dis time de cotton gin wuz run by horse power instid of steam an' wid good steady work dey would gin 'bout four bales a day. De gin house wuz built square, an' de top of hit wuz cut into stalls, de gin stand would set in de top story of de gin, an' de bottom of de house wuz whar de machinery wuz kept. Dey had a big wheel to which de horse wuz hitched to de leavers, de cotton wuz thrown into de lint room after hit wuz ginned an' den dey carried hit up-stairs to de press whar hit wuz put into de box to press. Dey would start de horse aroun' in a circle an' den de follow block, dey called hit, would cum down an' press de bale.

"Dey would tie de bales wid a rope, dese bales weigh 'bout four hundred pounds. During de war dey did'nt have any baggin' or ropes, so dey tie de bales wid hickory switches, an' put boards aroun' de bales. After de war wuz over dey had to rebale hit an' den dey ship hit to de old country hit still sold for high prices like fifty cents to a dollar a bale, an' wuz high for good many years after de war.

"W'en dey send dey cattle to de market from East Texas, San Antonio wuz not as good den as New Orleans, befo' dey started de Chissum Trail from dis country dey would drive dem down de Trinity on down along Sabine Lake thro' Port Arthur an' along de Louisiana coast. W'en de tide had been high or de waters had been up from de rivers, de hard beach shifted an' left stretches of smooth looking sand dat covered up deep bogs an' quicksand an' dis caused dem to lose dey cattle by dem gittin' bogged up. So dis caused them to send de cattle up to Kansas. Dey wuz a way to New Orleans dat led by de old Spanish Trail we call hit now thro' Beaumont an' Orange Texas.

"De old records show dat de toll charges wuz considered fair over de rivers, de ferryman wuz forced by law to keep de cattle pens at de crossings. Each one of de ferrymen had at least one pair of oxen which dey used to lead de ones de cattle men bring to de ferry, de tame oxen would be put in de pen wid de new ones to be shipped, an' driven down a chute into de water, as soon as dey would hit de water dey would start swimming for de other side, den de cowboys would crowd de rest of de cattle down de chute an' dey would fol-low de ferryman's oxen across. In keepin' dem from turning back down de river de wrong way de men would follow dem in boats on bof' sides of de herd an' prod dem wid long poles. One queer thing, de herd would not swim wid de sun in dey eyes an' so dey never crossed de rivers going east in de mornings.

"A charge of a few cents wuz made by de head for herds crossing de rivers, an' de ferryman wuz made to keep de men, boats, cattle pens, an' de tame oxen ready for de use of any one who cum wid a herd. Sometimes dey has to stay over a night or two to cross if de river be up, so dey has to have dese pens.

"Den dey wuz de "Broomtail ponies of East Texas" dat dey would take to de markets an' sell, hit wuz on one of dese trips dat a fellow by de name of Steve Jackson wuz takin' a bunch to find a pasture, dey rode into a fine lookin' lake after dey had cum from a long days ride, so dey stop to water dey horses, but de horses jes took a sniff an' waded out widout drinkin' so dis fellow dat is takin' dem figures dat he kin take a drink if de horses could'nt, so he takes one big mouthful an' let's out a yell, an' tell's de other men dat he is poisoned, so dey think he is going to die but 'stid of dying he feels better next day. Dey decides dat dis is a lake of mineral water, so de story goes dat he bought a big tract of land an' dey bore wells dat has been used for a health resort.

"While I am telling you 'bout de way dey lived I must tell yer 'bout how w'en hit wuz hard to git salt dat dey find hit at a place called Horsehead

Crossing on de Pecos River, hit wuz a long an' dangerous trip an' go on out to de Pecos for salt. De men would got to de salt beds whar de salt an' de water wuz mixed an' wade out an' pile hit into big heaps an' leave hit untill de water an' de sand run out of hit, dis left de salt dat wuz loaded into wagons to take back wid dem.

"Sometimes after dis dey discovered dat dey could make salt by de use of large pots an' de evaporation by steam on Salt Creek in Lampasas county near de present town of Lometa, an' dis made hit lots easier for de folks in dis part of Texas to have de salt, but dis wuz one of de things dat dey had to do wid out durin' de war an' one of de things dat wuz needed de most.

"But I must tell yer more 'bout Fairfield, but de things dat I has told yer 'bout how far dey had to go jes for dese little things dat we has at our door now is de truth, de folks now-a-days does not know how easy dey lives to what dey did den.

"In Fairfield dey had a Baptist school dey called de Fairfield Baptist College, de girls building wuz 'bout five miles east of town, an' de boys building wuz in town, de young folks dat cum from other towns boarded in dese halls for de young men an' de wimmen, dey had 'bout fifty boarders at each one of de halls de bes' dat I kin recolleck. I has heard dem talk 'bout w'en dey had de examinations dey has de pupils folks to cum if dey can, an' dey gives de examinations publicly.

"De way dey cooked for de College dey had de kitchen set off from de house in de back yard, dey cooked on a big hearth wid de iron kettles hung from de pot rack or skillets set over de coals of fire, den dey would heap de coals on de lid of de oven. De groceries wuz kept in a big smoke house near de kitchen an' dey kept hit locked 'ceptin' w'en dey go to git de groceries. De nigger slaves would bring de food into de dining room an' as dey did'nt have any screens a nigger girl would stand at de head of de table an' wave a fan or pine bough to keep de flies away from de table while dey wuz eating.

"W'en de Civil War cum de wimmin made de canteen covers, knitted de socks an' helped to git de men ready for de first call for volunteers. De folks in Fairfield gave a big barbecue to de company of soljers dat went from Fairfield an' de country 'round hit. Miss Mollie Graves, a school teacher in de College gave de company a flag an' de boys marched away wid hit wavin' over dem.

"W'en de older men left at de last call den de wimmen had to manage by demselves except de help of de slaves who kept de work on de plantations going, for dey had to keep on livin' an' some one had to do dis work, de slaves whar I lived jes stayed on an' took keer of thing for de Master while dey wuz away to de war.

"De wimmen spun an' weve de cloth for de clothes for de men an' sent to dem in de army, as well as for de use of de folks at home. Some of dese men wuz stationed at Galveston. Calico wuz a dollar a yard an' hit took ten yards to make a ladies dress. During de war if a man had a fambly sometimes dey would hire a man to go in his place, den dey would take dey slaves to go an' build de breastworks, dey wuz two dat went from de Stroud fambly, dey wuz John an' Noel Stroud. One got killed an' de [sic] cum back.

"Dey wuz de Stroud an' Oliver famblies, w'en Rod Oliver died I fell to one of his son-in-laws, by de name of Stroud. I lived on de Stroud plantation, 'bout eight miles north of Fairfield untill freedom cum. After freedom I left an' cum to de old Springfield community, dis wuz six miles north of whar Grosbeck is now, dey wuz no Grosbeck den. De town of Grosbeck wuz not started until de year 1870 w'en de Houston an' Texas Central railroad cum thro' hit.

"My last Massa's father Logan Stroud had a hundred slaves, today dey is three living, Lunny Giddins, (who took de name of de first man dat owned him) an' Hickory Giddins, an' myself. My mammy Nelly Simpson wuz de mother of thirteen chillun, I am de only one living. She died in 1886.

"During de war dey wuz a man by de name of Jerry Steward, he wuz a w'ite man an' lived 'bout six miles from de Stroud place. He kept blood hounds to track de run-a-way slaves. I kin 'member dey names as well as if hit wuz today, dey wuz named Milo, Jenny Lane, Rock an' Red. I kin hear in my memory how dey would go thro' de country a yelpin' as dey chase de niggers thro' de bottom an' den w'en dey had him up a tree yer could tell by de way dey would bark.

"W'en dey ketch de nigger dey bring him back an' turn him over to de overseer, an' sometimes dey would lock him up or give him a whippin' an' send him to de field. Dey jes had to whip de lazy ones an' de ones dat would not work. De Massa Stroud an' Oliver, all dey had mostly wuz good niggers dat stayed wid dem. Maybe because dey wuz good to de slaves.

"Yes, Mam, I kin 'member de Indian tales dat wuz handed down to us from de Tehuacana tribe of Indians lived in de Tehuacana Hills, close to whar I lived all dese years dat I been tellin' yer 'bout. De one dat I like de best is 'bout de young Indian chief called Takiti, dis wuz de story 'bout de Spanish Traders hidin' de gold in de Tehuacana Hills.

"De tribe of Tehuacana Indians wuz in dis section long befo' de w'ite man cum. De town of Tehuacana, south of Mexia, de Tehuacana Creek dat run thro' dis country on down in 'bout six or eight miles of Waco, whar de old Indian trading house Tehuacana Trading House, wuz located, run close to de Brazos river near dis place, wuz all named after dis tribe of Tehuacana Indians.

"De story dat I has been told 'bout what becum of dese Tehuacana Indians wuz dat dey headquarters wuz in de Tehuacana Hills whar de town of Tehuacana is now, dey wuz friendly to de w'ite man, but when de Cherokee Indians cum down into Texas from Arkansas to live, dey wuz attacked by de Waco's, an' de Waco's took a fine lot of horses from dem, jes as dey wuz 'bout to win in a fight to git dey horses back de Tehuacana's cum to de help of de Waco's, and dis caused de Waco to win dis fight, so de Cherokees vowed to have dey revenge on de Tehuacana's.

"De next summer dey make an' attack on de Tehuacana's in dey fort dis Indian fort wuz built of de limestone rock dat Limestone County takes hit's name from, de Tehuacana's wuz holding' out, for dey had dey provisions in de fort, so de Cherokees decided to smoke dem out. Dey bring de grass an' put in de windows an' set fire to hit, an' so w'en de Tehuacana's had to cum out dey massacreed all but 'bout a dozen dat made dey escape.

"So dis Takiti wuz de son of de chief, an' one of de braves dat escaped tell Takiti 'bout de Spanish gold dat wuz buried in de Tehuacana Hills. He is dying an' he tells Takiti de secret of how he watched from behind a tree de Spanish Traders who once traveled across de blue bonnet valleys below de high hills an' had found de buffalo tracks dat led to de spring an' made dey camp. De Tehuacana's had planned to attack dem but de Spaniards had been warned so dey slip away, but befo' dey do dis dey take de sacks from de pack mules an' bury dem, de sacks wuz heavy an' de yellow gold shone in de light as one of de sacks cum open.

"Dey had buried hit near de spring an' marked de spot wid de rocks, dey wuz big rocks dat dey call boulders now. Dey took three of dese big rocks an' laid dem in a circle around de spot dey buried de gold, on each one of dese rocks dey carved a snake wid de head pointing to de center of de pile, for years dis old Indian brave kept his secret, but befo' he died he had told Takiti 'bout hit an' how to find de place. He told him dat "as de son of de old chief hit wuz his duty to go an' find dis gold an' bring hit to his people so dey could live in peace wid de white man an' not have to rob an' steal for dey livin.'"

"He told Takiti de curse dat rested on de spot, for de spirits of de Spaniards kept watch over hit at night, hit would have to be dug in de daytime an' not after dark or by de light of de moon for dis wuz de time de ghosts of de Spaniards walked. So now, after many moons had passed Takiti wuz on his way an' nearly at de end of his journey jes befo' de sun had set. As he climbed de hill de valley turned to blue mists befo' him, an' de sounds of de night cumin' on seemed to whisper in de voice of de birds an' de wind an' de trees words of courage from his people. Dis wuz de first time he had seen de

Tehuacana Hills whar he roamed as a boy since he escaped from de Cherokees wid de few others, an' de sight of de Hills made him happy.

"On de eastern slope of de hill Takiti stopped an' looked an' looked, he could not believe what he saw, could dis land whar for ages his people had celebrated dey tribe dances on dirt dat wuz carried from dey long hunting trips to make a dirt floor, de ground dat had been made sacred by de spirits of de braves who had gone on to de happy huntin' grounds be ruined by a plow? Yes hit wuz so an' towards him a white man wuz walking who spoke to Takiti, but if he answered him hit would be a betrayal of de spirits dat seemed to be whisperin' to him.

"Below, a little ways to de left wuz de spring an' de three big rocks, an' under dem wuz de gold dat would save de few of de tribe dat wuz left, but de white man guarded de spot. Takiti knew dat he could not dig de gold before de white man, an' to wait an' dig hit by de light of de moon, de spirits of de Spaniards dat guarded hit would be there, so dey wuz nothin' he could do but to go back to his people an' try to lead dem on de best he could 'till de bitter end.

"De white man who walked behind Takiti could not know de grief dat wuz in de heart of dis Indian brave as he walked away over de hills wid his eyes on de valley of de land dat his folks had once owned, wid sorrow in his heart he chanted de death song dat go like dis in de English language.

"Oh, Sun, you remain forever, but we Tehuacana's must die,

"Oh, Earth, you remain forever, but we Tehuacana's must die.

"Dey is other legends of de tribe of Tehuacana's handed down by de ones who cum first, but to me dis is one dat always wuz next my heart in de days w'en de Indian legends wuz told 'round de chimbley fire, as de Indians wuz sent to de reservations in my boyhood days."

Van Buren, Nettie
Age: 62
Clarendon, Arkansas
Interviewer: Irene Robertson
[M:11: pt. 7: 5–6]

"My mother was named Isabel Porter Smith. She come from Springville. Rev. Porter brought her to Mississippi close to Holly Springs. Then she come to Batesville, Arkansas. He owned her. He was a circuit rider. I think he was a Presbyterian minister. I heard her say they brought her to Arkansas when she was a small girl. She nursed and cooked all the time. After freedom she went with Reverend Porter's relatives to work for them. I know so very little about what she said about slavery.

"My father was raised in North Carolina. His name was Jerry Smith and his master he called Judge Smith. My father made all he ever had farmin'. He knew how to raise cotton. He owned a home. This is his home (a nice home on River Street in Clarendon) and 80 acres. He sold this farm two miles from here after he had paralasis, to live on.

"My parents had two girls and two boys. They all dead but me. My mother's favorite song was "Oh How I Love Jesus Because He First Loved Me." They come here because my mother had a brother down here and she heard it was such fine farmin' land.

"When I was a little girl my father was a Presbyterian so he sent me to boardin' school in Cotton Plant and then sent me to Jacksonville, Illinois. I worked my board out up there. Mrs. Dr. Carroll got me a place to work. My sister learned to sew. She sewed for the public till her death. She sewed for both black and white folks. I stretches curtains now if I can get any to stretch and I irons. It give me rheumatism to wash. I used to wash and iron.

"My husband cooks on a Government derrick boat. He gits $1.25 and his board. They have the very best things to eat. He likes the work if he can stay well. He can cook pies and fancy cookin'. They like that. Say they can't hardly get somebody work long because they want to be in town every night.

"We have one child. I used to be a primary teacher here at Clarendon.

"I never have voted. My husband votes but I don't know what he thinks about it.

"I try to look at the present conditions in an encouraging way. The young people are so extravagant. The old folks in need. The thing most discouraging is the strangers come in and get jobs home folks could do and need and they can't get jobs and got no money to leave on nor no place to go. People that able to work don't work hard as they ought and people could and willin' to work can't get jobs. Some of the young folks do sure live wild lives. They think only of the present times. A few young folks are buying homes but not half of them got a home. They work where they let 'em have a room or a house. Different folks live all kinds of ways."

Jefferson County

Baltimore, William
Age: 103
Pine Bluff, Arkansas
Interviewer: R. S. Taylor
[S2:1 (AR): 19–24]
[See also M:8: pt. 1: 97–100]

"Uncle" William Baltimore. Twenty Eight Years in Slavery, Never was bought, Never was sold, Threatened once but never was whipped.

Living on Route 1 Pine Bluff, there is a remarkable old negroe called Uncle William Baltimore, who is nearing his one hundred and fourth birthday, he has been totally blind for about twenty three years, blindness in his case occured as the result of a nine months sickness in 1914.

Uncle William was born on what was known as the Dr Waters place, he gives the location of the place as about 12 miles out of Pine Bluff, on the east side of Noble Lake.

His Grandfather & Grandmother, also his Father & Mother were slaves on the Waters plantation before him, so being born in slavery & gaining his liberty at the close of the Civil War, he says, that while he was a slave, he never was bought or sold as such.

He adds to this distinction the statement that he was never whipped, not hiding the fact that he was threatened with a severe whipping once at the same time telling the incident with evident delight.

Dr Waters he says was a very kindhearted man, who never spoke of his "SLAVES", always referring to them as the "SERVANTS", whipping rarely ever being resorted to as a means of punishment. Uncle William who was very well liked by his master, perhaps due to the fact that he was a very capable man, had incurred the displeasure of the overseer for some reason or another. Dr Waters being gone one day this man sought to give some orders to Uncle William who already had orders enough from Dr Waters to keep him busy all day, and insisted on carrying out the first orders, the overseer at once declared he would whip him and make him do as he was told, then got ready to apply the lash, at this point Uncle William straightened up and told the overseer that he would have to prove the better man if the whipping took place. The incident closed at this turn of the tide. As Uncle William told the writer of this experience he added the statement, Mr. Taylor, I was much of a man at that time, even now with 103 years behind him this old fellow retains all the appearance of once having had great muscular power.

At the outbreak of the Civil War Uncle William was taken into the ranks of the Confederacy, being assigned to the duties of a servant, serving in this capacity until 1863, when he was captured by the Yankees who took him to Little Rock, where he was sworn in as a Union Soldier, being kept in the service until 1866, when he was mustered out at Little Rock, the date being September 16.

Uncle William never took part in any fighting but was always kept busy with the countless and never ending tasks peculiar to the army.

He tells of marching from Pine Bluff, on through Ft Smith and the Indian territory of Oklahoma, thence to Leavenworth Kansas and back again to Jefferson County Ark. making the entire journey "on these foot's"

He tells that on this march they camped about 30 miles from Ft Smith, he had had nothing to eat for three days and started out to try and get something. After a while he got hold of a sheep and started back to camp in great glee at the prospects of a big feed of mutton. No sooner had he reached camp and let the sheep down from his shoulders than he was sent on picket duty. Some hours later being relieved from duty he made haste to where he expected to find a chunk of mutton only to find out it had been dressed, cooked and eaten. He never even got a grease spot on his fingers from it.

After being mustered out he went back to Jefferson County and started farming. Some years later he went to Desha County where he opened up a *general blacksmith shop*, he having served as a *blacksmith* while he belonged to Dr Waters.

He tells when you care to question him that there was nothing in the general blacksmith or wagon building business that he was not familiar with, Dr Waters having placed him under the instruction of a highly skilled man to learn this trade, when he was in his early teens.

He made all his own tools. Once when needing a hacksaw, he made one out of an old file, the only material at hand at the time. He recalls making a cotton scraper out of hardwood then putting a steel edge on it, from time to time making anything and everything that was needed in the way of farm tools.

I asked him about wagon building, only to be told he had made more than one wagon out of the raw materials, one piece excepted, the hubs for the wheels being the only parts that were bought ready made.

I visited many a time at McArthur, Desha Co., where he had his shop. Many of the men of that place spoke to me of the skill and excellent workmanship of Uncle William as a blacksmith and wagon builder.

When I first got to know this well liked old fellow I heard of how he patched his own clothes. I also saw specimens of this work, but could never understand how he threaded his needle, but had heard of a little instrument he had made to thread needles with. I tried to figure out what this would be like, but failed to get the idea. One day when calling on him I asked him to let me see his needle threader. He arose and went to a drawer and felt around a bit, then pulled out a very tiny little half arrow, which he had made out of a bit of tin with a pair of scissors and a fine file. He pushed this through the eye of the needle, then hooked the thread on it and pulled it back again, threading his needle as fast as if he had good eyesight.

The patches and the stitches in them were not as neat as his little tool for threading his needle, but he at least covered the holes in his clothes.

Uncle William says his grandmother lived to be well up over 100 years of age, his mother was 100 and his father 96 when they died. He was the eldest of twelve children.

Uncle William's wife died about 20 years ago. She was blind also for several years before she died. Of his boyhood friends he does not know even one now living.

Uncle William and his wife had 12 children, one son and four daughters still living. He came out of Desha County in 1927 during the flood, at that time taking up his residence in Pine Bluff, where he now lives with a grandson.

He joined the Baptist Church in 1870, and has a fairly good grasp of the scriptures, although, having been blind so long he gets his quotations mixed up quite a bit at times.

It may be said that he was very fortunate in having been captured by the Yankees during the war. After he lost his sight he got into pretty hard circumstances, being unable to do any work. The white folks were very good to him in his distress, but it was a sort of a hit and miss way of being cared for. Ultimately some of them got his war record dug up and took his case up with the U.S. government and got him a substantial pension about 16 years ago, so that in his closing days he is well cared for.

It was an interesting experience to visit with this old fellow, truly a link through which you are connected with the past. He not only listens well while you talk to him, but being a good talker himself and having a remarkable memory especially regarding the times and incidents of his life as a slave, and the days that were so trying after the close of the Civil War, a couple of hours with him seems but a little while, and brings many words of gratitude to his lips.

He is very comfortable with his grandson and his wife. Both of them seem very devoted to their grandfather, and extremely courteous to visitors, Quite recently I took some of my Pine Bluff friends with me to visit him. They got a "great kick" out of the visit, but not as much as Uncle William. He having lifted up his heart to God in prayer, giving thanks for the visit of these "white folks" ere we left the house.

Benson, George
Age: 80
Ezell Quarters
Pine Bluff, Arkansas
Interviewer: Mrs. Bernice Bowden
[M:8: pt. 1: 153–54]

"I was here in slavery days—yes ma'm, I was here. When I come here, colored people didn't have their ages. The boss man had it. After surrender, boss man told me I ought to keep up with my age, it'd be a use to me some day, but I didn't do it.

"I member the soldiers would play with me when they wasn't on duty. That was the Yankees.

"I was born down here on Dr. Waters' place. Born right here in Arkansas and ain't been outa Arkansas since I was born. So far as I know, Dr. Waters was good to us. I don't know how old I was. I know I used to go to the house with my mother and piddle around.

"My father jined the Yankees and he died in the army. I heered the old people talkin', sayin' we was goin' to be free. You know I didn't have much sense cause I was down on the river bank and the Yankees was shootin' across the river and I said, 'John, you quit that shootin'!' So you know I didn't have much sense.

"I can remember old man Curtaindall had these nigger dogs. Had to go up a tree to keep em from bitin' you. Dr. Waters would have us take the cotton and hide it in the swamp to keep the Yankees from burnin' it but they'd find it some way.

"Never went to school over two months in all my goin's. We always lived in a place kinda unhandy to go to school. First teacher I had was named Mr. Bell. I think he was a northern man.

"All my life I been farmin'—still do. Been many a day since I sold a bale a cotton myself. White man does the ginnin' and packin'. All I do is raise it. I'm farmin' on the shares and I think if I raise four bales I ought to have two bales to sell and boss man two bales, but it ain't that way.

"I voted ever since I got to be a man grown. That is—as long as I could vote. You know—got so now they won't let you vote. I don't think a person is free unless he can vote, do you? The way this thing is goin', I don't think the white man wants the colored man to have as much as the white man.

"When I could vote, I jus' voted what they told me to vote. Oh Lord, yes, I voted for Garfield. I'se quainted with him—I knowed his name. Let's see—Powell Clayton—was he one of the presidents? I voted for him. And I voted for McKinley. I think he was the last one I voted for.

"I been farmin' all my life and what have I got? Nothin'. Old age pension? I may be in glory time I get it and then what would become of my wife?"

Bertrand, James
Age: 68
1501 Maple Street
Pine Bluff, Arkansas
Interviewer: Samuel S. Taylor
[M:8: pt. 1: 157–58]

"I have heard my father tell about slavery and about the Ku Klux Klan bunch and about the paterole bunch and things like that. I am sixty-eight years old now. Sixty-eight years old! That would be about five years after the War that I was born. That would be about 1870, wouldn't it? I was born in Jefferson County, Arkansas, near Pine Bluff.

"My father's name was Mack Bertrand. My mother's name was Lucretia. Her name before she married was Jackson. My father's owners were named Bertrands. I don't know the name of my mother's owners. I don't know the names of any of my grandparents. My father's owners were farmers.

"I never saw the old plantation they used to live on. My father never told me how it looked. But he told me he was a farmer—that's all. He knew farming. He used to tell me that the slaves worked from sunup till sundown. His overseers were very good to him. They never did whip him. I don't know that he was ever sold. I don't know how he met my mother.

"Out in the field, the man had to pick three hundred pounds of cotton, and the women had to pick two hundred pounds. I used to hear my mother talk about weaving the yarn and making the cloth and making clothes out of the cloth that had been woven. They used to make everything they wore—clothes and socks and shoes.

"I am the youngest child in the bunch and all the older ones are dead. My mother was the mother of about thirteen children. Ten or more of them were born in slavery. My mother worked practically all the time in the house. She was a house worker mostly.

"My father was bothered by the pateroles. You see they wouldn't let you go about if you didn't have a pass. Father would often get out and go 'round to see his friends. The pateroles would catch him and lash him a little and let him go. They never would whip him much. My mother's people were good to her. She never did have any complaint about them.

"For amusement the slaves used to dance and go to balls. Fiddle and dance! I never heard my father speak of any other type of amusement.

"I don't remember what the old man said about freedom coming. Right after the War, he farmed. He stayed right on with his master. He left there before I was born and moved up near Pine Bluff where I was born. The place my father was brought up on was near Pine Bluff too. It was about twenty miles from Pine Bluff.

"I remember hearing him say that the Ku Klux Klan used to come to see us at night. But father was always orderly and they never had no clue against him. He never was whipped by the Ku Klux.

"My father never got any schooling. He never could read or write. He said that they treated him pretty fair though on the farms where he worked after freedom. As far as he could figure, they didn't cheat him. I never had any personal experience with the Ku Klux. I never did do any sharecropping. I am a shoemaker. I learned my trade from my father. My father was a shoemaker as well as a farmer. He used to tell me that he made shoes for the Negroes and for the old master too in slavery times.

"I have lived in Little Rock thirty years. I was born right down here in Pine Bluff like I told you. This is the biggest town—a little bigger than Pine Bluff. I run around on the railroad a great deal. So after a while I just come here to this town and made it my home."

Blackwell, Boston
Age: 98
320 Plum
North Little Rock, Arkansas
Interviewer: Beulah Sherwood Hagg
[M:8: pt. 1: 168–74]

Make yourself comfoble, miss. I can't see you much 'cause my eyes, they is dim. My voice, it kinder dim too. I knows my age, good. Old Miss, she told me when I got sold—"Boss, you is 13—borned Christmas. Be sure to tell your new misses and she put you down in her book." My borned name was Pruitt 'cause I got borned on Robert Pruitt's plantation in Georgia,—Franklin County, Georgia. But Blackwell, it my freed name. You see, miss, after my mammy got sold down to Augusta—I wisht I could tell you the man what bought her, I ain't never seed him since,—I was sold to go to Arkansas; Jefferson county, Arkansas. Then was when old Miss told me I am 13. It was before the Civil War I come here. The onliest auction of slaves I ever seed was in Memphis, coming on to Arkansas. I heerd a girl bid off for $800. She was about fifteen, I reckon. I heerd a woman—a breeding woman, bid off for $1500. They always brought good money. I'm telling you, it was when we was coming from Atlanta.

Do you want to hear how I runned away and jined the Yankees? You know Abraham Lincoln 'claired freedom in '65, first day of January. In October '63 I runned away and went to Pine Bluff to get to the Yankees. I was on the Blackwell plantation south of Pine Bluff in '63. They was building a new house; I wanted to feel some putty in my hand. One early morning I clim a ladder to get a little chunk and the overseer man, he seed me. Here he come, yelling me to get down; he gwine whip me 'cause I'se a thief, he say. He call a slave boy and tell him cut ten willer whips; he gwine wear every one out on me. When he's gone to eat breakfas', I runs to my cabin and tells my sister, "I'se leaving this here place for good." She cry and say, "Overseer man, he kill you." I says, "He kill me anyhow." The young boy what cut the whips—he named Jerry—he come along wif me, and we wade the stream for long piece. Heerd the hounds a-howling, getting ready for to chase after us. Then we hide in dark woods. It was cold, frosty weather. Two days and two nights we traveled. That boy, he so cold and hongry, he want to fall out by the way, but I drug him on. When we gets to the Yankee camp all our troubles was over. We gets all the contraband we could eat. Was they more run-aways there? Oh, Lordy, yessum. Hundreds, I reckon. Yessum, the Yankees feeds all them refugees on contraband. They made me a driver of a team in the quatemasters department. I was always keerful to do everything they told me. They told me I was free when I gets to the Yankee camp, but I couldn't go outside much. Yessum, iffen you could get to the Yankee's camp you was free right now.

That old story 'bout 40 acres and a mule, it make me laugh. Yessum, they sure did tell us that, but I never knowed any pusson which got it. The officers told us we would all get slave pension. That just exactly what they tell. They sure did tell me I would get a passel (parcel) of ground to farm. Nothing ever hatched out of that, neither.

When I got to Pine Bluff I stayed contraband. When the battle come, Captain Manly carried me down to the battle ground and I stay there till fighting was over. I was a soldier that day. No'um, I didn't shoot no gun nor cannon. I carried water from the river for to put out the fire in the cotton bales what made the breas'works. Every time the 'Federates shoot, the cotton, it come on fire; so after the battle, they transfer me back to quartemaster for driver. Captain Dodridge was his name. I served in Little Rock under Captain Haskell. I was swored in for during the war (Boston held up his right hand and repeated the words of allegiance). It was on the corner of Main and Markham street in Little Rock I was swored in. Year of '64. I was 5 feet, 8 inches high. You says did I like living in the army? Yessum, it was purty good. Iffen you obeyed them Yankee offices they treated you purty good, but iffen you didn't, they sure went rough on you.

You says you wants to know how I live after soldiers all go away? Well, firstes thing, I work on the railroad. They was just beginning to come here. I digged pits out, going along front of where the tracks was to go. How much I get? I get $1.00 a day. You axes me how it seem to earn money? Lady, I felt like the richess man in the world! I boarded with a white fambly. Always I was a watching for my slave pension to begin coming. 'Fore I left the army my captain, he told me to file. My file number, it is 1,115,857. After I keeped them papers for so many years, white and black folks bofe told me it ain't never coming—my slave pension—and I reckon the chilren tored up the papers. Lady, that number for me is filed in Washington. Iffen you go there, see can you get my pension.

After the railroad I went steamboating. First one was a little one; they call her Fort Smith 'cause she go from Little Rock to Fort Smith. It was funny, too, her captain was name Smith. Captain Eugene Smith was his name. He was good, but the mate was sure rough. What did I do on that boat? Missy, was you ever on a river boat? Lordy, they's plenty to do. Never is no time for rest. Load, onload, scrub. Just you do whatever you is told to do and do it right now, and you'll keep outen trouble, on a steamboat, or a railroad, or in the army, or wherever you is. That's what I know.

Yessum, I reckon they was right smart old masters what didn't want to let they slaves go after freedom. They hated to turn them loose. Just let them work on. Heap of them didn't know freedom come. I used to hear tell how the govmint had to send soldiers away down in the far back country to make them turn the slaves loose. I can't tell you how all them free niggers was living; I was too busy looking out for myself. Heaps of them went to farming. They was share croppers.

Yessum, miss, them Ku-Kluxers was turrible,—what they done to people. Oh, God, they was bad. They come sneaking up and runned you outen your house and taken everything you had. They was rough on the women and chilren. People all wanted to stay close by where soldiers was. I sure knowed they was my friend.

Lady, lemme tell you the rest about when I runned away. After peace, I got with my sister. She's the onliest of all my people I ever seed again. She telled me she was skeered all that day, she couldn't work, she shake so bad. She heerd overseer man getting ready to chase me and Jerry. He saddle his horse, take his gun and pistol, bofe. He gwine kill me on sight, but Jerry, he say he bring him back, dead or alive, tied to his horse's tail. But he didn't get us, Ha, Ha, Ha. Yankees got us.

Now you wants to know about this voting business. I voted for Genral Grant. Army man come around and registered you before voting time. It wasn't no trouble to vote them days; white and black all voted together. All you had to do was tell who you was vote for and they give you a colored ticket. All the men up had different colored tickets. Iffen you're voting for Grant, you get his color. It was easy. Yes Mam! Gol 'er mighty. They was colored men in office, plenty. Colored legislaturs, and colored circuit clerks, and colored county clerks. They sure was some big officers colored in them times. They was all my friends. This here used to be a good county, but I tell you it sure is tough now. I think it's wrong—exactly wrong that we can't vote now. The Jim Crow law, it put us out. The Constitution of the United States, it give us the right to vote; it made us citizens, it did.

You just keeps on asking about me, lady. I ain't never been axed about myself in my whole life! Now you wants to know after railroading and steam-boating what. They was still work the Yankee army wanted done. The war had been gone for long time. All over every place was bodies buried. They was bringing them to Little Rock to put in Govmint graveyard. They sent me all over the state to help bring them here. Major Forsythe was my quartemaster then. After that was done, they put me to work at St. John's hospital. The work I done there liked to ruin me for life. I cleaned out the water closets. After a while I took down sick from the work—the scent, you know—but I keep on till I get so for gone I can't stay on my feets no more. A misery got me in the chest, right here, and it been with me all through life; it with me now. I filed for a pension on this ailment. I never did get it. The Govmint never took care of me like it did some soldiers. They said I was not a 'listed man; that I was a employed man, so I couldn't get no pension. But I filed, like they told me. I telled you my number, didn't I? 1,115,827, Boston Blackwell. I give my whole time to the govmint for many years. White and black bofe always telling me I should have a pension. I stood on the battlefield just like other soldiers. My number is in Washington. Major Forsythe was the one what signed it, right in his office. I seed him write it.

Then what did I do? You always asking me that. I was low er long time.

When I finally get up I went to farming right here in Pulaski county. Lordy, no, miss, I didn't buy no land. Nothing to buy with. I went share cropping with a white man, Col. Baucum. You asking me what was the shares? Worked on halvers. I done all the work and fed myself. No'um, I wasn't married yit. I took the rheumatiz in my legs, and got short winded. Then I was good for nothing but picking cotton. I kept on with that till my eyes, they got so dim I couldn't see to pick the rows clean. Heap o'times I needed medicine—heap o'times I needed lots of things I never could get. Iffen I could of had some help when I been sick, I mought not be so no account now. My daughter has taked keer of me ever since I not been able to work no more.

I never did live in no town; always been a country nigger. I always worked for white folks, nearly. Never mixed up in big crowds of colored; stayed to myself. I never been arrested in my whole life; I never got jailed for nothing. What else you want to know, Miss?

About these days, and the young folks! Well, I ain't saying about the young folks; but they—no, I wouldn't say. (He eyed a boy working with a saw.) Well, I will say, they don't believe in hard work. Iffen they can make a living easy, they will. In old days, I was young and didn't have nothing to worry about. These days you have to keep studying where you going to get enough to eat.

Buttler, Henry H.
Age: 87
1308 E. Bessie Street
Fort Worth, Texas
Interviewer: Sheldon F. Gauthier
[S2:3 (TX, pt. 2): 551–59]

Henry H. Buttler, 87, venerable graduate of Washburn College in Topeka, Kansas, and ex-school teacher of the Sherman and Ft. Worth, Texas colored school systems, was born a slave to Mr. George Sullivan on his 300 acre plantation located at the base of Bull Mountain in Farquier Co., Va. Mr. Sullivan owned about 30 slaves including Henry's bother, sister, and mother. His father was owned by Mr. John Rector, who was related by marriage to the Sullivans and owned the adjacent plantation with a similar set of slaves that were constantly intermingling with the Sullivan slave workers. Henry and a number of slaves were transported to Arkansas by their master in 1863 to prevent their capture by the Federal soldiers in the Civil War. After his arrival in Arkansas, Henry escaped and joined the Federal Army and fought in The Battle of Pine Bluff and a number of other battles. In 1880, he married Lucia Brown and they were blessed with three children who are now dead. They now reside at

1308 E. Bessie St., Ft. Worth, Tex. Their sole support now is a Union soldier's pension received monthly from the U. S. Government for the past 30 years. His story:

"My name is Henry H. Buttler, and I am past 87 years of age. That figure may not be accurate, but it is approximately correct. You must realize that there were no authentic records made of slave births. Therefore, one is compelled to approximate such events. I estimate my age on the work I was doing at the commencement of the Civil War, and the fact that I was large enough to be accepted as a soldier, in the Union Army, in the year of 1864.

"I was born on the plantation of George Sullivan in Fauquier County, Virginia. The plantation was situated in the valley at the base of Bull Mountain. A place with the mountain as a background that presented a beautiful picture, especially in the spring of the year. The plantation consisted of about 300 acres, with about 30 slaves as workers. The number of slaves varied due to the Master's trading activities. Sometimes the number would reach fifty. Master Sullivan owned my mother and her children, two boys and one girl. My father was owned by Mr. John Rector, who also owned thirty slaves and was an extensive trader.

"Adjacent to the Sullivan's plantation was located the Rector's place of about the same size. The two families were related by marriage and they cooperated in the cultivation of their lands to a great extent. Therefore, there existed a constant exchange of workers and great intimacy among the slaves as well as the two families.

"The slaves, of course, as customary, were housed in quarters especially constructed for that purpose. The quarters consisted of a group of one-room log cabins, usually one for each family, and as you may assume, not pretentious. The cabins contained no flooring. The Master contended that a dirt floor served the negro better than wood. I have heard that same contention in regards to mules, but I have never understood the reason for such application to the negro. The furnishings for the cabins were very crude. There were bunks for sleeping purposes, benches for seats, and a general purpose table. The fire place provided the means for cooking and heating when necessary.

"The food was wholesome and of sufficient quantity. The fact is, in that period, about all the food consumed was produced and processed on the plantations, which eliminated any reason for failure to provide ample food, except the happening of some unavoidable event. I believe, as a whole, the food we ate in those days was more wholesome and tasty than that which we have at our disposal today. All our meat was home cured, the ham and bacon certainly was superior in flavor, the cornmeal and flour likewise. The clothing was plain home spun, but warm and durable, and we were always provided with the necessary amount.

"In the matter of maintaining discipline, there existed a vast difference in the methods employed on the two planations. On the Sullivan place, there existed consideration for human feelings, and the treatment accorded was such as a human should receive. On the Rector place, neither the Master nor the overseer seemed to understand that slaves were human beings.

"I shall relate an instance of punishment administered to one old slave we called Jim. He had committed some infraction of a rule, or an order given. It was early one morning that they ordered him to strip. They tied him to the whipping post and from morning until noon, at intervals, the lash was applied to his back. I, myself, saw and heard many of the lashes as they connected with Jim's back. Yes, and I heard his cries for mercy. He would repeat over and over, "Have mercy, oh Marster, have mercy on me."

"I shall relate another instance where I was concerned. One morning, a number of us were ordered to lay a fence row on the Rector place. Others were ordered to cut and supply us with the rails. The overseer drove up and said, "This row must be laid to the branch and leave in sufficient time to roll those logs that are cut in the back woods." Well, it was sun down when we laid the last rail. True to his word, the overseer put us to rolling logs without any supper. It was eleven o'clock when we completed the task. Old Pete, who was the ox driver, had been engaged in hauling rails and then assisting us with the log rolling, became so exhausted by the time we had finished, that he fell asleep without unyoking the oxen. For that infraction of a rule, he was given 100 lashes. I could relate numerous other incidents of extreme cruelty, but the above should give a sufficient idea of the inconsiderate treatment accorded the slaves on the Rector place.

"In regards to the domestic relations existing among the slaves, that is a question that requires considerable explanation to be understood properly. I shall attempt to answer it briefly, and of course covering only the Sullivan and Rector plantations. The slaves were allowed to marry, but were compelled to first obtain permission from the Master, and he would not consent unless he considered it a proper mating. The position taken by the Master was not wholly due to a disregard for the negro's feelings, nor a disregard for the sacred bonds of matrimony. The main factor involved was the desire on the part of the Master to rear negroes with perfect physiques. However, on neither plantation was there any thought or compassion in evidence when the matter of a sale or trade was in question. I have witnessed the separation of husband

and wife, child and mother. I have witnessed the extreme grief of the parties involved because of such separations, and then witnessed the lash administered to the grieving party because they were neglecting their work. All of which made the marriage a farce, and more so because there was a purported ceremony performed by an alleged preacher, a white man who owned an adjoining plantation.

"Allow me to digress here just a moment to talk about that preacher. He preached a sermon each Sunday to the slaves of the neighborhood. The place of congregation was the Sullivan plantation. He was very inconsiderate in the treatment of his own slaves, therefore his brotherly talk was not taken seriously by most of the colored folks. One one occasion, a listener laughed at the minister's remarks during a discourse on kindness. The purported minister administered twenty-five lashes to the unfortunate negro.

"Now back to where we were. After the commencement of the Civil War, conditions changed to some extent on each plantation. There were several appropriations of food made by the army, which created a scarcity and some privation until the following crop was harvested. With this one exception, things went on as usual.

"In 1863, Master Sullivan transported about forty of us slaves to Arkansas, locating us on a farm near Pine Bluff. It was done for the purpose of avoiding the possibility of us slaves being taken by the Federal soldiers. The general faithfulness of the slave was well illustrated during that time as there was an opportunity for deserting the Master and going to the free states. I believe that I was the only one of that crowd of negroes that took advantage of the opportunity.

"Before I continue about my deserting, I shall mention an incident which further illustrates how faithful the average negro was to his Master. You recall Pete, the old negro that received a lashing that lasted from morning until noon. Well, he was given a letter with instructions to deliver it to General Price's headquarters, south of Pine Bluff. He could have gone to the Federal headquarters at Fort Smith and would have been freed. Naturally one would think in retaliation for the cruel treatment he had received, that he would do so, but he was faithful and delivered the letter as ordered.

"Now I shall return to my deserting Master Sullivan. I availed myself of the opportunity and went to the Federal headquarters at Fort Smith, Arkansas. I was received and mustered into the army. That was in the early part of 1864. I remained until the close of the war and was mustered out of service at Pine Bluff.

"During my service with the army, we campaigned in Arkansas and the adjacent territory. We fought small battles and skirmishes up and down the White River. The major battle that I was engaged in was the battle of Pine Bluff, which lasted one day and a part of one night.

"The battle of Pine Bluff was a desperately fought battle while it lasted. I shall give you my impression received as a fighting soldier. We were expecting a battle early on a Sunday morning in November 1864. Our anticipations were realized when orders came to fall in formation for battle. It was a little before sunrise, and by sunrise fighting had commenced. Both armies kept advancing slowly in the face of terrific firing until we met. Then it was largely hand to hand fighting. The men fought with bayonets, pistols, knives, clubs, and in the absence of any other implement, the fist was resorted to. Each side fought with an energy and determination that manifested a desire to exterminate their antagonist. The battle waged back and forth; first one side would give a little ground, then regain it, then the other side would do likewise. Neither side seemed to be able to deliver the decisive blow. About the middle of the afternoon, men began to drop from exhaustion. They would rest a little while, then return to the front line. More and more men began to fall because of fatigue. With the number killed and wounded, our line began to weaken. The Confederates indicated the same condition and it appeared that it was a question of endurance, and up to the last man before victory for either side could be determined.

"When it seemed to be a hopeless struggle, there appeared on the field, a large number of women who had organized themselves into squads. They were carrying small platforms, two to a platform, upon which was coffee, sandwiches and other eatables. These women went among the men feeding the soldiers the food and at the same time, they kept up a constant encouraging talk, as follows: "Stand up to them, men. Be real men. Be whole men. Don't give up. Fight them, men. We are behind you. Show your stuff. Fight them to the last man, you have them whipped. Just stay in there and fight, just a little longer."

"Those women kept us fighting on into the night, and then the Confederates began to give ground, which continued into a general retreat. They had no sandwich squad. If anyone should ask you who won the battle of Pine Bluff, tell them that Henry Buttler said that it was the women's sandwich squad that joined the Union forces, armed with food and encouraging words.

"I was mustered out of the army in 1865 in the city of Pine Bluff. I immediately set out to obtain an education. A determination I possessed, partly because of my own volition and partly because of what my father had told me. That was to educate myself if I had the opportunity.

"I entered the grade school at Pine Bluff, and worked after school hours at any job I could secure. I succeeded in graduating from the high school. Then I entered the Washburn College located at Topeka, Kansas. I majored in English, my purpose was to become a teacher and assist my race to improve their station and to become more useful men and women. I succeeded in college and completed my work. Completing my college work, I followed steam engineering for a period of four years. In 1875, I went to Sherman, Texas and taught school there for six months. Then I went to Fort Worth, and spent twenty-two years in educational work among my people. I exerted my best efforts to advance my race.

"I was married in 1880 to Lucia Brown. We were blessed with three children, but unfortunately they are all dead. There is just my wife and me left of the Buttler family. Our sole support now is a $75.00 per month Union soldier's pension that I have been receiving from the Federal Government for the past thirty years.

Hardridge, Mary Jane
Age: 85
1501 East Barraque Street
Pine Bluff, Arkansas
Interviewer: Mrs. Bernice Bowden
[M:9: pt. 3: 157–59]

"Oh don't ask me that, honey. Yes, I was here in slavery days. I reckon I was here before the Civil War; I was born in '58. I'm right now in my birth county about four miles from this city.

"I can remember my young masters that went to war. One was named Ben and one Chris. Old master's name was James Scull. He was kinda mixed up—he wasn't the cruelest one in the world. I've heard of some that was worse than he was. I never suffered for nothin' to eat.

"I can tell you about myself as far back as I can remember. I know I was about thirteen or fourteen when the war ended.

"My father's birth home was in Virginia. His name was Flem(?) Price and his father was a doctor and a white man. Mother's name was Mary Price and she was half Indian. You can tell that by looking at her picture. She was born in Arkansas.

"I can remember seeing the soldiers. I had to knit socks for them. Used to have to knit a pair a week. Yes ma'm I used to serve them. I had it to do or get a whippin'. I nursed and I sewed a little. My mother was a great seamstress. We did it by hand too. They didn't have no sewing machines in them times.

"When my white folks went on summer vacations—they was rich and traveled a great deal—mama always went along and she just left us children on the plantation just like a cow would leave a calf. She'd hate to do it though. I remember she went off one time and stayed three months and left me sick in the white folks house on a pallet. I know I just hollered and cried and mama cried too. There was another old colored lady there and she took me to her house. We lived right on the river where the boat landed and I remember the boat left at high noon and I cried all the rest of the afternoon.

"I remember the first Yankee I ever saw. They called him Captain Hogan. I had a white chile in my arms. He set there and asked the boss how many Negroes did he have and the boss said what was the news. He come out to let the Negroes know they was as free as he was and told Marse Jim to bring all of them back from Texas. I know I run and told mama and she said 'You better hush, you'll get a whippin.'

"They sho didn't burn up nothin'—just took the mules and horses. Now I remember that—they didn't burn up nothin' where I lived.

"I heard of the Ku Klux but I never seen any. We was expectin' em though at all times.

"My grandmother belonged to Creed Taylor and after freedom mama got her and she lived there with the Sculls two years. My mother and father was paid a salary and they paid me too—four dollars a month. And I remember mama never would let me have it—just give me what she wanted me to have. They treated us better than they did before the war. Cose they was a little rough, but they couldn't whip you like they did. They could threaten it though.

"I went to school just a little after freedom. Mama and papa wasn't able to send me. Wasn't no colored teachers competent to teach then and we had to pay the white teacher a dollar a month.

"I had very strict parents and was made to mind. When I went out I knew when I was comin' in. I had one daughter who died when she was eight years old and if I could bring her back now, I wouldn't do it cause I know she would worry me to death.

"I used to sew a lot for people in Pine Bluff but I am too old now. I own my home and I have some rooms rented to three young men students and I get a little help from the Welfare so I manage to get along.

"Well good-bye—I'm glad you come."

Harris, Mary
Age: 82
713 W. Plum Street
Pine Bluff, Arkansas

Interviewer: Mrs. Bernice Bowden
[M:9: pt. 3: 177–78]

"I was born right here in Arkansas and I remember they was havin' somethin'. I remember when they taken this town (Pine Bluff). The people what owned me was the parson of the Methodist church—Parson Walsh. Yes ma'm I knowed the Union soldiers was dressed in blue and the Secessors was called Greybacks. My father was with the Yankee soldiers. I don't know how he got with em but I know he was gone away from this town three years. He come back here after he was mustered out in Vicksburg.

"I remember the Yankee soldiers come and took the colored folks away if they wanted to go. That was after surrender. They carried us to the 'county band' and fed us.

"I know the day the Yankees taken Pine Bluff; it was on Sunday and Marse Jesse went to services. The Secessor soldiers left Pine Bluff. Of course I didn't understand what it was all about cause in them times people didn't enlighten children like they does now. They know everything now, ain't no secrets.

"Most work I've done is washin' and ironin' since I been a full-grown, married woman. I was twenty some odd when I was married. I know I was out of my teens.

"I went to school a good while after the war. My first teacher was Mr. Todd from the North.

"I used to do right smart sewing. I did sewing before machines come to this town. The frocks they used to make had from five to ten yards.

"We is livin' now in a time of worry. What they is doin' is told about in the scripture."

Haskell, Hetty
Age: 85
1416 W. Pullen
Pine Bluff, Arkansas
Interviewer: Mrs. Bernice Bowden
[M:9: pt. 3: 193–94]
[See also S2:1: 19–24]

"Yes'm, I reckon I was about twelve when the Civil War ended. Oh, I could nurse a little.

"No ma'am, I wasn't born in Arkansas. I was born in Tennessee, but I was brought here when I was a baby. Come here before the war. The old master had sold 'em.

"We was bought by Will Nichols. You ever hear of this here Dick Lake? Well, that's the place.

"They taken my father and my sister to Texas and stayed till after freedom. My mother was sick and they didn't carry her and I was too little, so they left me. They was pretty good to us as far as I know.

"I remember when the Yankees come through. Oh, yes'm, I was scared. I used to hide under the bed. I wouldn't give 'em a chance to talk to me.

"Our folks stayed on the Nichols' place about two years. Then they farmed on the shares till he got able to buy him a mule, then he rented.

"After the war the cholera disease come along. My mother and sister died with it.

"Somebody said if you would hang up some beef outdoors between the road and the house, it would stop the disease. I know old master hung up about a half a quarter and it seemed to work. The meat would turn green.

"The Yankees took things to eat but the Rebels would take the women's clothes—and the men's too. I guess they just took 'em 'cause they could.

"Biggest work I've done is farm work.

"My daddy said I was sixteen when I married. I had thirteen children but they ain't all livin'.

"I remember when they said they was free. Some of the folks left the place and never come back and some of 'em stayed.

"Sometimes I had a pretty good time and sometimes pretty tough.

"I'm gettin' along all right now. I stay here with my son part of the time and then I go to the country and stay with my daughter."

Hill, Elmira
Age: 97
1220 North Willow
Pine Bluff, Arkansas
Interviewer: Mrs. Bernice Bowden
[M:9: pt. 3: 252–55]

"I'm one of em. Accordin' to what they tell me, I think I'll be ninety-eight the ninth day of February. I was born in Virginia in Kinsale County and sold from my mother and father to Arkansas.

"The Lord would have it, old man Ed Lindsey come to Virginia and brought me here to Arkansas. I was here four years before the Old War ceasted and I was twelve when I come here.

"I was right there standin' behind my mistis' chair when Abe Lincoln said, 'I 'clare there shall be war!' I was was right here in Arkansas—eighteen miles from Pine Bluff when war ceasted. The Lord would have it. I had a good master and mistis. Old master said, 'Fore old Lincoln shall free my niggers, I'll free em myself.' They might as well a been free, they had a garden and if they raised cotton in that garden they could sell it. The Lord bless His Holy Name! We didn't know the difference when we got free. I stayed with my mistis till she went back to Virginia.

"Yes, honey, I was here in all the war. I was standin' right by my mistis' chair. I never heard old master make a oaf in his life, but when they brought the paper freein' the slaves, he said, "Dad burn it.'

"I member a man called Jeff Davis. I know they sung and said, 'We'll hand old Jeff Davis to the sour apple tree.'

"I been here a long time. Yes, honey, I been in Arkansas so long I say I ain't goin' out—they got to bury me here. Arkansas dirt good enough for me. I say I been here so long I got Arkansas 'stemper (distemper).

"My old master in Virginia was Joe Hudson. My father used to ketch oysters and fish. We could look up the Patomac river and see the ships comin' in. In Virginia I lived next to a free state and the runaways was tryin' to get away. At Harper's Ferry—that's where old John Brown was carryin' em across. My old mistis used to take the runaway folks when the dogs had bit their legs, and keep em for a week and cure em up. This time o' year you could hear the bull whip. But I was lucky, they was good to me in Virginia and good to me in Arkansas.

"Yes, chile, I was in Alexandria, Virginia in Kinsale County when they come after me by night. I was hired out to Captain Jim Allen. I had been nursin' for Captain Allen. He sailed on the sea. He was a good man. He was a Christian man. He never whipped me but once and that was for tellin a story, and I thank him for it. He landed his boat right at the landin' on Saturday. Next day he asked me bout somethin' and I told him a story. He said, 'I'm gwine whip you Monday morning!' He wouldn't whip me on Sunday. He whipped me and I thank him for it. And to this day the Lindsey's could trust me with anything they had.

"I was in Virginia a play-chile when the ships come down to get the gopher wood to build the war ships. Old mistis had a son and a daughter and we all played together and slep together. My white folks learned me my A B C's.

"They come and got me and carried me to Richmond—that's where they sold em. Sold five of us in one bunch. Sold my two brothers in New Orleans—Robert and Jesse. Never seen them no more. Never seed my mother again after I was sold.

"Yes, chile, I was here in Arkansas when the war started, so you know I been here a long time.

"I was here when they fit the last battle in Pine Bluff. They called it Marmaduke's Battle and they fit it on Sunday morning. They took the old cotehouse for a battery and throwed up cotton bales for a breastworks. They fit that Sunday and when the Yankees started firin' the Rebels went back to Texas or wherever they come from.

"When we heard the Yankees was comin' we went out at night and hid the silver spoons and silver in the toilet and buried the meat. After the war was over and the Yankees had gone home and the jayhawkers had went in— then we got the silver and the meat. Yes, honey, we seed a time—we seed a time. I ain't grumblin'—I tell em I'm havin' a wusser time now than I ever had.

"Yankees used to call me a 'know nothing' cause I wouldn't tell where things was hid.

"Yes, chile, I'm this way—I like everbody in this world. I never was a mother, but I raised everbody else's chillun. I ain't nothin' but a old mammy. White and black calls me mamma. I'll answer at the name.

"I was married twice. My last husband and me lived together fifty years. He was a preacher. My first husband, the old rascal—he was so mean to me I had to get rid of him.

"Yes, I been here so long. I think the younger generation is goin' the downward way. They ain't studyin' nothin' but wickedness. Yes, honey, they tell me the future generation is goin' a do this and goin' a do that and they ain't done nothin'. And God don't like it.

"My white folks come to see me and say as long as they got bread, I got it.

"I went to school the second year after surrender. I can read but I ain't got no glasses now. I want you to see this letter my mother sent me in 1867. My baby sister writ it. Yes, honey, I keeps it for remembrance.

"Don't know nothin' funny that happened 'ceptin stealin' my old master's company's hoss and running a race. White chillun too. Them as couldn't ride sideways ridin' straddle. Better *not* ride Rob Roy—that was old master's ridin' hoss and my mistis saddle hoss. That was the hoss he was talkin' bout ridin' to the war when the last battle was fit in Helena. But he was too old to go to war.

"Well, goodbye, honey—if I don't see you no more, come across the Jordan."

Hinton, Charlie
Age: 89
Old River Road
Pine Bluff, Arkansas

Interviewer: Mrs. Bernice Bowden
[M:9: pt. 3: 279–80]

"Oh Lordy, lady, I was pickin' cotton durin' the war. I was here before the first gun was fired. When the war came they sent my mother and father and all the other big folks to Texas and left us undergrowth here to make a crop.

"My mother's name was Martha and my father was named Peter Hinton. Now I'm just goin' to tell you everything—I'm not ashamed. I've got the marks of slavery on me. My old marster and Miss Mary, they was good to me, but the old cook woman throwed me off the porch and injured my back. I ain't never been able to walk just right since.

"Now, here's what I remember. Our marster, we thought he was God.

"They pretty near raised us with the pigs. I remember they would cook a great big oven of bread and then pour a pan full of buttermilk or clabber and we'd break off a piece of bread and get around the pan of milk jest like pigs. Yes mam, they did that.

"Let's see now, what else occurred. Old marster would have my father and Uncle Jacob and us boys to run foot races. You know—they was testin' us, and I know I was valued to be worth five hundred dollars.

"But my folks was good to me. They wouldn't have no overseer what would be cruel. If he was cruel he would have to be gone from there.

One time old marster say "Charlie how come this yard so dirty?" You know there would be a little track around. I said, will you give me that old gray horse after I clean it and he said "Yes". So I call up the boys and we'd clean it up, and then the old gray horse was mine. It was just the old worn out stock you understand.

"I want to tell you when the old folks got sick they would bleed them, and when the young folks got sick they give you some blue mass and turn you loose.

"I remember when old marster's son Sam went to war and got shot in the leg. Old marster was cryin' "Oh, my Sam is shot". He got in a scrummage you know. He got well but he never could straighten out his leg.

"When freedom come, I heard 'em prayin' for the men to come back home. Miss Mary called us all up and told us our age and said, "You are all free and can go where you want to go, or you can stay here."

"Oh yes, the Ku Klux use to run my daddy if they caught him out without a pass, but I remember he could outrun them—he was stout as a mule.

"I been here so long and what little I've picked up is just a little fireside learnin'. I can read and write my name. I can remember when we thought a newspaper opened out was a bed-cover. But a long time after the war when the public school come about, I had the privilege of going to school three weeks. Yes mam, I was swift and I think I went nearly through the first reader.

"I am a great lover of the Bible and I'm a member of Mount Calvary Baptist Church.

"I'm glad to give you some kind of idea 'bout my age and life. I really am glad. Goodbye."

Lucas, Louis
Age: 83
1320 Pulaski Street
Pine Bluff, Arkansas
Interviewer: Samuel S. Taylor
[M:9: pt. 4: 297–303]

Masters, Birth, Parents, Grandparents
"I was born in 1855 down on Bayou Bartholomew near Pine Bluff, Jefferson County.

"My mother's name was Louisa. She married a man named Bill Cardrelle after freedom. Her husband in slavery time was Sam Lucas. He belonged to a man by the name of O'Neil. They took him in the War and he never did come back to her. (He didn't much believe he was my father, but I went in his name anyway.)

"My mother's father's name was Jacob Boyd. I was young, but I know that. He was free and didn't belong to nobody. That was right here in Arkansas. He had three other daughters besides my mother, and all of them were slaves because their mother was a slave. His wife was a woman by the name of Barclay. Her master was Antoine Barclay (?). She was a slave woman. She died down there in New Casgogne. That was a good while ago.

"The French were very kind to their slaves. The Americans called all us people that belonged to the Frenchmen free people. They never gave the free Negroes among them any trouble. I mean the Frenchmen didn't give them no trouble.

"The reason we finally left the place after freedom was because of the meanness of a colored woman, Amanda Sanders. I don't know what she had against us. The old mistress raised me right in the house and fed me right at the table. When she died, this woman used to beat the devil out of me. We had good owners. They never had no overseers until just before the War broke out, and they never beat nobody.

"The first overseer was on a boat named the Quapaw when the mate knocked him in the head and put him in a yawl and took him to the shore. The boss saw it and took four men and went and got him and had the doctor attend to him. It was a year before he could do anything. He didn't stay there long before they had him in the War. He just got to oversee a short time after he got well. He was in the cavalry. The other boys went off later. They took the cavalry first. None of them ever came back. They were lost in the big fight at Vicksburg. My *paran*, Mark Noble, he was the only one that got back.

"I don't remember my father's father. But I know that his mother went in the name of Rhoda. I don't know her last name. She was my grandma on his side.

"I belonged to a man named Brumbaugh. His first name was Raphael. He was a all right man. He had a *colored man for an overseer* before this here white man I was tellin' you about came to him. 'Uncle' Jesse was the foreman. He was not my uncle. He was related to my wife though; so I call him uncle now. Of course, I didn't marry till after freedom came. I married in 1875.

Early Days
"When I was a little child, my duty was to clean up the yard and feed the chickens. I cleaned up the yard every Friday.

House, Furniture, and Food
"My mother lived in a cabin—log, two rooms, one window, that is one window in each room.

"They didn't have anything but homemade furniture. We never had no bed bought from the store—nothin' like that. We just had something sticking against the wall. It was built in a corner with one post out. They made their table and used benches—two-legged and sometimes four-legged. The two-legged benches was a long bench with a wide plank at each end for legs.

"For food we got just what the white folks got. We didn't have no quarters. They didn't have enough hands for that. They raised their own meat. They had about seven or eight. There was Dan, Jess, Bill, Steve. They bought Bill and Steve from Kentucky.

"Old 'Free Jack' Jenkins, a colored man, sold them two men to ol' master. Jenkins was the only *Negro slave trader* I ever knowed. He brought them down one evening and the old man was a long time trading. He made them run and jump and do eveything before he would buy them. He paid one thousand five hundred dollars for each one of them. 'Free Jack' made him pay it part in silver and some in gold. He took some Confederate paper. It was circulating then. But he wouldn't take much of that paper money.

"He stole those boys from their parents in Kentucky. The boys said he fooled them away from their homes with candy. Their parents didn't know where they were.

"Then there were my brothers—two of them, John Alexander and William Hamilton. They were half-brothers. That makes six men altogether on the place. I might have made a miscount. There was old man Wash Pearson and his two boys, Joe and Nathan. That made ten persons with myself.

"Brumbaugh didn't have such a large family. I never did know how large it was.

Soldiers

"The rebel soldiers were often at my place. A bad night the jayhawkers would come and steal stock and the slaves too, if they got a chance. They cleaned the old man's stock out one night. The Yankees captured them and brought them back to the house. They gave him his stallion, a great big fine horse. They offered him five thousand dollars for him but he wouldn't take it. They kept all the other horses and mules for their own use, but they gave the stallion back to the old man. If they hadn't give him back the stallion, the old man would have died. That stallion was his heart. The Yankees didn't do nobody any harm.

"When the soldier wagons came down to get the feed, they would take one crib and leave one. They never bothered the smokehouse. They took all the dry cattle to feed the people that were contrabands. But they left the milk cows. The quartermaster for the contrabands was Captain Mallory. The contrabands were mostly slaves that they kept in camps just below Pine Bluff for their own protection.

How Freedom Came

"It was martial law and twelve men went 'round back and forth through the country. They come down on a Monday, and told the children they were free and told them they had no more master and mistress and told them what to call them. No more master and mistress, but Mr. and Mrs. Brumbaugh. Then they came down and told them that they would have to marry over again. But my ma never had a chance to see the old man any more. She didn't marry him over again because he didn't come back to her. But they advised them to stay with their owners if they wanted to. They didn't say for none of the slaves to leave their old masters and go off. We wouldn't have left but that old colored woman beat me around so all the time, so my mother came after me and took me home since I wanted to go. The Yankees' officer told her it would be good to move me from that place so I wouldn't be so badly treated. The white folks was all right; it was that old colored woman that beat on me all the time.

Right after Freedom

"Right after freedom my mother married Bill Cardrelle. She moved from the O'Neil place and went up to a place called the Dr. Jenkins' place. She kept house for her husband in the new place. I didn't do much there of anything. After they moved away from there when I was twelve years old, they taught me to plow (1867). I went to school in the contraband camp. Mrs. Clay and Mr. Clay, white folks from the North, were my teachers. At that time, the colored people weren't able to teach. I went a while to school with them. I got in the second reader—McGuffy's—that's far as I got.

"I stayed with my mother and stepfather till I was about sixteen years old. She sent me away to come up here to my father, Sam Lucas. My oldest brother brought me here and I worked with him two years. Then I went to a man named Cunningham and stayed with him about six months. He paid me fifteen dollars a month and my board. He was going to raise my wages when his wife decided she wanted women to do the work. The women would slip things away and she wouldn't mention them to her husband till weeks afterwards. Then long after the time, she would accuse me. Those women would have the keys. When they went in to get soap, they would take out a ham and carry it off a little ways and hide. By the time his wife would tell him about it, you wouldn't be able to find it nowhere.

"He owed me for a month's work. She told him not to pay it, but he paid it and told me not to let her know he did it. I didn't either.

"When I left him, I came over the river here down here below Fourche Dam. I stayed there forty or fifty years in that place. When I was between thirty-two and thirty-three years old, I married, and I stayed right on in that same place. I farmed all the time down there. I had to go in a lawsuit about the last crop I made. Then I came here to Little Rock in 1904 and followed ditching with the home water company. Then I did gas ditching with the gas people. Then I worked on the street car line for old man White. I come down then—got broke down, and couldn't do much. The relief folks gave me a labor card; then they took it away from me—said I was too old. I have done a heap of work here in this town. I got old and had to stop.

"I get old age assistance from the Welfare. That is where I get my groceries—through them. I wouldn't be able to live if it wasn't for them.

Opinions

"There is a big difference between the young people now and what they used to be. The old folks ain't the same neither."

Interviewer's Comment

Lucas told his story very fluently but with deliberation and care. The statement about his father on the first page was not a slip. He told what he wanted to tell but he discouraged too much effort to go into detail on those matters. One senses a tragedy in his life and in the life of his mother that is poignant and appealing. Although he states no connection, one will not miss the impression that his stepfather was hostile. Suddenly we find his mother sending him to his father. But after he reached his father, there is little to indicate that his father did anything for him. Then, too, it is evident that his father deliberately neglected to remarry his mother after freedom.

McClendon, Charlie
Age: 77
708 E. Fourth Avenue
Pine Bluff, Arkansas
Interviewer: Mrs. Bernice Bowden
[M:10: pt. 5: 1–3]

"I don't know exactly how old I am. I was six or seven when the war ended. I member dis—my mother said I was born on Christmas day. Old master was goin' to war and he told her to take good care of that boy—he was goin' to make a fine little man.

"Did I live up to it? I reckon I was bout as smart a man as you could jump up. The work didn't get too hard for *me*. I farmed and I sawmilled a lot. Most of my time was farmin'.

"I been in Jefferson County all my life. I went to school three or four sessions.

"About the war, I member dis—I member they carried us to Camden and I saw the guards. I'd say, 'Give me a pistol.' They'd say, 'Come back tomorrow and we'll give you one.' They had me runnin' back there every day and I never did get one. They was Yankee soldiers.

"Our folks' master was William E. Johnson. Oh Lord, they was just as good to us as could be under slavery.

"After they got free my people stayed there a year or two and then our master broke up and went back to South Carolina and the folks went in different directions. O Lord, my parents she was well treated. Yes ma'm. If he had a overseer, he wouldn't low him to whip the folks. He'd say, 'Just leave em till I come home.' Then he'd give em a light breshin'.

"My father run off and stay in the woods one or two months. Old master say, 'Now, Jordan, why you run off? Now I'm goin' to give you a light breshin' and don't you run off again.' But he'd run off again after awhile.

"He had one man named Miles Johnson just stayed in the woods so he put him on the block and sold him.

"I seed the Ku Klux. We colored folks had to make it here to Pine Bluff to the county band. If the Rebels kotch you, you was dead.

"Oh Lord yes, I voted. I voted the Publican ticket, they called it. You know they had this Australia ballot. You was sposed to go in the caboose and vote. They like to scared me to death one time. I had a description of the man I wanted to vote for in my pocket and I was lookin' at it so I'd be sure to vote for the right man and they caught me. They said, 'What you doin' there? We're goin' to turn you over to the sheriff after election! They had me scared to death. I hid out for a long time till I seed they wasn't goin' to do nothin'.

"My wife's brother was one of the judges of the election. Some of the other colored folks was constable and magistrates—some of em are now— down in the country.

"I knew a lot about things but I knew I was in the United States and had to bow to the law. There was the compromise they give the colored folks— half of the offices and then they got em out afterwards. John M. Clayton was runnin' for the senate and say he goin' to see the colored people had equal rights, but they killed him as he was gwine through the country speakin'.

"The white people have treated me very well but they don't pay us enough for our work—just enough to live on and hardly that. I can say with a clear conscience that if it hadn't been for this relief, I don't know what I'd do—I'm not able to work. I'm proud that God Almighty put the spirit in the man (Roosevelt) to help us."

Mann, Lewis
Age: 81
1501 Bell Street
Pine Bluff, Arkansas
Interviewer: Mrs. Bernice Bowden
[M:10: pt. 5: 47–48]

"As nigh as I can come at it, I was bout five or six time of the war. I remember when the war ceased. I was a good-sized chap.

"Durin' the war my mother's master sent us to Texas; western Texas is whar they stopped me. We stayed there two years and then they brought us back after surrender.

"I remember when the war ceasted and I remember the soldiers refugeein' through the country. I'm somewhar round eighty-one. I'm tellin' you the truf. I ain't just now come here.

"I was born right here in Arkansas. My mother's master was old B. B. Williams of Tennessee and we worked for his son Mac H. Williams here in Arkansas. They was good to my mother. Always had nurses for the colored childrun while the old folks was in the field.

"After the war I used to work in the house for my white folks—for Dr. Bob Williams way up there in the country on the river. I stayed with his brother Mac Williams might near twenty-five or thirty years. Worked around the house servin' and doin' errands different places.

"I went to school a little bit a good piece after the war and learned to read and write.

"I've heard too much of the Ku Klux. I remember when they was Ku Kluxin' all round through here.

"Lord! I don't know how many times I ever voted. I used to vote every time they had an election. I voted before I could read. The white man showed me how to vote and asked me who I wanted to vote for. Oh Lord, I was might near grown when I learned to read.

"I been married just one time in my life and my wife's been dead thirteen years.

"I tell you, Miss, I don't know hardly what to think of things now. Everything so changeable I can't bring nothin' to remembrance to hold it.

"I didn't do nothin' when I was young but just knock around with the white folks. Oh Lord, when I was young I delighted in parties. Don't nothin' like that worry me now. Don't go to no parades or nothin'. Don't have that on my brain like I did when I was young. I goes to church all the place I does go.

"I ain't never had no accident. Don't get in the way to have no accident cause I know the age I is if I injure these bones there ain't anything more to me.

"My mother had eight children and just my sister and me left. I can't do a whole day's work to save my life. I own this place and my sister-in-law gives me a little somethin' to eat. I used to be on the bureau but they took me off that."

Perry, Dinah
Age: 78
1800 Ohio Street
Pine Bluff, Arkansas

Interviewer: Mrs. Bernice Bowden
[M:10: pt. 5: 318–21]

"Yes ma'am, I lived in slavery times. They brought me from Alabama, a baby, right here to this place where I am at, Mr. Sterling Cockril.

"I don't know zackly when I was born but I member bout the slave times. Yes ma'am, I do. After I growed up some, I member the overseer—I do. I can remember Mr. Burns. I member when he took the hands to Texas. Left the chillun and the old folks here.

"Oh Lord, this was a big plantation. Had bout four or five hundred head of niggers.

"My mother done the milkin' and the weavin'. After free times, I wove me a dress. My mother fixed it for me and I wove it. They'd knit stockin's too. But now they wear silk. Don't keep my legs warm.

"I member when they fit here in Pine Bluff. I member when 'Marmajuke' sent word he was goin' to take breakfast with Clayton that mornin' and they just fit. I can remember that was 'Marmajuke.' It certainly was 'Marmajuke.' The Rebels tried to carry me away but the wagon was so full I didn't get in and I was glad they didn't. My mother was runnin' from the Rebels and she hid under the cotehouse. After the battle was over she come back here to the plantation.

"I·had three brothers and three sisters went to Texas and I know I didn't know em when they come back.

"I member when they fit here a bum shell fell right in the yard. It was big around as this stovepipe and was all full of chains and things.

"After free time my folks stayed right here and worked on the shares. I was the baby chile and never done no work till I married when I was fifteen.

"After the War I went to school to white teachers from the North. I never went to nothin' but them. I went till I was in the fifth grade.

"My daddy learned me to spell 'lady' and 'baker' and 'shady' fore I went to school. I learned all my ABC's too. I got out of the first reader the second day. I could just read it right on through. I could spell and just stand at the head of the class till the teacher sent me to the foot all the time.

"My daddy was his old mistress' pet. He used to carry her to school all the time and I guess that's where he got his learnin'.

"After I was married I worked in the field. Rolled logs, cut brush, chopped and picked cotton.

"I member when they had that 'Bachelor' (Brooks-Baxter) War up here at Little Rock.

"After my chillun died, I never went to the field no more. I just stayed round mongst the white folks nussin'. All the chillun I nussed is married and grown now.

"All this younger generation—white and colored—I don't know what's gwine come of em. The poet says:

'Each gwine a different way
And all the downward road.'"

"I's bawn in Alabama and brought here to Arkansas a baby. I couldn't tell what year I was bawn 'cause I was a baby. A chile can't tell what year he was bawn 'less they tells him and they sure didn't tell me.

"When I'd wake up in the mawnin' my mother would be gone to the field.

"Some things I can remember good but you know old folks didn't 'low chillun to stand around when they was talking' in dem days. They had to go play. They had to be mighty particular or they'd get a whippin'.

"Chillun was better in them days 'cause the old folks was strict on 'em. Chillun is raisin' theirselves today.

"I 'member one song they used to sing

'We'll land over shore
We'll land over shore;
And we'll live forever more.'

They called it a hymn. They'd sing it in church, then they'd all get to shoutin'.

"Superstitions? Well, I seen a engineer goin' to work the other day and a black cat ran in front of him, and he went back 'cause he said he would have a wreck with his train if he didn't. So you see, the white folks believes in things like that too.

"I never was any hand to play any games 'cept 'Chick, Chick.' You'd ketch 'hold a hands and ring up. Had one outside was the hawk and some inside was the hen and chickens. The old mother hen would say

'Chick-ama, chick-a-ma, craney crow,
Went to the well to wash my toe;
When I come back my chicken was gone,
What time is it, old witch?'

One chicken was s'posed to get out and then the hawk would try to ketch him.

"We was more 'ligious than the chillun nowadays. We used to play preachin' and baptisin'. We'd put 'em down in the water and souse 'em and we'd shout just like the old folk. Yes ma'am."

Rassberry, Senia
Age: 84
810 Catalpa Street
Pine Bluff, Arkansas
Interviewer: Mrs. Bernice Bowden
[M:10: pt. 6: 14–16]

"Yes'm, I know what I hear em say. Well, in slavery times I helped make the soldiers' clothes.

"I was born on the old Jack Hall place on the Arkansas River in Jefferson County.

"I know I was 'leven years old when peace declared. I reckon I can member fore the War started. I know I was bastin' them coats and pants.

"My old master's name was Jack Hall and old mistress' name was Priscilla. Oh, yes'm, they was good to me—just as good to me as they could be. But ever' once in awhile they'd call me and say, 'Senia.' I'd say, 'What you want?' They say, 'Wasn't you out there doin' so and so?' I'd say, 'No.' They say, 'Now, you're tellin' a lie' and they'd whip me.

"I was the house girl, me and my sister. My mammy was the cook.

"Old master had two plantations. Sometimes he had a overseer and sometimes he didn't.

"Oh, they had plenty to eat, hog meat and cracklin' bread. Yes ma'am, I loved that, I reckon. I et so much of it then I don't hardly ever want it now. They had so much to eat. Blackberry cobbler? Oh Lawd.

"How many brothers and sisters? Me? My dear, I don't know how many I had but I heard my mother say that all the chillun she did have, that she had 'leven children.

"Our white folks took us to Texas durin' of the War. I think my old master said we stayed there three years. My mother died there with a congestive chill.

"We come back here to Arkansas after freedom and I think my father worked for Jack Hall three or four years. He wouldn't let him leave. He raised my father and thought so much of him. He worked on the shares.

"After freedom I went to school. I learnt to read and write but I just wouldn't *do* it. I learnt the other chillun though. I did *that*. I was into ever'thing. I learnt them that what I could do. Blue Back? Them's the very ones I studied.

"In slavery times I had to rise as early as I could. Old master would give me any little thing around the house that I wanted. They said he was too old to go to war. Some of the hands run off but I didn't know where they went to.

"Some of the people was better off slaves than they was free. I don't study bout things now but sometimes seems like all them things comes before me.

"I used to hear em talking bout old Jeff Davis. I didn't know what they was talkin' bout but I heered em.

"I was sixteen when I married and I had eleven chillun. All dead but four.

"Yes'm, I been treated good all my life by white and black. All of em loved me seemed like.

"I been livin' in Arkansas all my life. I never have worked in the field. I always worked in the house. I always was a seamstress—made pants for the men on the place.

"After I come here to Pine Bluff I worked for the white folks. Used to cook and wash and iron. Done a lot of work. I did that.

"I been blind 'leven years but I thank the Lord I been here that long. Glory to Jesus! Oh, Lord have mercy! Glory, glory, glory to Jesus!'"

Stanford, Kittie
Age: 104
309 Missouri Street
Pine Bluff, Arkansas
Interviewer: Mrs. Bernice Bowden
[M:10: pt. 6: 214–15]

"Yes'm, I used to be a slave. My mother belonged to Mrs. Lindsey. One day when I was ten years old, my old mistress take me over to her daughter and say 'I brought you a little nigger gal to rock de cradle.' I'se one hundred and four years old now. Miss Etta done writ it down in the book for me.

"One time a lady from up North ask me did I ever get whipped. Honey, I ain't goin' tell you no lie. The overseer whipped us. Old mistress used to send me to her mother to keep the Judge from whippin' me. Old Judge say 'Nigger need whippin' whether he do anything or not.'

"Some of the hands run away. Old Henry run away and hide in the swamp and say he goin' stay till he bones turn white. But he come back when he get hongry and then he run away again.

"When the war come some of the slaves steal the Judge's hosses and run away to Pine Bluff and he didn't never find 'em. The Judge think the Yankees goin' get everything he got so we all left Arkansas and went to Texas. We in Texas when freedom come. We come back to Arkansas and I stay with my white folks awhile but I didn't get no pay so I got a job cookin' for a colored woman.

"I been married fo' times. I left my las' husband. I didn't leave him cause he beat me. I lef' him cause he want too many.

"No'm I never seen no Ku Klux. I heard 'bout 'em but I never seen none that I knows of. When I used to get a pass to go to 'nother plantation I always come back fo' dark.

"This younger generation is beyond my understanding. They is gettin' weaker and wiser.

"I been ready to die for the last thirty years. 'Mary (her granddaughter with whom she lives), show the lady my shroud.' I keeps it wrapped up in blue cloth. They tells me at the store to do that to keep it from turning yellow. 'Show her that las' quilt I made.' Yes'm I made this all by myself. I threads my own needle, too, and cuts out the pieces. I has worked hard all my life.

"Now the Welfare gives me my check. My granddaughter good to me. I goes to church on the first and third Sundays.

"Lady, I glad you come to see me and God bless you. Goo' bye."

Thomas, Tanner
Age: 78
1213 Louisiana
Pine Bluff, Arkansas
Interviewer: Mrs. Bernice Bowden
[M:10: pt. 6: 304–05]

"I was born down here at Rob Roy on the river on the Emory place. My mother's name was Dinah Thomas and my father's name was Greene Thomas. He taken sick and died in the War on the North side. That's what my mother told me. I was born under Mars Jordan Emory's administration.

"I 'member somebody brought me here to Pine Bluff to Lawyer Bell's house. I stayed two or three months, then Mars Jordan sent for me and carried me back out to Rob Roy and I stayed with my mother. She had done married again but I stayed with her all the time till I got grown and I married.

"I come here in 1892 and I been here ever since—forty-six years. Oh, whole lots of the white folks know me.

"I worked at the Standard Lumber Company and Bluff City Lumber Company and Dilley's foundry. Then I went to the oil mill. I was the order man. I was the best lumber grader on the place.

"'Course I knows lots of white folks and they knows me too. I done a heap of work 'round here in different places in forty-six years.

"I went to school a little but I didn't learn nothin'.

"My mother said they come and pressed my daddy in the War. 'Course I don't know nothin' 'bout that but my mother told me.

"Now, what is this you're gettin' up? Well, I was born in slavery times. You know I was when my daddy was in the War.

"Oh Lord yes, I voted. I voted Republican. I didn't know whether it would do any good or not but I just voted 'cause I had a chance. My name's been in Washington for years 'cause I voted, you know.

"My way is dark to the younger generation now. I don't have much dealin' with them. They are more wiser. Education has done spread all over the country.

"God intended for every man in the world to have a living and to live for each other but too many of 'em livin' for themselves. But everything goin' to work out right after awhile. God's goin' to change this thing up after awhile. You can't rush him. He can handle these people. After he gets through with this generation, I think he's goin' to make a generation that will serve him."

Tucker, Mandy
Age: 80?
1021 E. 11th Street
Pine Bluff, Arkansas
Interviewer: Mrs. Bernice Bowden
[M:10: pt. 6: 357–59]

"I was here in slavery times but I don't know what year I was born. War? I was in it!

"I member old master and old mistis too. I member I didn't know nothin' bout my mother and father cause it was night when they went to work and night when they come in and we chilluns would be under the bed asleep.

"I know the white folks had a kitchen full of we chilluns. We went over to the kitchen to eat.

"My mother belonged to the Cockrills and my father belonged to the Armstrongs. They were cousins and their plantations joined.

"I was large enough to know when they took my parents to Texas, but I didn't know how serious it was till they was gone. I member peepin' through the crack of the fence but I didn't know they was takin' em off.

"They left me with the old doctor woman. She doctored both white and colored. I stayed there till I was fourteen years old.

"I know we had our meals off a big wooden tray but we had wooden spoons to eat with.

"I member when they was fightin' here at Pine Bluff. I was standin' at the overseer's bell house waitin' for a doll dress a girl had promised me and the guns was goin' just like pop guns. We didn 't know what it was to take off our shoes and clothes for six months. We was ready to run if they broke in on us.

"The Yankees had their headquarters at the big house near the river. All this was in woods till I growed up. We used to have our picnic here.

"I was standin' right at the post when they run the bell in the bell house when peace declared. I heered the old folks sayin', 'We is free, we is free!'

I know before freedom they wouldn't let us burn a speck of light at night. Had these little iron lamps. They'd twist wicks and put em in tallow. I don't know whether it was beef or sheep tallow but they had plenty of sheeps on the place.

"Colonel Cockrill would have us come up to the big house every Sunday mornin' and he'd give us a apple or a stick of candy. But them that was big enough to work wouldn't get any. They worked on Sunday too—did the washin' every Sunday evenin'.

"Oh Lord, they had a big plantation.

"After the War I went to school some. We had white teachers from the North. I didn't get to go much except on rainy days. Other times I had to work. I got so I could read print but I can't read writin'. I used to could but since I been sick seems like my mind just hops off.

"After freedom my parents rented land and farmed. I stayed with the old doctor woman till I was fourteen then I went to my parents.

"I married when I was eighteen and had five chillun. When I worked for my father he'd let us quit when we got tired and sit under the shade bushes. But when I married I had to work harder than ever. My husband was just a run-around. He'd put in a crop and then go and leave it. Sometimes he was a constable. Finally he went off and took up with another woman.

"I been here in Arkansas all my life except eight months I lived in St. Louis, but I didn't like it. When I was in St. Louis I know it started to snow. I thought it was somebody pickin' geese. I said, 'What is that?' and my granddaughter said, 'Gal, that's snow.'

"I don't know what to think of the younger generation. I think they is just goin' out to nothin'. They say they are gettin' weaker and wiser but I think they are weaker and foolish—they are not wise in the right way. Some are very good to their parents and some are not.

"Honey, I don't know how things is goin'—all I know is they is mighty tight right now."

Washington, Parrish
Age: 86
812 Spruce Street
Pine Bluff, Arkansas
Interviewer: Mrs. Bernice Bowden
[M:11: pt. 7: 60–61]

"I was born in 1852—born in Arkansas. Sam Warren was my old master.
"I remember some of the Rebel generals—General Price and General Marmaduke.
"We had started to Texas but the Yankees got in ahead of us in the Saline bottoms and we couldn't go no further.
"My boss had so much faith in his own folks he wouldn't leave here 'til it was too late. He left home on Saturday night and got into the bottoms on Sunday and made camp. Then the Yankees got in ahead of him and he couldn't go no further, so we come back to Jefferson County.
"The Yankees had done took Little Rock and come down to Pine Bluff.
"My father died in 1860 and my mother in 1865.
"I can remember when they whipped the slaves. Never whipped me though—they was just trainin' me up.
"Had an old lady on the place cooked for the children and we just got what we could.
"I remember when peace was declared, the people shouted and rejoiced—a heavy load had fell off.
"All the old hands stayed on the place. I stayed there with my uncle and aunt. We was treated better then. I was about 25 years old when I left there.
"I farmed 'til '87. Then I joined the Conference and preached nearly forty years when I was superannuated.
"I remember when the Rebels was camped up there on my boss's place. I used to love to see the soldiers. Used to see the horses hitched to the artillery.
"Two or three of Sam Warren's hands run off and joined the Yankees. They didn't know what it was goin' to be and two of 'em come back—stayed there too.
"I used to vote the Republican ticket. I was justice of the peace four years—two terms.
"I went to school here in Pine Bluff about two or three terms and I was school director in district number two about six or seven years.
"I have great hope for the young people of the future. 'Course some of 'em are not worth killin' but the better class—I think there is a bright future for 'em.

"But for the world in general, if they don't change they goin' to the devil. But God always goin' to have some good people in reserve 'til the Judgment."

Williams, Horatio W.

Age: 83
Jasper, Texas
12 September 1937
Interviewer: Letha K. Hatcher, P.W.
[M:5: pt. 4 (TX): 164–65]
[See also S2:10 (TX, pt. 2): 4087–89]

Horatio W. Williams, known as "Rash" to his friends, is 83 years old. He was a slave of Woodruff Norseworthy, in Pine Bluff, Arkansas. Horatio has lived in Jasper, Texas, for many years.

"I was born in slavery in Pine Bluff in de state of Arkansas, on July 2, 1854, and dey tells me dat make me 'bout 84 years old. Woodruff Norseworthy was my owner and boss all de time I a slave. I marry in 1875 and I lost my wife two year ago, and when a man loses a good woman he loses somethin'. Us had 13 chillen, but only two of dem alive now.

"My boss man was mean to he niggers and I 'member crawlin' down through de woods and listenin' one time when he had a nigger. Every time he hit him he pray. Boss have 15 slaves and I recollect one time he gwine beat my mother. She run to kitchen and jump behin' de door and cover herself up in de big pile of dirty clothes. Dey never think to look for her there and she stay there all day. But de next day dey cotch her and whip her.

"Dem what runs away, dey gits bloodhounds after 'em. Dey clumb de tree when dey heered dem hounds comin' but de massa make dem git down and dey shoot dem, iffen dey didn't. When dey gits down de dogs jumps all over dem and would tear dem to pieces, but de massa beats dem off.

"Once de boss has company and one our niggers sleeps on de porch outside de company's room, and in de night he slip in dat room and thiefed de fine, white shirt out de suitcase and wears it round de next mornin'.

"Course he couldn't read and he ain't know de white man have he name on dat shirt. When de boss find it out he takes dat nigger down in de bottom and I crawls through de bresh and watches. Dey tie he foots together over de limb and let he head hang down and beat him till de blood run down on de roots of dat tree. When dey takes him down he back look like raw meat and he nearly die.

"Sometimes when de nigger won't mind dey puts de chain to one foot and a ball on it 'bout big as a nigger's head, and he have to drag it down with him wherever he go.

"My white folks moved to Bastrop in Louisiana and den to Texas and brung me with them. When us work in de field us have de cook what put us food on big trays and carry it to de field, den we stop and eat it under shade of a tree, if dey any. Dey give us bread and meat and syrup for dinner and us has bacon long as it last.

"When I's free I rents land and crops 'round, after I gits marry. Befo' dat, I was here, dere and yonder, for my board and clothes and four bits de day. I give all my chillen de eddication, leastwise dey all kin read and write and dat's what I cain't do.

"I 'longs to de Meth'dist church and I don't unndestan' some dese other churches very well. Seems strange to me dat at dis late time dey's tryin' find new ways of gittin' to Heaven."

Williams, Hulda
Age: 81
1155 No. Lansing Street
Tulsa, Oklahoma
Interviewer: L. P. Livingston
[OK: 484–85]

My mammy use to belong to the Burns plantation back in old Mississippi; that was before I was born, but the white overseer, a man named Kelly, was my father, so my mammy always said. She stayed with the Burns' until her Master's daughter married a man named Bond and moved to Jefferson County, Arkansas, about 25 miles south of Little Rock. The Old Master give mammy and two other slaves to the girl when she married—that's how come mammy to be in Arkansas when I was born, in 1857. The record says July 18. Mammy was named Emmaline and after she got to Arkansas she married one of the Bond slaves, George Washington Bond.

My step-father told me one time that Master Bond tell him to get some slippery-elm bark, but step-paw forget it. And it seem like the Master done forgot it too, but on the next Sunday morning he called out for step-pappy. "Come here," he said. "I'm going to give you a little piece of remembrance!" That was a good flogging, and some of the white neighbors look on and laugh.

But there was one slave, Boyl Green, who lived on a plantation nearby that my husband told me about after we was married. That Negro said he never would let nobody whip him. One day the Master got killing mad about something and told his overseer to bring in Boyl from the field. When he come in there was his Master waiting with a whip and gun. He handed the gun to the overseer and spoke to the slave, "Boyl, you're going to get a good whipping or a shooting—which you going have!"

Boyl he just look straight at his Master and said, "You never going whip me! Nobody going whip me!" The Master motion and the overseer raise the gun and shoot Boyl right through the heart—that's the way some Masters done.

My husband, Nason Bond, told me about his uncle Cal, a man whose face was all mashed in, one-sided like, like maybe his jaw was done broken by the kick of a mule.

It seemed like Uncle Cal hated his Mistress, even after she died. She was buried by a willow tree 'longside of a road, and everytime Cal would ride by the tree he would stop and swear at the grave something awful. One day he sitting on his mule, cussing the woman buried by the tree, when some-thing smack him side of the head and he roll off the mule, nearly dead. Whatever hit him change his face—he went through life marked by the Spirits! . . . everybody said.

After my husband's brother buried his wife, the man was so sad and lonely he would go to her grave every evening and pray. One time in the middle of his prayer he heard a voice: "What are you doing here? This is a place for the dead! The living folks has no business here!" He jumped up and looked around, but there was nobody to see. He run from the grave and never went back no more for prayers.

During War times there was a concentration camp for the Slaves at Pine Bluff. We was in the camp; there was lots of guns and soldiers. The soldiers give each family one piece of wood every day for the camp fire, and just enough food stuff to keep the Negroes from starving. I remember my mammy would slip out at night and steal wood and scraps from the soldier's kitchen. That's all I remember about the War—if I saw any battles I done forgot.

The young darkies these days says they are modern; sass their mammy, too. When I was raising up, the children mind their folks—my mammy was the boss, and she whip me for something when I was 27-year old! The girls nowadays strip their shoulders and bare their legs so's they can catch a man. That's the wrong way to live, and I'm glad I'm a Christian. It makes your heart soft and kind, makes you do good things, and it's the sacrificing of personal pleasure and time that please the Lord!

Williams, Jackson Barkley
Age: 76
Jefferson County Hospital
Pine Bluff, Arkansas
Interviewer: Bernice Bowden
[S2:1 (AR): 250–51]

Jackson Barkley Williams is my name—I sign it J. B. Williams. I was born in 'sixty-two, April the 12th.

I was born in the upper part of the state near the Missouri line and come down here in my mother's arms in slavery times.

I was a little bit of a boy runnin' around and I can remember seein' 'em dance around sayin' they was free. O yes ma'm!

Me and Leo M. Andrews was play-boys together. Me and him use to play marbles together.

I use to go to the country school and then I come in to Pine Bluff to go to school. Professor M. W. Martin was a white man from the north. It was a free school. I went part of four years here in town. I was in Mr. Guffy's sixth reader and the Blue-back speller when I quit. I started to town school in 'seventy-four but I went in the country before that.

The biggest kind of work I ever done is farming.

My folks stayed on the Fish place after freedom but they farmed for themselves and some of 'em worked by the day.

There was three brothers of us and two sisters. Colonel Fish bought my mother from a man in Washington County.

After freedom she went over here on the Warren road on a place my brother-in-law's father bought.

I'm the onliest one of the brothers living.

I use to work in the gin house. I pressed the cotton. I aint been able to work since 'thirty-three. Last place I farmed was at Fairfield.

I guess I'm about five feet six. I use to weigh two hundred and two when I was young.

I did belong to the Woodmen but it went down. I haven't jined no church. No ma'm. I aint got no family. No ma'm I never did marry.

Extra Comment
This man is about five feet six inches tall and weighs between one hundred sixty-five and one hundred seventy. Dark complexion—white hair. Walks with a cane.

He lives at the Jefferson County Hospital which has just recently been completed.

Johnson County

Lee, Mandy
Age: 85
Coal Hill, Arkansas
Interviewer: Sallie C. Miller
[M:9: pt. 4: 250]

"Yes'm I was a slave. I been here. I heard the bugles blowing, the fife beat, the drums beat, and the cannons roar. We started to Texas but never got across the river. I don't know what town it was but it was just across the river from Texas. My white folks was good to me. I staid with them till they died. Missy died first, then master died. I never was away from them. They was both good. My mammy was sold but I never was. They said they was surrendered when we come back from Texas. I heard the drums beat at Ft. Smith when we come back but I don't know what they was doing. I worked in the house with the children and in the field too. I help herd the horses. I would card and spin and eat peaches. No, that wasn't all I had to eat. I didn't have enough meat but I had plenty of milk and potatoes. I was born right here in Coal Hill. I ain't never lived anywhere else except when we went South during the war.

"Law woman I can't tell you what I think of the present generation. They are good in their way but they don't do like we did. I never did go naked. I don't see how they stand it.

"I could sing when I was young. We sang everything, the good and bad."

Strayhorn, Eva
Age: 79
1016 E. Grand Ave.
McAlester, Oklahoma
Interviewer: Mrs. Jessie R. Ervin
[OK: 411–17]

When I was a child in Arkansas we used to go to camp-meetings with the white folks. We went right along by they side till we got to church and we set down on the back seat. We took part in all services. When they wasn't any church our old Master would call us in on Sunday morning and read the Bible to us and we would sing some good old songs and den go 'bout our ways. Some of the songs that we sung still ring in my ears and I still remember the words to some of them:

> "Must Jesus bear the cross alone
> And all the world go free ...
> No, there's a cross for everyone
> And there's a cross for me."

Another one was:

> "Oh, Jesus is a rock in a weary land,
> A weary land, a weary land,
> Jesus is a rock in a weary land
> A shelter in the time of storm."

We sung a lot of others such as: "I Am Bound for the Promised Land," "The Old Time Religion," and "When I Can Read My Title Clear, To Mansions in the Skies." My favorites was the ones I just give you and they are still my favorite songs.

I was born in Johnson County, Clarksville, Arkansas. My father was Henry and my mother was Cindy Newton. Master Bill Newton owned them both.

Father was owned by a man named Perry when he first married my mother and he had to have a pass every time he come to visit her. The Patrollers give him so much trouble dat Old Man Bill Newton just put a stop to it by buying father from his master.

Master Newton let my father build a nice little two-room log house just outside the regular quarters and he went with him to the Turners and had two nice bedsteads made, the kind that had ropes laced across for springs. Father then made some white-oak chairs with split bottoms. Mother made some rag rugs and they settled down to keeping house. We had a nice big fireplace and we had a cozy little home and was as happy as the day was long.

Our old Master was a really good man. He was kind to us and provided well for us. He never allowed his slaves to be whipped and if any of them was sick he saw to it that they was well cared for and had a doctor if dey needed one.

Mother was the cook for the white folks and all the food for everybody was cooked in the kitchen at the big house. The white folks' food was carried to the dining room and our food was carried to our homes. I reckon we had the same food that dey had for I know we always had plenty of good food.

We had a nigger overseer. Some folks called colored overseers "nigger drivers" or "nigger overlookers." This overseer had complete charge of the plantation and the hands, for old Master was hardly ever at home. He was a Legislator at Little Rock.

The overseer's name was Solomon and he had the right name for he sure was a smart man. When he was a young boy he used to take his young mistress, Miss Liza, to school. She was jest a little girl and if the road was muddy he would carry her on his shoulder. She was his special charge and he would a died for her. Dey would sit down to rest by de roadside and she would learn him out of her books. Dey would do this every day and soon he could read as good as she could. As she growed up she kept learning more and Solomon had married and Miss Liza would go down to his cabin every night and teach im some more. His wife learned to read a little.

Miss Liza finally married and went away and nobody knowed Solomon could read, as Miss Liza never had said anything about teaching him for she was afraid her pappy wouldn't like it. One night old Master went down to his house to give him orders for the next day and there set Sol with the Bible on his lap. Old Master said, "Sol, what are you doing with that Book?" Sol say, "I'ze reading it, Marse Bill. I ain't going to tell you no lie about it." Master Bill say, "How on earth did you learn to read?" Sol told him that Miss Liza learnt him when he used to tote her to school. Master Bill set there a minute and he said, "I want you to read it to me." Sol read it to him jest like he was talking it off. This sure did tickle Master Bill and he told him that he wanted him to practice up good, that he was going to have his head examined on Sunday. This sort of scared old Sol but he went ahead and sure enough on Sunday they was several men come out from town and old Master had Sol read for dem. A Dr. Weems was in the crowd. He had Sol set down in a chair and he felt all over his head and talked all de time he was examining them. He told old Master that Sol was an on-commonly smart man.

I never did have no regular job. There was two other children that lived with us, one a girl about my age and size. Her name was Ann. Me and her had to run errands for our old Miss and my mother. We swept and dusted the white folks' house, swept the yards, carried water from the spring and drove the calves to the pasture and any other little job dat we was big enough to do. Sometimes mother would let us help her cook and we liked that best of all.

The country began to be all torn up and everybody was talking about war. Dey commenced recruiting soldiers and all de young men went off to de army.

Old Master had two sons, Robert and William. Dey had been to California to the gold fields for two or three year. When they come home old

Master hoped dey would settle down and stay at home so he give dem some slaves. He gave my old grandmother and two of her children to Master William and he gave Hannah and her brother to master Robert. Dey kept dem for awhile and den dey said de war was coming on and dey would be likely to lose dem anyway so dey was going to sell dem and realized something from dem. Old Master tried to get dem to keep dem but dey wouldn't do it. My grandmother and her children sold together for $1,100. The other poor woman, Hannah, was sold away from her children. Ann was about seven year old and Frank was five. When she left she said to my mother, "Cindy, be a mother to my children, will you. I hate to leave dem, poor little things, but I can't help myself. Dere poor father is dead and only God knows what will become of dem," and dey took her away to Texas.

Mother kept her promise and took de two children into our house and looked after dem jest like dey was hers. Old Miss Tessie and Master Bill loved dem and was awful good to dem, too.

Both of Master Bill's boys went to de army. Dere wasn't no men or boys at home during de war. The white men dat was not too old was in de army and de colored men and boys had been refugeed to Texas. Dere owners thought dat if dey could get dem to Texas dey wouldn't have to free dem. De women had to do all de work. Mother had to work mighty hard as she had to cut wood and haul it in with a team of oxen. Us children helped her all we could.

Master Bill and Miss Tessie talked things over and dey decided that Master Bill would slip away after night with his colored men and boys and keep dem in Texas for awhile and maybe dey could save dem dat way. He thought dat Miss Tessie would be safe at home with mother and us children. One night about midnight he took father and Jim and Sol and all the boys over ten year old and dey left for Texas and we never saw dem anymore for a long time.

Young Master William was shot in the war and dey brought him home. He lived about a week after dey brought him back. Master Robert found out dat his brother was about to die and he and a squad of men slipped back home to see him. Dey dassent stay at home but scouted 'round in the woods nearby.

One morning 'bout daylight my mother called me and Ann and told us to go to the big house, dat Miss Tessie had something to tell us. She told us that she wanted us to go on up on de hill and for me to stand at de corner of the field and for Ann to go a little further on and for us to watch for the blue-coated soldiers. She had heard dat dere was a squad scouting around in de neighborhood trying to catch Master Robert and his friends. Well, me and Ann went to our posts and set down to watch. I was too young and sleepy to bother much about soldiers or anything else so I put my head down on my knees and went fast asleep. The next thing I knew I heard guns popping all 'round me right over my head. I jumped up and looked down de road and saw my mother with her hands full of food and coffee. She was on her way to take food to Master Robert and de soldiers had seen her and were shooting at her. I jumped up and ran to her jest as fast as I could and de soldiers quit shooting when dey saw me. Mother stood right still and de soldiers rode right by us jest like we wasn't dere. Dey rode in the direction dat mother was going and found de boys and Master Robert. Dey started runnin' but most of dem was captured but none of dem was killed. Dey shot a fine black horse down from under one man and it fell on him and of course dey got him, Master Robert and one of de boys jumped in a creek and hid under a a big drift and dey didn't catch dem.

Mother was wearing a white sunbonnet and it had three holes shot in it, one in the tail and two in the crown. Dey put out poor spies when dey put me and Ann out to watch.

All the colored people in the country, men, women and children, 'cept mother and her children and de two little children dat Hannah left in her care, had gone wid de soldiers to de north where dey would be set free. Mother wouldn't leave for she told de officers, "Henry is in de South and I'll never see him again if I leave de old home place for he won't know where to find me." De officer told her dat he was coming back de next day after us and for her to be ready to go. Mother told Miss Tessie dat she was going to town and take the oath of peace and dey couldn't make her leave. Old Miss told her to go on, so that night she hitched up the oxen and took her children and set out to Dover, Arkansas, twelve miles away, to see the bureau man and take the oath.

We traveled till 'bout midnight and come to a man's house that we knew. He let us stay all night and we was up by good daylight and on our way again. We come to a creek and it was up. It was runnin' wild and mother was afraid to try to cross it. A man come along and he tied de wagon bed down with hickory withes so we could cross. Mother drove in and de oxen swum and drug de wagon along behind dem. We crossed safely and drove till we come to a narrow pass in de mountains. Blue coat soldiers began to pass us, walking two and two. Mother stopped de wagon and when dey would come up to it dey would separate and one would go on one side of de wagon and one on de other, but dey didn't say anything to us. It seemed like dey was in a great hurry. We set dere in de wagon till late dat evening before de soldiers quit passing us and den it was too late for us to go on. We went about a mile and come to a house and dey let us stay all night and de next morning we drove on into town. It was de first time any of us ever had been to town and I know mother was scared but she was determined to take de oath so she could stay on wid old Miss Tessie. She left us children in de wagon while she went in to talk to de bureau man.

Mother was awfully light, had gray eyes and straight hair and when she got to see de bureau man he said, "What are you coming here for, you ain't no nigger, you are a darned Sesesh white and I ain't got no time to fool wid you." Mother done everything she could to convince him dat she was a colored woman but she couldn't do it. She had an aunt 'bout ten miles from town and she decided to go dere and if she hadn't gone away she would get her to come back wid her and swear dat she was a colored woman. She took us away and we went again to try to find her aunt Susan. We got dere about dark and sure enough aunt Susan was still dere and her master let her go back wid us. Aunt Susan was dark and she swore that mother was her sister's child and dey finally let her sign the oath.

The oath of peace was dat you would obey de law and wouldn't harbor no Rebel soldiers nor no bushwhackers or do nothing dat was wrong or would hinder de cause of de North.

When we got back home we didn't have no home. De very night dat we left, de bushwhackers, or toe-burners as dey was called, come to our house and told Miss Tessie dat dey wanted her money. She told dem dat she didn't have any but dey didn't believe her and told her dat dey would burn her if she didn't give dem her money. She kept tellin' dem dat she didn' have any money and dey took everything dey wanted and den jerked the curtains off de windows and piled dem in de middle of de room and de furniture on top of dem and set dem afire and burned everything 'cept the nigger quarters. It was a pity to burn dat big pretty two-story house, but dey done it.

Mother and us children went to live on the side of de mountain in a little cabin by ourselves and Miss Tessie went to live wid Miss Liza, her daughter. Mother had to keep her oath and she was afraid dat if she went wid Miss Tessie dat Master Robert might come home and they would say she had broke her oath and make her leave. One night mother was spinnin' and I was cardin' and everything was jest as quiet and we heard somebody tap in de door. We set real quiet and den we heard it again. You dassent speak above a whisper so mother went to de door and say real low, "Who's dere?" "It's your old Master Bill Newton." Mother forgot and said louder, "Is that really you Master Bill, and how did you know where I was?" He told her to open de door and let him in and he would tell her. She opened de door and sure enough it was Master Bill. He had come back to see how we was all gettin' along and found his house burnt. Somebody told him dat his wife was at Miss Liza's so he went dere and she told him where we was. He told mother dat he wanted her to go to his brother Nazor's and wait for him dere and he would take us to where father was. She hitched up de oxen and we went down to Uncle Nazor's and one night Old Master and Miss Tessie slipped in dere and got us and took us to Texas. We found father and we was all happy again.

I never had seen slaves punished before we went to Texas but I saw a woman tied down and whipped one day. Old Master was jest as good to us as he always had been and never punished any of us. Dey say dat de people in Texas was a lot harder on dere slaves during de war dan they ever had been before.

Old Miss Tessie had kept de two little children wid her after de house was burned and took dem wid her when we went South. After peace was made and we started back home she heard from somebody dat my grandmother was down dere pretty close to where dey were so dey went by dere and found grandmother and Hannah, too. She almost died she was so happy to see her little children again. She thanked mother and Miss Tessie over and over for taking care of her children for her.

After peace was made old Master called us all to him and told us dat we was free now, jest as free as he was, and dat he had some things dat he wanted to tell us. He talked to us jest like we was his own children wid tears running down his cheeks. He said, "Cindy, I've raised you from a baby and you, Henry, since you was a young man. I've tried to be good to you and take good care of you in return for de good work you have always done for me. I want you to go out in de worl' now and make good citizens. Be honest and respectable and don't turn against the good raisin' you have had and remember dat me and my wife loves you all."

We all went back wid dem to de old home place in Arkansas, and father went on 'bout 50 miles and got a job and come back after mother and us children. Young Master Robert bought a plantation 'bout fifteen miles from where we lived and old Master and Miss Tessie lived wid him. She got down low sick and begged and begged mother to come take care of her. Master Robert come and told mother and father hitched up the oxen and dey left dat night. Old Master said de very sight of Lucindy cured Miss Tessie. She got well and lived 'bout ten year after dat. When she took sick again mother went back and took care of her as long as she lived. Old Master lived several year after Miss Tessie died.

I married when I was fifteen. I remembered what a fine wedding Miss Liza had and I said I was going to git Old Master to let me have one jest like hers. I married in my mother and father's home and I had my wedding jest as near like Miss Liza's as I could. I had a long white dress and a long veil and a big bouquet of flowers. I didn't have things as fine as she did but I done my best. She had roses and I had jest common paper flowers. Her dress was satin and mine was cotton, my veil was cotton, too, but I thought it was fine and so did everybody else. We married on Christmas night and we had a big supper. Dey was as many white folks dere as colored and we had a grand time. De next day we went to housekeepin' and we lived together till nineteen year ago when my husband died. I had fifteen children but dere is only three living today.

Lee County

Thomas, Omelia
Age: 63
1014 W. Fifth Street
Little Rock, Arkansas
Interviewer: Samuel S. Taylor
[M:10: pt. 6: 300–303]

"I was born in Marianna, Lee County, in Arkansas. I wasn't born right in the town but out a piece from the town in the old Bouden place, in 1875. My father kept a record of all births and deaths in his Bible. He never forgot whenever a new baby would come to get down his glasses and pen and ink and Bible. My daddy learned to read and write after the emancipation.

"My father's name was Frank Johnson and my mother's name was Henrietta Johnson. I don't know the given names of my father's and mother's parents. I do know my mother's mother's name, Lucinda, and my father's mother was named Stephens. I don't know their given names. My mother's master was a Trotter.

"My father was a free man. He hired his own time. He told me that his father hired his own time and he would go off and work. He made washpots. He would go off and work and bring back money and things. His mother was free too. When war was declared, he volunteered to go. He was with the Yankees. My father worked just like my grandfather did. Whenever he had a job to do. He never had a lick from anybody, carried his gun strapped down on his side all the time and never went without it.

"After the War, he worked on a steamboat. They used to kick the roustabouts about and run them around but they never laid the weight of their hands on him.

"They wouldn't allow him to go to school in slavery time. After the War, he got a Blue Back Speller and would make a bowl of fire and at night he would study—sometimes until daybreak. Then he found an old man that would help him and he studied under him for a while. He never went to any regular school, but he went to night school a little. Most of what he got, he got himself.

"He was born in Louisville, Kentucky. I don't know how he happened to meet my mother. During the time after the War, he went to running on the boat from New Orleans to Friars (Friar) Point, Mississippi. Then he would come over to Helena. In going 'round, he met my mother near Marianna and married her.

"Mother never had much to say, and the other girls would have a big time talking. He noticed that she was sewing with ravelings and he said, 'Lady, next time I come I'll bring you a spool of thread if you don't mind.' He brought the thread and she didn't mind, and from then on, they went to courting. Finally they married. They married very shortly after the War.

"My mother was a motherless girl. My daddy said he looked at her struggling along. All the other girls were trying to have a good time. But she would be settin' down trying to make a quilt or something else useful, and he said to a friend of his, 'That woman would make a good wife; I am going to marry her.' And he did.

"She used to spin her fine and coarse sewing thread and yarn to make socks and stockings with. Her stockings and socks for the babies and papa would always be yarn. She could do pretty work. She had a large family. She had seventeen children and she kept them all in things she made herself. She raised ten of them. She would make the thread and yarn and the socks and stockings for all of these. I have known the time when she used to make coats and pants for my father and brothers. She would make them by hand because they didn't have any machines then. Of course, she made all the underwear. She put up preserves and jellies for us to eat in the winter. She used to put up kraut and stuff by the barrel. I have seen some happy days when I was with my daddy and mother. He raised pigs and hogs and chickens and cows. He raised all kinds of peas and vegetables. He raised those things chiefly for the home, and he made cotton for money. He would save about eight or ten bales and put them under his shed for stockings and clothes and everything. He would have another cotton selling in March.

"When my father was in the army, he would sometimes be out in the weather, he told us, and he and the other soldiers would wrap up in their blankets and sleep right in the snow itself.

"I farmed all my life until 1897. I farmed all my life till then. I was at home. I married in 1895. My first husband and I made three crops and then he stopped and went to public work. After that I never farmed any more but went to cooking and doing laundry work. I came from Clarendon here in 1901.

"I never had any experiences with the Yankees. My mother used to tell how they took all the old master's stuff—mules and sugar—and then throwed it out and rode their horses through it when they didn't want it for theirselves.

"I married a second time. I have been single now for the last three years. My husband died on the twentieth of August three years ago. I ain't got no business here at all. I ought to be at my home living well. But I work for what I get and I'm proud of it.

"A working woman has many things to contend with. That girl downstairs keeps a gang of men coming and going, and sometimes some of them sometimes try to come up here. Sunday night when I come home from church, one was standing in the dark by my door waiting for me. I had this stick in my hand and I ordered him down. He saw I meant business; so he went on down. Some of them are determined.

"There's no hope for tomorrow so far as these young folks are concerned. And the majority of the old people are almost worse than the young ones. Used to be that all the old people were mothers and fathers but now they are all going together. Everything is in a critical condition. There is not much truth in the land. All human affection is gone. There is mighty little respect. The way some people carry on is pitiful."

Interviewer's Comment

The men who bother Omelia Thomas probably take her for a young woman. She hasn't a gray hair in her head, and her skin is smooth and must be well kept. She looks at least twenty-five years younger than she is, and but for the accident of her presence at another interview, I would never have dreamed that she had a story to tell.

I went to see her in the quarters where she lives—over the garage in the back yard of the white people she works for. When I got halfway up the stairs, she shouted, "You can't come up here." I paused in perplexity for a moment, and she stuck her head out the door and looked. Then she said, "Oh, I beg pardon; I thought you were one of those men that visit downstairs." I had noticed the young lady below as I entered. She is evidently a hot number, and as troublesome as a sore thumb to the good old lady above her.

White, Lucy
Age: 74
Marianna, Arkansas
Interviewer: Irene Robertson
[M:11: pt. 7: 134–35]

"I was born on Jim Banks' place close to Felton. His wife named Miss Puss. Mama and all of young master's niggers was brought from Mississippi. I reckon it was 'fore I was born. Old master name Mack Banks. I never heard mama say but they was good to my daddy. They had a great big place in Mississippi and a good big place over here.

"I recollect seeing the soldiers prance 'long the road. I thought they looked mighty pretty. Their caps and brass buttons and canteens shining in the sun. They rode the prettiest horses. One of 'em come in our house one day. He told Miss Puss he was goiner steal me. She say, 'Don't take her off.' He give me a bundle er bread and I run in the other room and crawled under the bed 'way back in the corner. It was dark up under there. I didn't eat the bread then but I et it after he left. It sure was good. I didn't recollect much but seeing them pass the road. I like to watch 'em. My parents was field folks. I worked in the field. I was raised to work. I keep my clothes clean. I washed 'em. I cooked and washed and ironed and done field work all. When I first recollect Marianna, Mr. Lon Tau and Mr. Free Landing (?) had stores here. Dr. Steven (Stephen?) and Dr. Nunnaly run a drug store here. There was a big road here. Folks started building houses here and there. They called the town Mary Ann fo' de longest time.

"Well, the white folks told 'em, 'You free.' My folks worked on fer about twenty years. They'd give 'em a little sompin outer dat crap. They worked all sorter ways—that's right—they sure did. They rented and share cropped together I reckon after the War ended.

"The Ku Klux never bothered us. I heard 'bout 'em other places.

"I never voted and I never do 'sepect to now. What I know 'bout votin'?

"Well, I tell you, these young folks is cautions. They don't think so but they is. Lazy, no'count, spends ever cent they gits in their hands. Some works, some work hard. They drink and carouse about all night sometimes. No ma'am, I did not do no sich er way. I woulder been ashamed of myself. I would. Times what done run away wid us all now. I don't know what to look fer now but I know times changing all the time.

"I gets ten dollars and some little things to eat along. I say it do help out. I got rheumatism and big stiff j'ints (enlarged wrist and knuckles)."

Little River County

Parker, Judy
Age: 77
618 Wade Street
Hot Springs, Arkansas
Interviewer: Mary D. Hudgins
[M:10: pt. 5: 249–54]

As the interviewer walked down Silver Street a saddle colored girl came out on a porch for a load of wood.

"I beg your pardon," she began, pausing, "can you tell me where I will find Emma Sanderson?"

"I sure can." The girl left the porch and came out to the street. "I'll walk down with you and show you. That way it'll be easier. Kind of cold, ain't it?"

"It surely is," this from the interviewer. "Isn't it too cold for you, can't you just tell me? I think I can find it." The girl had expected to be only on the porch and didn't have a coat.

"No, ma'am. It's all right. Now we're far enough for you to see. You see those two houses jam up against one and 'tother? Well Miz Parker lives in the one this way. I goes down to look after her most every day. That's where you'll find her.—No ma'am—'twaren't no bother."

The gate sagged slightly at the house "this way" of the "two jam up against one and 'tother." A large slab from an oak log in the front yard near a wood-pile bore mute evidence of many an ax blow. (Stove wood is generally split in the rural South—one end of the "stick" resting against the ground, the other atop a small log.

Up a couple of rickety steps the interviewer climbed. She knocked three times. When she was bade to enter she opened the door to find an old woman sitting near a wood stove combing her long, white hair.

Mrs. Parker was expecting the visit. A few days before the interviewer had had a visit from a couple of colored women who had "heard tell how you is investigating the old people—been trying to get on old age pension for a long time—glad you come to get us on.—No? Oh, I see you is the Townsend woman." (An explanation of her true capacity was almost impossible for the interviewer.)

Mrs. Parker, however, seemed to comprehend the idea perfectly. She expected nothing save the chance to tell her story. Her joy at the gift of a quarter (the amount the interviewer set aside from her salary for each interviewee) was pitiful. Evidently it had been a long time since she had possessed a similar sum to spend exactly as she pleased.

"I don't rightly know how old I is. My mother used to tell me that I was a little baby, six months old when our master, Joe Potts was his name, got ready to clear out of Florida. You see he had heard tell of the war scare. So he started drifting out of the way. Bet it didn't take him long after he made up his mind. He was a right decided man, Mister Joe was.

How did we like him? Well, he was always good to us. He was well thought of. Seemed to be a pretty clever man, Mr. Joe did." ("Clever" in plantation language like "smart" refers more to muscular than mental activity. They might almost be used as synonyms for "hard working" on the labor level.)

So Mr. Joe got ready to go to Texas. Law, Miss, I don't rightly know whether he had a family or not. Never heard my Mother say. Anyhow he come through Arkansas intending to drift on out into Texaas. But when he got near the border 'twix't and between Arkansas and Texas he stopped. The talk about war had settled down. So he stopped. He stopped near where the big bridge is. You know where Little River County is don't you? He stopped and he started to work. Started to make a crop. 'Course I can't remember none about that. Just what my Mother told me. But I remembers him from later.

He went at it the good way. Settled down and tried to open up a home. They put in a crop and got along pretty good. Time passed and the war talk started floating again. That time he didn't pay much attention and it got him. It was on a Sunday morning when he went away. I never knew whether they made him go or not. But I kind of think they must of. Cause he wouldn't have moved off from Florida if he had wanted to go to war.

He took my daddy with him. Ma'am—did he take him to fight or to wait on him—Don't know ma'am, but I sort of think he took him to wait on him. But he didn't bring him back. My daddy got killed in the war. No ma'am. I don't rightly know how he got killed. Never heard nobody say. I was just a little girl—nobody bothered to tell me much.

Yes, that we did. We stayed on on the farm and we made a crop—the old folks did. Mr. Joe, when he went off, said "Now you stay on here, you make a crop and you use all you need. Then you put up the rest and save for me. He was a right good man, Mr. Joe was.

No, we didn't never see no fighting. There wasn't nothing to be scared of. Didn't see no Yankees until the war was through. Then they started passing. Lawsey, I couldn't tell how many of them there was. More than you could count.

We had all stayed on. I was the oldest of my mother's children. But she had two more after me. There was our family and my two uncles and my grandmother. Then there was some other colored folks. But we wasn't scared of the Yankees. Mr. Joe was there by that time. They camped all around in the woods near us. They got us to do their washing. Lawsey they was as filthy as hogs. I never see such folks. They asked Mr. Joe if we could do their washing. Everything on the place that come near those clothes got lousey. Those men was covered with them. I never see nothing like it. We got covered with them. No, ma'am, we got rid of 'em pretty easy. They ain't so hard to get rid of, if you keep clean.

After it was all over Master Joe got ready to go back to Florida. He took Warley and Jenny with him. They was children he had had by a black woman—you know folks did such things in them days. He asked the rest of us if they wanted to go back too. But my folks made up their minds they didn't. You see, they didn't know how they'd get along and how long it would take them to pay for the trip back, so they stayed right where they was.

Lots of 'em went to Rondo and some of us worked for Herb Jeans—he lived farther up Red River. After my mother died I was with my grandmother. She washed and cooked for Herb Jeans's family. I stayed on with her, helped out until I got married. I was about fifteen when that time came.

My man owned his place. Sure he did. Owned it when I married him. He owned it himself and farmed it good. Yes ma'am we stayed with the land. He made good crops—corn and cotton, mostly. Course we raised potatoes and the truck we needed—all stuff like that. Yes, ma'am we had thirteen children. Just three of them's living. All of them is boys.

Yes ma'am we got along good. My husband made good crops and we got along just good. But 'bout eight years ago my husband he got sick. So he sold out the farm—sold out everything. Then he come here.

Before he died he spent every last cent—every last cent—left me to get along the very best way I kin. I stays with my son. He takes care of me. He don't make much, but he does the best he kin.

No ma'am, I likes living down in the country. Down there near Red River it's soft and sandy. Up here in Hot Springs the rocks tear up your feet. If you's country raised—you like the country. Yes ma'am, you like the country."

As she left the interviewer handed her a quarter. At first the old woman's face was expressionless. But she moved the coin nearer to her eyes and a smile broke and widened until her whole face was a wrinkle of joy. When she turned in the doorway, the interviewer noticed that the hand jammed into an apron pocket was clutched into a possessive fist, cradling the precious twenty-five cents.

Lonoke County

Jones, Evelyn
Age: 70?
815 Arch Street
Little Rock, Arkansas
Interviewer: Samuel S. Taylor
[M:9: pt. 4: 145–47]

"I was born in Lonoke County right here in Arkansas. My father's name—I don't know it. I don't know nothin' 'bout my father. My mother's name was Mary Davis.

"My daddy died when I was five weeks old. I don't know nothin' 'bout 'im. Just did manage to git here before he left. I don't know the date of my birth. I don't know nothin' 'bout it and I ain't goin' to tell no lie.

"I have nineteen children. My youngest living child is twenty-eight years old. My oldest living is fifty-three. I have four dead. I don't know how old the oldest's one is. That one's dead.

"I have a cousin named Harry Jordan. He lives 'round here somewheres. You'll find him. I don't know where he lives. He says he knows just how old I am, and he says that I'm sixty-eight. My daughter here says I'm seventy. And my son thinks I'm older. Don't nobody know. My daddy never told me. My mama was near dead when I was born; what could she tell me? So how am I to know?

"My mother was born in slavery. She was a slave. I don't know nothing' 'bout it. My mother came from Tennessee. That's what she told me. I was born in a log cabin right here in Arkansas. I was born in a log cabin right in front of the white folks' big house. It was not far from the white folks' graveyard. You know they had a graveyard of their own. Old Bill Pemberton, that was the name of the man owned the place I was born on. But he wasn't my mother's owner.

"I don't know where my father come from. My mother said she had a good time in slavery. She spoke of lots of things but I don't remember them.

"My granma told me about when she went to church she used to carry her good clothes in a bundle. When she got near there, she would put them on, and hide her old clothes under a rock. When she come out from the meeting, she would have to put on her old clothes again to go home in. She didn't dare let the white folks see her in good clothes.

"I think my mother's white people were named Jordans. My mother and them all belonged to the young mistress. I think her name was Jordan. Yes, that's what it was—Jordan.

"Grandmammy had so many children. She had nineteen children—just like me. My grandmammy was a great big old red woman. She had red hair too. I never heard her say nothin' 'bout nobody whippin' her and my granddaddy. They whipped all them children though. My mama just had six children.

"Mama said her master tried to keep her in slavery after freedom. My mama worked at the spinning-wheel. When she heard the folks say they was through with the War, she was at the spinning-wheel. The white folks ought a tol' them they was free but they didn't. Old Jordan carried them down in De Valls Bluff. He carried them down there—called hisself gittin' away from the Yankees. But the Yankees told mama to quit workin'. They tol' her that she was free. My mama said she was in there at the wheel spinning and the house was full of white men settin' there lookin' at her. You don't see that sort of thing now.

"They had a man—I don't know what his name was. He stalled them steers, stalled 'em twice a day. They used to pick cotton. I dreamed about cotton the other night.

"My father farmed after slavery. I never heard them say they were cheated out of nothin'. I don't know whether they was or not. I'll tell you the truth. I didn't pay them no 'tention. Mighty little I can remember."

Waddill, Emiline
Age: 106 (deceased)
Lonoke County, Arkansas
Interviewer: Mrs. Blanche Edwards
Interviewee: Mrs. John G. High
20 October 1938
[M:11: pt. 7: 13–13B]

Emiline Waddell, a former slave of the L.W.C. Waddell family, lived to be 106 years old, and was active up to her death.

She was born a slave in 1826 at Raben county, Georgia, a slave of Claybourne Waddell, who emigrated to Brownsville [Lonoke County], in 1851, in covered wagons, oxen drawn.

Her "white folks" were three weeks making the trip from the ferry across the Mississippi to old Brownsville; after traveling all day through the bad and boggy woods, at the end of their rough journey at eventide, the movers dismounted and began hasty preparations for the night. While the men were feeding the stock and providing temporary quarters, the women assisted the slaves in preparing the evening meal, of hoe-cake, fried venison and coffee. Then the women and children would sleep in the wagons while the men kept watch for wild life.

Mammy Emiline was a faithful old black mammy, true to life and traditions, and refused her freedom, at the close of the war, as she wanted to stay and raise "Ole Massa's chilluns," which she did, for she was nursing her sixth generation in the Waddell family at the time of her death. Even to that generation there was a close tie between the southern child and his or her black mammy. A strange almost unbelievable thing happened to Emiline; she was born a deaf-mute, but her hearing and speech was restored many years before her death, when lightening struck a tree under which she was standing.

Superstitious beliefs were strong in her and her tales of "hants" were to "her little white chilluns", really true but hair-raising. Then she would talk and live again the "days that are no more", telling them of the happy prosperous, sunny land, in her negro dialect, and then tell of the ruin and desolation behind the Yankees; the hard times my white folks had in the reconstruction days—negro and carpetbag rule; then give them glimpses of good—much courage, some heart and human feeling; perhaps ending with an outburst of the negro spiritual, her favorite being, "Swing low, sweet chariot, coming for to carry me home."

After a faithful service of 106 years, Emiline died in 1932 at the home of Mrs. John High, a great-granddaughter of L.W.C. Waddell living nine miles north of Lonoke, and the grown up great-great-grandchildren still miss Mammy.

[Editor's note: another interview offers an alternate spelling, Emmeline Wadille.]

Marion County

Elgin, Tempe
Age: 75
Austin, Texas
Interviewer: Alfred E. Menn
25 February 1933
[S2:4 (TX, pt. 3): 1292–98]

Tempe Elgin, seventy-five, was born a slave on November 25, 1862, on the cotton plantation of Charley Primm, in Marion County, Arkansas. William

Tyson, Primm's son-in-law, became the owner of Tempe, her mother, Harriet King, and her sister, Julia. They were brought to a cotton plantation in Burleson County, Texas. Tempe's father, John King, belonged to a man by the name of King, and he was not brought to Texas. John followed his wife on horseback for sixty miles, pleading with her to run away with him so they would not have to part, but Harriet told him she couldn't leave her two little girls, Tempe and Julia. Harriet never saw her husband again, although she heard from him once. She then married James Parker, who was cruel to his two step-daughters. Tempe's mother died when she was twenty-seven years old. Tempe and Julia worked at odd jobs. When she was sixteen she married Sylvester Elgin. They had five children, three boys and two girls, of whom only two boys still are living. Her husband died on November 25, 1937. Tempe lives at 1616 East 3rd Street, Austin, and receives a monthly pension of eleven dollars from the State of Texas.

"Dat sure has been a long time since freedom cried out. It has sure been a long time since de slavery days.

"I don't remembah my pappy. I know dat his name was John King. I always heard mammy say dat pappy belonged to a Mawster King down in Marion County, Arkansas. Mammy would tell us how pappy loved her so much dat when she and two of her girls, me and Julia, was brought on down to Texas he follered 'em fo' about sixty miles.

"'Harriet,' he'd say, 'come on wid me. Let's run away f'om yo' mawster, and we'll live together.'

"'I kain't John,' mammy tole him, 'cause I got to look out fo' my little Tempe and Julia.'

"'Goodbye Harriet,' pappy said.

"So pappy rode away on his hoss and mammy never did see him again. She got jes' about one letter f'om him. Later in life we tried to look up some of de King fambles in Arkansas but we never did find no trace of pappy. I reckon dat he's been dead fo' a long time.

"My mammy was Harriet King. She was of a putty good size. She done mos' any kind of work durin' her life. She didn't live long, only twenty-seben years. When she was in Texas, she up and married James Parker. He was a worker on mawster James Parker's cotton plantation down in Burleson County. Parker was so mean to us kids dat his boss man run him off of de place. Dat step-pappy of our'n sure was rough.

"Dey done named me Tempe Salina Bettie King. Dat was my name when I was a girl. Mos' folks jes' called me Tempe. I don't know jes' why dey called me Tempe.

"I was bawn on November 25, 1862. Dat means dat I'm goin' to be seventy-six years old dis year. Oh, my and how I've been bustled around in all of dat time. I was bawn on de Charley Primm cotton plantation in Marion County, Arkansas. He was mammy's mawster. Pappy's mawster was a Mr. King.

"Den Mawster Primm's son-in-law, William Tyson, bought us. He was comin' to Texas. Me, Julia, and mammy was brought along. He den run a cotton plantation in Burleson County. He had only a few slave families.

"I was about sixteen years old, in 1878, when I got married. My husband's name was Sylvester Elgin. Instead of callin' him Sylvester, we always jes' shortened it to Bess. Dat's it—Bess.

"Bess rented two hosses and we rode all of de way to Bryan, in Brazos County, to git married. A Jedge Connell, I think it was, married us. We didn't pay nothin' fo' de marryin' but Bess had to pay about a dollah and a half fo' de license. Den we rode back to de place where we worked on de Jedge Davis cotton fahm, in Burleson County.

"We worked jes' lak always. Yo' see dat's where I met my husband. After slavery when our step-pappy was run off'n his boss man's place me and Julie den worked fo' a lot of other famblies.

"I stahted to work fo' Jedge Davis. I chopped and picked cotton. De jedge give me four bits a day fo' choppin' de cotton, f'om sun to sun, but fo' pickin' cotton I got fifty cents fo' each hunnert pounds dat I picked. Of cose, at dat time I couldn't pick more'n a hunndert or a hunnert and ten pounds a day. I was jes' a girl. But when I got older I got so dat I could pick three and four hunnertpounds a day. I always did lak to pick cotton.

"Dere wasn't much to pickin' cotton in de early days but I had to make a livin'. I lived wid de other workers in some cabins on de fahm. We wasn't chahged no rent but we had to buy our own groceries, sich as bacon, molasses, coffee, meal, and flour. If we had flour-biscuits fo' our Sunday dinner, we thought it was cake.

"De men folks on de place worked by de month. Yo' see dis was after slavery. Each man got fifteen dollahs a month, his rent and food was free. Every week each man was rationed about four pounds of bacon, a peck of meal, a little bucket of molasses, some flour and a few other things dat he might need. De way he got lard was to keep de grease f'om de fried bacon, or if de boss man kilt a hog he would give de man meaty bones, some fat f'om de guts, and give him plenty of cracklin's.

"Dat's away folks lived even after slavery. Dem whut never had no hosses had to walk to de places dat dey had to go to. I remembah how dem whut walked toted bundles and boxes of groceries on dere heads. And if dey was bringin' home some eats de kids was always waitin' to see if dere was any candy in dem boxes.

"Bess worked by de month fo' Jedge Davis. He plowed de fields, and planted and chopped de crops. I didn't have to go into de fields, cause Bess was gittin' paid by de month, but when I did I got paid fo' de work dat I done.

"Me and Bess stayed on dis place till 1882. I was twenty years old. Den we moved on up here to Austin. Bess picked cotton, worked at de Butler's Brick Works, den at de city water works, den fo' truck-gardeners hereabouts. He worked in de truck-gardens fo' years. Den in his last years he worked fo' de Austin Oil Mill Company. He worked mos' of de time in de hull house where he kept de seeds swept up. He kept de office clean, too.

"While Bess was doin' them kind of jobs me and de kids—dere was five of 'em, three boys and two girls—would go out to de cotton patch and pick cotton. We'd staht in August up in Taylor, Williamson County, and work on up through Paris, up in northeast Texas, around to Dallas and back to Austin in November.

"On each cotton fahm was some houses fo' de pickers. Each house had a wood-burnin' stove and there was plenty of wood but, of 'cose, we had to buy our own groceries.

"One fall me and de kids made one hunnert and ninety dollahs over all of our expenses. By us pickin' cotton f'om August to November and by me takin' in washin' and ironin' durin' de rest of de time, me and Bess was able to pay off dis little place of our'n here. Dis used to be a nigger section around here, but now de Mexicans has moved in.

"In November 1937 Bess got down bad sick. He had a stroke. He got so dat he couldn't walk across dis here yard. I'd have to help him. It got so dat I was always sick and nervous. De doctah told me dat I would have to calm down. I was walkin' all humped over.

"Bess was always so big-boned and healthy dat I didn't never think dat he was very sick. He would lay in his bed and watch me when I'd come into de room.

"'Mama,' he always called me mama, 'yo' sure have been a good wife to me,' he said one day. 'Yo' wore yo' sef out fo' me. If I live mama, I'll try to help yo.'

"'Don't worry Bess,' I told him, 'but jes' try to git well and try to serve de Lawd.'

"Den one day, November 25, right on my birthday, he called to me that he waz hongry.

"'Yo' is Bess?' I said. 'Well, all right, whut would yo' lak, a glass of milk?'

"'No, mama.'

"'A poached egg Bess?'

"'A poached egg is all right mama,' he told me.

"I still had some fire in my stove so I poached de egg, and brought it to him. He et it. Den I come back and he had throwed it up. I wiped his face.

"My son and daughter-in-law was now in de room wid me and Bess. Bess looked twice at each one of us, never said a word, den turned his head to one side and was still. I knowed dat he was dead. My son tried to tell me different.

"Den de doctah come.

"'Dis man is dead,' he said.

"I never did git to go to school in de early days. My white folks never did show me my A, B, C's. I was jes' a ignorant little girl. But here a few years back, I went to whut dey called de night school. I liked it all right. I went up to whut is de fourth grade. Den I got cataracts in my eyes, and I couldn't read much no mo'e. I reckon dat by now I would of been in de fifth or sixth grade."

Miller County

Cummins, Albert
Age: 86
Laurel Street
Texarkana, Arkansas
Interviewer: Mrs. V. M. Ball
[M:8: pt. 2: 70–71]

An humble cottage, sheltered by four magnificent oak trees, houses an interesting old negro, Albert Cummins.

Texarkana people, old and young, reverence this character, and obtain from him much valuable information concerning the early life of this country. This ex-slave was freed when he was fifteen years old, but continued to live in the same family until he was a man. He says: "All de training an' advice I evah had come from mah mistress. She was a beautiful Christian; if I am anybody, I owe it to her. I nevah went to school a day in mah life; whut I know I absorbed frum de white folks! Mah religion is De Golden Rule. It will take any man to heaben who follows its teachings.

"Mah mahster was kilt in de battle fought at Poison Springs, near Camden. We got separated in de skirmish an' I nevah did see him again. Libin' at that time wuz hard because dere wuz no way to communicate, only to sen' messages by horseback riders. It wuz months befo' I really knew dat mah mahster had been kilt, and where.

"Mr. Autrey bought mah mother when I wuz an infant, and gave us de protection an' care dat all good slave owners bestowed on their slaves. I worshipped dis man, dere has nevah been anudder like him. I sees him often in mah dreams now, an' he allus appears without food an' raiment, jus' as de South wuz left after de war."

"I come heah when Texarkana wuz only three years old, jus' a little kindly village, where we all knew each udder. Due to de location an' de comin' ob railroads, de town advanced rapidly. Not until it wuz too late did de citizens realize whut a drawback it is to be on de line between two states. Dis being Texarkana's fate, she has had a hard struggle overcoming dis handicap for sixty-three years. Still dat State Line divides de two cities like de "Mason and Dixon Line" divides the North an' South.

Living on the Arkansas side of this city, Albert Cummins is naturally very partial to his side. "The Arkansas side is more civilized", according to his version. "Too easy fo' de Texas folks to commit a crime an' step across to Arkansas to escape arrest an' nevah be heard ob again."

Quinn, Doc
Age: 93
1207 Ash Street
Texarkana, Arkansas
Interviewer: Cecil Copeland
[S1:2: AR, pt. 2: 19–21]

Doc Quinn, one of the oldest living residents of Miller County, tells some interesting stories of the early days of this section. Being one of many slaves on Col. Ogburn's plantation, he can recall many incidents that happened during this period. The Ogburn plantation is now a part of the Adams farm, which is located between Index and Fulton, on Red River.

When Doc first came here, this section was an immense canebrake, and a favorite retreat of bears and other wild animals. In order to prevent heavy losses from the depredations of predatory animals, the plantation owner would have the hogs, and other livestock rounded up, and herded into pens. Several slaves would be designated as guards to keep an all-night vigil over the pens.

Some of the bears' actions were almost human. Doc recalls, one day, coming upon a bear in the cornfield. The bear picked off an ear of corn and put it in his bended arm. He repeated this action until he had an armful, and then waddled over to the fence. Standing by the fence, he carefully threw the corn on the other side, ear by ear. The bear then climbed the fence, much in the same manner of a human being, retrieved the corn, and went on his way.

The plantation owned about twenty bloodhounds. The dogs were in charge of a slave, whose sole duties were to hunt predatory animals. Doc says that he has been forced to seek refuge in trees several times from angry bears, always selecting a small tree that a bear could not hug, so was unable to climb.

The following is an incident which occurred on the Ogburn plantation, as related by Doc Quinn:

"Late one ebenin', me an' anudder nigger named Jerry wuz comin' home frum fishin'. Roundin' a bend in de trail, whut do we meet almos' face to face?—A great big ole bar! Bein' young, an' blessed wid swif' feet, I makes fo' de nearest tree, and hastily scrambles to safety. Not so wid mah fat frien'. Peerin' outen thru de branches ob de tree, I sees de bar makin' fo' Jerry, an' I says to mahself: "Jerry, yo' sins has sho' kotched up wid yo' dis time." But Jerry, allus bein' a mean nigger, mus' hab had de debbil by he side. Pullin' outen his Bowie knife, dat nigger jumps to one side as de bar kum chargin' pas', and' stab it in de side, near de shoulder. As de bar started toinin' roun' to make anudder lunge at de nigger he notice de blood spurtin' frum de shoulder. An' whut do yo' think happen'? Dat ole bar forgets all about Jerry. Hastily scramblin' aroun', he begins to pick up leaves, an' trash an' clamps dem on de wound, tryin' to keep frum bleedin' to deaf. Yo' ax did de bar die? Well, suh, I didn' wait to see de result. Jerry, he done lef' dem parts, an' not wantin' to stay up in dat tree alnight by mahself, I scrambles down an' run fo' mile home in double quick time!"

Monroe County

Burgess, Jeff
Clarendon, Arkansas
Age: 74?
Interviewer: Miss Irene Robertson
[M:8: pt. 1: 334–35]

"I was born in Granville, Texas. My master was Strathers Burgess and mistress Polly Burgess. My master died 'fore I was born. He died on the way to Texas, trying to save his slaves. Keep them from leaving him and from going into the war. They didn't want to fight. His son was killed in the war. My folks didn't know they was free till three years after the war was over. They come back to Caloche Bay, the old home place. There was a bureau at De Valls Bluff. They had to let the slaves go and they was citizens then. My folks wasn't very anxious to leave the white owners because times was so funny and they didn't have nowhere to go. The courts was torn up powerful here in Arkansas.

"Heap of meanness going on right after the war. One man tell you do this and another man say you better not do that you sho get in trouble. It was hard to go straight. They said our master was a good man but awful rough wid his slaves and the hands overseeing too. Guess he was rough wid his family too.

"Times is hard with me. I get $10 pension every month. I got no home now. I got me three hogs. I lives three miles from here (Clarendon).

"If I wasn't so old and no account I'd think the times the best ever. It's bad when you get old. I jess sees the young folks. I don't know much about them. Seems lack they talk a lot of foolish chat to me. I got a lot and a half in town. They tore down my house and toted it off for fire wood. It was rented. Then they moved out and wouldn't pay no rent. They kept doing that way. I never had a farm of my own.

"I was good with a saw and axe. I cleared land and farmed. Once I worked on the railroad they was building. I drove pile mostly. Farming is the best job and the best place to make a living. I found out that myself."

Cotton, T. W.
Age: 80
Helena, Arkansas
Interviewer: Irene Robertson
[M:8: pt. 2: 39–41]

"I was born close to Indian Bay. I belong to Ed Cotton. Mother was sold from John Mason between Petersburg and Richmond, Virginia. Three sisters was sold and they give grandma and my sister in the trade. Grandma was so old she wasn't much account fer field work. Mother left a son she never seen ag'in. Aunt Adeline's boy come too. They was put on a block but I can't recollect where it was. If mother had a husband she never said nothing 'bout him. He muster been dead.

"Now my papa come from La Grange, Tennessee. Master Bowers sold him to Ed Cotton. He was sold three times. He had one scar on his shoulder. The patrollers hit him as he went over the fence down at Indian Bay. He was a Guinea man. He was heavy set, not very tall. Generally he carried the lead row in the field. He was a good worker. They had to be quiet wid him to get him to work. He would run to the woods. He was a fast runner. He lived to be about a hundred years old. I took keer of him the last five years of his life. Mother was seventy-one years old when she died. She was the mother of twenty-one children.

"Sure, I do remember freedom. After the Civil War ended, Ed Cotton walked out and told papa: 'Rob, you are free.' We worked on till 1866 and we moved to Joe Lambert's place. He had a brother named Tom Lambert. Father never got no land at freedom. He got to own 160 acres, a house on it, and some stock. We all worked and helped him to make it. He was a hard worker and a fast hand.

"I farmed all my life till fifteen years ago I started trucking down here in Helena. I gets six dollars assistance from the Sociable Welfare and some little helpouts as I calls it—rice and potatoes and apples. I got one boy fifty-five years old if he be living. I haven't seen him since 1916. He left and went to Chicago. I got a girl in St. Louis. I got a girl here in Helena. I jus' been up to see her. I had nine children. I been married twice. I lived with my first wife thirteen years and seven months. She died. I lived with my second wife forty years and some over—several weeks. She died.

"I was a small boy when the Civil War broke out. Once I got a awful scare. I was perched up on a post. The Yankees come up back of the house and to my back. I seen them. I yelled out, 'Yonder come Yankees.' They come on cussing me. Aunt Ruthie got me under my arms and took me to Miss Fannie Cotton. We lived in part of their house. Walter (white) and me slept together. Mother cooked. Aunt Ruthie was a field hand. Aunt Adeline must have been a field hand too. She hung herself on a black jack tree on the other side of the pool. It was a pool for ducks and stock.

"She hung herself to keep from getting a whooping. Mother raised (reared) her boy. She told mother she would kill herself before she would be whooped. I never heard what she was to be whooped for. She thought she would be whooped. She took a rope and tied it to a limb and to her neck and then jumped. Her toes barely touched the ground. They buried her in the cemetery on the old Ed Cotton place. I never seen her buried. Aunt Ruthie's grave was the first open grave I ever seen. Aunt Mary was papa's sister. She was the oldest.

"I would say anything to the Yankees and hang and hide in Miss Fannie's dress. She wore long big skirts. I hung about her. Grandma raised me on a bottle so mother could nurse Walter (white). There was something wrong wid Miss Fannie. We colored children et out of trays. They hewed them out of small logs. Seven or eight et together. We had our little cups. Grandma had a cup for my water. We et with spoons. It would hold a peck of something to eat. I nursed my mother four weeks and then mama raised Walter and grandma raised me. Walter et out of our tray many and many a time. Mother had good teeth and she chewed for us both. Henry was younger than Walter. They was the only two children Miss Fannie had. Grandma washed out our tray soon as ever we quit eating. She'd put the bread in, then pour the meat and vegetables over it. It was good.

"Did you ever hear of Walter Cotton, a cancer doctor? That was him. He may be dead now. Me and him caused Aunt Sue to get a whooping. They had a little pear tree down twix the house and the spring. Walter knocked one of the sugar pears off and cut it in halves. We et it. Mr. Ed asked 'bout it. Walter told her Aunt Sue pulled it. She didn't come by the tree. He whooped her her declaring all the time she never pulled it nor never seen it. I was scared then to tell on Walter. I hope eat it. Aunt Sue had grown children.

"The Ku Klux come through the first and second gates to papa's house and he opened the door. They grunted around. They told papa to come out. He didn't go and he was ready to hurt them when they come in. He told them when he finished that crop they could have his room. He left that year. They come in on me once before I married. I was at my girl's house. They wanted to be sure we married. The principal thing they was to see was that you didn't live in the house wid a woman till you be married. I wasn't married but I soon did marry her. They scared us up some.

"I don't know if times is so much better for some or not. Some folks won't work. Some do work awful hard. Young folks I'm speaking 'bout. Times is might fast now. Seems like they get faster and faster every way. I'll be eighty years old this May. I was born in 1858."

Hudgens, Molly
Age: 70
DeValls Bluff, Arkansas
Interviewer: Irene Robertson
[M:9: pt. 3: 345–46]

"I was born in Clarendon in 1868. My mother was sold to Judge Allen at Bihalia, N. C. and brought to Arkansas. The Cunninghams brought father from Tennessee when they moved to this State. His mother died when he was three months old and the white mistress had a baby three weeks older en him so she raised my father. She nursed him with Gus Cunningham. My father had us call them Grandma, Aunt Indiana, and Aunt Imogene.

"When I was seven or eight years old I went to see them at Roe. When I first come to know how things was, father had bought a place—home and piece of land west of Clarendon and across the river. I don't know if the Cunninghams ever give him some land or a mule or cow or not. He never said. His owner was Moster John Henry Cunningham.

"My father was a medium light man but not as light as I am. My mother was lighter than I am. I heard her say her mother did the sewing for all on her owner's place in North Carolina. My mother was a house girl. The reason she was put up to be sold she was hired out and they put her in the field to work. A dispute rose over her some way so her owner sold her when she was eighteen years old. Her mother was crying and begging them not to sell her but it didn't do no good she said. After the war was over she got somebody to write back and ask about her people. She got word about her sister and aunt and uncle. She never seen none of them after she was sold. Never did see a one of her people again. She was sold to Judge Allen for a house girl. His wife was dead. My mother sewed at Judge Allen's and raised two little colored children he bought somewhere cheap. He had a nephew that lived with him.

"Mr. Felix Allen and some other of his kin folks, one of them made me call him 'Tuscumby Bob.' I said it funny and they would laugh at me. Judge Allen went to Memphis and come home and took smallpox and died. I heard my mother say she seen him crying, sitting out under a tree. He said he recken he would give smallpox to all the colored folks on his place. Some of them took smallpox.

"We have been good living colored folks, had a right smart. I farmed, cooked, sewed a little along. I washed. I been living in DeValls Bluff 38 years. I got down and they put me on the relief. Seems I can't get back to going agin.

"Don't get me started on this young generation. I don't want to start talking about how they do. Times is right smartly changed somehow. Everybody is in a hurry to do something and it turns out they don't do nuthin'. Times is all in a stir it seem like to me.

"I don't vote. I get $8 and demodities and I make the rest of my keepin.'"

Lambert, Solomon
Age: 89
Holly Grove, Arkansas
Interviewer: Irene Robertson
[M:9: pt. 4: 229–34]

"My parents belong to Jordon and Judy Lambert. They (the Jordon family) had a big family. They never was sold. I heard 'em say that. They hired their slaves out. Some was hired fer a year. From New Year day to next New Year day. That was a busy day. That was the day to set in workin' overseers and ridin' bosses set in on New Year day. My parents' name was Fannie and Ben Lambert. They had eight children.

"How did they marry? They say they jump the brookstick together! But they had brush brooms so I recken that whut they jumped. Think the moster and mistress jes havin' a little fun outen it then. The brooms the sweep the floor was sage grass cured like hay. It grows four or five feet tall. They wrap it with string and use that fer a handle. (Illustration—[not present]) The way they married the man ask his moster then ask her moster. If they agree it be all right. One of 'em would 'nounce it 'fore all the rest of the folks up at the house and some times they have ale and cake. If the man want a girl and ther be another man on that place wanted a wife the mosters would swop the women mostly. Then one announce they married. That what they call a double weddin'. Some got passes go see their wife and family 'bout every Sunday and some other times like Fourth er July. They have a week ob rest when they lay by the crops and have some time not so busy to visit Christmas.

"I never seen no Ku Klux. There was Jay Hawkers. They was folks on neither side jes goin' round, robbin' and stealin', money, silver, stock or anything else they wanted. We had a prutty good time we have all the hands on our place at some house and dance. We made our music. Music is natur'l wid our color. They most all had a juice (Jew's) harp. They make the fiddle and banjo. White folks had big times too. They had mo big gatherins than they have now. They send me to Indian Bay once or twice a week to get the mail. I had no money. They give my father little money long and give him some 'bout Christmas. White folks send their darkies wid a order to buy things. I never seen a big town till I started on that run to Texas. They took the men 450 miles to Indian Nation to make a crop. We went in May and came back in October. They hired us out. Mr. Jo Lambert and Mr. Beasley took us. One of 'em come back and got us. That kept us from goin' to war. They left the women, children and old men, too old fer war.

"How'd I know 'bout war? That was the big thing they talk 'bout. See 'em. The first I seen was when I was shuckin' corn at the corn pin (crib) a man come up in gray clothes. (He was a spy). The way he talk you think he a southern man 'cept his speech was hard and short. I noticed that to begin wid. They thought other rebels in the corn pin but they wasn't. Wasn't nobody out there but me. Then here come a man in blue uniform. After while here come the regiment. It did scare me. Bob and Tom (white boys) Lambert gone to war then. They fooled round a while then they galloped off. I show was glad when the last man rid off!

Moster Lambert then hid the slaves in the bottoms. We carried provisions and they sent more 'long. We stay two or three days or a week when they hear a regiment comin' through or hear 'bout a scoutin gang comin' through. They would come one road and go back another road. We didn't care if they hid us. We hear the guns. We didn't wanter go down there. That was white man's war. In 1862 and 1863 they slipped off every man and one woman to Helena. I was yokin' up oxen. Man come up in rebel clothes. He was a spy. I thought I was gone then but and a guard whut I didn't see till he left went on. I dodged round till one day I had to get off to mill. The Yankees run up on me and took me on. I was fifteen years old. I was mustered in August and let out in 1864 when it was over. I was in the Yankee army 14 months. They told me when I left I made a good soldier. I was with the standing army at Helena. They had a batttle before I went in. I heard them say. You could tell that from the roar and cannons. They had it when I was in Texas. I wasn't in a battle. The Yankees begin to git slim then they made the darkies fill up and put them in front. I heard 'em say they had one mighty big battle at Helena. I had to drill and guard the camps and guard at the pickets (roads into Helena). They never let me go scoutin'. I walked home from the army. I was glad to get out. I expected to get shot 'bout all the time. I aint seen but mighty little difference since freedom. I went back and stayed 45 years on the Lambert place. I moved to Duncan. Moster died foe the Civil War. Some men raised dogs-hounds. If something get wrong they go get the dogs and use 'em. If some of the slaves try to run off they hunt them with the dogs. It was a big loss when a hand run off they couldn't ford that thing. They whoop 'em mostly fer stealin'. They trust 'em in everything then they whoop 'em if they steal. They knew it wrong. Course they did. The worse thing I ever seen in slavery was when we went to Texas we camped close to Camden. Camden, Arkansas! On the way down there we passed by a big house, some kind. I seen mighty little of it but a big yard was pailened in. It was tall and fixed so they couldn't get out. They opened the big gate and let us see. It was full of darkies. All sizes. All ages. That was a *Nigger Trader Yard* the worst thing I ever seen or heard tell of in my life. I heard 'em say they would cry 'em off certain times but you could buy one or two any time jes by agreement. I nearly fell out wid slavery then. I studied 'bout that heap since then. I never seen no cruelty if a man work and do right on my moster's place he be honored by both black and white. Foe moster died I was 9 year old, I heard him say I valued at $500.00. I never was sold.

"When I was small I minded the calves when they milk, pick up chips to dry fer to start fires, then I picked up nuts, helped feed the stock, learned all I could how to do things 'bout the place. We thought we owned the place. I was happy as a bird. I didn't know no better than it was mine. All the home I ever knowed. I tell you it was a good home. Good as ever had since. It was thiser way yo mama's home is your home. Well my moster's home was my home like dat.

"We et up at the house in the kitchen. We eat at the darkey houses. It make no diffurence—one house clean as the other. It haft to be so. They would whoop you foe your nasty habits quick as anything and quicker. Had plenty clothes and plenty to eat. Folk's clothes made out more lastin' cloth than now. They last longer and didn't always be gettin' more new ones. They washed down at the spring. The little darkies get in (tubs) soon as they hang out the clothes on the ropes and bushes. The suds be warm, little darkies race to get washed. Folks raced to get through jobs then and have fun all time.

"Foe I jined the Yankees I had hoed and I had picked cotton. Moster Lambert didn't work the little darkies hard to to stunt them. See how big I am? I been well cared fur and done a sight er work if it piled up so it could be seen. (Solomon Lambert is a large well proportioned negro.) In 1870 the railroad come in here by Holly Grove. That the first I ever seen. The first cars. They was small.

"I never knowd I oughter recollect what all they talked but she said they both (mother and father) come from Kentucky to Tennessee, then to Arkansas in wagons and on boats too I recken. The Lamberts brought them from Kentucky. For show I can't tell you no more 'bout them. I heard 'em say they landed at the Bay (Indian Bay).

"Fine reports went out if you jin the army whut all you would get. I didn't want to be there. I knew whut I get soon as ever I got way from them. Course I was goin' back. I had no other place to go. The government give out rations at Indian Bay after the war. I didn't need none. I got plenty to eat. Two or three of us colored folks paid Mr. Lowe $1.00 a month to teach us at night. We learned to read and calculate better. I learned to write. We stuck to it right smart while.

"I been married twice. Joe Yancey (white) married me to my first wife at the white folk's house. The last time Joe Lambert (white) married me in the church. I had 2 boys they dead now and 1 girl. She is living.

During slavery I had a cart I drove a little mule to. I took a barrel of water to the field. I got it at the well. I put it close by in the shade of a tree. Trees was plentiful! Then I took the breakfast and dinner in my cart. I done whatever come to my lot in Indian Nation. After the war I made a plowhand. "*Say there, from 1864 to 1937 Sol Lambert farmed.*" Course I hauled and cut wood, but my job is farmin'. I share croppe. I worked fer ⅓ and ¼ and I have rented. Farmin' is my talent. That whar all the darkey belong. He is made so. He can stand the sun and he needs meat to eat. That is where the meat grows.

"I got chickens and a garden. I didn't get the pigs I spoke fer. I got a fine cow. I got a house—10 1/2 acres of ground. That is all I can look after. I caint get 'bout much. I rid on a wagon (to town) my mare is sick I wouldn't work er. I got a buggy. Good nough fer my ridin' I don't come to town much. I never did.

I get a Federal soldier's pension. I tell you 'bout it. White folks tole me 'bout it and hope me see 'bout gettin' it. I'm mighty proud of it. It is a good support for me in my old helpless days. I'm mighty thankful for it. I'm glad you sent me word to come here I love to help folks. They so good to me.

"I vote a Republican ticket. I don't vote. I did vote when I was 21 years old. It was stylish then and I voted some since then along. I don't bother with votin' and I don't know nuthin 'bout how it is done now. I tried to run my farm and let them hired run the governmint. I knowed my job like he knowed his job. I come back to tell you one other thing. My Captain was Edward Boncrow.

"I told you all I know 'bout slavery less you ask me 'bout somethin' I might answer: We ask if we could go to white church and they tell us they wanted certain ones to go today so they could fix up. It was after the war new churches and schools sprung up. Not fast then.

Prices of slaves run from $1000 to $2000 fer grown to middle age. Old ones sold low, so did young ones. $1600 was a slow bid. That is whut I heard.

Roberts, J.
Age: 45 or 50
Brinkley, Arkansas
Interviewer: Miss Irene Robertson
[M:10: pt. 6: 53]

"My father was a Federal soldier in the Civil War. He was from Winston, Virginia. He went to war and soon after the end he came to Holly Grove. He was in Company 'K'. He signed up six or seven papers for men in his company he knew and they all got their pensions. Oh yes! He knew them. He was an awful exact honest man. He was a very young man when he went into the war and never married till he come to Arkansas. He married a slave woman. She was a field woman. They farmed. Father sat by the hour and told how he endured the war. He never expected to come out alive after a few months in the war.

"John Roberts Collins was his owner in slavery. I never heard why he cut off the Collins. I call my own self J. Roberts.

"The present times are hard times. Sin hath caused it all. Machinery has taken so much of the work.

"The present generation are fair folks but wild. Yes, the young folks today are wilder than my set was. I can't tell you how but I see it every way I go."

Smith, J. L.
Age: 76
1215 Pulaski Street
Little Rock, Arkansas
Interviewer: Samuel S. Taylor
[M:10: pt. 6: 198–202]

"I was born in 1862 in the month of September on the fifteenth. I was born at a place they call Indian Bay on White River down here in Arkansas. My mother was named Emmaline Smith and she was born in Tennessee. I don't know really now what county or what part of the state. My father's name was John Smith. He was born in North Carolina. I don't know nothing about what my grandfather's name and grandmother's names were. I never saw them. None of my folks are old aged as I am. My father was sixty years old when he died and my mother was only younger than that.

Experience of Father
"I heard my father say that he helped get out juniper timber in North Carolina. The white man me and my sister worked with after my father died was the man my father worked with in the juniper swamp. His name was Alfred Perry White. As long as he lived, we could do work for him. We didn't live on his place but we worked for him by the day. He is dead now—died way back yonder in the seventies. There was the Brooks and Baxter trouble in 1874, and my father died in seventy-five. White lived a little while longer.

"My father was married twice before he married my mother. He had two sets of children. I don't know how many of them there were. He had four children by my mother. He had only four children as far as I can remember.

"I don't know how my father and my mother met up. They lived on the same plantation and in the same house. They were owned by the same man after freedom came. I don't know how they got together. I have often wondered about that. One from Tennessee and the other from North Carolina, but they got together. I guess that they must have been born in different places and brought together through being bought and sold.

"My mother was a Murrill. My father was a Cartwright. My father's brother Lewis was a man who didn't take nothing much from anybody, and especially didn't like to take a whipping. When Lewis' master wanted to whip him, he would call his mother—the master's mother—and have her whip him because he figured Uncle Lewis wouldn't hit a woman.

"I have six children altogether. Two of them are dead. There are three girls and one boy living. The oldest is fifty-seven; the next, fifty; and the youngest, forty-eight. The youngest is in the hospital for nervous and mental diseases. She has been there ever since 1927. The oldest had an arm and four ribs broken in an auto accident last January on the sixteenth of the month. She didn't get a penny to pay for her trouble. I remember the man did give her fifteen cents once. The truck struck her in the alley there and knocked her clean across the street. She is fifty-seven years old and bones don't knit fast on people that old. She ain't able to do no work yet. All of my daughters are out of work. I don't know where the boy is. He is somewheres up North.

Slave Houses

"I have seen some old log houses that they said the slaves used to live in. I was too young to notice before freedom. I have seen different specimens of houses that they lived in. One log house had a plank house builded on to the end of it. The log end was the one lived in during slavery times and the plank end was built since. That gal there of mine was born in the log end. There were round log houses and sawed log houses. The sawed log houses was built out of logs that had been squared after the trees had been cut down, and the round log houses was built out of logs left just like they was when they was trees. There's been quite an improvement in the houses since I was a kid.

Food

"I have heard my father and mother talking among themselves and their friends, but they never did tell me nothing about slave times. They never did sit down and talk to me about it. When they'd sit down and start talkin', it would always be, 'Now you children run on out and play while we old folks sit here and talk.' But from time to time, I would be sitting on the floor playing by myself and they would be talking 'monst themselves and I would hear them say this or that. But I never heered them say what they et in slave times.

Work

"My father worked in the juniper swamp in North Carolina, like I told you. I think I heard my mother say she cooked. Most I ever heard them say was when they would get with some one else and each would talk about his master.

Cruelties

"I heard my mother say that her mistress used to take a fork and stick it in her head—jog it up and down against her head. I don't know how hard she punched her. My mother was very gray—all her hair was gray and she wasn't old enough for that. I reckon that was why.

How Freedom Came
"I don't remember how freedom came. They were refugeed—I call it that—my father and mother were. My sister was born in Texas, and they were back in Arkansas again when I was born. I was born and raised right here in Arkansas. They were running from one place to the other to keep the Yankees from freeing the slaves. I never even heard them say where they were freed. I don't know whether it was here or in Texas.

Right after the War
"I have no knowledge of what they did right after the war. The first thing I remember was that they were picking cotton in Pine Bluff or near there. It was a smoky log house I had to stay in while they were out in the field and the smoke used to hurt my eyes awful.

Ku Klux and Patrollers
"I don't remember nothing about the Ku Klux. I heard old folks say they used to have passes to keep the pateroles from bothering them. I remember that they said the pateroles would whip them if they would catch them out without a pass. When I first heard of the Ku Klux Klan, I thought that it was some kind of beast the folks was talking about. I didn't hear nothing special they did.

Occupational Experiences
"When I got old enough, I worked a farm—picked cotton, hoed, plowed, pulled corn—all such things. That is about all I ever did—farming. Farming was always my regular occupation. I never did anything else—not for no regular thing.

Marriage
"I married in 1879. My father and mother married each other too after freedom. I remember that. It was when the government was making all those that had been slaves marry. I have been married just the one time. My wife died in April 1927.

Present Condition
"I am not able to do anything now. I don't even tote a chair across the room, or spade up the ground for a garden, or hoe up the weeds in it. I am

ruptured and the doctor says it is the funniest rupture he ever seen. He says that there's a rupture and fat hanging down in the rupture. They have to keep me packed with ice all the time. The least little thing brings it down. I can't hold myself nor nothing. Have to wear something under my clothes.

"I don't get a pension."

Interviewer's Comment

Smith is sensitive about his first name—doesn't like to give it—and about his condition. He doesn't like to mention it or to have it referred to.

He has an excellent memory for some things and a rather poor one for some others. He got angry when his granddaughter supplied data about his wife which he apparently could not recall.

His physical condition is deplorable and his circumstances extremely straitened.

Taylor, Lula
Age: 71
R.F.D., east of town
Brinkley, Arkansas
Interviewer: Miss Irene Robertson
[M:10: pt. 6: 266–68]

"My mother was sold five times. She was sold when she was too little to remember her mother. Her mother was Charity Linnerman. They favored. She was dark and granny was light colored. My mother didn't love her mother like I loved her.

"Granny lived in a house behind the white church (?) in Helena. After freedom we kept writing till we got in tetch with her. We finally got granny with us on the Jefferies place at Clarendon.

"A man (Negro) come by and conjured my mother. She was with Miss Betty Reed (or Reid) up north of Lonoke. They was my mother's last owners. That old man made out like she stole things when he stole them his own black self. He'd make her hide out like she stole things. She had a sweetheart and him and his wife. She had to live with them. They stole her off from her last owner, Miss Betty Reed. They didn't like her sweetheart. They was going to marry. He bought all her wedding clothes. When she didn't marry him she let him have back all the weddin' clothes and he buried his sister in them. This old man was a conjurer. He give my mother a cup of some kind of herbs and made her drink it. He tole her all her love would go to Henry Deal. He liked him. He was my papa. Her love sure did leave her sweetheart and go to my papa. He bought her some nice clothes. She married in the clothes he got her. She was so glad to let go that old man and woman what conjured her away from her white folks to wait on them.

"Granny's head was all split open. I lived to see all that. White folks said her husband done it but she said one of her old master's struck her on the head with a shoe last.

"My papa said he'd hit boards and stood on them all day one after another working cold days.

"Master Wade Deal at freedom give papa a pair of chickens, goats, sheep, turkeys, a cow; and papa cleared ten acres of ground to pay for his first mule. He bought the mule from Master Wade Deal.

"Old Master Deal used to run us from behind him plowing. We tease him, say what he'd say to the horse or mule. He'd lock us up in the smoke-house. We'd eat dried beef and go to sleep. He was a good old man.

"Grandpa Henry Pool went to war. Papa was sold from the Pools to the Deals. Grandpa played with us. He'd put us all up on a horse we called Old Bill. He said he got so used to sleeping on his blanket on the ground in war times till he couldn't sleep on a bed. He couldn't get off asleep.

"Grandpa found a pitcher of gold money been buried in old Master Pool's stable. He give it to them. They knowed it was out there.

"Mother was with Miss Betty Reed in most of war times. Miss Betty hid their jewelry and money. She spoke of the Yankees coming and kill pretty chickens and drink up a churn of fresh milk turned ready for churning. It be in the chimney corner to keep warm. They'd take fat horses and turn their poor ones in the lot. They never could pass up a fat hog. They cleaned out the corn crib.

"All my kin folks was field hands. I ploughed all day long.

"Papa said his ole Mistress Deal was out under an apple tree peeling apples to dry. A white crane flew over the tree and fluttered about over her. Next day she died. Then the old man married a younger woman.

"It is so about the pigeons at Pigeon Roost (Wattensaw, Arkansas). They weighted trees down till they actually broke limbs and swayed plenty of them. That was the richest land you ever seen in your life when it was cleared off. Folks couldn't rest for killing pigeons and wasted them all up. I was born at Pigeon Roost on Jim High's place. I seen a whole washpot full of stewed pigeon. It was fine eating. It was a shame to waste up all the pigeons and clear out the place."

Ouachita County

Junell, Oscar Felix
Age: 60
1720 Brown Street
Little Rock, Arkansas
Interviewer: Samuel S. Taylor
[M:9: pt. 4: 173–74]

"My father's name was Peter Junell, Peter W. Junell. I don't know what the W. was for. He was born in Ouachita County near Bearden, Arkansas. Bearden is an old town. It is fourteen miles from Camden. My dad was seventy-five years old when he died. He died in 1924. He was very young in the time of slavery. He never did do very much work.

"His master was named John Junell. That was his old master. He had a young master too, Warren Junell. His old master given him to his young master, Warren. My father's mother and father both belonged to the Junells. His mother's name was Dinah, and his father's name was Anthony. All the slaves took their last names after their owners. They never was sold, not in any time that my father could remember.

"As soon as my father was large enough to go to walkin' about, his old master given him to his son, Master Warren Junell. Warren would carry him about and make him rassle (wrestle). He was a good rassler. As far as work was concerned, he didn't do nothing much of that. He just followed his young master all around rasslin.

"His masters was good to him. They whipped slaves sometimes, but they were considered good. My father always said they was good folks. He never told me how he learnt that he was free.

"Pretty well all the slaves lived in log cabins. Even in my time, there was hardly a board house in that county. The food the slaves ate was mostly bread and milk—corn bread. Old man Junell was rich and had lots of slaves. When he went to feed his slaves, he would feed them jus like hogs. He had a great long trough and he would have bread crumbled up in it and gallons of milk poured over the bread, and the slaves would get round it and eat. Sometimes they would get to fighting over it. You know, jus like hogs! They would be eatin and sometimes one person would find somethin and get holt of it and another one would want to take it, and they would get to fightin over it. Sometimes blood would get in the trough, but they would eat right on and pay no 'tention to it.

"I don't know whether they fed the old ones that way or not. I just heered my father tell how he et out of the trough hisself.

"I have heered my father talk about the pateroles too. He talked about how they used to chase him. But he didn't have much experience with them, because they never did catch him. That was after the war when the slaves had been freed, but the pateroles still got after them. My father remember how they would catch other slaves. One night they went to an old man's house. It was dark and the old man told them to come on in. He didn't have no gun, but he took his ax and stood behind the door on the hinge side. It was after slavery. When he said for them to come in, they rushed right on in and the old man killed three or four of them with his ax. He was a old African, and they never had been able to do nothin' with him, not even in slavery time. I never heard that they did nothin' to the old man about it. The pateroles was outlaws anyway.

"I heard my father say that in slavery time, they took the finest and portlies' looking Negroes—the males—for breeding purposes. They wouldn't let them strain themselves up nor nothin like that. They wouldn't make them do much hard work."

Osbrook, Jane
Age: 90
302 E. 21st Avenue
Pine Bluff, Arkansas
Interviewer: Mrs. Bernice Bowden
[M:10: pt. 5: 232–33]

"Yes, ma'm, I was livin' in slavery days. I was borned in Arkansas I reckon. I was borned within three miles of Camden but I wasn't raised there. We moved to Saline County directly after peace was declared.

"I don't know what year I was born because you see I'm not educated but I was ninety the 27th of this last past May. Yes ma'm, I'm a old bondage woman. I can say what a heap of em can't say—I can tell the truth bout it. I believe in the truth. I was brought up to tell the truth. I'm no young girl.

"My old master was Adkison Billingsly. My old mistress treated us just like her own children. She said we had feelin's and tastes. I visited her long after the war. Went there and stayed all night.

"I member when they had the fight at Jenkins Ferry. Old Steele had 30,000 and he come down to take Little Rock, Pine Bluff and others. Captain

Webb with 1,500 Rebels was followin' him and when they got to Saline River they had a battle.

"The next Sunday my father carried all us children and some of the white folks to see the battle field. I member the dead was lyin' in graves, just one row after another and hadn't even been covered up.

"Oh yes, I can tell about that. Nother time there was four hundred fifty colored and five white Yankee soldiers come and ask my father if old mistress treated us right. We told em we had good owners. I never was so scared in my life. Them colored soldiers was so tall and so black and had red eyes. Oh yes ma'm, they had on the blue uniforms. Oh, we sure was fraid of em—you know them eyes.

"They said, 'Now uncle, we want you to tell the truth, does she feed you well?' My ma did all the cookin' and we had good livin'. I tole my daughter we fared ten thousand times better than now.

"I come up in the way of obedience. Any time I wanted to go, had to go to old mistress and she say, 'Don't let the sun go down on you.' And when we come home the sun was in the trees. If you seed the sun was goin' down on you, you run.

"I ain't goin' tell nothin' but the truth. Truth better to live with and better to die with.

"Some of the folks said they never seed a biscuit from Christmas to Christmas but we had em every day. Never seed no sodie till peace was 'clared—used saleratus.

"In my comin' up it was Whigs and Democrats. Never heard of no Republicans till after the war. I've seed a man get upon that platform and wipe the sweat from his brow. I've seed em get to fightin' too. That was done at our white folks house—arguin' politics.

"I never did go to school. I married right after the war you know. What you talkin' bout—bein' married and goin' to school? I was housekeepin'! Standin' right in my own light and didn't know it."

Phillips County

Barber, Mollie
Age: 79
1602 N. 5th Street
Muskogee, Oklahoma
Interviewer: Ethel Wolfe Garrison
20 October 1938
[S1:12: pt. 1: 28–31]

Two year before de War broke out I was born, four mile north of Helena, Arkansas, on de old plantation of Nat Turner who was stomped to death by a bull 'bout 15-year ago—I read about it in de Arkansas papers.

My father was Reuben Turner; before dat he was a Slade and maybe some other names too, for he was sold lots of times. When de War come 'long he went off to de North, fought in de War, and never come back.

Mammy was Satira Turner, and she was taken from her folks in Missouri and sold when she was a child. She was sold two-three times in her life, once at Jefferson, Texas, to a Master King who live someplace dey called Black Jack. During de War she was run, with some other slaves, from Missouri to Mississippi, Holly Springs she thought it was, den over into Arkansas, down to Texas, back to Arkansas, and all 'round.

My birth month is de lucky month of July, on de last day of it, Mammy told me. I always been lucky too, wid plenty to eat, plenty to wear, and a good clean house to live in. Dat's about de luck folks can figure on anyways.

Dere was but one more child dan me; his name is Lucius, living down 'round Sulphur Spring, Texas, de last time I hear.

De Old Master's wife was Emma Turner, and Ann Turner was deir daughter. Dey wouldn't let any of de slaves learn reading and such, and dey had a white overseer to run things. He picked out de biggest slave man on de place and made him de "whip-man." When de overseer or de Master figured a slave was due a beating, dey call in de whip man and he lay on de lash.

My mammy work 'round de house and in de fields too; seem lak she done 'bout ever'thing. Before he run off to de North, father would haul de cotton and grain to Helena for Master, and at night he work some more to make "out money", which de Old Master keep part of and let my father keep de rest. Made boots and shoes, mostly.

Money makes me 'member 'bout dat 'Federate money. It got so dead dey give it to de chillen to make doll dresses wid; dat money was real no 'count stuff—wid a wagon-load of it, you was still poor!

Sometimes de white masters would sell de slaves, put 'em on de block and bid you off, de way Mammy told me 'bout it. When de slave was put on de block de white folks gather 'round and de bidding would start. De owner talk about de sale dis-a-way:

"I got dis 'ere Negro woman, wid sound teeth; she a good cook, and can have some good little Negroes. What I offered for her?"

Den some man in de crowd say, "Fifty dollar; I give fifty!" De owner say: "We start at dat. Fifty Dollar. . . . . Waiting for de next bid!" And 'fore de bidding off is done, dat woman bring in maybe one thousand dollars.

Dat's de way de Turner's done; ever'time dey need some money, off dey sell a slave, jest like now dey sell cows and hogs at de auction places.

'Nother time, mammy said, one of de slave women was bid off for six-hundred dollars single; dat mean widout her chillen. De woman went 'round her new Master's house crying all de day, and he asks her: "Aint I bein' a good Master? Don't you like me fo' a Master?"

"You is a good Master", de woman told him, "but I is crying 'bout my babies. I got six pair o' twins, some of dem not yet six-month old, and I don't like bein' sold f'om chillen!"

What my mother say is—her new Master went back and brought ever' child of hers and keep dem all together til dey was free.

Freedom come a year before my mammy knew 'bout it, and she learn 'bout it accidental-like. She was cooking de Christmas dinner for her Mistress, and she went out to de yard for something when a colored man come by. Dey got to talking and he told her 'bout de Freedom—dat she was free jest like all de folks dat had been slaves. She run back in de house, grab up what little clothes she had, make a bundle and leave dat place with de dinner 'most ready. Bless her old black heart! She was glad to be free!

Most of our masters was white—Caucasians, dey call theyselves—but somewheres in de selling and trading we had some Creek Indian folks and dey give us 60-acre of land.

I married "Doc" Barber at Helena, Arkansas, but he been dead a long time now. My son, Sam, lives part time wid me, but work keeps him 'way most de time.

De colored Methodist church is where I go, and I try to live right. I know if I live for Jesus he will show me de Way.

Brown, Peter
Age: 86
Helena, Arkansas
Interviewer: Irene Robertson
[M:8: pt. 1: 311–14]

"I was born on the Woodlawn place. It was owned by David and Ann Hunt. I was born a slave boy. Master Hunt had two sons and one girl. Bigy and Dunbar was the boys' names. Annie was the girl's name.

"My parents' names was Jane and William Brown. Papa said he was a little shirt tail boy when the stars fell. Grandma Sofa and Grandpa Peter Bane lived on the same place. I'm named after him. My papa come from Tennessee to Mississippi. I never heard ma say where she come from.

"My remembrance of slavery is not at tall favorable. I heard the master and overseers whooping the slaves b'fore day. They had stakes fixed in the ground and tied them down on their stomachs stretched out and they beat them with a bull whoop (cowhide woven). They would break the blisters on them with white oak paddles that had holes in it so it would suck. They be saying, 'Oh pray, master.' He'd say, 'Better pray for yourself.' I heard that going on when I was a child morning after morning. I wasn't big enough to go to the field. I didn't have a hard time then. Ma had to work when she wasn't able. Pa stole her out and one night a small panther smelled them and come on a log up over where they slept in a canebrake. Pa killed it with a bowie knife. Ma had a baby out there in the canebrake. Pa had stole her out. They went back and they never made her work no more. She was a fast breeder; she had three sets of twins. They told him if he would stay out of the woods they wouldn't make her work no more, take care of her children. They prized fast breeders. They would come to see her and bring her things then. She had ten children, three pairs of twins. Jonas and Sofa, Peter and Alice, Isaac and Jacob.

"When I was fifteen years old, mother said, 'Peter, you are fifteen years old today; you was born March 1, 1852.' She told me that two or three times and I kept up wid it. I am glad I did; she died right after that.

"Ma and pa et dinner, well as could be. Took cholera, was dead at twelve o'clock that night. It was on Monday. Ike and Jake took it. They got over it. I waited on the little things. One of them said, 'Peter, I'm hungry.' I broiled some meat, made a ash cake and put the meat in where I split the ash cake. He et it and went to sleep. He started mending. Sister come and got the children and took them to Lake Providence. I fell in the hands then of some cruel people. They had a doctor named Dr. Coleman come to see ma and pa. He said, 'Don't eat no fruit, no vegetables.' He said, 'Eat meat and bread.' I et green plums and peaches like a boy fifteen years old then would do. I never did have cholera. A boy fifteen years old didn't know as much as boys do now that age. The master died b'fore the cholera disease come on. We had moved from the hill place to a place in the bottoms. It was on the same place. None of his family had cholera but neighbors had it. We buried ma and pa on the neighbor's place. We had kin folks on the Harris place. While we was at the graveyard word come to dig two or three more graves.

"Master's house was sot on fire, the smokehouse emptied, the gin burned and the cotton. The mules was drove out of the lot. That turned me ag'in' the Yankees. We helped raise that meat they stole. They left us to starve and fed their fat selves on what was our living. I do not believe in parts of slavery. That whooping was cruel, but I know that the white man helped the slave in ways. The slaves was worked too hard. Men was no better than they are now.

"My owner had two fine black horses name Night and Shade. Glen was a white driver. We lived close to Fiat where they had horse races. He told Glen to get Night ready to win some money. He told Glen not to let nobody have their hand on the horse. Glen slept in the stable with the horse. They had three horses on the track. They made three rounds. Night lost three times, but on Friday Night come in and won the money. He made two or three thousand dollars and paid Glen. I never heard how much.

Freedom

"Some man come to our house searching for arms. We had a chest. They threw things winding. Said it was freedom. We didn't think much of such freedom. Had to take it. We didn't have no arms in the house. We never seen free times and didn't know what to look for nohow. We never felt times as good. We moved to the bottoms and I lost my parents.

"I fell in the hands of some mean people. They worked me on the frozen ground barefooted. My feet frostbit. I wore a shirt dress and a britches leg cap on my head and ears. I had no shoes, no underwear. I slept on a bed made in the corner of a room called a bunk. It had bagging over straw and I covered with bagging. Aunt July (Julie) and Uncle Mass Harris come for me. Sister brought my horse pa left for me. They took me from them folks to stay at Mr. W. C. Winters. He was good to me. He give me fifty dollars and fed me and my horse. He give me good clothes and a house in his yard. I was hungry. He fattened me and my horse both.

"They broke the Ku Klux up by putting grapevines across the roads. I know about that. I never seen one of them in my life.

"Election days years gone by was big times. I did vote. I voted regular a long time. The last President I voted for was Wilson.

"I farmed and worked on steamboats on the Mississippi River. I was what they called rousterbout. I loaded and unloaded freight. I worked on the Choctaw, Jane White, Kate Adams, and other little boats a few days at a time. Kate Adams burnt at Moons Landing. I stopped off here at Helena for Christmas. Some people got drowned and some burned to death. The head [?] clerk got lost. He went in and got two bags of silver money, put them in his pockets. The stave plank broke and he went down and never come up. He was at the shore nearly but nobody knew he had that silver in his pockets. He never come up and he drowned. People seen him go in but the others swum out. He never come up. They missed him and found him dead and the two bags of silver. I was due to be on there but I wanted to spend Christmas with grandma and my wife. The Choctaw carried ten thousand bales of cotton at times. I worked at the oil mill sixteen or seventeen years. I night watched on the transfer twenty-two years. I come to Helena when I was thirty years old. I'm eighty-six now. The worst thing I ever done was drink whiskey some. I done quit it. I have asthma. The doctors say whiskey is bad on that disease. I don't tetch it now.

"I think the present generation is crazy. I wish I had the chance they have now. The present times is getting better. I ask the Lord to spare me to be one hundred years old. I'm strong in the faith. I pray every day. He will open the way. The times have changed in my life."

Chambers, Lula
Age: 90+
2627 Thomas Street
St. Louis, Missouri
Interviewer: Grace E. White
[M:11: pt. 8: 79–83]

The subject of this sketch is Lula Chambers who is not certain of her age. However she knows she is past ninety and that she was born in Galatin County, Kentucky near Virginia. She lives with a granddaughter, Genevieve Holden, 2627 Thomas Street, St. Louis.

Lying ill in a three-quarter metal bed in the front hall room of her granddaughter's 4-room brick apartment, the old lady is a very cheerful person, with an exceptionally fair complexion. Her brown hair is mixed with gray and she wears it quite long. Her room is neatly furnished.

"I was born in Galatin County, Kentucky, more than ninety years ago, slaves didn't know dere age in them days when I come along. I do know I was born in July and my mammy's name was Patsy Lillard. I don't know nothing at all about no kind of father. Course, I had one but who he was I never knew. "I ain't never even seen my mother enough to really know her, cause she was sold off the plantation where I was raised, when I was too young to remember her, and I just growed up in the house with the white folks dat owned me. Dere names was Dave Lillard. He owned more dan one hundred slaves. He told me dat my mother had seven children and I was de baby of 'em all and de onliest one living dat I knows anything about. They sold my mother down de river when I was too young to recollect a mother. I fared right well with my white masters. I done all de sewing in de house, wait on de table, clean up de house, knit and pick wool, and my old miss used to carry me to church with her whenever she went. She liked lots of water, and I had to bring her water to her in church. I had so much temper dey never bothered me none about nursing de children. But I did have a heap of nursing to do with de grown ups.

I used to get a whipping now and den but nothing like de other slaves got. I used to be scared to death of those old Ku Klux folks with all dem hoods on dere heads and faces. I never will forget, I saw a real old darkey woman slave down on her knees praying to God for his help. She had a Bible in front of her. Course she couldn't read it, but she did know what it was, and she was prayin' out of her very heart, until she drawed the attention of them old Ku Klux and one of 'em just walked in her cabin and lashed her unmerciful. He made her get up off her knees and dance, old as she was. Of course de old soul couldn't dance but he just made her hop around anyhow.

De slave owners in de county where I was raised—de well-to-do ones I mean, did not abuse de slaves like de pore trash and other slave holders did. Of course dey whipped 'em plenty when dey didn't suit. But dey kind of taken care of 'em to sell. Dey had a great slave market dere dat didn't do nothing but sell slaves, and if dey wanted a good price for dem de slave would have to be in a purty good condition. Dat's what saved dere hides. My owners had a stock farm and raised de finest stock in Kentucky. Dey didn't raise any cotton at all, but dey shore did raise fine wheat, barley and corn, just acres and acres of it. De worse lashing our slaves ever got was when dey got caught away from home without a pass. Dey got whipped hot and heavy den.

In Arkansas many of de slave owners would tie dere slaves to a wagon and gallop 'em all over town and dey be banged up. I saw a strange niggah come to town once and didn't know where he was going and stepped in the door of a white hotel. When he saw all white faces, he was scared most to death. He didn't even turn around he just backed out and don't you know dem white folks kilt him for stepping inside a white man's hotel by mistake, yes they did.

"I can't tell you any pleasure I had in my early days honey, cause I didn't have none. If I had my studyin' cap on, and hadn't just got over dis terrible sick spell, I could think of lots of things to tell you, but I can't now. Right after de war dey sent colored teachers through de South to teach colored people and child, do you know, dem white folks just crucified most of 'em. I don't know how to read or write. Never did know. I am de mother of five children, but dey is all dead now. I have two grandchilren living, and have been in St. Louis seven years. I come here from Helena, Arkansas. My husband was a saloon keeper and a barber. He died in 1880 in Brinkley, Arkansas. I nursed and cooked in Brinkley after he died for fifteen years for one family.

"I wears glasses sometime. I have been a member of de church over fifty years. My membership is in Prince of Peace Baptist Church now and has been every since I been in St. Louis. God has been so good to me, to let me live all dese years. I just want to be ready to meet him when he is ready for me. My only trouble will be to love white folks, dey have treated my race so bad. My pastor, Rev. Fred McDonald always tells me I will have to forgive them and love dem if I wants to go to heaven. But honey, dat's goin to be a lifetime job. I don't care how long God lets me live, it will still be a hard job.

"I gets an old age pension. It is very little, but I thank God for dat. I have nothing left to do now in this world but to pray. Thank God for his goodness to me and be ready when He comes.

"Dis rhemetis serves me so bad I can't be happy much. Wish I could remember more to tell you but I can't."

The old woman is well preserved for her years.

Davis, Jeff
Age: 78
R.F.D., five miles south
Marvell, Arkansas
Interviewer: Watt McKinney
[M:8: pt. 2: 117–21]

"I'se now seventy-eight year old an' gwine on seventy-nine. I was borned in de Tennessee Valley not far from Huntsville, Alabama. Right soon atter I was borned my white folks, de Welborns, dey left Alabama an' come right here to Phillips County, Arkansas, an' brung all the darkies with 'em, an' that's how come me here till dis very day. I is been here all de time since then an' been makin' crops er cotton an' corn every since I been old enough. I is seen good times an' hard times, Boss, all endurin' of those years followin' de War, but de worst times I is ever seen hab been de last several years since de panic struck.

"How-some-ever I is got 'long first rate I reckon 'cause you know I owns my own place here of erbout eighty acres an' has my own meat an' all such like. I really ain't suffered any for nothin'. Still they has been times when I ain't had nary a cent an' couldn't get my hands on a dime, but I is made it out somehow. Us old darkies what come up with de country, an' was de fust one here, us cleared up de land when there wasn't nothin' here much, an' built de log houses, an' had to git 'long on just what us could raise on de land an' so on. Couldn't mind a panic bad as de young folks what is growed up in de last ginnyration.

"You see, I was borned just three years before de darkies was sot free. An' course I can't riccolect nothin' 'bout de slavery days myself but my mammy, she used to tell us chillun 'bout dem times.

"Like I first said, us belonged to de Welborns an' dey was powerful loyal to de Souf an' er heap of de young ones fit in de army, an' dey sont corn an' cows an' hogs an' all sich like supplies to de army in Tennessee an' Georgia. Dat's what my mammy tole me an' I know dey done dem things, an' dey crazy 'bout Mr. Jefferson Davis, de fust an' only President of de Confederacy, an' dat's how come me got dis name I got. Yas suh, dat is how come me named 'Jeff Davis'. An' I always has been proud of my name, 'cause dat was a sure great one what I is named after.

"My pappy was a white man, dat's what my mammy allus told me. I knows he bound to been 'cause I is too bright to not have no white blood in me. My mammy, she named 'Mary Welborn'. She say dat my pappy was a white man name 'Bill Ward' what lived back in Alabama. Dat's all my mammy ever told me about my pappy. She never say iffen he work for de Welborns er no, er iffen he was an overseer or what. I don't know nothin' 'bout him scusin' dat he is er white man an' he named 'Bill Ward'. My steppappy, he was name John Sanders, an' he married my mammy when I 'bout four year old, an' dat was atter de slaves taken outen dey bondage.

"My steppappy, he was a fine carpenter an' could do most anything dat he want to do with an axe or any kind of a tool dat you work in wood with. I riccolect dat he made a heap of de culberts for de railroad what was built through Marvell from Helena to Clarendon. He made dem culberts outen logs what would be split half in two. Then he would hew out de two halves what he done split open like dey used to make a dug-out boat. Dey would put dem two halves together like a big pipe under de tracks for de water to run trough.

"There was several white mens dat I knowed in dis part of de county what raised nigger famblys, but there wasn't so many at dat. I will say this for them mens though. Whilst it wasn't right for dem to do like dat, dem what did have em a nigger woman what dey had chillun by sure took care of de whole gang. I riccolect one white man in particular, an' I knows you is heered of him too. How-some-ever, I won't call no names. He lived down on de ribber on de island. Dis white man, he was a overseer for a widder woman what lived in Helena an' what owned de big place dat dis man overseer was on. Dis white man, he hab him dis nigger woman for de longest. She have five chillun by him, three boys an' two gals.

"After a while dis man, he got him a place up close to Marvell where he moved to. He brought his nigger fambly with him. He built dem a good house on his farm where he kept them. He give dat woman an' dem chillun dey livin' till de chillun done grown an' de woman she dead. Then he married him a nice white woman after he moved close to Marvell. He built him a house in town where his white wife live an' she de mammy of a heap of chillun too by dis same man. So dis man, he had a white fambly an' a half nigger fambly before. De most of de chillun of dis man is livin' in this county right now.

"Yas suh, Boss, I is sure 'nough growed up with dis here county. In my young days most all de west end of this county was in de woods. There wasn't no ditches or no improvements at all. De houses an' barns was most all made of logs, but I is gwine to tell you one thing, de niggers an' de white folks, dey get erlong more better together then dan dey does at dis time. De white folks then an' de darkies, dey just had more confidence in each other seems like in dem days. I don't know how 'twas in de other states after de War, but right here in Phillips County de white folks, dey encouraged de darkies to buy 'em a home. Dey helped dem to git it. Dey sure done dat. Mr. Marve Carruth, dat was really a good white man. He helped me to get dis very place here dat I is owned for fifty years. An' then I tell you dis too, Boss, when I was coming up, de folks, dey just worked harder dan dey do these days. A good hand then naturally did just about three er four times as much work in a day as dey do now. Seems like dis young bunch awful no 'count er bustin' up and down de road day and night in de cars, er burnin' de gasoline when dey orter be studyin' 'bout making er livin' an' gettin' demselves er home.

"Yas suh, I riccolect all 'bout de time dat de niggers holdin' de jobs in de courthouse in Helena, but I is never took no part in that votin' business an' I allus kept out of dem arguments. I left it up to de white folks to 'tend to de 'lectin' of officers.

"De darkies what was in de courthouse dat I riccolect was: Bill Gray, he was one of de clerks; Hanse Robinson, Dave Ellison, an' some more dat I don't remember. Bill Gray, he was a eddycated man, but de res', dey was just plain old ex-slave darkies an' didn't know nothing. Bill Gray, he used to be de slave of a captain on a steamboat on de ribber. He was sorter servant to he mars on de boat where he stayed all the time. The captain used to let him git some eddycation. Darkies, dey never last long in de courthouse. Dey soon git 'em out.

"I gwine tell yo somepin else dat is done changed er lot since I was comin' up. Dat is, de signs what de folks used to believe in dey don't believe in no more. Yet de same signs is still here, an' I sure does believe in 'em 'cause I done seen 'em work for all dese years. De Lawd give de peoples a sign for all things. De moon an' de stars, dey is a sign for all them what can read 'em an' tells you when to plant de cotton an' de taters an' all your crops. De screech owls, dey give er warnin' dat some one gwine to die. About de best sign dat some person gwine die 'round close is for a cow to git to lowin' an' a lowin' constant in de middle of de night. Dat is a sign I hardly ever seen fail an' I seen it work out just a few weeks ago when old Aunt Dinah died up de road. I heered dat cow a lowin' an' a lowin' an' a walkin' back an' forth down de road for 'bout four nights in a row, right past Aunt Dinah's cabin. I say to my old woman dat somepin is sure gwine to take place, an' dat some pusson gwine die soon 'cause dat cow, she givin' de sign just right. Dere wasn't nobody 'round sick a tall an' Aunt Dinah, she plumb well at de time. About er week from then Aunt Dinah, she took down an' start to sinkin' right off an' in less than a week she died. I knowed some pusson gwine die all right, yet an' still I didn't know who it was to be. I tell you, Boss, I is gittin' uneasy an' troubled de last day or two, 'cause I is done heered another cow a lowin' an' a lowin' in de middle of de night. She keeps a walkin' back an' forth past my house out there in de road. I is really troubled 'cause me an' de old woman both is gittin' old. We is both way up in years an' whilst both of us is in real good health, Aunt Dinah was too. Dat cow a lowin' like she do is a bad sign dat I done noticed mighty nigh allus comes true."

Davis, Rosetta
Age: 55
Marianna, Arkansas
Interviewer: Irene Robertson
[M:8: pt. 2: 130]

"I was born in Phillips County, Arkansas. My folks' master was named Dr. Jack Spivy. Grandma belong to him. She was a field woman. I don't know if he was a good master or not. They didn't know it was freedom till three or four months. They was at work and some man come along and said he was going home, the War was over. Some of the hands asked him who win and he told them the Yankees and told them they was free fer as he knowed. They got to inquiring and found out they done been free. They made that crap I know and I don't recollect nothing else.

"I farmed at Foreman, Arkansas for Taylor Price, Steve Pierce, John Huey. I made a crap here with Bill Dale. I come to Arkansas twenty-nine years ago. I come to my son. He had a cleaning and pressing shop here (Marianna). He died. I hired to the city to work on the streets. I never been in jail. I owned a house here in town till me and my wife separated. She caused me to lose it. I was married once.

"I get ten dollars a month from the gover'ment.

"The present time is queer. I guess I could git work if I was able to do it. I believe in saving some of what you make along. I saved some along and things come up so I had to spend it. I made so little.

"Education has brought about a heap of unrest somehow. Education is good fer some folks and not good fer some. Some folks git spoilt and lazy. I think it helped to do it to the people of today."

Gill, James
Age: 86
Marvell, Arkansas
Interviewer: Watt McKinney
[M:9: pt. 3: 19–26]

"Uncle Jim" Gill, an ex-slave eighty-six years of age, owns a nice two hundred acre farm five miles north of Marvell where he has lived for the past thirty-five years. "Uncle Jim" is an excellent citizen, prosperous and conservative and highly respected by both white and colored. This is molasses making time in the South and I found "Uncle Jim" busily engaged in superintending the process of cooking the extracted juice from a large quantity of sorghum cane. The familiar type of horse-power mill in which the cane is crushed was in full operation, a roaring fire was blazing in the crudely constructed furnace beneath the long pen that contained the furiously foaming, boiling juice and that "Uncle Jim" informed me was "nigh 'bout done" and ready to drain off into the huge black pot that stood by the side of the furnace. The purpose of my visit was explained and "Uncle Jim" leaving the molasses making to some younger Negro accompanied me to the shade of a large oak tree that stood near-by and told me the following story:

"My ole mars, he was name Tom White and my young mars what claimed me, he was name Jeff. Young mars an' me was just 'bout same age. Us played together from time I fust riccolect till us left de old home place back in Alabama and lit out for over here in Arkansas.

"Ole mars, he owned a heap of niggers back dere where us all lived on de big place but de lan', it was gittin' poor an' red and mought near wore out; so old mars, he 'quired a big lot of lan' here in Arkansas in Phillips County, but you know it was all in de woods den 'bout fifteen miles down de ribber from Helena and just thick wid canebrakes. So he sont 'bout twenty famblies ober here and dats how us happened to come 'cause my pappy, he was a extra blacksmith and carpenter and old mars knowed he gwine to haf to hab him to 'sist in buildin' de houses and sich like.

"Though I was just 'bout seven year ole den, howsomever, I 'member it well an' I sure did hate to leave de ole home where I was borned and I didn' want leave Mars Jeff either and when Mars Jeff foun' it out 'bout 'em gwine take me he cut up awful and just went on, sayin' I his nigger and wasn't gwine 'way off to Arkansas.

"Ole mars, he knowed my mammy and pappy, dey wasn't gwine be satisfied widout all dere chillun wid 'em, so en course I was brung on too. You see, ole mars and he fambly, dey didn' come and we was sont under de overseer what was name Jim Lynch and us come on de train to Memphis and dat was when I got so skeered 'cause I hadn' nebber seen no train 'fore den an' I just hollered an' cried an' went on so dat my mammy say if I didn' hush up she gwine give me to de paddy rollers.

"Dey put us on de steamboat at Memphis and de nex' I 'member was us gittin' off at the landin'. It was in de winter time 'bout las' of January us git here and de han's was put right to work clearin' lan' and buildin' cabins. It was sure rich lan' den, boss, and dey jus' slashed de cane and deaden de timber and when cotton plantin' time come de cane was layin' dere on de groun' crisp dry and dey sot fire to it and burned it off clean and den planted de crops.

"Ole mars, he would come from Alabama to see 'bout de bixness two an' three times every year and on some of dem 'casions he would bring Mars Jeff wid him and Mars Jeff, he allus nebber failed to hab somethin' for me, candy and sich like, and dem times when Mars Jeff come was when we had de fun. Us just run wild playin' and iffen it was in de summer time we was in de bayou swimmin' er fishin' continual but all dem good times ceasted atter a while when de War come and de Yankees started all dere debbilment. Us was Confedrits all de while, leastwise I means my mammy an' my pappy and me an' all de res' of de chillun 'cause ole mars was and Mars Jeff would er fit 'em too and me wid him iffen we had been ole enough.

"But de Yankees, dey didn' know dat we was Confedrits, dey jus' reckon we like most all de res' of de niggers. Us was skeered of dem Yankees though 'cause us chillun cose didn' know what dey was and de oberseer, Jim Lynch, dey done tole us little uns dat a Yankee was somepin what had one great big horn on he haid and just one eye and dat right in de middle of he breast and, boss, I sure was s'prized when I seen a sure 'nough Yankee and see he was a man just like any er de res' of de folks.

"De war tore up things right sharp yit an' still it wasn't so bad here in Arkansas as I hear folks tell it was back in de yolder states like Tennessee, Alabama, and Georgia. De bes' I riccolect de Yankees come in here 'bout July of de year and dey had a big scrap in Helena wid 'em and us could hear de cannons fifteen miles off and den dey would make dere trips out foragin' for stuff, corn and sich, and dey would take all de cotton dey could fin', but our mens, dey would hide de cotton in de thickets an' canebrakes iffen dey had time or either dey would burn it up 'fore de Yankees come if dey could. I 'member one day we had on han' 'bout hundred bales at de gin and a white man come wid orders to de oberseer to git rid of it, so dey started to haulin' it off to de woods and dey hauled off 'bout fifty bales and den dey see dey wasn't goin' to have time to git de res' to de woods and den dey commenced cuttin' de ties on de bales so dey could set fire to dem dat dey hadn' hid yet and 'bout dat time here come one of Mr. Tom Casteel's niggers just a flyin' on a mule wid a letter to de white men. Mr. Tom Casteel, he had he place just up de ribber from us, on de island, and when he gived de letter to de man en de man read it, he said de Yankees is comin' and he lit out for de ribber where de boat was waitin' for him and got 'way and dere was all dat loose cotton on de groun' and us was skeered to set fire to de cotton den and 'bout dat time de Yankees arive and say don' you burn dat cotton and dey looked all ober de place and find de bales dat was hid in de woods and de nex' day dey come and haul it off and dey say us niggers can hab dat what de ties been cut on and my mammy, she set to work and likewise de odder women what de Yankees say can had de loose cotton and tie up all dey can in bags and atter dat us sold it to de Yankees in Helena for a dollar a poun' and dat was all de money us had for a long time.

"How-some-ever us all lived good 'cause dere was heap of wild hogs an' 'possums and sich and we had hid a heap of corn and us did fine. Sometimes de war boats, dey would pass on de ribber—dat is de Yankee boats—and us would hide 'hind de trees and bushes and see dem pass. We wouldn't let dem see us though 'cause we thought they would shoot. Heap en heap er times sojers would come by us place. When de Yankees ud come dey would ax my mammy, 'Aunt Mary, is you seen any Se-cesh today?' and mammy, she ud say

'Naw suh' eben iffen she had seen some of us mans, but when our sojers ud come and say, 'Aunt Mary, is you seen ary Yankee 'round here recent?' she ud allus tell dem de truf. Dey was a bunch of us sojers, dat is the Confedrits, what used to stay 'round in de community constant, dat we knowed, but dey allus had to be on de dodge 'cause dere was so many more Yankees dan dem.

"Some of dese men I 'member good 'cause dey was us closest neighbors and some of dem libed on 'j'ining places. Dere was Mr. Lum Shell, Mr. Tom Stoneham, Mr. Bob Yabee, Mr. Henry Rabb and Mr. Tom Casteel. Dem I 'member well 'cause dey come to us cabin right of 'en and mammy, she ud cook for 'em and den atter de niggers git dey freedom dey could leave de place any time dey choose and every so of 'en mammy ud go to Helena and gin'rally she took me wid her to help tote de things she get dere. Old Mr. Cooledge, he had de biggest and 'bout de onliest store dat dere was in Helena at dat time. Mr. Cooledge, he was a old like gentleman and had everything most in he store—boots, shoes, tobacco, medicine en so on. Cose couldn't no pusson go in an' outen Helena at dat time—dat is durin' war days—outen dey had a pass and de Yankee sojer dat writ de passes was named Buford en he is de one what us allus git our passes from for to git in en out and 'twasn't so long 'fore Mr. Buford, he git to know my mammy right well and call her by her name. He, just like all de white mens, knowed her as 'Aunt Mary', but him nor none of de Yankees knowed dat mammy was a Confedrit and dats somepin I will tell you, boss.

"Dese sojers dat I is just named and dat was us neighbors, dey ud come to our cabin sometimes en say, 'Aunt Mary, we want you to go to Helena for us and git some tobacco, and mebbe some medicine, and so on, and we gwine write old man Cooledge er note for you to take wid you; and mammy, she ud git off for town walking and ud git de note to ole man Cooledge. Ole man Cooledge, you see, boss, he sided wid de Confedrites too but he didn't let on dat he did but all de Confedrit sojers 'round dar in de county, dey knowed dey could 'pend on him and when my mammy ud take de note in old man Cooledge, he ud fix mammy up in some of dem big, wide hoop skirts and hide de things 'neath de skirts dat de men sont for. Den she and sometimes me wid her, us would light out for home and cose we allus had our pass and dey knowed us and we easy git by de pickets and git home wid de goods for those sojer men what sont us.

"Speakin' from my own pussonal 'sperience, boss, de niggers was treated good in slavery times, dat is dat was de case wid my mars' peoples. Our mars wouldn't hab no mistreatment of his niggers but I'se heered tell dat some of the mars was pretty mean to dere niggers, but twasn't so wid us 'cause us had good houses and plenty somepin to eat outen de same pot what de white folks' victuals cooked in and de same victuals dat dey had. You see dat ole kittle settin' ober dar by de lasses pan right now? Well, I is et many a meal outen dat kittle in slavery times 'cause dat is de very same kittle dat dey used to cook us victuals in when us belonged to ole mars, Tom White, and lived on he place down on de ribber. It was den, boss, just same wid white men as 'tis in dis day and time. Dere is heap of good white folks now and dere is a heap of dem what ain't so good. You know dat's so, boss, don't you?

"When de niggers been made free, de oberseer, he called all de peoples up and he says, 'You all is free now and you can do like you please. You can stay on here and make de crops ur you can leave which-some-ever you want to do.' And wid dat de niggers, dat is most of dem, lef' like when you leave de let gate open where is a big litter of shotes and dey just hit de road and commenced to ramble. Most of 'em, dey go on to Helena and gits dey grub from de Yankees and stay dar till de Yankees lef'.

"But us, we stay on de place and some more, dey stay too and you know, boss, some of dem niggers what belonged to old mars and what he was so good to, dey stole mighty nigh all de mules and rode dem off and mars, he never git he mules back. Naw suh, dat he didn'. De war, it broke ole mars up and atter de surrender he jus' let he Arkansas farm go an' never come back no more. Some of de older peoples, dey went back to Alabama time er two and seen old mars but I nebber did git to see him since us was sot free. But Mars Jeff, he comed here all de way from de home in Alabama way atter he was growed. It's been 'bout fifty year now since de time he was here and I sure was proud to see him, dat I was, boss, 'cause I sure did love Mars Jeff and I loves him yet to dis day iffen he still lives and iffen he daid which I ain't never heered er not, den I loves and 'spects he memory.

"Yas suh, boss, times is changed sure 'nough but like I 'splained 'bout white folks and it's de same wid niggers, some is good and trys to lib right en some don' keer and jus' turns loose en don' restrain demselves.

"You know, boss, dere is heaps of niggers wid white blood in 'em and dat mess was started way back yonder I reckon 'fore I was ever borned. Shucks, I knowed it was long afore den but it wasn't my kine er white folks what 'sponsible for dat, it was de low class like some of de oberseers and den some of de yother folks like for instance de furriners what used to come in de country and work at jobs de mars ud give 'em to do on the places like carpentrying an' sich. I knowed one bad case, boss, dat happened right dere by us place and dat was de oberseer who 'sponsible for dat and he was de oberseer for a widow oman what lived in Helena and dis white man runned de place an' he hab he nigger oman and she de mama of 'bout six chillun by dis man I tellin' you 'bout, three gals and three boys, and dem chillun nigh 'bout white and look just like him and den he move off to some yother part of de county and he git married dere to a white oman but he take he nigger fambly wid him just de same and he built dem a house in de middle of de places he done bought and he keep 'em dere eben though he done got him a white wife who he lib wid also and, boss, since I done told you he name don't tell I said so 'cause de chillun, dey is livin' dere yet and some of dem is gettin' old deyselves now but, boss, I don't 'spect I is tellin' you much you don't already know 'bout dat bunch."

Johnson, Ella
Age: 85
913 ½ Victory Street
Little Rock, Arkansas
Interviewer: Samuel S. Taylor
[M:9: pt. 4: 77–83]

"I was born in Helena, Arkansas. Not exactly in the town but in hardly not more than three blocks from the town. Have you heard about the Grissoms down there? Well, them is my white folks. My maiden name was Burke. But we never called ourselves any name 'cept Grissom.

"My mother's name was Sylvia Grissom. Her husband was named Jack Burkes. He went to the Civil War. That was a long time ago. When they got up the war, they sold out a lot of the colored folks. But they didn't get a chance to sell my mother. She left. They tell me one of them Grissom boys has been down here looking for me. He didn't find me and he went on back.

"My mother's mistress was named Sylvia Grissom too. All of us was named after the white folks. All the old folks is dead, but the young ones is living. I think my mother's master was named John. They had so many of them that I forgit which is which. But they had all mama's children named after them. My mother had three girls and three boys.

"When the war began and my father went to war, my mother left Helena and came here. She run off from the Grissoms. They whipped her too much, those white folks did. She got tired of all that beating. She took all of us with her. All six of us children were born before the war. I was the fourth.

"There is a place down here where the white folks used to whip and hang the niggers. Baskin Lake they call it. Mother got that far. I don't know how. I think that she came in a wagon. She stayed there a little while and then she went to Churchill's place. Churchill's place and John Addison's place is close together down there. That is old time. Them folks is dead, dead, dead. Churchill's and Addison's places joined near Horse Shoe Lake. They had hung and burnt people—killed 'em and destroyed 'em at Baskin Lake. We stayed there about four days before we went on to Churchill's place. We couldn't stay there long.

"The ha'nts—the spirits—bothered us so we couldn't sleep. All them people that had been killed there used to come back. We could hear them tipping 'round in the house all the night long. They would blow out the light. You would kiver up and they would git on top of the kiver. Mama couldn't stand it; so she come down to General Churchill's place and made arrangements to stay there. Then she came back and got us children. She had an old man to stay there with us until she come back and got us. We couldn't stay there with them ha'nts dancing 'round and carryin' us a merry gait.

"At Churchill's place my mother made cotton and corn. I don't know what they give her for the work, but I know they paid her. She was a hustling old lady. The war was still goin' on. Churchill was a Yankee. He went off and left the plantation in the hands of his oldest son. His son was named Jim Churchill. That is the old war; that is the first war ever got up—the Civil War. Ma stayed at Churchill's long enough to make two or three crops. I don't know just how long. Churchill and them wanted to own her—them and John Addison.

"There was three of us big enough to work and help her in the field. Three—I made four. There was my oldest sister, my brother, and my next to my oldest sister, and myself—Annie, John, Martha, and me. I chopped cotton and corn. I used to tote the leadin' row. Me and my company walked out ahead. I was young then, but my company helped me pick that cotton. That nigger could pick cotton too. None of the rest of them could pick anything for looking at him .

"Mother stayed at Churchill's till plumb after the war. My father died before the war was over. They paid my mother some money and said she would get the balance. That means there was more to come, doesn't it? But they didn't no more come. They all died and none of them got the balance. I ain't never got nothin' either. I gave my papers to Adams and Singfield. I give them to Adams; Adams is a Negro that one-legged Wash Jordan sent to me. They all say he's a big crook, but I didn't know it. Adams kept coming to my house until he got my papers and then when he got the papers he didn't come no more.

"After Adams got the papers, he carried me down to Lawyer Singfield's. He said I had to be sworn in and it would cost me one dollar. Singfield wrote down every child's name and everybody's age. When he got through writing, he said that was all and me and Pearl made up one dollar between us and give it to him. And then we come on away. We left Mr. Adams and Mr. Singfield in Singfield's office and we left the papers there in the office with them. They didn't give me no receipt for the papers and they didn't give me no receipt for the dollar. Singfield's wife has been to see me several times to sell me something. She wanted to git me to buy a grave, but she ain't never said nothin' about those papers. You think she doesn't know 'bout 'em? I have seen Adams once down to Jim Perry's funeral on Arch Street. I asked him about my papers and he said the Government hadn't aswered him. He said, 'Who is you?' I said, 'This is Mrs. Johnson.' Then he went on out. He told me when he got a answer, it will come right to my door.

"I never did no work before goin' on Churchill's plantation. Some of the oldest ones did, but I didn't. I learned how to plow at John Addison's place. The war was goin' on then. I milked cows for him and churned and cleaned up. I cooked some for him. Are you acquainted with Blass? I nursed Julian Blass. I didn't nurse him on Addison's place; I nursed him at his father's house up on Main Street, after I come here. I nursed him and Essie both. I nursed her too. I used to have a time with them chillen. They weren't nothin' but babies. The gal was about three months old and Julian was walkin' 'round. That was after I come to Little Rock.

"My mother come to Little Rock right after the war. She brought all of us with her but the oldest. He come later.

"She went to work and cooked and washed and ironed here. I don't remember the names of the people she worked for. They all dead—the old men and the old ladies.

"She sent me to school. I went to school at Philander and down to the end of town and in the country. We had a white man first and then we had a colored woman teacher. The white man was rough. He would fight all the time. I would read and spell without opening my book. They would have them blue-back spellers and McGuffy's reader. They got more education then than they do now. Now they is busy fighting one another and killin' one another. When you see anything in the paper, you don't know whether it is true or not. Florence Lacy's sister was one of my teachers. I went to Union school once. I don't know how many grades I finished in school. I guess it was about three altogether. I had to git up and go to work then.

"You remember Reuben White? They tried to bury him and he came to before they got him in the grave. He used to own the First Baptist Church. He used to pastor it too. He sent for J. P. Robinson by me. He told Robinson he wanted him to take the Church and keep it as long as he lived. Robinson said he would keep it. Reuben White went to his brother's and died. They brought him back here and kept his body in the First Baptist Church a whole week. J. P. carried on the meetin', and them sisters was fightin' him. They went on terrible. He started out of the church and me and 'nother woman stopped him. At last they voted twice, and finally they elected J. P. He was a good pastor, but he hurrahed the people and they didn't like that.

"Reuben White didn't come back when they buried him the second time. They were letting the coffin down in the grave when they buried him the first time, and he knocked at it on the inside, knock, knock. (Here the old lady rapped on the doorsill with her knuckles—ed.) They drew that coffin up and opened it. How do I know? I was there. I heard it and seen it. They took him out of the coffin and carried him back to his home in the ambulance. He lived about three or four years after that.

"I had a member to die in my order and they sent for the undertaker and he found that she wasn't dead. They said she died after they embalmed her. That lodge work ran my nerves down. I was in the Tabernacle then. Goodrich and Dubisson was the undertakers that had the body. Lucy Tucker was the woman. I guess she died when they got her to the shop. They say the undertaker cut on her before he found that she was dead.

"After I quit school, I nursed mighty nigh all the time. I cooked for Governor Rector part of the time. I cooked for Dr. Lincoln Woodruff. I cooked for a whole lot of white folks. I washed and ironed for them Anthonys down here. She like to had a fit over me the last time she saw me. She wanted me to come back, but my hand couldn't stand it. I cooked for Governor Rose's wife. That's been a long time back. I wouldn't 'low nobody to come in the kitchen when I was working. I would say, 'You goin' to come in this kitchen, I'll have to git out.' The Governor was awful good to me. They say he kicked the res' of them out. I scalded his little grandson once. I picked up the teakettle. Didn't know it had water in it and it slipped and splashed water over the little boy's hand. If'n it had been hot as it ought to have been, it would have burnt him bad. He went out of that kitchen hollerin'. The Governor didn't say nothin' 'cept, 'Ella, please don't do it again.' I said, 'I guess that'll teach him to stay out of that kitchen now.' I was boss of that kitchen when I worked there.

"We took the lock off the door once so the Governor couldn't git in it.

"I dressed up and come out once and somebody called the Governor and said, 'Look at your cook.' And he said, 'That ain't my cook.' That was Governor Rector. I went in and put on my rags and come in the kitchen to cook and he said, 'That is my cook.' He sure wanted me to keep on cookin' for him, but I just got sick and couldn't stay.

"I hurt my hand over three years ago. My arm swelled and folks rubbed it and got all the swelling down in one place in my hand. They told me to put fat meat on it. I put it on and the meat hurt so I had to take it off. Then they said put the white of an egg on it. I did that too and it was a little better. Then they rubbed the place until it busted. But it never did cure up. I poisoned it by goin' out pullin up greens in the garden. They tell me I got dew poisoning.

"I don't git no help from the Welfare or from the Government. My husband works on the relief sometimes. He's on the relief now.

"I married—of, Lordy, lemme see when I did marry. It's been a long time ago, more 'n thirty years it's been. It's been longer than that. We married up here on Twelfth and State Street, right here in Little Rock. I had a big wedding. I had to go to Thompson's hall. That was on Tenth and State Street. They had to go to git all them people in. They had a big time that night.

"I lived in J. P. Robinson's house twenty-two years. And then I lived in front of Dunbar School. It wasn't Dunbar then. I know all the people that worked at the school. I been living here about six months."

Interviewer's Comment

Ella Johnson is about eighty-five years old. Her father went to war when the War first broke out. Her mother ran away then and went to Churchill's farm not later than 1862. Ella Johnson learned to plow then and she was at least nine years old she says and perhaps older when she learned to plow. So she must be at least eighty-five.

Martin, Josie
Age: 86
Madison, Arkansas
Interviewer: Irene Robertson
[M:10: pt. 5: 51–52]

"I was born up near Cotton Plant but took down near Helena to live. My parents named Sallie and Bob Martin. They had seven children. I heard mother say she was sold on a block in Mississippi when she was twelve years old. My father was a Creek Indian; he was dark. Mother was a Choctaw Indian; she was bright. Mother died when I was but a girl and left a family on my hands. I sent my baby brother and sister to school and I cooked on a boarding train. The railroad hands working on the tracks roomed and et on the train. They are all dead now and I'm 'lone in the world.

"My greatest pleasure was independence—make my money, go and spend it as I see fit. I wasn't popular with men. I never danced. I did sell herbs for diarrhea and piles and 'what ails you.' I don't sell no more. Folks too close to drug stores now. I had long straight hair nearly to my knees. It come out after a spell of typhoid fever. It never come in to do no good." (Baldheaded like a man and she shaves. She is a hermaphrodite, reason for never marrying.) "I made and saved up at one time twenty-three thousand dollars cooking and field work. I let it slip out from me in dribs.

"I used to run from the Yankees. I've seen them go in droves along the road. They found old colored couple, went out, took their hog and made them barbecue it. They drove up a stob, nailed a piece to a tree and stacked their guns. They rested around till everything was ready. They et at one o'clock at night and after the feast drove on. They weren't so good to Negroes. They was good to their own feelings. They et up all that old couple had to eat in their house and the pig they raised. I reckon their owners give them more to eat. They lived off alone and the soldiers stopped there and worked the old man and woman nearly to death.

"Our master told us about freedom. His name was Master Martin. We come here from Mississippi. I don't recollect his family.

"I get help from the Welfare. I had paralysis. I never got over my stroke. I ain't no 'count to work."

Myers, Betty
Age: 80+
Helena, Arkansas
Interviewer: Irene Robertson
[S2:1 (AR): 107–08]
[See also S1:2 (AR): 17–18]

"I was born in Helena. Old woman we called grandma had me with her children. She died. Then Mr. Charlie Wooten's mother come and got me. I was a orphant child. She learned me everything. She took care of me nicely. Mr. Charlie Wooten is a cotton buyer here in Helena now. His mother name Miss Violet. I lived in a room in her house till I married. I been married once. She was nice to me. My husband was a lumber stacker. Miss Violet built me a house in her yard after I married. Ed Pillows brought my husband with him from Nashville, Tennessee when he was a young man. We married in Mrs. Wooten's dining-room. Mr. Charlie's preacher married us. He was the white folks' Baptist preacher. I lived with him till he died. It was about thirty years. He made me a good living. After my husband died I went back to Miss Louise and lived there twenty-one years. Miss Violet was blind. Every morning she tell them to tell me to come to see her, she want to squeeze my hand. She got blind and was ninety-nine years old when she died. She lacked a few months of being a hundred years old. She would squeeze my hand and say, 'God bless you.' I never knowed no father nor mother. I sprung up in her hands good fashion. I took Mr. Charlie to my church (Negro church) every Sunday to Sunday-school. He got three children of his own now.

"Miss Violet married a Smith the first time. They was rich people. He died. Then she married Mr. Wooten. They had two children but the girl died. They been mighty nice to me, kept me nicely. Good as could be to me. I never went to school a day in my life—only Sunday-school where I took Mr. Charlie when he was a little boy. Miss Violet learned me to work. I could cook, wash, iron, keep house. That all was better than going to school. They look after me. They are always sending me something nice. They send me nice dinners on Sunday. But they don't send nice bread like I cook for them. The cook don't make it is the reason. I cooked for them as long as I was able.

"I never seen a Ku Klux. I heard talk of them.

"I get ten dollars a month from the Gover'ment. I was sick and I have someone to see after me now. Mr. Charlie helps me. He gets my medicine if the doctor think I need it. He gets my doctor. They take care of me mighty nicely. I never had a child. I didn't see the War. I lived out from here then. The War didn't 'fect me. We lived in the country and in Helena both all along. I might not 'come with Miss Violet when the War was in Helena."

Peters, Mary Estes
Age: 78
5115 W. 17th Street
Little Rock, Arkansas
Interviewer: S. S. Taylor
[M:10: pt. 5: 323–31]

Biographical
Mary Estes Peters was born a slave January 30, 1860 in Missouri somewhere. Her mother was colored and her father white, the white parentage being very evident in her color and features and hair. She is very reticent about the facts of her birth. The subject had to be approached from many angles and in many ways and by two different persons before that part of the story could be gotten.

Although she was born in Missouri, she was "refugeed" first to Mississippi and then here, Arkansas. She is convinced that her mother was sold at least twice after freedom,—once into Mississippi, once into Helena, and probably once more after reaching Arkansas, Mary herself being still a very small child.

I think she is mistaken on this point. I did not debate with her but I cross-examined her carefully and it appears to me that there was probably in her mother's mind a confused knowledge of the issuance of the Emancipation Proclamation in 1862. Lincoln's Compensation Emancipation plan advocated in March 1862, the Abolition in the District of Columbia in 1862 in April, the announcement of Lincoln's Emancipation intention in July 1862, the prohibition of slavery in present and future territories, June 19, 1862, together with the actual issuance of the Emancipation in September 1862, and the effectiveness of the proclamation in January 1, 1863, would well give rise to an impression among many slaves that emancipation had been completed.

As a matter of fact, Missouri did not secede; the Civil War which nevertheless ensued would find some slaveholders exposed to the full force of the 1862 proclamation in 1863 at the time of its first effectiveness. Naturally it did not become effective in many other places till 1865. It would very naturally happen then that a sale in Missouri in the latter part of 1862 or any time thereafter might be well construed by ex-slaves as a sale after emancipation, especially since they do not as a rule pay as much attention to the dates of occurrences as to their sequence. This interpretation accords with the story. Only such an explanation could make probable a narrative which places the subject as a newborn babe in 1860 and sold after slavery had ceased while still too young to remember. Her earliest recollections are recollections of Arkansas.

She has lived in Arkansas ever since the Civil War and in Little Rock ever since 1879. She made a living as a seamstress for awhile but is now unable to sew because of fading eyesight. She married in 1879 and led a long and contented married life until the recent death of her husband. She lives with her husband's nephew and ekes out a living by fragmentary jobs. She has a good memory and a clear mind for her age.

Slave after Freedom

"My mother was sold after freedom. It was the young folks did all that devilment. They found they could get some money out of her and they did it. She was put on the block in St. Louis and sold down into Vicksburg, Mississippi. Then they sold her into Helena, Arkansas. After that they carried her down into Trenton (?), Arkansas. I don't know whether they sold her that time or not, but I reckon they did. Leastways, they carried her down there. All this was done after freedom. My mother was only fifteen years old when she was sold the first time, and I was a baby in her arms. I don't know nothing about it myself, but I have heard her tell about it many and many a time. It was after freedom. Of course, she didn't know she was free.

"It was a good while before my mother realized she was free. She noticed the other colored people going to and fro and she wondered about it. They didn't allow you to go round in slave times. She asked them about it and they told her, 'Don't you know you are free?' Some of the white people too, told her that she was free. After that, from the way she talked, I guess she stayed around there until she could go some place and get wages for her work. She was a good cook.

Mean Mistress
"I have seen many a scar on my mother. She had mean white folks. She had one big scar on the side of her head. The hair never did grow back on that place. She used to comb her hair over it so that it wouldn't show. The way she got it was this:

"One day her mistress went to high mass and left a lot of work for my mother to do. She was only a girl and it was too much. There was more work than she could get done. She had too big a task for a child to get done. When her old mistress came back and the work was not all done, she beat my mother down to the ground, and then she took one of the skillets and bust her over the head with it—trying to kill her, I reckon. I have seen the scar with my own eyes. It was an awful thing.

"My mother was a house servant in Missouri and Mississippi. Never done no hard work till she came here (Arkansas). When they brought her here they tried to make a field hand out of her. She hadn't been used to chopping cotton. When she didn't chop it fast as the others did, they would beat her. She didn't know nothing about no farmwork. She had all kinds of trouble. They just didn't treat her good. She used to have good times in Missouri and Mississippi but not in Arkansas. They just didn't treat her good. In them days, they'd whip anybody. They'd tie you to the bed or have somebody hold you down on the floor and whip you till the blood ran.

"But, Lawd, my mother never had no use for Catholics because it was a Catholic that hit her over the head with that skillet—right after she come from mass.

Food
"My mother said that they used to pour the food into troughs and give it to the slaves. They'd give them an old wooden spoon or something and they all eat out of the same dish or trough. They wouldn't let the slaves eat out of the things they et out of. Fed them just like they would hogs.

"When I was little, she used to come to feed me about twelve o'clock every day. She hurry in, give me a little bowl of something, and then hurry right on out because she had to go right back to her work. She didn't have time to stay and see how I et. If I had enough, it was all right. If I didn't have enough, it was all right. It might be pot liquor or it might be just anything.

"One day she left me alone and I was lying on the floor in front of the fireplace asleep. I didn't have no bed nor nothing then. The fire must have popped out and set me on fire. You see they done a whole lot of weaving in them days. And they put some sort of lint on the children.

"I don't reckon children them days knowed what a biscuit was. They just raked up whatever was left off the table and brung it to you. Children have a good time nowadays.

"People goin' to work heard me hollering and came in and put out the fire. I got scars all round my waist today I could show you.

"Another time my mother had to go off and leave me. I was older then. I guess I must have gotten hungry and wanted to get somethin' to eat. So I got up and wandered off into the woods. There weren't many people living round there then. (This was in Trenton (?), Arkansas, a small place not far from Helena.). And the place wasn't built up much then and they had lots of wolves. Wolves make a lot of noise when they get to trailin' anything. I got about a half mile from the road and the wolves got after me. I guess they would have eat me up but a man heard them howling, and he knew there wasn't no house around there but ours, and he came to see what was up, and he beat off the wolves and carried me back home. There wasn't nare another house round there but ours and he knew I must have come from there.

"Mother was working then. It was night though. They brung the news to her and they wouldn't let her come to me. Mother said she felt like getting a gun and killin' them. Her child out like that and they wouldn't let her go home.

"That must have happened after freedom, because it was the last mistress she had. Almost all her beatings and trouble came from her last mistress. That woman sure gave her a lot of trouble.

Age, Good Masters

"All I know about my age is what my mother told me.

"The first people that raised my mother had her age in the Bible. She said she was about fifteen years old when I was born. From what she told me, I must be about seventy-eight years old. She taught me that I was born on Sunday, on the thirtieth of January, in the year before the War.

"My mother's name was Myles. I don't know what her first master's name was. She told me I was born in Phelps County, Missouri; I guess you'd call it St. Louis now. I am giving you the straight truth just as she gave it to me.

"From the way she talked, the people what raised her from a child were good to her. They raised her with their children. Them people fed her just like they fed their own children.

Color and Birth

"There was a light brownskin boy around there and they give him anything that he wanted. But they didn't like my mother and me—on account of my color. They would talk about it. They tell their children that when I got big enough, I would think I was good as they was. I couldn't help my color. My mother couldn't either.

"My mother's mistress had three boys, one twenty-one, one nineteen, and one seventeen. Old mistress had gone away to spend the day one day. Mother always worked in the house. She didn't work on the farm in Missouri. While she was alone, the boys came in and threw her down on the floor and tied her down so she couldn't struggle, and one after the other used her as long as they wanted for the whole afternoon. Mother was sick when her mistress came home. When old mistress wanted to know what was the matter with her, she told her what the boys had done. She whipped them and that's the way I come to be here.

Sales and Separations

"My mother was separated from her mother when she was three years old. They sold my mother away from my grandmother. She don't know nothing about her people. She never did see her mother's folks. She heard from them. It must have been after freedom. But she never did get no full understanding about them. Some of them was in Kansas City, Kansas. My grandmother, I don't know what became of her.

"When my mother was sold into St. Louis, they would have sold me away from her but she cried and went on so that they bought me too. I don't know nothing about myself, but my mother told me. I was just nine months old then. They would call it refugeeing. These people that had raised her wanted to get something out of her because they found out that the colored people was going to be free. Those white people in Missouri didn't have many slaves. They just had four slaves—my mother, myself, another woman and an old colored man called Uncle Joe. They didn't get to sell him because he bought hisself. He made a little money working on people with rheumatism. They would run the niggers from state to state about that time to keep them from getting free and to get something out of them. My mother was sold into Mississippi after freedom. Then she was refugeed from one place to another through Helena to Trenton (?), Arkansas.

Marriages

"My mother used to laugh at that. The master would do all the marryin'. I have heard her say that many a time. They would call themselves jumpin' the broom. I don't know what they did. Whatever the master said put them together. I don't know just how it was fixed up, but they holt the broom and master would say, 'I pronounce you man and wife' or something like that.

Ku Klux

"My mother talked about the Ku Klux but I don't know much about them. She talked about how they would ride and how they would go in and destroy different people's things. Go in the smoke house and eat the people's stuff. She said that they didn't give the colored people much trouble. Sometimes they would give them something to eat.

"When they went to a place where they didn't give the colored people much to eat, what they didn't destroy they would say, 'Go get it.' I don't know how it was but the Ku Klux didn't have much use for certain white people and they would destroy everything they had.

"I have lived in Arkansas about all my life. I have been in Little Rock ever since January 30, 1879. I don't know how I happened to move on my birthday. My husband brought me here for my rheumatism.

"I married in 1879 and moved here from Marianna. I had lived in Helena before Marianna.

Voting

"The niggers voted in Marianna and in Helena. They voted in Little Rock too. I didn't know any of them. It seems like some of the people didn't make so much talk about it. They did, I guess, though. Many of the farmers would tell their hands who they wanted them to vote for, and they would do it.

"Them was critical times. A man would kill you if he got beat. They would say, 'So and so lost the 'lection,' and then somebody would go to Judgment. I remember once they had a big barbecue in Helena just after the 'lection. They had it for the white and for the colored alike. We didn't know there was any trouble. The shooting started on a hill where everybody could see. First thing you know, one man fell dead. Another dropped down on all fours bleeding, but he retch in under him and dragged out a pistol and shot down the man that shot him. That was a sad time. Niggers and white folks were all mixed up together and shooting. It was the first time I had ever been out. My mother never would let me go out before that.

Seamstress

"I ain't able to do much of anything now. I used to make a good living as a dressmaker. I can't sew now because of my eyes. I used to make many a dollar before my eyes got to failing me. Make pants, dresses, anything. When you get old, you fail in what you been doing. I don't get anything from the government. They don't give me any kind of help."

Rhone, Shepherd
Age: 75
10th and Kentucky
Pine Bluff, Arkansas
Interviewer: Bernice Bowden
[M:10: pt. 6: 33–34]

"Yes, ma'am, I was bred and born in 'sixty-three in Phillips County, Arkansas, close to Helena, on old Judge Jones' plantation. Judge Jones, he was a lawyer. Remember him? I ought to, he whipped me enough. His wife's name was Caroline Jones. She used to smack my jaws and pull my ears but she was a pretty good woman. The old judge was a raw one though. You had to step around or he'd step around for you.

"I stayed right there till I was grown. My mother was named Katie Rhone and my father was named Daniel Rhone. My mother was born in Richmond, Virginia and my father in Petersburg, Virginia.

"Judge Jones brought em here to Arkansas. My father was a bodyguard for old Judge Jones' son Tom in the War. My father stuck with him till peace declared—had to do it.

"They was thirteen of us chillun and they is all gone but me, and I'll soon be gone.

"I know when the Yankees come I run from em. When peace declared, the Yankees come all through our house and took everything they could get hold of to eat.

"The only reason the Yankees whipped the South was they starved em.

"I know one time when peace declared I caught afire and I run and jumped in a tub of water and I had sense enough not to tell my mother. A girl I was raised up with went and told her though.

"After freedom I worked for old Judge Jones on the half system. He give me everthing that was due me. When he was eighty years old, he called all his old tenants up and give em a mule and twenty-five dollars. He was pretty good to em after all.

"I went to free school in the summertime after the crops was laid by. I can read and write pretty good.

"I came here to Jefferson County in 'eighty-six and I put in thirty-six years at the Cotton Belt Shops. When that strike come on they told us colored folks to quit and I never went back. I worked for em when she was a narrow gauge.

"I worked in the North three years. I nightwatched all over St. Louis and Madison, Illinois. I liked it fine up there—white folks is more familiar up there and seems like you can get favors. If I don't get somethin' here, I'm goin' back up there.

"When I got big enough I voted the Republican ticket and after they got this primary. I think the colored people ought to vote now cause they make em pay taxes.

"I'll tell you right now, the younger generation is goin' to the dogs. We'll never make a nation of em as long as they go out to these places at night. They ought to be a law passed. When nine o'clock comes they ought to be home in bed, but they is just gettin' started then.

"I belong to the Catholic Church. I think it's a pretty good church. We have a white priest and I'll tell you one thing—you can't get a divorce and marry again and stay in the Catholic Church."

Stiggers, Liza
Age: 70+
Forrest City, Arkansas
Interviewer: Irene Robertson
[M:10: pt. 6: 238]

"I was born in Poplar Grove, Arkansas on Col. Bibbs' place. Mama was sold twice. Once she was sold in Georgia, once in Alabama, and brought to Tennessee, later to Arkansas. Master Ben Hode brought her to Arkansas. She had ten children and I'm the only one living. Mama was a dancing woman. She could dance any figure. They danced in the cabins and out in the yards.

"The Yankees come one day to our house and I crawled under the house. I was scared to death. They called me out. I was scared not to obey and scared to come on out. I come out. They didn't hurt me. Mr. Ben Hode hid a small trunk of money away. He got it after the War. The slaves never did know where it was hid. They said the hair was on the trunk he hid his money in. It was made out of green hide for that purpose.

"Mama had a slave husband. He was a field hand and all kind of a hand when he was needed. Mama done the sewing for white and black on the place. She was a maid. She could cook some in case they needed her. She died first. Papa's foot got hurt some way and it et off. He was so old they couldn't cure it. He was named Alfred Hode. Mama was Viney Hode. She said they had good white folks. They lived on Ben Hode's place two or three years after freedom.

"I farmed, cooked, and ironed all my life. I don't know how to do nothing else.

"I live with my daughter. I got a son."

Turner, Henry
Age: 93
Turner, Arkansas
Interviewer: Watt McKinney
[S2:1 (AR): 135–41, 132–34]
[See also M:10: 363–68]

> I'm gettin' old and feeble now and cannot walk no more
> And I've laid the rusty-bladed hoe to rest.
>
> Ole marster and old missus are sleeping side by side
> And their spirits are a-roamin' with the blest.

The above lines, had they been composed today, might well have been written with reference to "Uncle" Henry Turner, ninety-three years of age, of Turner, Arkansas, in Phillips County, and among the very few remaining ex-slaves, especially of those who were old enough at the time of their emancipation to have now a clear recollection of conditions, customs, events, and life during those days long past immediately preceding and following the Civil War. "Uncle" Henry's eyes have now grown dim and he totters slightly as, supported by his cane, he slowly shuffles along the path over a short distance between the clean, white-washed cabin where he lives with a daughter and the small, combination store and post office, on the porch of which he is accustomed to sit in an old cane-bottomed chair for a few hours each day and the white folks in passing stop to speak a few words and to buy for him candy, cold drinks, and tobacco.

Though "Uncle" Henry is approaching the century mark in age, his mind is remarkably clear and his recollection is unusually keen. He was born a slave in northern Mississippi near the small towns of Red Banks and Byhalia, was the property of his owner, Edmond Turner, and was brought to Phillips

County by "his white folks" some months before the war. Turner, who owned some fifty other slaves besides Henry, settled with his family on a large acreage of land that he had purchased about fifteen miles west of Helena near Trenton. Both Turner and his wife died soon after taking up residence in Arkansas leaving their estate to their two sons, Bart and Nat, who were by that time grown young men, and being very capable and industrious soon developed their property into one of the most valuable plantations in the County.

As "Uncle" Henry recalls, the Turner place was, it might be said, a world within itself, in the confines of which was produced practically everything essential in the life of its inhabitants and the proper and successful conduct of its operations. Large herds of cattle, hogs, sheep, and goats provided a bountiful supply of both fresh and salt meats and fats. Cotton and wool was carded, spun and woven into cloth for clothes, fast colored dyes were made by boiling different kinds of roots and barks, various colored berries were also used for this purpose. Medicine was prepared from roots, herbs, flowers, and leaves. Stake and rider fences enclosed the fields and pastures and while most of the houses, barns and cribs were constructed of logs, some lumber was manufactured in crude sawmills in which was used what was known as a "slash saw". This was something like the crosscut saws of today and was operated by a crank that gave the saw an alternating up and down motion. Wheat was ground into flour and corn into meal in mills with stone burrs similar to those used in the rural districts today, and power for this operation was obtained through the use of a treadmill that was given its motion by horses or mules walking on an inclined, endless belt constructed of heavy wooden slats. Candles for lighting purposes were made of animal fats combined with beeswax. Plows, harrows and cultivating implements were made on the plantation by those Negroes who had been trained in carpentry and blacksmithing. Plows for breaking the land were sometimes constructed with a metal point and a wooden moldboard and harrows were made of heavy timbers with large, sharpened wooden pegs for teeth. Hats of straw and corn shucks were woven by hand.

Small, crude cotton gins were powered by horses or mules hitched to a beam fastened to an upright shaft around which they traveled in a circle and to which was attached large cogwheels that multiplied the animal's power enormously and transmitted it by means of a belt to the separating machinery where the lint was torn from the seed. No metal ties were available during this period and ropes of cotton were used to bind the bales of lint. About three bales was the daily capacity of a horse-powered plantation gin.

It was often difficult to obtain the services of a competent doctor and except in cases of serious illness home remedies were administered.

Churches were established in different communities throughout the County and the Negro slaves were allowed the privilege of attending the services, certain pews being set apart from them, and the same minister that attended the spiritual needs of the master and his family rendered like assistance to his slaves.

No undertaking establishments existed here at this time and on the death of a person burial was made in crude caskets built of rough cypress planks unless the deceased was a member of a family financially able to afford the expensive metal caskets that were available no nearer than Memphis. "Uncle" Henry Turner recalls the death of Dan Wilborn's little six-year-old boy, Abby, who was accidentally killed when crushed by a heavy gate on which he was playing, and his burial in what "Uncle" Henry described as a casket made of the same material as an old-fashioned door knob; and while I have no other authority than this on the subject, it is possible that in that day caskets were made of some vitrified substance, perhaps clay, and resembling the present day tile.

The planters and slaveowners of this period obtained the greater share of their recreation in attendance at political rallies, horse races, and cock fights. Jobe Dean and Gus Abington who came to Trenton from their home near La Grange, Tennessee were responsible for the popularity of these sports in Phillips County and it was they who promoted the most spectacular of these sporting events and in which large sums of money were wagered on the horses and the game cocks. It is said that Marve Carruth once owned an Irish Grey Cock on which he bet and won more than five thousand dollars one afternoon at Trenton.

No Negro slave was allowed to go beyond the confines of his owner's plantation without written permission. This was described by "Uncle" Henry Turner as a "pass"; and on this "pass" was written the name of the Negro, the place he was permitted to visit, and the time beyond which he must not fail to return. It seems that numbers of men were employed by the County or perhaps by the slaveowners themselves whose duty it was to patrol the community and be on constant watch for such Negroes who attempted to escape their bondage or overstayed the time limit noted on their "pass". Such men were known then as "Paddy Rolls" by the Negroes and in the Southern states are still referred to by this name. Punishment was often administered by them, and the very mention of the name was sufficient to cause stark terror and fear in the hearts of fugitive slaves.

At some time during that period when slavery was a legal institution in this country, the following verse was composed by some unknown author and set to a tune that some of the older darkies can yet sing:

Run nigger run, the Paddy Roll will get you
Run nigger run, it's almost day.
That nigger run, that nigger flew
That nigger tore his shirt [in two].
Run nigger run, the Paddy Roll will get you
Run nigger run, it's almost day.

Both Bart Turner and his brother Nat enlisted in the services of the Confederacy. Nat Turner was a member of the First Arkansas Volunteers, a regiment organized at Helena and of which Patrick R. Cleburne was colonel. Dick Berry and Milt Wiseman, friends and neighbors of the Turners, also volunteered and enlisted in Cleburne's command. These three stalwart young men from Phillips County followed Cleburne and fought under his battle flag on those bloody fields at Shiloh, Murfreesboro, Ringgold gap, and Atlanta; and they were with him that day in November in front of the old gin house at Franklin as the regiment formed for another and what was to be their last charge. The dead lay in heaps in front of them and almost filled the ditch around the breastworks, but the command though terribly cut to pieces was forming as cooly as if on dress parade. Above them floated a peculiar flag, a field of deep blue on which was a crescent moon and stars. It was Cleburne's battle flag and well the enemy knew it; they had seen it so often before. "I tip my hat to that flag" said the Federal General Sherman years after the war. "Whenever my men saw it they knew it meant fight." As the regiment rushed on the Federal breastworks a gray clad figure on a chestnut horse rode across the front of the moving column and toward the enemy's guns. The horse went down within fifty yards of the breastworks. The rider arose, waved his sword, and led his men on foot to the very ramparts. Then he staggered and fell, pierced with a dozen balls. It was Cleburne, the peerless field-marshal of Confederate brigade commanders. The Southern cause suffered a crushing defeat at Franklin and the casualty list recorded the names of Nat Turner, Dick Berry, and Milt Wiseman, who like their beloved commander had given their life for their country. There is an inscription on the stone base of the magnificent bronze statue of General N . B. Forrest astride his war horse in Forrest Park in Memphis that could well be placed above the graves of Cleburne, Turner, Berry, and Wiseman, those brave, heroic soldiers from Phillips County. The inscription in verse is as follows:

Those hoof beats die not on fame's crimson sod
But will live on in song and in story.
He fought like a Trojan and struck like a god
His dust is our ashes of glory.

Bart Turner served for a time with the troops in Arkansas but since he had married a few weeks prior to the beginning of the Civil War afterwards came back to their plantation home and moved his family, Negroes, livestock, and all belongings to Texas in order to escape the plundering raids of the invading Federal army. Bart Turner located near Daingerfield in Texas where he was engaged for two years in producing supplies for the Confederate troops. It was on this journey to Texas that Turner either bought or traded for a Negro named Bryant Singfield, a mulatto one-quarter white. Singfield was much more intelligent than the Negroes of unmixed blood and Bart Turner appointed him foreman of the field hands. However, after the return to Arkansas and the slaves had obtained their freedom, Bryant Singfield showed his true nature. He became surly, impudent and disobedient and Bart Turner ordered him from his place.

After leaving the Turner plantation Singfield became active as a leader and agitator among the former slaves who remained with their masters and who had entered into contracts to work their crops on a share basis, and in these activities he was in a large measure encouraged and assisted by the commanders of the Federal soldiers who were garrisoned at Helena for many months after the close of the war. Negroes as individuals and as a race are easily led and persuaded especially by one of their own color who possesses a superior intelligence and this was indeed true in this case and Singfield was successful in inducing large numbers of ex-slaves to desert their former owners and join a colony that he had established midways between Trenton and Helena. Even those Negroes who did not join Singfield's group became restless and dissatisfied with their lot and a general discontent prevailed among them due to his disturbing influence and the landowners were faced with a serious labor shortage and a very serious Negro question that threatened the peace and welfare of the county.

One still, dark, moonless night in late summer a number of grim, determined men said to have been led by Bart Turner, Marve Carruth, and Carter Reed, all of whom were mounted and heavily armed, called at the homes of Bryant Singfield and of several other Negroes who had been engaged in similar activities. What befell these Negroes that night was never definitely known; however, it was the general opinion that all were killed as none of them were ever seen in Phillips County from that night. There is a broad, sweeping, lonesome bend in Big Creek only a few miles below Trenton and known as "The Basin" where the giant alligator, gar flounce lazily and the scaly, venomous moccasin lay unmolested on partially submerged logs and tops of fallen trees and where along the shores ancient cypresses standing as silent sentinels rear gaunt and ghost-like against the sky that Negroes contend is haunted and where it is said that in the dark stillness of a moonless summer night the ghost of Bryant Singfield can be seen to emerge from the murky depths and a terrifying voice can be heard pleading vainly for mercy.

During that unsettled period following the close of the Civil War Bart Turner was prominent in all movements looking toward the restoration of peace, law and order, and was one of the leaders of that organization known locally as the "Red Shirts" who were so largely instrumental in lifting the yoke of the carpetbaggers and Negroes from the state and county governments and restoring control to the white Democrats.

Bart Turner served several terms as sheriff of Phillips County and was the father of the late Renfro Turner of Earle, Arkasas, prominent planter and several times county judge of Crittenden County.

Wilborn, Dock
Age: 95
Marvell, Arkansas
Interviewer: Watt McKinney
[M:11: pt. 7: 142–46]

Dock Wilborn was born a slave near Huntsville, Alabama on January 7, 1843, the property of Dan Wilborn who with his three brothers, Elias, Sam, and Ike, moved to Arkansas and settled near Marvell in Phillips County about 1855.

According to "Uncle Dock" the four Wilborn brothers each owning more than one hundred slaves acquired a large body of wild , undeveloped land, divided this acreage between them and immediately began to erect numerous log structures for housing themselves, their Negroes, and their stock, and to deaden the timber and clear the land preparatory to placing their crops the following season. The Wilborns arrived in Arkansas in the early fall of the year and for several months they camped, living in tents until such time that they were able to complete the erection of their residences. Good, substantial, well constructed and warm cabins were built in which to house the slaves, much better buildings "Uncle Dock" says than those in which the average Negro sharecropper lives today on Southern cotton plantations. And these Negores were given an abundance of the same wholesome food as that prepared for the master's family in the huge kettles and ovens of the one common kitchen presided over by a well-trained and competent cook and supervised by the wife of the master.

During the period of slavery the more apt and intelligent among those of the younger Negroes were singled out and given special training for those places in which their talents indicated they would be most useful in the life of the plantation. Girls were trained in housework, cooking, and in the care of children while boys were taught blacksmithing, carpentrying, and some were trained for personal servants around the home. Some were even taught to read and write when it was thought that their later positions would require this learning.

According to "Uncle Dock" Wilborn, slaves were allowed to enjoy many pleasures and liberties thought by many in this day, especially by the descendants of these slaves, not to have been accorded them, were entirely free of any responsibility aside from the performance of their alloted labors and speaking from his own experience received kind and just treatment at the hands of their masters.

The will of the master was the law of the plantation and prompt punishment was administered for any violation of established rules and though a master was kind, he was of necessity invariably firm in the administration of his government and in the execution of his laws. Respect and obedience was steadfastly required and sternly demanded, while indolence and disrespect was neither tolerated or permitted.

In refutation to often repeated expressions and beliefs that slaves were cruelly treated, provided with insufficient food and apparel and subjected to inhuman punishment, it is pointed out by ex-slaves themselves that they were at that time very valuable property, worth on the market no less than from one thousand to fifteen hundred dollars each for a healthy, grown Negro and that it is unreasonable to suppose that these slaveowners did not properly safeguard their investments with the befitting care and attention such valuable property demanded or that these masters would by rule or action bring about any condition adversely effecting the health, efficiency or value of their slaves.

The spiritual and religious needs of the slaves received the attention of the same minister who attended the like needs of the master and his family, and services were often conducted on Sunday afternoons exclusively for them at which times the minister exhorted his congregation to live lives of righteousness and to be at all times obedient, respectful and dutiful servants in the cause of both their earthly and heavenly masters.

In the days of slavery, on occasion of the marriage of a couple in which the participants were members of slave-owning families, it was the custom for the father of each to provide the young couple with several Negroes, the number of course depending on the relative wealth or affluence of their respective families. It seems, however, that no less than six or eight grown slaves were given in most instances as well as a like number of children from two to four years of age. This provision on the part of the parents of the newly-wedded pair was for the purpose as "Uncle Dock" expressed it to give them a "start" of Negroes. The children were not considered of much value at such an age and the young master and his wife found themselves possessed with the responsibility attached to their proper care and rearing until such time as they reached the age at which they could perform some useful labor. These responsibilities were bravely accepted and such children received the best of care and attention, being it is said often kept in a room provided for them in the master's own house where their needs could be administered to under the watchful eye and supervision of their owners. The food given these young children according to informants consisted mainly of a sort of gruel composed of whole milk and bread made of whole wheat flour which was set before them in a kind of trough and from which they ate with great relish and grew rapidly.

Slaveowners, as a rule, arranged for their Negroes to have all needed pleasure and enjoyment, and in the late summer after cultivation of the crops was complete it was the custom for a number of them to give a large barbecue for their combined groups of slaves, at which huge quantities of beef and pork were served and the care-free hours given over to dancing and general merry-making. "Uncle Dock" recalls that his master, Dan Wilborn, who was a good-natured man of large stature, derived much pleasure in playing his "fiddle" and that often in the early summer evenings he would walk down to the slave quarters with his violin remarking that he would supply the music and that he wished to see his "niggers" dance, and dance they would for hours and as much to the master's own delight and amusement as to theirs.

Dock Wilborn's "pappy" Sam was in some respects disobedient, prompted mainly so it seems by his complete dislike for any form of labor and which Dan Wilborn due to their mutual affection appeared to tolerate for long periods or until such time that his patience was exhausted when he would then apply his lash to Sam a few times and often after these periodical punishments Sam would escape to the dense forests that surrounded the plantation where he would remain for days or until Wilborn would enlist the aid of Nat Turner and his hounds and chase the Negro to bay and return him to his home.

"Uncle Dock" Wilborn and his wife "Aunt Becky" are among the oldest citizens of Phillips County and have been married for sixty-seven years. Dan Wilborn performed their marriage ceremony. The only formality required in uniting them as man and wife was that each jump over a broom that had been placed on the floor between them. This old couple are the parents of four children, the eldest of whom is now sixty-three. They live alone in a small white-washed cabin only a mile or so from Marvell being supported only by a small pension they received each month from the Social Security Board. They have a garden and a few chickens and a hog or two and are happy and content as they dip their snuff and recall those days long past during which they both contend that life was at its best. "Aunt Becky" is religious and a staunch believer, a long-time member of Mount Moriah Baptist Church while "Uncle Dock" who has never been affiliated with any religious organization is yet as he terms himself "a sinner man" and laughingly remarks that he is going to ride into heaven on "Aunt Becky's" ticket to which comment she promptly replies that her ticket is good for only one passage and that if he hopes to get there he must arrange for one of his own.

Young, Louis
Age: 88
5523 Bonnell Street
Fort Worth, Texas
12 September 1937
Interviewer: Sheldon F. Gauthier
[M:5: pt. 4 (TX): 232–234]
[See also S2:10 (TX, pt. 9): 4307–13]

Louis Young, 88, was born a slave of Hampton Atkinson, on a small farm in Phillips County, Arkansas. When Louis was twelve, his master sold him and his mother to Tom Young, who took them to Robinson Co., Texas. Louis now lives at 5523 Bonnell St., Fort Worth, Tex.

"Mammy done put my age in de Bible and I'm eighty-eight years old now. I'm born in 1849. But I can git around. Course, I can't work now, but, shucks, I done my share of work already. I works from time I'm eight years old till I'm eighty past, and I'd be workin' yet if de rheumatis' misery didn't git me in de arms and legs. It make me stiff, so I can't walk good.

"Yes, suh, I starts to work when eight on dat plantation where I'm born. Dat in Arkansaw, and Massa Hampton own me and my mammy and eight other niggers. My pappy am somewhere, but I don't know where or nothin' 'bout him.

"Us all work from light to dark and Sunday, too. I don't know what Sunday am till us come to Texas, and dances and good things, I don't know nothin' 'bout dem till us come to Texas. Massa Hampton, he am long on de work and short on de rations, what he measure out for de week. Seven pounds meat and one peck meal and one quart 'lasses, and no more for de week. If us run out, us am out, dat's all.

"One day us gets sold to Massa Tom Young. He feels mammy's muscles and looks on her for marks of de whip. Massa Young say he give $700, but Massa Hampton say no, he want $1,000. He say, 'yous takin' dem to Texas, where dey sho' to be slaves, 'spite de war.'

"Finally Massa Young gives $900 for us and off us go to Texas. Dat in 1861, de fall de year, and it am three teams mules and three teams oxen hitch to wagons full of farm things and rations and sich. Us on de road more'n three weeks, maybe a month, befo' us git to Robinson County.

"When us git dere, de work am buildin' de cabins and house and den clear de land, and by Spring, us ready to put in de crops, de corn and cotton. Massa Young am good and give us plenty to eat. He has 'bout twenty slaves and us works reason'ble, and has good time 'pared with befo'. On Saturday night it am dancin' and music and singin', and us never heared of sich befo'.

"One day Massa Young call us to de house and tell us he don't own us no more, and say us can stay and he pay us some money, if us wants. He ask mammy to stay and cook and she does, but I'm strongheaded and runs off to Calvert and goes to work for Massa Brown, and dere I stays till I'm growed. He paid me $10.00 de month and den $15.00.

"When I's twenty-five I marries Addie Easter and us have no chillen and she dies ten years after. Den I drifts 'round, workin' here and yonder and in 1890 I marries dat woman settin' right dere. Den I rents de farm and if de crops am good, de prices am bad, and if de prices am good, de crops am bad. So it go and us lives, and not too good, at dat. I quits in 1925 and comes to Fort Worth and piddles at odd jobs till my rheumatis' git so bad five years ago.

"I done forgit to tell you 'bout de Klux. Dem debbils causes lots of trouble. Dey done de dirty work at night, come and took folks out and whip dem.

"Some cullud folks am whip so hard dey in bed sev'ral weeks and I knowed some hanged by dey thumbs. Maybe some dem cullud folks gits out dere places, but mostest dem I knows gits whip for nothin'. It jus' de orneriness dem Klux. It so bad de cullud folks 'fraid to sleep in dey house or have parties or nothin' after dark. Dey starts for de woods or ditches and sleeps dere. It git so dey can't work for not sleepin', from fear of dem Klux. Den de white folks takes a hand and sojers am brung and dey puts de stop to dem debbils.

"'Bout de livin' now, us jus' can't make it. Us lives on what de pension am and dat $30.00 de month, and it might close us has to live to git by on sich. I thinks of Massa Young, and us live better den dan now.

"I never votes, 'cause I can't read and dat make troublement for me to vote. How I gwine make de ticket for dis and dat? For dem what can read, dey can vote.

Pope County

Little, William
Age: 83
Atkins, Arkansas
Interviewer: Thomas Elmore Lucy
[M:9: pt. 4: 262–63]

"I was born on the plantation of Dr. Andrew Scott, but my old ma'ster was Col. Ben T. Embry. The 14th of March, in the year 1855, was my birthday. Yes suh, I was born right here at old Galla Rock! My old Ma'ster Embry had a good many slaves. He went to Texas and stayed about three years. Took a lot of us along, and de first work I ever done after I was set free was pickin' cotton at $2 a hundred pounds. Dere was seventy-five or a hundred of us freed at once. Yes suh! Den we drove five hundred miles back here from Texas, and drove five hundred head of stock. We was refigees—dat's de reason we had to go to Texas.

"Father and mother both passed away a good many years ago. Oh, yes, dey was mighty well treated while dey was in slavery; never was a kinder mas'r anywhere dan my old mas'r. And he was wealthy, too—had lots of land, and a store, and plenty of other property. Many of the slaves stayed on as servants long after the War, and lived right around here at old Galla Rock.

"No suh, I never belonged to no chu'ch; dey thought I done too much of the devil's work—playin' the fiddle. Used to play the fiddle for dances all around the neighborhood. One white man gave me $10 once for playin' at a dance. Played lots of the old-time pieces like 'Turkey in the Straw', 'Dixie', and so on.

"We owns our home here, and I has another one. Been married twice and raised eighteen chillun. Yes suh, we've lived here eighteen years, and had fine health till last few years, but my health is sorter po'ly now. Got a swellin' in my laigs.

"(Chuckling) I sure remembers lots of happy occasions down here in days before the War. One day the steamboat come up to the landin'. It was named the Maumelle—yes suh, Maumelle, and lots of horses and cattle was unloaded from the steamer. Sure was busy days then. And our old mas'r was mighty kind to us."

NOTE: "Uncle Bill" did not know how he came about the name "Little."

Perhaps it was a nickname bestowed upon him to distinguish him from some other William of larger stature. However, he stands fully six feet in height, and has a strong, vigorous voice. He is the sole surviving ex-slave of the Galla Rock community.

Russell, Henry
Age: 72
Russellville, Arkansas
Interviewer: Thomas Elmore Lucy
[M:10: pt. 6: 109–10]

"My father's name was Ed Russell, and he was owned by Dr. Tom Russell, de first pioneer settler of Russellville—de man de town got its name from. My name is Henry, and some folks call me 'Bud.' I was born at Old Dwight de 28th of October, 1866. Yes suh, dat date is correct.

"I was too young to remember much about happenin's soon after de War, but I kin riccollect my father belongin' to de militia for awhile during de Reconstruction days. Both Negroes and whites were members of de militia.

"My folks come here from Alabama, but I don't know much about them except dat my grandmother, Charlotte Edwards, give me an old wash pot dat has been in de family over one hundred years. Yes suh, it's out here in de ya'd now. Also, I owns an old ax handle dat I keep down at de store jist for a relic of old days. It's about a hundred years old, too.

"My wife was Sallie Johnson of Little Rock, and she was a sister of Mrs. Charley Mays, de barber you used to know, who was here sich a long time.

"For a long time I worked at different kinds of odd jobs, sometimes in de coal mines and sometimes on de farms, but for several years I've run a little store for de colored folks here in Russellville. Ain't able to do very much now.

"I remember very well de first train dat was ever run into Russellville. Must have been 68 or 69 years ago. A big crowd of people was here from all over de country. Of course dere was only a few families living in de town, and only one or two families of colored folks. People come in from everywhere, and it was a great sign. Little old train was no bigger dan de Dardanelle & Russellville train. (You remember de little old train dey used to call de 'Dinkey' don't you?) Well, it wasn't no bigger dan de Dinkey, and it didn't run into de depot at all, stopped down where de dump is now. Sure was a sight. Lot of de folks was afraid and wouldn't go near it, started to run when two men got off. I saw only two men working in front of it, but I remember it very plain. Dey was working with wheelbarrows and shovels to clear up de track ahead.

"Another thing I remember as a boy was de 'sassination of President Gyarfield. I can't read or write but very little, but I remember about dat. It was a dull, foggy mornin', and I was crossin' de bayou with Big Bob Smith. (You remember 'Big Bob' dat used to have the merry-go-'round and made all de county fairs.) Well, he told me all about de killing of de President. It was about 1881 wasn't it?

"I think times was better in de old days because people was better. Had a heap more honor in de old days dan dey have now. Not many young folks today have much character.

"All right. Come back again. Whenever I kin help you out any way, I'll be glad to."

NOTE: Henry Russell is quite proud of the fact that his ancestors were the first families of Russellville. He is a polite mulatto, uneducated, and just enough brogue to lend the Southern flavor to his speech, but is a fluent conversationalist.

Scott, Sam
Age: 79
Russellville, Arkansas
Interviewer: Thomas Elmore Lucy
[M:10: pt. 6: 131–33]

"Hello, dar, Mistah L—! Don' you dare pass by widout speakin' to dis old niggah friend of yo' chil'hood! No suh! Yuh can't git too big to speak to me!

"Reckon you've seen about all dar is to see in de worl' since I seen you, ain't you? Well, mos' all de old-time niggahs and whites is both gone now. I was born on de twentieth of July, 1879. Count up—dat makes me 79 (born 1859), don't it? My daddy's name was Sam, same as mine, and mammy's was Mollie. Dey was slaves on de plantation of Capt. Scott—yes suh, Capt. John R. Homer Scott—at Dover. My name is Sam, same as my father's, of course. Everybody in de old days knowed Sam Scott. My father died in slavery times, but mother lived several years after.

"No, I never did dance, but I sure could play baseball and make de home runs! My main hobby, as you calls it, was de show business. You remember de niggah mistrels we used to put on. I was always stage manager and could sing baritone a little. Ed Williamson and Tom Nick was de principal dancers, and Tom would make up all de plays. What? Stole a uniform coat of yours? Why, I never knowed Tom to do anything like that! Anyway, he was a good-hearted niggah—but you dunno what he might do. Yes, I still takes out a show occasionally to de towns around Pope and Yell and Johnson counties, and folks treat us mighty fine. Big crowds—played to $47.00 clear money at Clarksville. Usually take about eight and ten in our comp'ny, boys and gals—and we give em a real hot minstrel show.

"De old show days? Never kin forgit em! I was stage manager of de old opery house here, you remember, for ten years, and worked around de old printin' office downstairs for seven years. No, I don't mean stage manager—I mean property man—yes, had to rustle de props. And did we have road shows dem days! Richards & Pringle's Georgia minstrels, de Nashville students, Lyman Twins, Barlow Brothers Minstrels, and—oh, ever so many more—yes, Daisy, de Missouri Girl, wid Fred Raymond. Never kin forgit old black Billy Kersands, wid his mouf a mile wide!

"De songs we used to sing in old days when I was a kid after de War wasn't no purtier dan what we used to sing wid our own minstrel show when we was at our best twenty-five and thirty years ago; songs like 'Jungletown,' 'Red Wing,' and 'Mammy's Li'l Alabama Coon.' Our circuit used to be around Holla Bend, Dover, Danville, Ola, Charleston, Nigger Ridge, out from Pottsville, and we usually starred off at the old opery house in Russellville, of course.

"I been married, but ain't married now. We couldn't git along somehow. Yes suh, I been right here workin' stiddy for a long time. Been janitor at two or three places same time; was janitor of de senior high school here for twenty-two years, and at de Bank of Russellville twenty-nine years.

"Folks always been mighty nice to me—and no slave ever had a finer master dan old Captain Scott.

"In de old show days de manager of de opery always said, 'Let de niggers see de show,' and sometimes de house was half full of colored folks—white folks on one side de house and niggahs on de other—and dere never was any disturbance of any kind. Ain't no sich good times now as we had in the old road show days. No suh!"

NOTE: Sam Scott, who has been personally known to the interviewer for many years, is above the average of the race for integrity and truthfulness. His statement that he was born a few years after slavery and that his father died during slavery was not questioned the matter being a delicate personal affair and of no special moment.

Starr, Milton
Age: 80
Gibson Station, Oklahoma

Interviewer: Ethel Wolfe Garrison
[OK: 408–10]

I was born a slave, but was not treated like other slaves and my folks never told me anything about slavery. So there is very little I can tell of those days. My birthplace was in the old Flint District of the Cherokee Nation; the nearest town was Russellville, Arkansas, and the farm was owned by Jerry Starr, half-breed Cherokee, who was my master and father. They told me I was born February 24, 1858, right in my master's house, and when I was a baby had the care of the average white child.

My mother was Jane Coursey of Tennessee, a slave girl picked up by the Starrs when they left that country with the rest of the Cherokee Indians. My mother wasn't bought, but was stole by the Indians, and when she was freed she went back to Tennessee; I stayed with Starr family and was raised by Millie and Jerry Starr.

Jerry Starr said when the Cherokees come to this country they crossed Barron Fork Creek east of Proctor (Okla.); they were riding in a government wagon and they crossed Barron Fork on ice so thick the mules and wagons didn't break through.

My master had a brother named Tom Starr, and he came to this country with some earlier Cherokees than did Jerry. Tom settled at Walking-Stick Spring east of Tahlequah, where he had 20 slaves working on a 40-acre patch of rocks and sand, or at least that's the way Jerry Starr always talked about Tom's place. He said all the slaves did was fish and hunt.

The Starrs got mixed up with some pretty bad folks, too, after the war. I heard about it when I was a young man; about how Tom Starr had a son named Sam who married a white woman the folks called Belle Starr. She was the baddest woman in the whole country before she got killed down on her farm near Briartown, about 1888, I think it was. Shot from her horse, but they never found out who killed her.

Old Tom was a kind of outlaw too, but not like his son's wife. He never went around robbing trains and banks, his troubles was all account of Indian doings long before the war, so they say. Seem like they said he killed a man name Buffington and run away to Texas for a long time, but he come back when the Cherokee Government send word for Tom to come back home and behave himself.

Jerry Starr was close kin to another mixed-blood Cherokee who was a bad man that most of the folks nowadays remember pretty well. He was Henry Starr and it ain't been long ago that he robbed a bank over in Arkansas and got hisself shot in the back before he could get away with the money. (Henry was killed at Harrison, Arkansas, in 1921, during an attempted bank robbery, but the old Negro couldn't remember the date.) The Starr boys always seem to be in pecks of trouble most of the time.

Jerry Starr was known best around the place of Tahlequah where we all moved to after the war. I saw a hanging there; Lizzie Redbird was hanged for selling dope of some kind. The hanging tree was an old oak that stood near the little creek that runs on the edge of town. Don't know if it's still there or not.

There's one Indian law I remember Jerry Starr told me about, and it was the death law. If an Indian found any silver, or gold, or any kind of mineral that was rich, he was to hide it and never tell anybody about it or where it was. If anybody went against that law he was bound to die.

My mistress and stepmother had three girls; Mamie, Ella and Tiger. They had some slave girls and one of them, Jessie, I married long after the war, in 1883. We went to Tyler, Texas, for awhile, but she died and years later I married Jenona Alberty. We had two girls, Irena and Esther, but they're both dead.

But, like I said, my folks never told me about slavery; they never whipped me, treated me like I was one of the family, because I was, so I can't tell anything about them days.

Prairie County

Braddox, George
Age: 81
Hazen, Arkansas
Interviewer: Irene Robertson
[M:8: pt. 1: 223–29]

George Braddox was born a slave but his mother being freed when he was eight years old they went to themselves—George had one sister and one brother. He doesn't know anything about them but thinks they are dead as he is the youngest of the three. His father's name was Peter Calloway. He went with Gus Taylor and never came back to his family. George said he had been to Chicago several times to see his father where he was living. But his mother let her children go by that name. She gave them a name Braddox when they were freed. Calloways lived on a joining plantation to John and Dave Gemes. John Gemes was the old master and Dave the young. George said they were mean to him. He can remember that Gus Taylor was overseer for the Gemes till he went to war. The Gemes lived in a brick house and the slaves lived in log houses. They had a big farm and raised cotton and corn. The cotton was six feet tall and had big leaves. They had to pull the leaves to let the bowls get the sun to open. They topped the cotton too. They made lots of cotton and corn to an acre. Dave Gemes had several children when George moved away, their names were Ruben, John, Margaret, Susie and Betty. They went to school at Marshall, Texas.

John Gemes had fine carriages, horses and mules. He had one old slave who just milked and churned. She didn't do anything else. When young calves had to be attended to somebody else had to help her and one man did all the feeding. They had lots of peafowles, ducks, geese and chickens. They had mixed stock of chickens and guineas—always had a drove of turkeys. Sometimes the turkeys would go off with wild turkeys. There were wild hogs and turkeys in the woods. George never learned to read or write. He remembers they built a school for white children on the Calloway place joining the Gemes place but he thought it was tuition school. George said he thought the Gemes and all his "kin" folks came from Alabama to Texas, but he is not sure but he does know this. Dr. Hazen came from Tennessee to Texas and back to Hazen, Arkansas and settled. His cousin Jane Hodge (colored) was working out near here and he came here to deer hunt and just stayed with them. He said deer was plentiful here. It was not cleared and so close to White, Cache, St. Francis and Mississippi rivers.

George said his mother cooked for the Gemes the first he could remember of her. That was all she had time to do. It was five miles to Marshall. They lived in Harrison County and they could buy somethings to eat there if they didn't raise enough. They bought cheese by the cases in round boxes and flour in barrels and sugar in barrels. They had fine clothes for Sunday. After his mother left the Gemes they worked in the field or did anything she could for a living.

George married after he came to Arkansas and bought a farm 140 acres of land 4 miles north of Hazen and a white man,—closed a mortgage out on him and took it. He paid $300.00 for a house in town in which he now lives. His son was killed in the World War and he gets his son's insurance every month.

George said when he came to Arkansas it was easy to live if you liked to hunt. Ship the skins and get some money when you couldn't be farming. Could get all the wood you would cut and then clear out land and farm. He hunted 7 or 8 years with Colonel A. F. Yopp and fed Colonel's dogs. He hunted with Mr. Yopp but he didn't think Colonel was a very good man. I gathered from George that he didn't approve of wickedness.

It is bad luck to dig a grave the day before a person is buried, or any time before the day of the burying. Uncle George has dug or helped to dig lots of graves. It is bad luck to the family of the dead person. The grave ought not to be "left open" it is called. He has always heard this and believes it, yet he can't remember when he first heard it.

He thinks there are spirits that direct your life and if you do wrong the evil fates let you be punished. He believes in good and evil spirits. Spirits right here among us. He says there is "bound to be spirits" or "something like 'em."

Most of the old songs were religious. I don't remember none much. When the war broke out my papa jess left and went on off with some people and joined the Yankee army. I went to see him since I been at Hazen. He lived in Chicago. Yes mam he's been dead a long time ago. Gus Taylor and Peter Calloway (white) took my papa with them for their helper. He left them and went with the Yankee army soon as he heard what they was fighting about. Peter Calloway lived on a big track of land joining Dave Genes land. It show was a big farm. Peter Calloway owned my papa and Dave Genes my mama. Gus Taylor was Dave Genes overseer. Peter Calloway never come back from the war. My folks come from Alabama with Dave Genes and his son John Genes. I was born in Harrison county, Texas. Gus Taylor was great big man. He was mean to us all. The Yankees camped there. It was near Marshall. I had some good friends among the Yankees. They kept me posted all time the war went on. Nobody never learnt me nothing. I can cipher a little and count money. I took that up. I learned after I was grown a few things. Just learned it myself. I never went to school a day in my life. The Genes had a brick, big red brick house. They sent their children to schools. They had stock, peafowls, cows, guineas, geese, ducks and chickens, hogs and everything. Old woman on the place just milked and churned. That is all she done.

I never heard of no plantations being divided. They never give us nothing, not nothing. Right after the war was the worse times we ever have had. We ain't had no sich hard times since then. The white folks got all was made. It was best we could do. The Yankees what camped down there told us about the surrender. If the colored folks had started an uprisin the white folks would have set the hounds on us and killed us.

I never heard of the Ku Klux Klan ever being in Texas. Gus Taylor was the ridin boss and he was Ku Klux enough. Everybody was scared not to mind him. He rode over three or four hundred acres of ground. He could beat any fellow under him. I never did see anybody sold. I never was sold. We was glad to be set free. I didn't know what it would be like. It was just like opening the door and lettin the bird fly out. He might starve, or freeze, or be killed pretty soon but he just felt good because he was free. We show did have a hard time getting along right after we was set free. The white folks what had money wouldn't pay nothing much for work. All the slaves was in confusion.

A cousin of mine saw Dr. Hazen down in Texas and they all come back to work his land. They wrote to us about it being so fine for hunting. I always liked to hunt so I rode a pony and come to them. The white folks in Texas told the Yankees what to do after the surrender; get off the land. We didn't never vote there but I voted in Arkansas. Mr. Abel Rinehardt always hope me. I could trust him. I don't vote now. No colored people held office in Texas or here that I heard of.

I got nothing to say bout the way the young generation is doing.

I farmed around Hazen nearly ever since the Civil War. I saved $300 and bought this here house. My son was killed in the World War and I get his insurance every month. I hunted with Colonel Yapp and fed his dogs. He never paid me a cent for taking care of the dogs. His widow never as much as give me a dog. She never give me nothing!

I'm too old to worry bout the present conditions. They ain't gettin no better. I sees dot.

Charleston, Willie Buck, Jr.
Age: 74
Biscoe, Arkansas
Interviewer: Irene Robertson
[M:8: pt. 2: 8–9]

"I was born up here on the Biscoe place before Mr. Biscoe was heard of in this country. I'm for the world like my daddy. He was light as I is. I'm jus' his size and make. There was three of us boys. Dan was the oldest; he was my own brother, and Ed was my half-brother. My daddy was a fellar of few words and long betwix' 'em. He was in the Old War (Civil War). He was shot in his right ankle and never would let it be took out. Mother had been a cook. She and my grandmother was sold in South Carolina and brought out here. Mother's name was Sallie Harry. Judging by them being Harrys that might been who owned them before they was sold. She was about as light as me. Mother died when I was a litter bit er of a feller. Then me and Dan lived from house to house. Grandma Harry and my Aunt Mat and Jesse Dove raised us. My daddy married right er way ag'in.

"I recollect mighty little about the war. We lived back in the woods and swamps. I was afraid of the soldiers. I seen them pass by. I was so little I can barely recollect seeing them and hiding from them.

"When we lived over about Forrest City I seen the Ku Klux whoop Joe Saw and Bill Reed. It was at night. They was tied to trees and whooped with a leather snake whoop. I couldn't say how it come up but they sure poured it on them. There was a crowd come up during the acting. I was scared to death then. After then I had mighty little use for dressed-up folks what go around at night (Ku Klux). I can tell you no sich thing ever took place as I heard of at Biscoe. We had our own two officers and white officers and we get along all the time tolerably well together."

Chase, Lewis
Age: 90?
Des Arc, Arkansas
Interviewer: Irene Robertson
[M:8: pt. 2: 10–12]

"I answer all your questions I knows lady.
"When de Civil War goin on I heard lots folks talking. I don't know what all they did say. It was a war mong de white folks. Niggers had no say in it. Heap ob them went to wait on their masters what went to fight. Niggers didn't know what the fight war bout. Yankey troops come take everything we had made, take it to the Bluff [DeValls Bluff], waste it and eat it. He claim to be friend to the black man an do him jes dater way. De Niggers what had any sense tall stuck to the white folks. Niggers what I knowed didn't spec nothin and they so didn't get nothin but freedom.

"I was sold. Yes mam I sho was. Jes put up on a platform and auctioned off. Sold rite here in Des Arc. Nom taint right. My old mistress [Mrs. Snibley] whoop me till I run off and they took me back when they found out where I lef from. I stayed way bout two weeks.

"One man I sho was glad didn't get me cause he whoop me. No'om he didn't get me. I heard him puttin up the prices and I sho hope he didn't get me.

"I don't know whar I come from. Old Missus Snibley kept my hat pulled down over my face so I couldn't see de way to go back. I didn't want to come and I say I go right back. Whar I set, right between old missus and master on de front seat ob de wagon and my ma set between missus Snibley's two girls right behind us. I recken it was a covered wagon. The girls name was Florence and Emma. Old master Snibley never whip me but old Missus sho did pile it on me. Noom I didn't lack her. I run away. He died fo the war was over. I did leave her when de war was over.

"I saw a heap ob bushwhackers and carpet bagger but I nebber seed no

Ku Klux. I heard battles of the bushwhackers out at the Wattensaw bridge [Iron bridge]. I was scared might near all de time for four years. Noom I didn't want no soldiers to get me.

"I recken I wo long britches when de war started cause when I pulled off dresses I woe long britches. Never wo no short ones. Nigger boys and white boys too wore loose dresses till they was four, five or six years old in them times. They put on britches when they big nough to help at the field.

"I worked at the house and de field. I'ze farmed all my life.

"I vote many a time. I don't know what I vote. Noom I don't! I recken I votes Democrat, I don't know. I don't do no good. Noom I ain't voted in a long time. I don't know nothin bout votin. I never did.

"Noom I never owned no land, noom no home neither. I didn't need no home. The man I worked for give me a house on his place. I work for another man and he give me a house on his land. I owned a horse one time. I rode her.

"I don't know nuthin bout the young generation. I takes care bout myself. Dats all I'm able to do now. Some ob dem work. Now they don't work hard as I did. I works now hard as they do. They ought to work. I don't know what going to become ob them. I can't help what they do.

"The times is hard fo old folks cause they ain't able to work and heap ob time they ain't no work for em to do.

"Noom I lived at Bells, Arkansas for I come to Hickory Plains and Des Arc. I don't know no kin but my mother. She died durin the war. Noom not all de white folks good to the niggers. Some mean. They whoop em. Some white folks good. Jes lak de niggers, deres some ob em mighty good and some ob em mean.

"I works when I can get a little to do and de relief gives me a little.

"I *am* er hundred years old! Cause I knows I is. White folks all tell you I am."

Vaden, Charlie
Age: 77
Hazen, Green Grove, Arkansas
Interviewer: Irene Robertson
[M:11: pt. 7: 1–2]

Charlie Vaden's father ran away and went to the war to fight. He was a slave and left his owner. His mother died when he was five years old but before she died she gave Charlie to Mrs. Frances Owens (white lady). She came to Des Arc and ran the City Hotel. He never saw his father till he was grown. He worked for Mrs. Owens. He never did run with colored folks then. He nursed her grandchildren, Guy and Ira Brown. When he was grown he bought a farm at Green Grove. It consisted of a house and forty-seven acres of land. He farmed two years. A fortune teller came along and told him he was going to marry but he better be careful that they would wouldn't live together or he might "drop out." He went ahead and married like he was "fixing" to do. They just couldn't get along, so they got divorced.

They had the wedding at her house and preacher Isarel Thomas (colored) married them and they went on to his house. He don't remember how she was dressed except in white and he had a "new outfit too."

Next he married Lorine Rogers at the Green Grove Church and took her home. She fell off the porch with a tub of clothes and died from it just about a year after they married.

He married again at the church and lived with her twenty years. They had four girls and four boys. She died from the change of life.

The last wife he didn't live with either. She is still living.

Had another fortune teller tell his fortune. She said, "Uncle, you are pretty good but be careful or you'll be walking around begging for victuals." He said it had nearly come to that now except it hurt him to walk. (He can hardly walk.) He believes some of what the fortune tellers tell comes true. He has been on the same farm since 1887, which is forty-nine years, and did fine till four years ago. He can't work, couldn't pay taxes, and has lost his land.

He was paralyzed five months, helpless as a baby, couldn't dress himself. An herb doctor settled at Green Grove and used herbs for tea and poultices and cured him. The doctors and the law run him out of there. His name was Hopkins from Poplar Bluff, Missouri.

Charlie Vaden used to have rheumatism and he carried a buckeye in each pants pocket to make the rheumatism lighter. He thought it did some good.

He has a birthmark. Said his mother must have craved pig tails. He never had enough pig tails to eat in his life. The butchers give them to him when he comes to Hazen or Des Arc. He said he would "fight a circle saw for a pig tail."

He can't remember any old songs or old tales. In fact he was too small when his mother died (five years old).

He believes in herb medicine of all kinds but can't remember except garlic poultice is good for neuralgia. Sassafras is a good tea, a good blood purifier in the spring of the year.

He knows a weather sign that seldom or never fails. "Thunder in the morning, rain before noon." "Seldom rains at night in July in Arkansas."

He has seen lots of lucky things but doesn't remember them. "It's bad luck to carry hoes and rakes in the living house." "It's bad luck to spy the new moon through bushes or trees."

He doesn't believe in witches, but he believes in spirits that direct your course as long as you are good and do right. He goes to church all the time if they have preaching. Green Grove is a Baptist church. He is not afraid of dead people. "They can't hurt you if they are dead."

Wesmoland, Maggie
Age: 85
Brinkley, Arkansas
Interviewer: Irene Robertson
[M:11: pt. 7: 99–103]

"I was born in Arkansas in slavery time beyond Des Arc. My parents was sold in Mississippi. They was brought to Arkansas. I never seed my father after the closing of the war. He had been refugeed to Texas and come back here, then he went on back to Mississippi. Mama had seventeen children. She had six by my stepfather. When my stepfather was mustered out at De Valls Bluff he come to Miss (Mrs.) Holland's and got mama and took her on wid him. I was give to Miss Holland's daughter. She married a Cargo. The Hollands raised me and my sister. I never seen mama after she left. My mother was Jane Holland and my father was Smith Woodson. They lived on different places here in Arkansas. I had a hard time. I was awfully abused by the old man that married Miss Betty. She was my young mistress. He was poor and hated Negroes. He said they didn't have no feeling. He drunk all the time. He never had been used to Negroes and he didn't like em. He was a middle age man but Miss Betty Holland was in her teens.

"No, mama didn't have as hard a time as I had. She was Miss Holland's cook and wash woman. Miss Betty told her old husband, 'Papa don't beat his Negroes. He is good to his Negroes.' He worked overseers in the field. Nothing Miss Betty ever told him done a bit of good. He didn't have no feeling. I had to go in a trot all the time. I was scared to death of him—he beat me so. I'm scarred up all over now where he lashed me. He would strip me start naked and tie my hands crossed and whoop me till the blood ooze out and drip on the ground when I walked. The flies blowed me time and again. Miss Betty catch him gone, would grease my places and pat turpentine on them to kill the places blowed. He kept a bundle of hickory switches at the house all the time. Miss Betty was good to me. She would cry and beg him to be good to me.

"One time the cow kicked over my milk. I was scared not to take some milk to the house, so I went to the spring and put some water in the milk. He was snooping round (spying) somewhere and seen me. He beat me nearly to death. I never did know what suit him and what wouldn't. Didn't nothing please him. He was a poor man, never been used to nothin' and took spite on me everything happened. They didn't have no children while I was there but he did have a boy before he died. He died fore I left Dardanelle. That is where he was so mean to me. He lived in the deer and bear hunting country.

"He went to town to buy them some things for Christmas good while after freedom—a couple or three years. Two men come there deer hunting every year. One time he had beat me before them and on their way home they went to the Freemens bureau and told how he beat us and what he done it for—biggetness. He was a biggity acting and braggy talking old man. When he got to town they asked him if he wasn't hiding a little Negro girl, ask if he sent me to school. He come home. I slept on a bed made down at the foot of their bed. That night he told his wife what all he said and what all they ask him. He said he would kill whoever come there bothering about me. He been telling that about. He told Miss Betty they would fix me up and let me go stay a week at my sister's Christmas. He went back to town, bought me the first shoes I had had since they took me. They was brogan shoes. They put a pair of his sock on me. Miss Betty made the calico dress for me and made a body out of some of his pants legs and quilted the skirt part, bound it at the bottom with red flannel. She made my things nice—put my underskirt in a little frame and quilted it so it would be warm. Christmas day was a bright warm day. In the morning when Miss Betty dressed me up I was so proud. He started me off and told me how to go.

"I got to the big creek. I got down in the ditch—couldn't get across. I was running up and down it looking for a place to cross. A big old mill was upon the hill. I could see it. I seen three men coming, a white man with a gun and two Negro men on horses or mules. I heard one say, 'Yonder she is.' Another said, 'It don't look like her.' One said, 'Call her.' One said, 'Margaret.' I answered. They come to me and said, 'Go to the mill and cross on a foot log.' I went up there and crossed and got upon a stump behind my brother-in-law on his horse. I didn't know him. The white man was the man he was share croppin' with. They all lived in a big yard like close together. I hadn't seen my sister before in about four years. Mr. Cargo told me if I wasn't back at his house New Years day he would come after me on his horse and run me every step of the way home. It was nearly twenty-five miles. He said he would give me the worst whooping I ever got in my life. I was going back, scared not to be back. Had no other place to live.

"When New Year day come the white man locked me up in a room in his house and I stayed in there two days. They brought me plenty to eat. I slept in there with their children. Mr. Cargo never come after me till March. He didn't see me when he come. It started in raining and cold and the roads was bad. When he come in March I seen him. I knowed him. I lay down and covered up in leaves. They was deep. I had been in the woods getting sweet-gum when I seen him. He scared me. He never seen me. This white man bound me to his wife's friend for a year to keep Mr. Cargo from getting me back. The woman at the house and Mr. Cargo had war nearly about me. I missed my whoopings. I never got none that whole year. It was Mrs. Brown, twenty miles from Dardanelle, they bound me over to. I never got no more than the common run of Negro children but they wasn't mean to me.

"When I was at Cargo's, he wouldn't buy me shoes. Miss Betty would have but in them days the man was head of his house. Miss Betty made me moccasins to wear out in the snow—made them out of old rags and pieces of his pants. I had risings on my feet and my feet frostbite till they was solid sores. He would take his knife and stob my risings to see the matter pop way out. The ice cut my feet. He cut my foot on the side with a cowhide nearly to the bone. Miss Betty catch him outer sight would doctor my feet. Seem like she was scared of him. He wasn't none too good to her.

"He told his wife the Freemens Bureau said turn that Negro girl loose. She didn't want me to leave her. He despised nasty Negroes he said. One of them fellows what come for me had been to Cargo's and seen me. He was the Negro man come to show Patsy's husband and his share cropper where I was at. He whooped me twice before them deer hunters. They visited him every spring and fall hunting deer but they reported him to the Freemens Bureau. They knowed he was showing off. He overtook me on a horse one day four or five years after I left there. I was on my way from school. I was grown. He wanted me to come back live with them. Said Miss Betty wanted to see me so bad. I was so scared I lied to him and said yes to all he said. He wanted to come get me a certain day. I lied about where I lived. He went to the wrong place to get me I heard. I was afraid to meet him on the road. He died at Dardanelle before I come away from there.

"After I got grown I hired out cooking at $1.50 a week. When I was a girl I ploughed some. I worked in the field a mighty little but I have done a mountain of washing and ironing in my life. I can't tell you to save my life what a hard time I had when I was growing up. My daughter is a blessing to me. She is so good to me.

"I never knowed nor seen the Ku Klux. The Bushwhackers was awful after the war. They went about stealing and they wouldn't work.

"Conditions is far better for young folks now than when I come on. They can get chances I couldn't get they could do. My daughter is tied down here with me. She could do washings and ironings if she could get them and do it here at home. I think she got one give over to her for awhile. The regular wash woman is sick. It is hard for me to get a living since I been sick. I get commodities. But the diet I am on it is hard to get it. The money is the trouble. I had two strokes and I been sick with high blood pressure three years. We own our house. Times is all right if I was able to work and enjoy things. I don't get the Old Age Pension. I reckon because my daughter's husband has a job—I reckon that is it. I can't hardly buy milk, that is the main thing. The doctor told me to eat plenty milk.

"I never voted."

Pulaski County

Anderson, R. B.
Age: 76
Route 4, Box 68 (near Granite)
Little Rock, Arkansas
Interviewer: Samuel S. Taylor
[M:8: pt. 1: 53–54]

"I was born in Little Rock along about Seventeenth and Arch Streets. There was a big plantation there then. Dr. Wright owned the plantation. He owned my mother and father. My father and mother told me that I was born in 1862. They didn't know the date exactly, so I put it the last day in the year and call it December 30, 1862.

"My father's name was William Anderson. He didn't go to the War because he was blind. He was ignorant too. He was colored. He was a pretty good old man when he died.

"My mother's name was Minerva Anderson. She was three-fourths Indian, hair way down to her waist. I was in Hot Springs blacking boots when my mother died. I was only about eight or ten years old then. I always regretted I wasn't able to do anything for my mother before she died. I don't know to what tribe her people belonged.

"Dr. Wright was awful good to his slaves.

"I don't know just how freedom came to my folks. I never heard my father say. They were set free, I know. They were set free when the War ended. They never bought their freedom.

"We lived on Tenth and near to Center in a one-room log house. That is the earliest thing I remember. When they moved from there, my father had accumulated enough to buy a home. He bought it at Seventh and Broadway. He paid cash for it—five hundred and fifty dollars. That is where we all lived until it was sold. I couldn't name the date of the sale but it was sold for good money—about three thousand eight hundred dollars, or maybe around four thousand. I was a young man then.

"I remember the Brooks-Baxter War.

"I remember King White fooled a lot of niggers and armed them and brought them up here. The niggers and Republicans here fought them and run them back where they come from.

"I know Hot Springs when the main street was a creek. I can't remember when I first went there. The government bath-house was called 'Rat Hole', because it was mostly people with bad diseases that went there.

"After the War, my father worked for a rich man named Hunter. He was yardman and took care of the house. My mother was living then.

"Scipio Jones and I were boys together. We slept on pool tables many a time when we didn't have no other place to sleep. He was poor when he was a boy and glad to get hold of a dime, or a nickel. He and I don't speak today because he robbed me. I had a third interest in my place. I gave him money to buy my place in for me. It was up for sale and I wanted to get possession. He gave me some papers to sign and when I found out what was happening, he had all my property. My wife kept me from killing him."

Interviewer's Comment
Occupation: Grocer, bartender, porter, general work

Bates, John
Age: 84
Corsicana, Texas
Interviewer: William E. Smith
6 August 1937
[S2:2 (TX, pt. 1): 212–19]
[See also M:4: pt. 1 (Texas): 51–53]

The story of John Bates.
My name is John Bates, I'se eighty four years ole, I was bo'n in Little Rock Arkansas in 1852. My father was Ike Bateman, his marsters name was Mock Bateman, my mothers name was Francis Bateman. My father and mother came from Tennessee. I had four brothers and six sisters, Frank, Mingo, George and Jeff were my brothers; my sisters names were Manda, and Lucy.

De other four was never named. Most of dese chilluns died when dey was babies, der is only two of us livin today.

Our home was a one room log house with a dirt floo and two families lived in dis. We had beds of shucks laid across some ropes dat was run through holes bored in boads and a few quilts. My grandma and grandpa I'se never seed them.

I'se done every kind of work on de plantation dar is to do. Sech as plow, hoe, cut wood and water, bale hay and eberything. We earned lots of money durin slave days, but we never did gits payed any. We jest got what we eats and wears fer our work. But we had plenty to eat most all de time, sech as beef, wild turkey, deer, goat, squirrel, po'k, chicken and all kinds of vegetables. It was all cooked in de big open fire place in de old fashun skillets and pots hung from racks. We had plenty of possum, rabbit, and fish too. I'se allus liked fish and turkey best. And de vegetables we eat we gots dem all at one big garden, every body goes to de garden every time dey wants to.

De clothes we wore was made on de plantation too, mos every body wore shoes. We made our own shoes der, I'se de shoe maker. We tanned and treated de leathah and cuts it out in shoes and harness, I'se done all dis mah self.

My weddin clothes was a pair of ole jeans britches and shirt, made at home and a pair of shoes made by myself. My mother belonged ter Harry Hogan and my father belonged ter Mock Bateman, dats what I got my name. We jest left de last part of de name off and says Bates, but I dont know much bout him cause we moved ter Limestone County Texas while I was small leavin my pappy in Arkansas. I's never seed him no more, but dis man marster Harry Hogan was a pretty good sort of feller, but he had a hart time like de rest of us de first wintah we moved to Texas, we shore went hongrey several days dat first wintah. An dat mistress of hisn shore was a good woman, she was good ter de chilluns specially. Dey had three chilluns, two girls and one boy.

Marster Hogan lived in a big log house with a hallways clear through, but dis house had a plank floo whar ourn didnt, and it had a porch in front clean cross, and it had an old fashun stick n' dirt chimley, dis chimley was big nuff ter burn cord wood in, shore did throw out de heat. Marster Harry er de young marster one of em an maybe both of dem was de over seer and drivah, dey didnt has no body else cause dey only had twelve slaves big nuff ter work.

Now bout de size of dis place, I jest dont know zactly how many acres but marster Harry jest rented places after he come ter Texas he never did owns a place of his own, but dis place was a good big place. De young marster usually comes out early in de mornin bout foah clock and hollers and dat means fer us ter git up, we would gits up and while de women foks was gitten breakfast, de men foks would do de milkin and feedin and den eats breakfast, and be in de field fore sun up and works til sun down. Dis man was a good man ter work, I never did hears him threatin ter whip one of us.

But I has heard dat some of de slave owners did whip some of de slaves ter death, but nothin lak dat happens roun marster Hogan. Now Marster Hogan did threatin ter take de food way from two or three of em fer three days if dey didnt do bettah, but deys do bettah and he never did do dat. He's done it and dey knowed it too. He never did sell any of his slaves either laks some people did, dem speckalators didnt do no good wid him. I saw bout two speckalators, but dey didnt have no slaves, I dont think dey did much good out dis far wes, dey allus travels on foot, dat is de big slaves did, de young uns de drivahs and de speckleters rode. I has heard dat some of dem was put in chains but I never did seed any of dem.

One of my young misses tried her dead level bes ter learn me to read and write but my head was jest too thick, I jest couldnt learn.

Some of de slaves allus reads de Bible, my Uncle Ben could read de Bible. He reads it all de time he wasnt working. He tole us all de time we was gonna be free, he says de Bible speaks of us bein freed and explainin it ter us and marster Harry was standin in de chimley corner listenin, finally marster Harry laughs, haw, haw, haw, what dat you tellin Ben. Hell no, you never will be free, you aint got sense nuff ter make a livin if you was free. No siree, you never will be free, you'll be a slave as long as you live. We allus went ter church til dis happen and after dat we wasnt lowed ter go. He even takes Uncle Ben's Bible away from him sayin dat book puts bad ideas in our heads, but Uncle Ben finally gits hold of another one, but he keeps dis one hid all de time.

We all goes ter a babtisin one time ter a big saw mill tank and seed fifty baptized. I was in dat bunch myself. Dey didn't have no funeral songs fer de slaves, dey jest bury dem likes you do a cow er horse dese days, jest digs a hole and rolls em in it and kivers em over wid dirt, I never did go ter a white funeral.

When de war comes on and sometimes before de war de slaves would try ter run away ter de north, some never would be heard of again, sometimes dey would be caught and be whipped to death and maybe other things would happen. Dey always knew dey had sumpin comin iffen dey was caught. Well durin dem times jest like today nearly everybody knew what was goin on, news traveled purty fast, iffen de slaves couldnt gits it ter each other by gitten a pass, dey would slip out after dark and go in ter another plantation from de back way ter gits it scattered and sometimes dey was caught and would gits a good whippen fer it.

After we worked all day in de fiels we had ter comes in and do up all de chores such as cuttin wood, toten it in, carry water, milk from eight ter twelve head of cows, feed bout fifty hogs, feeds de mules and hosses, chickens, separate de calves and cows, maybe doctor some stock fer screw worms and jest anything that happens ter need ter be done, and de same thing fore we goes ter work in the morning. We worked every day in de fiels if it warnt rainin and if we was in de grass, but if we wasnt in de grass, we was alowed ter knock off Satdy evenin and fore Uncle Ben got his Bible took way from him we would go ter preachin on Satdy nights if there was any, but after dat, we jest sets round and talks and de same things on Sundays.

We allus got de Foath of July, Christmas and Thanksgiving off. We allus had big dinners on dem days and dat was bout all. But we shore had ter put in a big day on New Years day. We allus gathered the corn shuck and all and shucked it in the crib on rainy days and bad weather.

When cotton pickin comes in de fall of the year, de chilluns and grown folks both picks cotton in big baskets and marster Harry Hogan hauled it over ter Mr. Logan Stroud ter gits it ginned as he didn't have no gin.

Mos of the weddins happen in de fall of the year, de older one of the Logan girls got married in de fall, it was October, clost ter Halloween and all de work was stopped and a big weddin was had with a big dinner and supper. All de slaves from de plantation of marster Harry went and all of master Logans slaves was present when dey was married and dat night de Logan boys and young marster Harry got some dem pumpkins and pine knots and fix dem inside some of the slaves cabins and after de supper was over, and everything de slaves started home, and when dey opens de doors and seed dem funny faces, dey jest scatters lak quails, but dey finally gits dem all back together.

When de slaves dies, deys carries dem off, digs a hole, puts dem and covers dem up, no funeral is held, just a buryin, and when dey marries, you jest answers a few questions fer your marster and jumps over a broom stick and you'se married.

We plays lots of make up games, jest games we done thought up ourselves. De chilluns of dem days was jes lak de chilluns of today, allus thinking up some meaness ter git into, and we would sing play songs and our mamas would sing songs ter us when we was little, but I done fergot all dem too. One time when I was about twelve years ole, a few of us boys went down to an ole log house to play. It sets out in de timber tween a quarter and a half mile from de quarters, cause we allus lak ter play here bettah than any were else cause dey all didnt want us to. There was an old dug well here, and de top was in bad shape and our folks and marster Harry was afraid we would fall in it, but we could allus have more fun there than any place else and we would jes slip off and go down there ter play. One day we thought we had slipped off and went down there ter play, we carried an ole coon with us, we was busy playin when our dog begins ter bark and he tucks his tail tween his legs and way he goes ter de house a barkin every time he hits de ground, we knows it was sumpin bad, and we begins ter look fer a bear or panther. We was afraid ter move, we jest stands there shakin and lookin and directly my cousin sees it, and he says there it is and points it out and de rest of us looks at it and it was sumpin white and bout ten feet high, it walks out from behind a big white oak tree, with its head rockin and bendin dis way and dat, looking about fer us. It was huntin fer us, we slips round behind de ole log house and starts fer home, and we hadn't got very fer when we looks back and it was up by de side of dis house lookin inside through de ole rotten roof, den it sees us in de timber and lets out a squeelin racket and bends way over and starts for us, and we lets out more racket den de dog and him both goin home. We was cryin, and hollerin and runnin lake a deer, all de slaves was workin in a corn fiel bout a quarter of a mile away, and dey comes runnin ter see what is wrong, but we couldnt tells dem fer bout hour I guess and Marster Harry and some of dem goes ter look fer it but it jest disappeared and we never did go back ter dis ole haunted house ter play no more. Dat was my first and last ghos. Us boys was afraids ter git out of de yard fer a long time, it nearly scares us sick.

When de slaves gits sick dey would gets de bittercrest weeds er bark dey could find and makes a tea outen it and takes it cause if dey gits too sick dey would gets a doctor. I aint had no doctor in twenty five years, when I gets ter feelin bad I goes out and gets some of dese ole bitter weeds we calls em, de kind dat makes your cows milk bitter, and boils it, makin a tea and takes it and in a few days I am all right. I got some layin over there now dat I went out in de pasture dis mornin and got. It is better den de patten medicine dat you buys.

Marster Harry was havin a purty hard time after we come ter Texas, and he hads ter do every way he could ter gits by, and den de war comes on and calls fer ever able bodied man, and it took money, hosses, food and feed and lots of things ter fight dis war, and the farmers had ter share der part, and marster Harry tried ter share his part and keep goin, and too, young marster Harry goes ter de war and take one of de slaves ter wait on him. Young marster Harry was wounded and we didnt have much ter eat after tryin ter send food and feed ter de soldiers, we shore did have a hard time. Then de news comes dat we was free, we was all glad ter hear dis but hated ter hear bout young marster Harry bein all shot up.

Blake, Henry
Age: 80+
Rear of 1300 Scott Street
Little Rock, Arkansas
Interviewer: Samuel S. Taylor
[M:8: pt. 1: 175–79]

"I was born March 16, 1853, they tell me. I was born in Arkansas right down here on Tenth and Spring Streets in Little Rock. That was all woods then. We children had to go in at night. You could hear the wolves and the bears and things. We had to make a big fire at night to keep the wolves and varmints away.

"My father was a skiffman. He used to cross the Arkansas River in a ferry-boat. My father's name was Doc Blake. And my mother's name was Hannah Williams before she married.

"My father's mother's name was Susie somethin'; I done forgot. That is too far back for me. My mother's mother was named Susie—Susie Williams.

"My father's master was named Jim Paty. My father was a slavery man. I was too. I used to drive a horsepower gin wagon in slavery time. That was at Pastoria just this side of Pine Bluff—about three or four miles this side. Paty had two places—one about four miles from Pine Bluff and the other about four miles from England on the river.

"When I was driving that horsepower gin wagon, I was about seven or eight years old. There wasn't nothin' hard about it. Just hitch the mules to one another's tail and drive them 'round and 'round. There wasn't no lines. Just hitch them to one another's tail and tell them to git up. You'd pull a lever when you wanted them to stop. The mule wasn't hard to manage.

"We ginned two or three bales of cotton a day. We ginned all the summer. It would be June before we got that cotton all ginned. Cotton brought thirty-five or forty cents a pound then.

"I was treated nicely. My father and mother were too. Others were not treated so well. But you know how Negroes is. They would slip off and go out. If they caught them, he would put them in a log hut they had for a jail. If you wanted to be with a woman, you would have to go to your boss man and ask him and he would let you go.

"My daddy was sold for five hundred dollars—put on the block, up on a stump—they called it a block. Jim Paty sold him. I forget the name of the man he was sold to—Watts, I think it was.

"After slavery we had to get in before night too. If you didn't, Ku Klux would drive you in. They would come and visit you anyway. They had something on that they could pour a lot of water in. They would seem to be drinking the water and it would all be going in this thing. They was gittin' it to water the horses with, and when they got away from you they would stop and give it to the horses. When he got you good and scared he would drive on away. They would whip you if they would catch you out in the night time.

"My daddy had a horse they couldn't catch. It would run right away from you. My daddy trained it so that it would run away from any one who would come near it. He would take me up on that horse and we would sail away. Those Ku Klux couldn't catch him. They never did catch him. They caught many another one and whipped him. My daddy was a pretty mean man. He carried a gun and he had shot two or three men. Those were bad times. I got scared to go out with him. I hated that business. But directly it got over with. It got over with when a lot of the Ku Klux was killed up.

"In slavery time they would raise children just like you would raise colts to a mare or calves to a cow or pigs to a sow. It was just a business. It was a bad thing. But it was better than the county farm. They didn't whip you if you worked. Out there at the county farm, they bust you open. They bust you up till you can't work. There's a lot of people down at the state farm at Cummins—that's where the farm is ain't it—that's raw and bloody. They wouldn't let you come down there and write no history. No Lawd! You better not try it. One half the world don't know how the other half lives. I'll tell you one thing, if those Catholics could get control there would be a good time all over this world. The Catholics are good folks.

"That gang that got after you if you let the sun go down while you were out—that's called the Pateroles. Some folks call 'em the Ku Klux. It was all the same old poor white trash. They kept up that business for about ten years after the War. They kept it up till folks began to kill up a lot of 'em. That's the only thing that stopped them. My daddy used to make his own bullets.

"I've forgot who it is that told us that we was free. Somebody come and told us we're free now. I done forgot who it was.

"Right after the War, my father farmed a while and after that he pulled a skiff. You know Jim Lawson's place. He stayed on it twenty years. He stayed at the Ferguson place about ten years. They're adjoining places. He stayed at the Churchill place. Widow Scott place, the Bojean place. That's all. Have you been down in Argenta to the Roundhouse? Churchill's place runs way down to there. It wasn't nothing but farms in Little Rock then. The river road was the only one there at that time. It would take a day to come down from Clear Lake with the cotton. You would start 'round about midnight and you would get to Argenta at nine o'clock the next morning. The roads were always bad.

"After freedom, we worked on shares a while. Then we rented. When we worked on shares, we couldn't make nothing—just overalls and something to eat. Half went to the other man and you would destroy your half if you weren't careful. A man that didn't know how to count would always lose. He might lose anyhow. They didn't give no itemized statement. No, you just had to take their word. They never give you no details. They just say you owe so much. No matter how good account you kept, you had to go by their account and now, Brother, I'm tellin' you the truth about this. It's been that way for a long time. You had to take the white man's word on notes and everything. Anything you wanted, you could git if you were a good hand. You could git anything you wanted as long as you worked. If you didn't make no money, that's all right; they would advance you more. But you better not leave him— you better not try to leave and get caught. They'd keep you in debt. They were sharp. Christmas come, you could take up twenty dollars in somethin' to eat and much as you wanted in whiskey. You could buy a gallon of whiskey. Anything that kept you a slave because he was always right and you were always wrong if there was difference. If there was an argument, he would get mad and there would be a shooting take place.

"And you know how some Negroes is. Long as they could git somethin', they didn't care. You see, if the white man came out behind, he would feed you, let you have what you wanted. He'd just keep you on, help you get on your feet—that is, if you were a good hand. But if you weren't a good hand, he'd just let you have enough to keep you alive. A good hand could take care of forty or fifty acres of land and would have a large family. A good hand could git clothes, food, whiskey, whenever he wanted it. My father had nine children and took care of them. Not all of them by one wife. He was married twice. He was married to one in slavery time and to another after the War. I was a child of the first one. I got a sister still living down there in Galloway station that is mighty nigh ninety years old. No, she must be a hundred. Her name is Frances Dobbins. When you git ready to go down there, I'll tell you how to find that place jus' like I told you how to fin' this one. Galloway is only 'bout four miles from Rose City.

"I been married twice in my life. My first woman, she died. The second lady, she is still iving. We dissolved friendship in 1913. Leastwise, I walked out and give her my home. I used to own a home at twenty-first and Pulaski.

"I belong to the Baptist Church at Wrightsville. I used to belong to Arch Street. Was a deacon there for about twelve years. But they had too much splittin' and goin' on and I got out. I'll tell you more sometime."

Interviewer's Comment
Henry Blake's age appears in excess of eighty. His idea of seventy-five is

based on what someone told him. He is certain that he drove a "Horsepower Gin Wagon" during "slavery times", and that he was seven or eight when he drove it. Even if that were in '65, he would be at least eighty years old—seventy-three years since the War plus seven years of his life. His manner of narration would indicate that he drove earlier.

The interview was held in a dark room, and for the first time in my life I took notes without seeing the paper on which I was writing.

Davis, Charlie
Age: 76
100 North Plum
Pine Bluff, Arkansas
Interviewer: Mrs. Bernice Bowden
[M:8: pt. 2: 99]

"They said I was born in 1862, the second day of March, in Little Rock.

"I 'member the War. I 'member the bluecoats. I knowed they was fightin' but I didn't know what about.

"My old master was killed in the War. I don't know his name, I just heered 'em call him old master.

"I know old missis kept lookin' for him all durin' the War and looked for him afterward. As long as I could understand anything she was still lookin'.

"Far as I know, my parents stayed with old missis after the war.

"I 'member my father hired me out when I was a little boy. They treated me good.

"Never have done anything 'cept farm work. I'm failin' now. Hate to say so but I found out I am.

"I never did want to go away from here. I could a went, but I think a fellow can do better where he is raised. I have watched the dumb beasts go off with others and see how they was treated, so I never did crave to go off from home. I have knowed people have went away and they'd bring 'em back dead, and I'd say to myself, 'I wonder how he died?' I've studied it over and I've just made myself satisfied.

"I went to school some but I was the biggest help the old folks had and they kept me workin'."

Dothrum, Silas
Age: 82 or 83
1419 Pulaski Street
Little Rock, Arkansas

Interviewer: Samuel S. Taylor
[M:8: pt. 2: 185–88]

"The white people that owned me are all dead. I am in this world by myself. Do you know anything that a man can put on his leg to keep the flies off it when it has sores on it? I had the city doctor here, but he didn't do me no good. I have to tie these rags around my foot to keep the flies off the sores.

"I worked with the white man nineteen years—put all that concrete down out there. He is still living. He helps me a little sometimes. If it weren't for him I couldn't live. The government allows me and my wife together eight dollars a month. I asked for more, but I couldn't get it. I get commodities too. They amount to about a dollar and a half a month. They don't give any flour or meat. Last month they gave some eggs and those were nice. What they give is a help to a man in my condition.

"I don't know where I was born and I don't know when. I know I am eighty-two or eighty-three years old. The white folks that raised me told me how old I was. I never saw my father and my mother in my life. I don't know nothin'. I'm jus an old green man. I don't know none of my kin people—father, mother, uncles, cousins, nothin'. When I found myself the white people had me.

"That was right down here in Arkansas here on old Dick Fletcher's farm. There was a big family of them Fletchers. They took me to Harriet Lindsey to raise. She is dead. She had a husband and he is dead. She had two or three daughters and they are dead.

Slave Houses
"I can remember what they used to live in. The slaves lived in old wooden houses. They ain't living in no houses now—one-half of them. They were log houses—two rooms. I have forgot what kind of floors—dirt, I guess. Food was kept in a smokehouse.

Relatives
"The whole family of Fletchers is dead. I think that there is a Jef Fletcher living in this town. I don't know just where but I met him sometime ago. He doesn't do nothing for me. Nobody gives me anything for myself but the man I used to work for—the concrete man. He's a man.

How Freedom Came
"All I remember is that they boxed us all up in covered wagons and carried us to Texas and kept us there till freedom came. Then they told us we were free and could go where wanted. But they kept me in bondage and a girl

that used to be with them. We were bound to them that we would have to stay with them. They kept me just the same as under bondage. I wasn't allowed no kind of say-so.

"After Dick Fletcher died, his wife and his two children fetched us back—fetched us back in a covered wagon.

"I am a Arkansas man. Was raised here. I am very well known here, too. Some years after that she turned us loose. I can't remember just how many years it was, but it was a good many.

Right after the War

"After Mrs. Fletcher turned us loose, we worked with some families. I was working by the year. If I broke anything they took it out of my wages. If I broke a plow they would charge me for it. I was working for niggers. I can't remember how much they paid, but it wasn't anything when they got through taking out. I'm dogged if I know how much they were supposed to pay; it has been so long. But know that if I broke anything—a tool or something—they charged me for it. I didn't have much at the end of the year. It would take me a lifetime to make anything if I had to do that.

Patrollers

"I have been out in the bushes when the pateroles would come up and gone into log houses and get niggers and whip their asses. They would surround all the niggers and make them go into the house where they could whip them as much as they wanted to. All that is been years and years ago. I never seen any niggers get away from them. I have heered of them getting away, but if they did I never knowed it.

Ku Klux Klan

"I heered of the Ku Klux, but they never bothered me. I never saw them do anything to anybody.

Recollections Relating to Parents

"I don't know who my parents were, but it seems like I heard them say my father was a white man, and I seem to remember that they said my mother was a dark woman.

Opinions

"The young people today ain't worth a shit. These young people going to school don't mean good to nobody. They dance all the night and all the time, and do everything else. That man across the street runs a whiskey house where they dance and do everything they're big enough to do. They ain't worth nothing."

Douglas, Steve
Age: 69
Abilene, Texas
Interviewer: Sheldon F. Gauthier
12 September 1937
[S2:4 (TX, pt. 3): 1225–29]

Steve Douglas, early day Texas trail driver and frontiersman, was born a slave on an Arkansas plantation near Little Rock in the year 1862. When the slaves were freed he came with his father, William Douglas, and family and some pioneer white settlers, to Parker County, Texas. They located seven miles east of Weatherford. Here his father was murdered by the Indians. Soon after this tragedy, the fourteen year old Steve ran away from home and never saw his family again. For the last twenty years Douglas has been a resident of Abilene, performing janitor services for the Central State Bank. Here he has won the highest respect among his white friends. "Uncle Steve" is a familiar figure, sitting on the veranda of his big two story house, 325 Willow Street, which is located on the "hill".

"I was bo'n on a plantation near Little Rock, Arkansas, soon after the big war was on. I wasn't much size when freedom came. Not so long after, my folks strike out for Texas. 'Cou'se all I know 'bout them times was just what I heard my mother and father talkin' about later on in my life. Now 'bout slavery; I wasn't big enough to see much what happened but I 'members hearin' my parents tell 'bout a widow woman back in Arkansas what owned a big plantation and had so many slaves and after her old man die, she bought some bloodhounds to chase her run-a-ways. She got 'em when they was pups and her boy, what was about nine year old, and a little nigger boy 'bout same size, it was they job to train 'em and make mean dogs. The white boy, he hold the pups and the black boy he take a run, way 'round and through the woods. After so long, the white boy he let go the pups and off they go with they nose to the ground on his trail, you know. Pretty soon the black boy turn up and twant long 'fore the pups run right on his trail. Then you know what the old woman made that little nigger do?—well, those pups had to be train right— she was makin' nigger chasers out of 'em. Yes sir, they had to have blood and that little black boy was held and the pups tasted blood right off his legs. Its terrible to believe, but thats right—just like I tell it to you. She had to guard those dogs her own self—fed 'em, no human ever touch 'em but her and her little boy. The niggers would kill 'em (the dogs) iffen they could.

"Then the first thing that stan' out in my min', and I never forget, is the Red Skin. It was this way—we came to the Weatherford Country just when the Indian seem lak he was his worse. I 'members how we built the log cabins—cut the oaks, hawl 'em up, make the house with a dirt floor, no windows, just a big door what we barred at night—(take us 'bout a week)—built a rail corral for our stock and not long—'fore it seem lak home. Then one day a whole lot of Red Skins—seem lak 'bout a hundred to me—they come yellin' and ridin' hard. We was all in the yard, three men, my father and two white men and some women, us chillun playin' pretty close by the corral. Bless your life! We ran hard as we could to the cabin and the grown folks just stan' there. Never turn they han' nor open they mouth. Those red devils drove our hosses, eight or nine head right off 'fore our eyes. I was lookin' out a big crack in the wall between the logs.

"Then 'fore many day, they back again and this time they steal three white chillun down close to Spring Creek. My father and four white men went on a search for them. It was down on Rush Creek, fifteen miles west of Weatherford, where they overtaken 'em. The Indians put a arrow through my father and killed two other white men. But anyway—they rescue the chillun and brought the bodies of the men home. Now that was sumpin' bad. We buried my father and the other two men. Seem lak I couldn't stay there after that, so soon as I come fourteen, I ran away. Not long after I turn up at Joe Loving's place in Lost Valley. I ride hosses, run cattle and help at 'most any job they put me to.

"Two times I went up the trail. In '76 we lef' in latter part of February. We fought the Indians nearly ever bit the way, seem lak. Soldiers went part of the way with us, it was like this—a bunch of soldiers from a fort would fall in along the side of us then they take us within a days ride of another fort, they turn back and we make it to the fort, there another bunch of soldiers fall in and on we go lak that 'til we come nearly to Abilene (Kansas). By that time our herd, what we started with so poor they can scasley walk, now so fat they can scasley walk.

"I didn't min' the cold of the weather—come night catch me a fresh hoss, change my saddle on him—place him close where I know I gonna need him 'fore come day. Fall into my tarpaulin with my clothes on (haven't change since left the ranch and don't, more'n likely, 'til I get back again), roll up, come rain, blue norther, don't care, sleep right on long as they let me. Call out in the night "Hey, Steve! Get on a move—Indians! Cattle on stampede!" Swing my hoss, never put bridle on him 'til I got better time, just use a hackamore, and off we go, tryin' to get 'em rounded up. Ho! cattle ho! sing all night tryin to quiet 'em. Ho! cattle ho! den I ride in a circle, win' up in the middle and a big bunch of longhorns all 'round. Believe I don't know where I am—I lost—I hunt the boys, they huntin' me and we all lost, maybe so—but bye'n bye get together again and move on up the trail. Then it come July and August and—'bout 'long that time we lan' in Abilene (Kansas)—sell our herd and then, back to Texas. Great days! Lawd Amighty! We never see 'em again—Then I follow that job, me and four other culled boys, with Loving's bunch, 'til those days are no more—then I settle down back among my white friends in Cisco, Texas and marry my first time—work for a Doctor name F. M. Oldam there, for years, janitored at his building. He was a real white man, and I say I don't put all white folks in one sack, but God made lots of good white men, same as the nigger. He made lots of good niggers—but you can't put all of them in one sack! But lissen, the white folks has always treated me right, I have no complaint and my best friends today are the whites. So back to slavery days, I believe the white man was yo' friend—you let him be. I'm this way, I lived my life the bes' I know how, got lots to think 'bout now and I'm old—to old to work I know. Gonna get a little pension (Old Age) money—got a paper here in my vest now, done tol' me so—and that will help and I'm very oblige to my Uncle Sam's Gove'nment.

Kinsey, Cindy
Age: 86
Florida
Interviewer: Barbara Darsey
[M:17: 190–93]

"Yes maam, chile, I aint suah ezackly, but I think I bout 85 mebby 86 yeah old. Yes maam, I wus suah bahn in de slavery times, an I bahn right neah de Little Rock in Arkansas, an dere I stay twell I comed right from dere to heah in Floridy bout foah yeah gone.

"Yes maam, my people de liv on a big plantation neah de Little Rock an we all hoe cotton. My Ma? Lawzy me, chile, she name Zola Young an my pappy he name Nelson Young. I had broddehs Danel, Freeman, George, Will, and Henry. Yes maam, Freeman he de younges an bahn after we done got free. An I had sistehs by de name ob Isabella, Mary, Nora,—dat aint all yet, you want I should name em all? Well then they was too Celie, Sally, and me Cindy but I aint my own sisteh is I, hee, hee, hee.

"My Old Massa, he name Marse Louis Stuart, an my Ole Missy, dat de real ole one you know, she name,—now-let-me-see, does-I-ricollek, lawzy me, chile, I suah fin it hard to member some things. O! yes,—her name hit war Missy Nancy, an her chilluns dey name Little Marse Sammie an Little Missy Fanny. I don know huccum my pappy he go by de name Young when Old Massa he name Marse Stuart lessen my pappy he be raised by nother Massa fore Marse Louis got him, but I disrememba does I eber heerd him say.

"Yes maam, chile I suah like dem days. We had lot ob fun an nothing to worrify about, suah wish dem days wus now, chile, us niggahs heaps better off den as now. Us always had plenty eat and plenty wearin close too, which us aint nevah got no more. We had plenty cahn pone, baked in de ashes too, hee, hee,hee, it shore wus good, an we had side meat, an we had other eatin too, what ever de Old Marse had, but I like de side meat bes. I had a good dress for Sunday too but aint got none dese days, jes looky, chile, dese ole rags de bes I got. My Sunday dress? Lawzy me, chile, hit were alway a bright red cotton, I suah member dat color, us dye de cotton right on de plantation mostly. Other close I dont ezackly ricollek, but de mostly dark, no colahs.

"My ma, she boss all de funerls ob de niggahs on de plantation an she got a long white veil for wearin, lawzy me, chile, she suah look bootiful, jes lak a bride she did when she boss dem funerls in dat veil. She not much skeered nether fo dat veil hit suah keep de hants away. Wisht I had me dat veil right now, mout hep cure dis remutizics in ma knee what ailin me so bad. I disrememba, but I sposen she got buried in dat veil, chile. She hoe de cotton so Old Marse Louis he always let her off fo de buryings cause she know how to manage de other niggahs and deep dem quiet at de funerls.

"No maam, chile, we didnt hab no Preacher-mans much, hit too fah away to git one when de niggah die. We sung songs and my ma she say a Bible vurs what Old Missy dont lernt her. De vurs, lawsy me, chile, suah wish I could member hit for you. Dem songs? I don jues recollek, but hit seem lak de called 'Gimme Dem Golden Slippahs', an a nother one hit wah 'Ise Goin to Heben in De Charot Ob Fiah', suah do wish I could recollek de words an sing em foh you, chile, but I caint no more, my min, hit aint no good lak what it uster be.

"Yes maam, chile, I suah heerd ob Mr. Lincoln but not so much. What dat mans wanter free us niggahs when we so happy an not nothing to worrify us. No maam, I didnt see none dem Yankee sojers but I heerd ob dem and we alwy afeerd dey come. Us all cotch us rabbits an weah de lef hine foots roun our nek wif a bag ob akkerfedity, yessum I guess dat what I mean, and hit shore smell bad an hit keep off de fevah too, an if a Yankee cotch you wif dat rabbit foots an dat akkerfedity bag roun youh nek, he suah turn you loose right now.

"Yes maam, chile, Ise a Baptis and sho proud ob it. Praise de Lord and go to Church, dat de onliest way to keep de debbil offen youh trail and den sometime he almos kotch up wif you. Lawsy me, chile, when de Preacher-mans baptiz me he had duck me under de wateh twell I mos dron, de debbil he got such a holt on me an jes wont let go, but de Preacher-mans he kep a duckin me an he finaly shuck de debbil loose an he aint bother me much sence, dat is not very much, an dat am a long time ago.

"Yes, maam, chile, some ob de niggahs dey run off from Ole Marse Louis, but de alway come back bout stahved, hee, hee, hee, an do dey eat, an Old Marse, he alway take em back an give em plenty eatins. Yes maam, he alway good to us and he suah give us niggahs plenty eatins all de time. When Crismus come, you know chile, hit be so cole, and Old Marse, he let us make a big fiah, a big big fiah in de yahd roun which us live, an us all dance roun de fiah, and Old Missy she brang us Crismus Giff. What war de giff? Lawzy me, chile, de mostly red woolen stockings and some times a pair of shoeses, an my wus we proud. An Old Marse Louis, he giv de real old niggahs, both de mens an de womans, a hot toddy, hee, hee, hee. Lawzy me, chile, dem wus de good days, who give an ole niggah like me a hot toddy dese days? An talking you bout dem days, chile, sho mek me wish dey wus now."

Logan, John H.
Age: 89
449 Gaines Avenue
Hot Springs, Arkansas
Interviewer: Mary D. Hudgins
[M:9: pt. 4: 274–80]

Gaines Avenue was once a "Quality Street". It runs on a diagonal from Malvern Avenue, a one-time first class residential thorofare, to the Missouri Pacific Tracks. Time was when Gaines led almost to the gates of the fashionable Combes Racetrack.

Built up during the days of bay windows Gaines Avenue has preserved half a dozen land marks of former genteelity. Long stretches between are filled "shot gun" houses, unaquainted for many years with a paintbrush.

Within half a block of the streetcar line on Malvern an early spring had encouraged plowing of a 200 foot square garden. Signs such as "Hand Laundry" appear frequently. But by far the most frequent placard is "FOR SALE" a study in black and white, the insignia of a local real estate firm specializing in foreclosures.

The street number sought proved to be two doors beyond the red brick church. A third knock brought a slight, wrinkled face to the door, its features aquiline, in coloring only the mildest of mocha. Its owner Laura Burton

Logan, after satisfying herself that the visitor wasn't just an intruder, opened the door wide and invited her to come inside.

"Logan, oh Logan, come on here, come on in here." she called to an old man in the next room. "Law, I don't know whether he can tell you anything or not. He's getting pretty feeble. Now five or six years ago he could have told you lots of things. But now—I don't know."

Into the "front room" hobbled the old fellow. His back was bent, his eyes dimmed with age. His face was the sort often called "good"—not good in the sense stupid acquiescence—but rather evidence of an intelligent, non-predatory meeting of the problems of life.

A quarter, handed the old fellow at the beginning of the interview remained clutched in his hand throughout the entire conversation. Because of events during the talk the interviewer reached for her change purse to find and offer another quarter. It was not in her purse. Getting up from her chair she looked on the floor about her. It wasn't there. Mrs. Logan, who had gone back to bed, wanted to know what the trouble was, and was worried when she found what was missing. By manner the interviewer put over the idea that she wasn't suspecting either of the two. But Logan, not having heard the entire conversation got to his feet and extended his hand—the one holding the quarter, offering it back to the interviewer.

When he rose, there was the purse as it had slipped down on the seat of the rocker which the interviewer had almost taken and in which she had probably carelessly tossed her purse. A second quarter, added to his first, brought a beaming smile from the old man. But for the rest of the afternoon there was a lump in the interviewer's throat. Here was a man, evidently terribly in need of money, ready, without even a tiny protest, to return a gift of cash which must have meant so much to him—on the barest notion in his mind that the interviewer wanted it back.

"Be patient with me ma'am," Logan began, "I can't remember so good. And I want to get it all right. I don't want to spoil my record now. I been honest all my life, always stood up and told the truth, done what was right. I don't want to spoil things and lie in my mouth now. Give me time to think.

I was born on—December—December 15. It was in 1848—I think. I was born in the house of Mrs. Cozine. She was living on Third Street in Little Rock. It was near the old Catholic Church. Was only a little ways from the State House. Mrs. Cozine, she was my first mistress. Then she sold me, me and my mother and a couple of brothers.

It was Governor Roane she sold me to. Don't know just how old I was—good sized boy, though. Guess I was five—maybe six years old. He was a fine man, Governor Roane was—a mighty fine man. He always treated me good. Raised me up to be a good man.

I remember when he gives us a free-pass. That was during the war. He said, Now boys, you be good. You stand for what is right, and don't you tell any stories. I've raised you up to do right.'

When he wasn't governor any more he went back to Pine Bluff. We lived there a long time. I was with Governor Roane right up until I was grown. I can't right correct things in my mind altogether, but I think I was with him until I was about 20.

When the war come on, Governor Roane helped to gather up troops. He called us in out of the fields and asked us if we wanted to go. I did. Right today I should be getting a pension. I was truly in the army. Ought to be getting a pension. Once a white man, Mr. Williams, I believe his name was, tried to get me to go with him to Little Rock. Getting me a pension would be easy he said. But somehow we never did go.

I worked in the powder factory for a while. Then they set me to hauling things—mostly food from the Brazos river to Tyler, Texas. We had hard times then—we had a time—and don't you let anybody tell you we didn't. Sometimes we didn't have any bread. And even sometimes we didn't have any water. I wasn't so old, but I was a pretty good man—pretty well grown up.

After the war I went back with my pappy. While I'd belonged to Governor Roane, Roane was my name. But when I went back with father, I took his name. We farmed for a while and later I went to Little Rock.

I did lots of things there. Worked in a cabinet maker's shop for one thing. Was classed as a good workman too. I worked the lathes. Did a good job of it. I never was the sort that had to walk around looking for work. Folks used to come and get me and ask me to work for them.

How'd I happen to come to Hot Springs? They got me to come to work on the water mains. Worked for the water works a long time. Then I worked for a Mr. Smith in the bath house. I fired the furnace for him. Then for about 15 years I kept the yard at the Kingsway—the Eastman it was then. I kept the lawn clean at the Eastman Hotel. That was about the last steady work I did.

Yes and in between I used to haul things. Had me an express wagon. Used to build rock walls too. Built good walls.

Who did you say you was, Miss? Your father was Jack Hudgins—Law, child, law—"

A feeble hand reached for the hand of the white woman and took it. The old eyes filled with tears and the face distorted in weeping. For a few minutes he sat, then he rose, and the young woman rose with him. For a moment she put a comforting arm around him and soon he was quieter.

"Law, so your father was Jack Hudgins. How well I does remember him. Whatever did become of that fine boy? Dead did you say? I remembers now. He was a fine man, a mighty—mighty fine man. Jack Hudgins girl!

Yes, Miss, I guess you has seen me around a lot. Lots of folks know me. They'll come along the street and they'll say, 'Hello Logan!' and sometimes I won't know who they are, but they'll know me.

I remember once, it's been years and years ago, a man come along Central Avenue—a white man. I was going along the street and suddenly he grabbed me and hugged me. It scared me at first. 'Logan,' he says, 'Logan' he says again. 'Logan, I'd know you anywhere. How glad I am to see you.' But I didn't recognize him. 'Wife,' he say 'wife, come on over and speak to Logan, he saved my life once.' Invited me to come and see him too, he did.

Things have been mighty hard for the last few years. Seems like we could get the pension. First they had a rule that we'd have to sign away the home if we got $9.00 a month. Well, my wife's daughter was taking care of us. Even if we got the $9 she'd still have to help. She wasn't making much, but she was dividing everything—going without shoes and everything. So we thought it wasn't fair to her to sign away our home after all she'd done for us—so that they'd just kick her out when we was dead—she'd been too good to us. So we says 'No!' We been told that they done changed that rule, but we can't seem to get help at all. Maybe, Miss, there's somthing you can do. We sure would be thankful, if you could help us get on.

All my folks is dead, my mother and my father and all my brothers, my first and my second wives and both my children. My wife's daughter helps us all she can. She's mighty good to us. Don't know what we'd do without her. Thank you, glad you come to see us. Glad to know you. If you can talk to them over at the Court House, we'd be glad. Good-bye. Come to see us again."

Rains, Eda
Age: 84
Douglasville, Texas
[M:5: pt. 3 (TX): 225–26]
[See also S2:8: 3221–26]

Aunt Eda Rains, 94, was born a slave in Little Rock, Arkansas, in 1853. In 1860 Eda, her brothers and mother, were bought by a Mr. Carter and brought to Texas. She now lives in Douglasville, Texas.

"I don't 'member my first marster, 'cause my mammy and Jim and John who was my brothers, and me was sold when I was seven and brought to

Douglass, in Texas, to hire out. Befo' we lef' Little Rock, whar I was born, we was vaccinated for smallpox. We came through in a wagon to Texas and camped out at night and we slep' on the groun'.

"When I's hired out to the Tomlins at Douglass I sho' got lonesome for I's jus' a little girl, you know, and wanted to see my mother. They put me to work parchin' coffee and my arm was still sore, and I'd pa'ch and cry, and pa'ch and cry. Finally Missus Tomlin say, "You can quit now." She looked at my arm and then put me to tendin' chillen. I was fannin' the baby with a turkey wing fan and I fell to sleep and when the missus saw me she snatched the fan and struck me in the face with it. This scar on my forehead is from that quill stuck in my head.

"I slep' on a pallet in the missus' room and she bought me some clothes. She had nine chillen, two boys and seven girls. But after awhile she sol' me to Marster Roack, and he bought my mother and my brothers, so we was togedder again. We had our own cabin and two beds. Every day at four they called us to the big house and give us milk and mush. The white chillen had to eat it, too. It was one of marster's ideas and he said he's raised thataway.

"Now, I mus' tell you all 'bout Christmas. Our bigges' time was at Christmas. Marster'd give us maybe fo'-bits to spend as we wanted and maybe we'd buy a string of beads or some sech notion. On Christmas Eve we played games, "Young Gal Loves Candy," or "Hide and Whoop." Didn' know nothin' 'bout Santa Claus, never was larned that. But we allus knowed what we'd git on Christmas mornin'. Old Marster allus call us togedder and give us new clothes, shoes too. He allus wen' to town on the Eve and brung back our things in a cotton sack. That old sack'd be crammed full of things and we knowed it was clothes and shoes, 'cause Marster didn' 'lieve in no foolishness. We got one pair shoes a year, at Christmas. Most times they was red and I'd allus paint mine black. I's one nigger didn' like red. I'd skim grease off dishwater, mix it with soot from the chimney and paint my shoes. In winter we wore woolen clothes and got 'em at Christmas, too.

"We was woke up in the mornin' by blowing of the conk. It was a big shell. It called us to dinner and if anything happened 'special, the conk allus blew.

"I seed runaway slaves and marster kep' any he caught in a room, and he chained 'em till he coul' reach their marsters.

"We didn' get larned to read and write but they took care of us iffen we was sick, and we made medicine outta black willow and outta black snake root and boneset. It broke fevers on us, but, Lawsy, it was a dose.

"After freedom they tol' us we could go or stay. I stayed a while but I married Clainborn Rains and lived at Jacksonville. We had ten chillen. The Lawd's been right good to me, even if I'm blind. Nearly all my old white folks and my chillen has gone to Judgment, but I know the Lawd won't leave me here too long 'fore I jines 'em.

Stephens, Charlotte
Age: 83
1420 West 15th Street
Little Rock, Arkansas
Interviewer: Beulah Sherwood Hagg
[M:10: pt. 6: 226–33]

"I was born right here in Little Rock. My father was owned by a splendid family—the Ashleys. The family of Noah Badgett owned my mother and the children. Pardon me, madam, and I shall explain how that was. In many cases the father of children born in slavery could not be definitely determined. There was never a question about the mother. From this you will understand that the children belonged to the master who owned the mother. This was according to law.

My father's family name was Andrews. How did it happen that it was not Ashley? .... Oh, my dear, you have been misinformed about all slaves taking the name of the master who owned them when peace came.... No, madam. My father was named William Wallace Andrews after his father, who was an English gentleman. He had come to Missouri in early days and owned slaves. ... Yes, my grandfather was white. The Ashleys brought my father to Arkansas Territory when they came. They always permitted him to keep his family name. Many other masters did the same.

From the standpoint of understanding between the white and colored races, Little Rock has always been a good place to live. The better class families did not speak of their retainers as slaves; they were called servants. Both my parents were educated by their masters. Besides being a teacher and minister my father was a carpenter and expert cabinet worker.

The first school for Negroes in Little Rock was opened in 1863 and was taught by my father. I went to school to him. A few months later there came from the north a company of missionary teachers and opened a school which I attended until 1867. My father was a minister of the Methodist Episcopal church for colored people on what is now Eighth and Broadway. He also had a chapel on the property of Mr. Ashley. You probably know that during slavery days the slaves belonged to and attended the same church as their white folks. They sat in the back, or in a balcony built for them. My father was considered the founder of Wesley Chapel, which was Methodist Episcopal. From that time until this day I have been a member of that church. Seventy-three years, I think it is. Before the break came in the Methodist church, you know, it was all the same, north and south. After the division on account of slavery the Methodist church in the south had the word "south" attached. For a long time my father did not realize that. In 1863 he and his church went back into the original Methodist church.

In 1867 the Society of Friends—we called them Quakers—came and erected a large two-story schoolhouse at Sixth and State streets. It was called Union school. When it was built it was said by the Quakers that it was to be for the use of colored children forever, but within a year or two the city bought the property and took charge of the school. As far as I can now recall, white and colored children never did attend the same school in Little Rock. There have always been separate schools for the races. I am able to remember the names of the first teachers in the Quaker school; J. H. Binford was the principal and his sister taught the primary department. Other teachers were Miss Anna Wiles (or Ware), Miss Louise Coffin, Miss Lizzie Garrison, and Sarah Henley.

I was about 11 years old when peace came and was living with my mother and the other children on the Badgett plantation about 7 miles east of Little Rock. Mother did laundry and general house work. Being a small child, all that was asked of me was to run errands and amuse the little white children. Madam, if I could tell you the great difference between slave owners it would help you in understanding conditions of today among the colored people. Both my father and my mother had peculiar privileges. The Ashley family were exceptional slave owners; they permitted their servants to hire their time. There was class distinction, perhaps to greater extent than among the white people. Yes, madam, the slaves who lived in the family with master and mistress were taught just about the same as their own children. At any rate, they imitated them in all matters; to speak with a low voice, use good English, the niceties of manners, good form and courtesy in receiving and attending guests.

I began teaching in Little Rock schools when I was 15 years old and am still teaching. In all, it is 69 years, and my contract is still good. My first experience as a teacher, (as I told you I was fifteen) was by substituting for a teacher in that first Missionary school, in 1869. For some reason, she did not return, and the School Board appointed me in her place. After one year I was given leave of absence to attend Oberlin College in Ohio. I spent three years there, but not in succession. When my money would give out I would come home and the School Board would provide work for me until I could earn enough to carry me through another term. I finished at Oberlin in 1873. I extended my work through courses at Normal schools and Teacher's Institutes. I have taken lecture courses in many colleges, notably the University of California in 1922. I have taught all grades from the first to the twelfth. My principal work, for the last 35 years, however, has been high school Latin and English and Science.

At present I am serving as librarian at the Senior high school and Junior College. I have twice served as principal of city schools in Little Rock. First at Capitol Hill. The Charlotte E. Stephens school at 18th and Maple was named in my honor. I have a book I have kept for 68 years regarding those first schools, and I'm told it is the only one in existence. I also have the first monthly report card ever issued in Little Rock. Mr. Hall (Superintendent of Little Rock City Schools) has asked me to will it to the School Board.

I could recall many interesting events of those early schools for the colored race. Old, old slaves came, desiring to learn to read and spell. They brought the only books they could find, many of which proved to be almanacs, paper bound novels discarded by their mistress and ancient dictionaries, about half of which might be missing.

Yes, madam, I do remember that the emancipated slaves were led to believe they would be given property and have just what their masters had been accustomed to enjoy. I remember hearing my mother tell, in later years, that she really had expected to live as her mistress had; having some one to wait upon her, plenty of money to spend, ride in a carriage with a coachman. But she always added that the emancipated ones soon found out that freedom meant more work and harder than they had ever done before.

What did they work at? Pardon me please for so often reminding you of conditions at that time. Few of the trades workers were white. Brick makers and brick layers, stone masons, lathers, plasters,—all types of builders were of the freed men. You must remember that slaves were the only ones who did this work. Their masters had used their labor as their means of income. Not all slaves were in the cotton fields, as some suppose. The slave owners of towns and villages had their slaves learn skilled trade occupations and made a great deal of money by their earnings. The Yankee soldiers and the many Northern people who lived here hired the freed men and paid them. Quite soon the colored people were buying homes. Many were even hired by their former masters and paid for the work they formerly did without pay under slavery. I remember Bill Read and Dave Lowe. They had been coachmen before freedom. By combining their first savings, they bought a hack, as it was called. It was more of a cab. For all those who did not have private conveyances, this was the only way of getting about town. It was Little Rock's first taxi-cab business, I should say. Bill and Dave made a fortune; they had a monopoly of business for years and eventually had enough cabs to take the entire population to big evening parties, theater, and all places where crowds would gather.

No, madam, I do not recall that we had any inconvenience from the Ku Klux Klan. If they made trouble in Little Rock I do not now remember it. I did hear that out in the country they drove people from their homes. Yes, madam, I do remember, quite distinctly, the times when colored men were voted into public offices. John C. Corbin was State Superintendent of Public Instruction. Phillips county sent two colored men to the legislature; they were W. H. Gray and H. H. White, both from Helena. J. E. Bush of this city followed M. W. Gibbs as Police Judge. After reconstruction when all colored people were eliminated from public life all these people returned to their trade.

I was 22 when I married. My husband was a teacher but knew the carpenter trade. During the time that Negroes served in public office he served as deputy sheriff and deputy constable. He was with me for 41 years before his death; we raised a family of six children and gave each one a college education.

Now, you have asked my opinion of present conditions of the younger generation. It seems to me they are living in an age of confusion; they seem to be all at sea as to what they should get for themselves. I do know this. In some respects the modern frankness is an improvement over the old suppression and repression in the presence of their elders. At the same time, I think the young people of today lack the proper reverence and respect for age and the experience it brings as a guide for them. During my long years of teaching I have had opportunity to study this question. I am still making a study of the many phases of modern life as it affects the young people. I do not like the trend of amusements of today; I would like for our young people to become interested in things more worth while; in a higher type of amusement. Conditions of morality and a lack of regard for conventions is deplorable. Smoking among the girls has increased the common use of liquor between the sexes.

Did you ask me about the voting restrictions for the colored race in this State? I will tell you frankly that I think the primary law here is unjust; most unjust. We are citizens in every other respect; the primary voting privilege should be ours also. This restriction has been explained as coming down from "the grandfather clause" inserted in early legislation. I cannot give you the exact wording of the clause but the substance was that no person whose ancestor—grandfather—was not entitled to vote *before* 1863 should have the right to the ballot. Of course it is readily seen that this clause was written purely for the purpose of denying the vote to the colored people.

Perhaps, madam, my talk has been too much along educational lines. You asked me about my life since freedom came and how I have lived to the present time. I have had the blessed privilege of being a teacher—of doing the work I love best of all in the world to do. I have written the story of my life work; it is all ready to be published. I have written "The Story of Negro Schools in Little Rock" and "Memoirs of Little Rock." Madam, I have written, I suppose, what would amount to volumes for our church papers and local Negro newspaper. My daughter was, at one time, editor of the Women's Page. No, I'm indeed sorry that I have not kept a scrapbook of such writings. In these latter years my friends scold me for having destroyed all the papers as fast as they were read. The most of the news in the articles, however, I have used in the manuscripts of the books I hope to have published.

Thomas, Rebecca
Age: 113
Travis County, Texas
Interviewer: Alfred E. Menn
15 April 1938
[S2:9: pt. 8 (TX): 3819–23]

Rebecca Thomas, 113, says she was born in 1825, in Little Rock, Arkansas. Rebecca looks her age. The skin on her arms is withered and dried. She has the high cheekbones and yellowish complexion of Indians. Rebecca can hardly see, and has been an invalid for many months. Her daughter, Tennie, takes care of her. There are only two small rooms in their house, and Rebecca lies on an old bed, next to the hot kitchen stove. Rebecca's master in Arkansas was Jake Saul. She said he believed in punishing his slaves, when they were unruly. She still has great respect for her mistress, Sukie, who was always kind to her. Saul brought his slaves to Texas before the Civil War. He located at Craft's Prairie, Caldwell County. Rebecca's parents were Champ and Aimee Hemphill. She has been married twice. Her first husband was John Cato. They had fourteen children. Henry Thomas was her second husband. They had no children. Rebecca lives at 1107 Rector Street, Austin, and receives a monthly pension of $9.00 from the State of Texas.

"Pappy's name was Champ Hemphill. I never did know why dey called him Champ. Maybe he was a good fighter. He was tall and of a good build. He was a field worker on Mawster Saul's cotton plantation. I reckon dat it must be more'n sixty years since he died.

"Aimee Hemphill was my mammy's name. Her chillun's name was: Rebecca, Maria, Gus, Hiram, Radin, Jane, Isaiah, we always called him Zair,

Emilie and Johanna. I was de oldest of de fambly, and Johanna was de youngest. Only three of us is still livin' today: Me, Rodin and Johanna. All of mammy's chillun was nothin' but hard workers. Mammy was fat and stout, and she was part Injun. I don't know whut tribe she belonged to. She had long, fine black hair, yaller skin and high cheek bones. Mammy died only about thirty years ago. She jes' died of old age. She jes' wo'e out, lak a old dress. She is buried in Lockhart, Caldwell County.

"When I was a girl, my name was Rebecca Saul, I reckon. Pappy took his name f'om some mawster that owned him at one time. I think dat is how he got his name. After de slavery days de colored folks took de name of some white folks.

"I was bawn in Little Rock, Arkansas, one hunnert and thirteen years ago. I was bawn in 1825. De way I got dat date, was when I asked fo' my pension, de folks up at de courthouse looked up de record, and said dat I was one hunnert and thutteen years old.

"I got a daughter dat is living dat is sebenty years old. Dere is six generations of us. Dat shows dat I'm old.

"Mawster Jake Saul had a big cotton plantation at Little Rock. He had a big orchard, too. He had plenty of everything. He had his niggers whooped when dey needed it.

"But Mistress Sukie was putty good to us. She always prayed to de Lawd dat she hoped she would live long enough to see her niggers set free. She lived to see it too. I remembah how Mistress Sukie raised whut yo' called coccoons. She had 'im on her place and she made her own silk f'om 'em, and made her own silk dresses. She never did let me help wid dis work. She had a lot of mulberry trees and she fed the leaves to dem coccoons.

"I was a house girl fo' awhile, and den I was a field hand fo' awhile. When I was doin' work in de house, I had to git a mulberry limb wid de leaves on it and fan Mistress Sukie wid it till she'd fall asleep; and den I'd fall asleep, too.

"I used to work de spinnin' wheel, and I wove my own clothes on de loom. I used one of dem big, hummin' wheels fo' my work, dat I had to turn by hand; but Mistress Sukie had a little black spinnin' wheel dat she worked wid her feet.

"When I was a girl, I was sich a good walker dat one day I had to go and help out some folks at another place. I was walkin' and de man of de fambly, dat I was to work fo' come along on his hoss. He didn't ride fast, and I beat him home. I walked all of de way.

"Mawster Saul brought us to Texas durin' slavery days. He brought us to whut was called Craft's Prairie, in Caldwell County. I kin still remembah how we travelled fo' many a day across de prairies, befo' we got to Caldwell County.

"He rented a fahm de first year, and raised a lot of cotton. He also raised some wheat and cawn. Dem slaves cut dat wheat wid whut yo' call sickles. Dere was times when at harvestin' time it turned out cold. It was den dat a jub of whiskey was brought along by de men, and dey'd take a drink after comin' out of each row.

"De most cotton dat I could pick was about three hunnert pounds a day. Dat wasn't much 'cause others could pick twice dat much.

"When I was young, I remembah dat I played wid Injun chillun. I even knowed how de Injuns sang and danced. I never danced with the Injuns, though. I know dat when dem Injuns was out on a battle and dey was figuring on killin' yo' dey's paint a spot of blood big as a half-dollah on dere cheeks. I know dat dey done dat, but I don't know if all tribes done dat. I use to make my chillun laugh, when I told 'em how de Injun mammies nussed some of dere chillun. Yo' know dat dey carried dere babies in a kind of satchel on de back. Dem Injun wimmen had sich long milk sacks, dat dey could throw 'em over dere shoulders and let de babies suck dem in dere satchels.

"After slavery, we rented a fahm f'om Isaiah Bean, near Waelder, Gonzales County. Fahmin' is de type of work dat I done all of my life, except fo' awhile when I was a house girl. But I kain't do nothin' now, and all dat I kin do is lay here in bed and eat and drink coffee and water.

"I use to go to a lot of dances in my good days. We'd dance the reels. Dere was times when de only music we had was played by a colored man on a reed. I could play a accordian and my first husband, John, could play de banjo, but we never did play at dances. I wish now dat I hadn't danced so much, and maybe my limbs wouldn't be so bad today. I never did let my girls go to dances, though, 'cause I didn't want no man to swing my girls around.

"I have been married two times. I was married durin' de war, and befor' I was set free. My first husband was John Cato. He was a fahmer. We had fourteen chillun, and about half of 'em died when dey was young. John died about fifty years ago.

"Tennie used to work in a house here in Austin where a lot of University boys lived. She said dat she'd lak to see if dem boys got up in life. One was goin' to be a doctah, and another one was goin' to be a lawyer. Dem boys sure did lak Tennie's cookin'. At meal time dey would yell, "All right, Tennie, bring on de good old hot biscuits and fresh butter.'

"Some of de boys would say, 'Tennie, dat sure was a good meal; here is a quarter fo' yo'.'

"Dat was about thutteen years ago, when Tennie worked out dere. She stays home now, and takes care of me."

White, Julia A.
Age: 79
3003 Cross Street
Little Rock, Arkansas
Interviewer: Beulah Sherwood Hagg
[M:11: pt. 7: 109–19]

Idiom and dialect are lacking in this recorded interview. Mrs. White's conversation was entirely free from either. On being questioned about this she explained that she was reared in a home where fairly correct English was used.

My cousin Emanuel Armstead could read and write, and he kept the records of our family. At one time he was a school director. Of course, that was back in the early days, soon after the war closed.

My father was named James Page Jackson because he was born on the old Jackson plantation in Lancaster County, Virginia. He named one of his daughters Lancaster for a middle name in memory of his old home. Clarice Lancaster Jackson was her full name. A man named Galloway bought my father and brought him to Arkansas. Some called him by the name of Galloway, but my father always had all his children keep the name Jackson. There were fourteen of us, but only ten lived to grow up. He belonged to Mr. Galloway at the time of my birth, but even at that, I did not take the name Galloway as it would seem like I should. My father was a good carpenter; he was a fine cook, too; learned that back in Virginia. I'll tell you something interesting. The first cook stove ever brought to this town was one my father had his master to bring. He was cook at the Anthony House. You know about that, don't you? It was the first real fine hotel in Little Rock. When father went there to be head cook, all they had to cook on was big fireplaces and the big old Dutch ovens. Father just kept on telling about the stoves they had in Virginia, and at last they sent and got him one; it had to come by boat and took a long time. My father was proud that he was the one who set the first table ever spread in the Anthony House.

You see, it was different with us, from lots of slave folks. Some masters hired their slaves out. I remember a drug store on the corner of Main and Markham; it was McAlmont's drug store. Once my father worked there; the money he earned, it went to Mr. Galloway, of course. He said it was to pay board for mother and us little children.

My mother came from a fine family,—the Beebe family. Angeline Beebe was her name. You've heard of the Beebe family, of course. Roswell Beebe at one time owned all the land that Little Rock now sets on. I was born in a log cabin where Fifth and Spring streets meet. The Jewish Synagogue is on the exact spot. Once we lived at Third and Cumberland, across from that old hundred-year-old-building where they say the legislature once met. What you call it? Yes, that's it; the Hinterlider building. It was there then, too. My father and mother had the kind of wedding they had for slaves, I guess. Yes, ma'am, they did call them "broom-stick weddings". I've heard tell of them. Yes, ma'am, the master and mistress, when they find a couple of young slave folks want to get married, they call them before themselves and have them confess they want to marry. Then they hold the broom, one at each end, and the young folks told to jump over. Sometimes they have a new cabin fixed all for them to start in. After Peace, a minister came and married my father and mother according to the law of the church and of the land.

The master's family was thoughtful in keeping our records in their own big family Bible. All the births and deaths of the children in my father's family was in their Bible. After Peace, father got a big Bible for our family, and—wait, I'll show you. . . . Here they are, all copied down just like out of old master's Bible. . . . Here's where my father and mother died, over on this page. Right here's my own children. This space is for me and my husband.

No ma'am, it don't make me tired to talk. But I need a little time to recall all the things you want to know 'bout. I was so little when freedom came I just can't remember. I'll tell you, directly.

I remember that the first thing my father did was to go down to a plantation where the bigger children was working, and bring them all home, to live together as one family. That was a plantation where my mother had been; a man name Moore—James Moore—owned it. I don't know whether he had bought my mother from Beebe or not. I can remember two things plain what happened there. I was little, but can still see them. One of my mother's babies died and Master went to Little Rock on a horse and carried back a little coffin under his arm. The mistress had brought mother a big washing. She was working under the cover of the wellhouse and tears was running down her face. When master came back, he said: "How come you are working today, Angeline, when your baby is dead?" She showed him the big pile of clothes she had to wash, as mistress said. He said: "There is plenty of help on this place what can wash. You come on in and sit by your little baby, and don't do no more work till after the funeral." He took up the little dead body and laid it in the coffin with his own hands. I'm telling you this for what happened later on.

A long time after peace, one evening mother heard a tapping at the door. When she went, there was her old master, James Moore. "Angeline," he said, "you remember me, don't you?" Course she did. Then he told her he was hungry and homeless. A man hiding out. The Yankees had taken everything he had. Mother took him in and fed him for two or three days till he was rested. The other thing clear to my memory is when my uncle Tom was sold. Another day when mother was washing at the wellhouse and I was laying around, two white men came with a big, broad-shouldered colored man between them. Mother put her arms around him and cried and kissed him goodbye. A long time after, I was watching one of my brothers walk down a path. I told mother that his shoulders and body look like that man she kissed and cried over. "Why honey," she says to me, "can you remember that?" Then she told me about my uncle Tom being sold away.

So you see, Miss, it's a good thing you are more interested in what I know since slave days. I'll go on now. The first thing after freedom my mother kept boarders and done fine laundry work. She boarded officers of the colored Union soldiers; she washed for the officers' families at the arsenal. Sometimes they come and ask her to cook them something special good to eat. Both my father and mother were fine cooks. That's when we lived at Third and Cumberland. I stayed home till I was sixteen and helped with the cooking and washing and ironing. I never worked in a cottonfield. The boys did. All us girls were reared about the house. We were trained to be lady's maids and houseworkers. I married when I was sixteen. That husband died four years later, and the next year I married this man, Joel Randolph White. Married him in March, 1879. In those days you could put a house on leased ground. Could lease it for five years at a time. My father put up a house on Tenth and Scott. Old man Haynie owned the land and let us live in the house for $25.00 a year until father's money was all gone; then we had to move out. The first home my father really owned was at 1220 Spring street, what is now. Course then, it was away out in the country. A white lawyer from the north—B. F. Rice was his name—got my brother Jimmie to work in his office. Jimmie had been in school most all his life and was right educated for colored boy then. Mr. Rice finally asked him how would he like to study law. So he did; but all the time he wanted to be a preacher. Mr. Rice tell Jimmie to go on studying law. It is a good education; it would help him to be a preacher. Mr. Rice tell my father he can own his own home by law. So he make out the papers and take care of everything so some persons can't take it away. All that time my family was working for Mr. Rice and finally got the home paid for, all but the past payment, and Mr. Rice said Jimmie's services was worth that. So we had a nice home all paid for at last. We lived there till father died in 1879, and about ten years more. Then sold it.

My father had more money than many ex-slaves because he did what the Union soldiers told him. They used to give him "greenbacks" money and tell him to take good care of it. You see, miss, Union money was not any good here. Everything was Confederate money. You couldn't pay for a dime's worth even with a five dollar bill of Union money then. The soldiers just keep on telling my father to take all the greenbacks he could get and hide away. There wasn't any need to hide it, nobody wanted it. Soldiers said just wait; some day the Confederate money wouldn't be any good and greenbacks would be all the money we had. So that's how my father got his money.

If you have time to listen, miss, I'd like to tell you about a wonderful thing a young doctor done for my folks. It was when the gun powder explosion wrecked my brother and sister. The soldiers at the Arsenal used to get powder in tins called canteens. When there was a little left—a tablespoon full or such like, they would give it to the little boys and show them how to pour it in the palm of their hand, touch a match to it and then blow. The burning powder would fly off their hand without burning. We were living in a double house at Eighth and Main then; another colored family in one side. They had lots of children, just like us. One canteen had a lot more powder in. My brother was afraid to pour it on his hand. He put a paper down on top of the stove and poured it out. It was a big explosion. My little sister was standing beside her brother and her scalp was plum blowed off and her face burnt terribly. His hand was all gone, and his face and neck and head burnt terribly, too. There was a young doctor live close by name Deuell. Father ran for him. He tell my mother if she will do just exactly what he say, their faces wll come out fine. He told her to make up bread dough real sort of stiff. He made a mask of it. Cut holes for their eyes, nose holes and mouths, so you could feed them, you see. He told mother to leave that on till it got hard as a rock. Then still leave it on till it crack and come off by itself. Nobody what ever saw their faces would believe how bad they had been burnt. Only 'round the edges where the dough didn't cover was there any scars. Dr. Deuell only charged my father $50.00 apiece for that grand work on my sister and brother.

Yes ma'am, I'll tell you how I come to speak what you call good English. First place, my mother and father was brought up in families where they heard good speech. Slaves what lived in the family didn't talk like cottonfield hands. My parents sure did believe in education. The first free schools in Little Rock were opened by the Union for colored children. They brought young white ladies for teachers. They had Sunday School in the churches on Sunday. In a few years they had colored teachers come. One is still living here in Little Rock. I wish you would go see her. She is 90 years old now. She founded the Wesley Chapel here. On her fiftieth anniversary my club presented her a gold medal and had "Mother Wesley" engraved on it. Her name is Charlotte E. Stevens. She has the first school report ever put out in Little Rock. It was in the class of 1869. Two of my sisters were graduated from Philander Smith College here in Little Rock and had post graduate work in Fisk University in Nashville, Tennessee. My brothers and sisters all did well in life. Allene married a minister and did missionary work. Cornelia was a teacher in Dallas, Texas. Mary was a caterer in Hot Springs. Clarice went to Colorado Springs, Colorado and was a nurse in a doctor's office. Jimmie was the preacher, as I told you. Gus learned the drug business and Willie got to be a painter. Our adopted sister, Milly, could do anything, nurse, teach, manage a hotel. Yes, our parents always insisted we had to go to school. It's been a help to me all my life. I'm the only one now living of all my brothers and sisters.

Well ma'am, about how we lived all since freedom; it's been good till these last years. After I married my present husband in 1879, he worked in the Missouri Pacific railroad shops. He was boiler maker's helper. They called it Iron Mountain shops then, though. 52 years, 6 months and 24 days he worked there. In 1922, on big strike, all men got laid off. When they went back, they had to go as new men. Don't you see what that done to my man? He was all ready for his pension. Yes ma'am, had worked his full time to be pensioned by the railroad. But we have never been able to get any retirement pension. He should have it. Urban league is trying to help him get it. He is out on account of disability and old age. He got his eye hurt pretty bad and had to be in the railroad hospital a long time. I have the doctor's papers on that. Then he had a bad fall what put him again in the hospital. That was in 1931. He has never really been discharged, but just can't get any compensation. He has put in his claim to the Railroad Retirement office in Washington. I'm hoping they get to it before he dies. We're both mighty old and feeble. He had a stroke in 1933, since he been off the railroad.

How we living now? It's mighty poorly, please believe that. In his good years we bought this little home, but taxes so high, road assessments and all make it more than we can keep up. My granddaughter lives with us. She teaches, but only has school about half a year. I was trying to educate her in the University of Wisconsin, but poor child had to quit. In summer we try to make a garden. Some of the neighbors take in washing and they give me ironing to do. Friends bring in fresh bread when they bake. It takes all my granddaughter makes to keep up the mortgage and pay all the rest. She don't have clothes decent to go.

I have about sold the last of the antiques. In old days the mistress used to give my mother the dishes left from broken sets, odd vases and such. I had some beautiful things, but one by one have sold them to antique dealers to get something to help out with. My church gives me a donation every fifth Sunday of a collection for benefit. Today I bought four cents worth of beans and one cent worth of onions. I say you have to cut the garment according to the cloth. You ain't even living from hand to mouth, if the hand don't have something in it to put to the mouth.

No ma'am, we couldn't get on relief, account of this child teaching. One relief worker did come to see us. She was a case worker, she said. She took down all I told her about our needs and was about ready to go when she saw my seven hens in the yard. "Whose chickens out there?" she asked. "I keep a few hens," I told her. "Well," she hollered, "anybody that's able to keep chickens don't need to be on relief roll," and she gathered up her gloves and bag and left.

Yes ma'am, I filed for old age pension, too. It was in April, 1935 I filed. When a year passed without hearing, I took my husband down so they could see just how he is not able to work. They told me not to bring him any more. Said I would get $10.00 a month. Two years went, and I never got any. I went my myself then, and they said yes, yes, they have my name on file, but there is no money to pay. There must be millions comes in for sales tax. I don't know where it all goes. Of course the white folks get first consideration. Colored folks always has to bear the brunt. They just do, and that's all there is to it.

What do I think of the younger generation? I wouldn't speak for all. There are many types, just like older people. It has always been like that, though. If all young folks were like my granddaughter—I guess there is many, too. She does all the sewing, and gardening. She paints the house, makes the draperies and bed clothing. She can cook and do all our laundry work. She understands raising chickens for market, but just don't have time for that. She is honest and clean in her life.

Yes ma'am, I did vote once, a long time ago. You see, I wasn't old enough at first, after freedom, when all the colored people could vote. Then, for many years, women in Arkansas couldn't vote, anyhow. I can remember when M. W. Gibbs was Police Judge and Asa Richards was a colored alderman. No ma'am! The voting law is not fair. It's most unfair! We colored folks have to pay just the same as the white. We pay our sales tax, street improvement, school tax, property tax, personal property tax, dog license, automobile license—they what have cars—; we pay utility tax. And we should be allowed to vote. I can tell you about three years ago a white lady come down here with her car on election day and ask my old husband would he vote how she told him if she carried him to the polls. He said yes and she carried him. When he got there they told him no colored was allowed to vote in that election. Poor old man, she didn't offer to get him home, but left him to stumble along best he could.

I'm glad if I been able to give you some help. You've been patient with an old woman. I can tell you that every word I have told you is true as the gospel.

Second Interview
December 1938
Interviewer: Samuel S. Taylor
[M:11: pt. 7: 120–33]

"I was born right here in Little Rock, Arkansas, eighty years ago on the corner of Fifth and Broadway. It was in a little log house. That used to be out in the woods. At least, that is where they told me I was born. I was there but I don't remember it. The first place I remember was a house on Third and Cumberland, the southwest corner. That was before the war.

"We were living there when peace was declared. You know, my father hired my mother's time from James Moore. He used to belong to Dick Galloway. I don't know how that was. But I know he put my mother in that house on Third and Cumberland while she was still a slave. And we smaller children stayed in the house with mother, and the larger children worked on James Moore's plantation.

"My father was at that time, I guess, you would call it, a porter at McAlmont's drug store. He was a slave at that time but he worked there. He was working there the day this place was taken. I'll never forget that. It was on September 10th. We were going across Third Street, and there was a Union woman told mamma to bring us over there, because the soldiers were about to attack the town and they were going to have a battle.

"I had on a pair of these brogans with brass plates on them, and they were flapping open and I tripped up just as the rebel soldiers were running by. One of them said, "There's a like yeller nigger, les take her." Mrs. Farmer, the Union woman ran out and said, "No you won't; that's my nigger." And she took us in her house. And we stayed there while there was danger. When my father came back from the drug store, she said she didn't see how he kept from being killed.

"At that time, there were about four houses to the block. On the place where we lived there was the big house, with many rooms, and then there was the barn and a lot of other buildings. My father rented that place and turned the outbuildings into little houses and allowed the freed slaves to live in them till they could find another place.

"My husband was an orphan child, and the people he was living with were George Phelps and Ann Phelps. They were freed slaves. That was after the war. They came here and had this little boy with them. That is how I come to meet that gentleman over there and get acquainted with him. When they moved away from there Phelps was caretaker of the Oakland Cemetery. We married on the twenty-seventh day of March, 1879. I still have the marriage license. I married twice; my first husband was George W. Glenn and my maiden name was Jackson. I married the first time June 10, 1875. I had two children in my first marriage. Both of them are dead. Glenn died shortly after the birth of the last child, February 15, 1878.

"Mr. White is a mighty good man. He is put up with me all these years. And he took mighty good care of my children, them by my first husband as well as his own. When I was a little girl, he used to tell me that he wouldn't have me for a wife. After we were married, I used to say to him, "You said you wouldn't have me, but I see you're mighty glad to get me.

"I have the marriage license for my second marriage.

"There's quite a few of the old ones left. Have you seen Mrs. Gillam, and Mrs. Stephen, and Mrs. Weathers? Cora Weathers? Her name is Cora not Clora. She's about ninety years old. She's at least ninety years old. You say she says that she is seventy-four. That must be her insurance age. I guess she is seventy-four at that; she had to be seventy-four before she was ninety. When I was a girl, she was a grown woman. She was married when my husband went to school. That has been more than sixty years ago, because we've been married nearly sixty years. My sister Mary was ten years older than me, and Cora Weathers was right along with her. She knew my mother. When these people knew my mother they've been here, because she's been dead since '94 and she would have been 110 if she had lived.

"My mother used to feed the white prisoners—the Federal soldiers who were being held. They paid her and told her to keep the money because it was Union Money. You know at that time they were using Confederate money. My father kept it. He had a little box or chest of gold and silver money. Whenever he got any paper money, he would change it into gold or silver.

"Mother used to make these ginger cakes—they call 'em stage planks. My brother Jimmie would sell them. The men used to take pleasure in trying to cheat him. He was so clever they couldn't. They never did catch him napping.

"Somebody burnt our house; it was on a Sunday evening. They tried to say it caught from the chimney. We all like to uv burnt up.

"My father was a carpenter, whitewasher, anything. He was a common laborer. We didn't have contractors then like we do now. Mother worked out in service too. Jimmie was the oldest boy. He taught school too.

"My father set the first table that was ever set in the Anthony Hotel, and was the cause of the first stove being brought here to cook on.

"Some of the children of the people that raised my mother are still living. They are Beebes. Roswell Beebe was a little one. They had a colored man named Peter and he was teaching Roswell to ride and the pony ran away. Peter stepped out to stop him and Roswell said, 'Git out of the way Peter, and let Willie Button come'.

"I get some commodities from the welfare. But I don't get nothing like a pension. My husband worked at the Missouri Pacific shops for fifty-two years, and he don't git nothing neither. It was the Iron Mountain when he first went there on June 8, 1879. He was disabled in 1932 because of injuries received on the job in March, 1931. But they hurried him out of the hospital and never would give him anything. That Monday morning, they had had a loving cup given them for not having had accidents in the plant. And at three P.M., he was sent to the hospital. He had a fall that injured his head. They only kept him there for two days and two hours. He was hurt in the head. Mr. Alkins himself came after him and let him set around in the tool room. He stayed there till he couldn't do nothing at all.

"In 1881, he got his eye hurt on the job in the service of the Missouri Pacific. It was the Iron Mountain then. He was off about three or four months. They didn't pay his wages while he was off. They told him they would give him a lifetime job, but they didn't. His eye gave him trouble for the balance of his life. Sometimes it is worse than others. He had to go to the St. Louis Hospital quite often for about three or four years.

"When the house on Third and Cumberland was burnt, he rebuilded it, and the owners charged him such rent he had to move. He rebuilt it for five hundred dollars and was to get pay in rent. The owners jumped the rent up to twenty-five dollars a month. That way it soon took up the five hundred dollars. Then we moved to Eighth and Main. My brother Jimmie was in an accident there.

"He was pouring powder on a fire from an old powder horn and the flames jumped up in the horn and exploded and crippled his hand and burnt his face. Dr. Duel, a right young doctor, said he could cure them if father would pay him fifty dollars a piece. My sister was burnt at the same time as my brother. He had them make a thin dough, and put it over their faces and he cut pieces out for their eyes, and nose, and mouth. They left that dough on their faces and chest till the dough got hard and peeled off by itself. It left the white skin. Gradually the face got back to itself and took its right color again, so you couldn't tell they had ever been burnt. The only medicine the doctor gave them was Epsom salts. Fifty dollars for each child. I used that remedy on a school boy once and cured him, but I didn't charge him nothing.

"I have a program which was given in 1874. They don't give programs like that now. People wouldn't listen that long. We each of us had two and three, and some of us had six and seven parts to learn. We learnt them and recited them and came back the next night to give a Christmas Eve program. You can make a copy of it if you want. [Copy not reprinted here.]

"A. C. Richmond is Mrs. Childress' brother. Anna George is Bee Daniels' mother (Bee Daniels is Mrs. Anthony, a colored public school teacher here). Corinne Jordan is living on Gaines between Eighth and Ninth streets. She is about seventy-five years old now. She was about Mollie's age and I was about five years older than Molly. Mary Riley is C. C. Riley's sister. C. C. Riley is Haven Riley's father. C. C. is dead now. Haven Riley was a teacher, at Philander Smith, for a while. He's a stenographer now. August Jackson and J. W. Jackson are my brothers. W. O. Emory became one of our pastors at Wesley. John Bush, everybody's heard of him. He had the Mosaic temple and got a big fortune together before he died, but his children lost it all. Annie Richmond is Annie Childress, the wife of Professor B. C. Childress, the State Supervisor. Corinne Winfrey turned out to be John Bush's wife. Billie Lane married W. O. Emery. Scipio Jordan became the big man in the Tabernacle. H. H. Gilkey went to the post office. He married Lizzie Bull. She's living still too. . . .

"The Commissary was on the northeast corner of Third and Cumberland. They used to call it the government commissary building. It took up a whole half block. Mrs. Farmer, the white woman, was living in what you call the old Henderliter Place, the building on the northwest corner, during the War. She was a Union woman, and was the one that took us in when the Confederate soldiers were passing and wanted to take us to Texas with them.

"I was so small I didn't know much about things then. When peace was declared a preacher named Hugh Brady, a white man, came here and he had my mother and father to marry over again.

"Mrs. Stephens' father was one of the first school-teachers here for colored people. There were a lot of white people who came here from the North to teach. Peabody School used to be called the Union School. Mrs. Stephens has the first report of the school dated 1869. It gives the names of the directors and all. J. H. Benford was one of the Northern teachers. Anna Ware and Louise Coffman and Miss Henley were teachers too.

"Mrs. Stephens is the oldest colored teacher in Little Rock. The A-B-C children didn't want the old men to teach us. So they would teach 'Lottie'— she was only twelve years old then—and she would hear our lessons. Then at recess time, we would all get out and play together. She was my play mama. Her father, William Wallace Andrews, the first pastor of Wesley chapel M. E. Church, was the head teacher and Mr. Gray was the other. They was teaching in Wesley Chapel Church. It was then on Eighth and Broadway. This was before Benford's time. It was just after peace had been declared. I don't know where Andrews come from, nor how much learning he had. Most of the people then got their learning from white children. But I don't know where he got his.

"Wesley was his first church as far as I know. Before the War all the churches were in with the white people. After freedom, they drew out. Whether Wesley was his first church or not, he was Wesley's first pastor. I got a history of the church.

"They had a real Sunday-school in those days. My sister when she was a child about twelve years old said three hundred Bible verses at one time and received a book as a prize. The book was named 'A Wonderful Deliverance' and other Stories, printed by the American Tract Society, New York, 150 Nassau Street. My sister's name was Mollie Jackson."

Randolph County

Allen, Hannah
Age: 107
Fredericktown, Missouri
Interviewer: J. Tom Miles
[S2:2: 138–42]

Note. Aunt Hannah, to date, is by far the oldest ex-slave that this writer has interviewed. She claims to be 107 years old, having been born on December 24th, 1830. When she made application for a marriage license in Fredericktown in 1912, she gave her age then as 82, according to the Madison County Recorder of Deeds. Since she receives an Old Age Pension further proof is being made to verify her age through the Old Age Assistance Office in Fredericktown.

From talking to some of the better informed persons in Fredericktown, the idea is confirmed; they are agreed the "Aunt" Hannah is probably 107 years old. She is still able to do the work around her house and, at times, walks up town. She can see very well without glasses and is not apparently feeble except for the fact that her feet bother her at times.

In a former report sent in it was stated that "Aunt" Hannah is not all negro. Her grandfather was a white man and she is far from a black person. Her face is comparatively free from wrinkles. Her bearing is splendid and her mind active. Possibly health can be attributed to several causes. She was treated well when young and a slave under the ownership of the Bollingers.

Being childless, she has never had to experience the tortures of childbirth. She has been content to live on the same spot for the last 71 years. And being a negro, she naturally does not take life too seriously but lives it as it comes.

Down in Pocahontas, Arkansas, a man had 400 slaves and the boss would allow an old colored man to have meetings every Saturday night and on Friday night they would have a class meeting. Several of them got religion right out in the field an would kneel down in the cornfield. The boss went home and told his wife he thought the slaves were losin' their minds cause they was all kneeling down in the field. The boss' daughter also got religion and went down to the mourners bench. The colored church finally made the boss and his whole family get religion. The ole white mistress would sing and pray while she washed dishes, milked the cows and made biscuits. So they called the doctor and the doctor come and said that God had got hold of her.

One of the darkies had a baby out in the field about eleven o'clock one morning. The doctor came out there to her. She was sick a long time cause she got too hot before the child was born. After this happened the boss got to be a better man. This old boss at first would not let the darkies have any church meetings.

On Sunday there at home the colored folks could get all the water that ran from the maple trees. The slaves would get through their work for the boss and then there would sometimes be three days when they could work for themselves. Then they would get paid for working for others and then buy clothes. They had the finest boots.

They did not want the mistress to tell me when we were free cause there was only two of us slaves left there. The other slaves had already run off. I did not want to leave. When I was a slave I learned to do a task right or do it over. I learned to sew, cook and spin. We set by the fireside and picked a shoe full of cotton and then we could go to bed. But you did a lot before you got that shoe full of cotton when it was pressed down. This was almost enough to pad a quilt with. The white children would be getting their lessons then and they used a pine torch for a light to see by.

I was paid nothin' after slavery but just stayed with the boss and they gave me things like a calf, clothes, and I got to go to church with them and to camp meetings and picnics. They would have big basket meetings with pies, hogs, sheep etc. They did not allow me to go with other colored girls if they had no character. We all set down and ate at the same table with the white folks and tended the sick together. Today if the parents would make their children do like they did in slavery, then we would have a better race. I was better off than the free people. I think that slavery taught me a lot.

In Fredericktown I worked for my mistress's sister and made $10.00 a month. My father told me to always keep myself clean and nice and to comb my hair. When I lived in Fredericktown the people I worked for always tried to keep me from going out with the low class. After I washed the supper dishes, I would have to go upstairs and cut out quilts and I did not like it but it was good for me.

My first husband gave $50.00 for this lot I am living on. This was just at the end of the war. He hauled the logs and chinked and whitewashed them and we had two rooms and a hall. It was a good, nice, warm house. He was a carpenter. About twenty-five years later my husband built him a frame house here and dug him a well. He had 4 dozen chickens, 15 head of hogs, 2 horses, 2 wagons, and a buggy to go back and forth to church at Libertyville, New Tennessee, or Pilot Knob. We lived together about fifty years before he died. He left me this home, three horses, three milk cows, three hogs.

We had no children but adopted a little boy. He was my husband's sister's child. The boy's mother took a notion that she wanted to work out and she was just a young girl so we took the boy at about the age of three and he was with us for about six years. He went to a colored school then but a white teacher taught him. We adopted a girl too from Marquand. The girl's father was a colored man but the mother was a white woman. The woman then married a white man in Marquand and her husband did not want the child so we took her at about three years old. We did not have her no time 'til she died. We have helped to raise about a dozen children. But I have quit doing that now. Mr. Allen is my second husband; he always liked to have children around but we had none of our own.

When my first husband died he did not owe fifteen cents. He just would not go in debt to nobody. He attended the Masonic lodge. After he died I then went to work. I bought wood, washed, ironed and cooked. I have made as high as $15.00 a week and board. I took care of a man's children after he and his wife separated. We have had two houses burn down right here. One of our houses was a little too close to Saline Creek and it was condemned and we tore it down and built the one we have now thirteen years ago. Harry Newberry has a mill and gave us the lumber to build this house.

We have a lot in the colored graveyard. I have no insurance but Mr. Allen had some kind of insurance, so if he gets hurt travelling he will get something. We are getting together $25.00 in pensions a month. We are living pretty well now. Some months we spend from seven to eight dollars a month on food. Almost everything is cash for us. I've been going barefoot for about ten years. I come very near going barefooted in the winter time. We have been getting a pension for about two years and were on relief for two or three years before that. Every two weeks we would then get five or six dollars worth of food. Our biggest debt is a doctor bill of about $60.00.

Some of the colored folks are better off today and some are worse. The young race says we who was slaves are ten times worse off than they cause we had bosses and couldn't read or write. But I say the young race has got all this to go by and they ought to be much better off than they are. We are better off in one sense than the young race cause about half of them don't know how to raise their children and they don't know how to do nothing. I think our folks have just as good a chance now as the white folks but they don't get cultivated. They say today that I don't know nothing cause I was a slave and all I learned was what the marster told me. But I know enough to keep out of devilment. I think all this speed shows that people ain't got no sense.

Sebastian County

Hart, Laura
Age: 85
Eleventh and Orange Street
Pine Bluff, Arkansas
Interviewer: Bernice Bowden
[M:9: pt. 3: 190–92]

"I just can't tell you when I was born cause I don't know. My mother said I was born on Christmas Eve morning. I'm a old woman. I was big enough to work in slave times.

"Yes ma'am, I member when the war started. I was born in Arkansas. I'm a Arkansas Hoosier. You know I had to have some age on me to work in slave times.

"I pulled corn, picked cotton and drive the mule at the gin. Just walked behind him all day. I've pulled fodder, pulled cotton stalks, chopped down corn stalks. I never worked in the house when I was a child while I was under the jurisdiction of the white folks.

"My old master was Sam Carson and his wife was named Phoebe Carson, boy named Andrew and a daughter named Mary and one named Rosie.

"We had plenty to eat and went to church on Sunday. After the white folks had their services we went in. The church was on his place right across the river. That's where I was when freedom taken place.

"When the war started—I remember that all right—cause when they was gettin' started old master sent a colored man to take his son's place in the war.

"I was born up here at Fort Smith and brought here to Jefferson County and sold—my mother and three chillun.

"Now wait—I'm goin' to give you the full history. My father's mother was a white woman from the North and my father was a colored man. Her folks run her here to Arkansas and she stayed with her brother till my father was nine months old and then she went back North and my papa stayed with his uncle.

"When his uncle died he willed my papa his place. He had it recorded at the cotehouse in Little Rock that my papa was a free man. But he couldn't stay in Arkansas free, so he just rambled till he found old man Carson and my mother. He offered to buy my mother but old master wouldn't sell her so he stayed with old man Carson till they was all free.

"My white folks was tollable fair—they didn't beat up the people.

"My mother was as bright as you are. She could sit on her hair. Her mother was a Creole and her father was a Frenchman. After freedom they would a killed my father if it hadn't been for old Sam Carson, cause they thought my mother was a white woman, she was so bright.

"Ku Klux? The Lord have mercy! I remember them. They came and surrounded the house, hundreds of em. We had a loose plank in the floor and we'd hide under the floor with the dogs and stay there, too, till they'd gone.

"My father was a gambler. He gambled and farmed. My mother was a Christian woman. When I got big enough to know anything, she was a Christian woman.

"I married when I was fourteen. We lived at a place called "Wildcat." Didn't have no school. Nothin' up there but saloons and gambling.

"Then we moved to what they called the Earl Wright place. I had four chillun—three boys and one girl. Most of my work was in the field.

"I been here in Pine Bluff gwine on seventy-one years. You know—I knowed this town when they wasn't but one store and two houses. I'm a old woman—I ain't no baby.

"Honey, I even remember when the Indians was run out o' this town!

"Well, I done told you all I know. In my comin' up, the colored people didn't have time to study bout the chillun's ages."

Sevier County

Miller, Nathan
Age: 76
Madison, Arkansas
Interviewer: Irene Robertson
[M:10: pt. 5: 93–94]

"Lady, I'll tell you what I know but it won't nigh fill your book.

"I was born in 1862 south of Lockesburg, Arkansas. My parents was Marther and Burl Miller.

"They told me their owners come here from North Carolina in 1820. They owned lots of slaves and lots of land. Mother was medium light—about my color. See, I'm mixed. My hair is white. I heard mother say she never worked in the field. Father was a blacksmith on the place. He wasn't a slave. His grandfather willed him free at ten years of age. It was tried in the Supreme Court. They set him free. Said they couldn't break the dead man's will.

"My father was a real bright colored man. It caused some disturbance. Father went back and forth to Kansas. They tried to make him leave if he was a free man. They said I would have to be a slave several years or leave the State. Freedom settled that for me.

"My great grandmother on my mother's side belong to Thomas Jefferson. He was good to her. She used to tell me stories on her lap. She come from Virginia to Tennessee. They all cried to go back to Virginia and their master got mad and sold them. He was a meaner man. Her name was Sarah Jefferson. Mariah was her daughter and Marther was my mother. They was real dark folks but mother was my color, or a shade darker.

"Grandmother said she picked cotton from the seed all day till her fingers nearly bled. That was fore gin day. They said the more hills of tobacco you could cultivate was how much you was worth.

"I don't remember the Ku Klux. They was in my little boy days but they never bothered me.

"All my life I been working hard—steamboat, railroad, farming. Wore clean out now.

"Times is awful hard. I am worn clean out. I am not sick. I'm ashamed to say I can't do a good day's work but I couldn't. I am proud to own I get commodities and $8 from the Relief."

Union County

Ames, Josephine
Age: ?
Fordville, Arkansas
Interviewer: Pernella Anderson
[M:8: pt. 1: 44–45]

Ah wuz bo'n de first year niggers wuz free. Wuz born in Caledonia at de Primm place. Mah ma belonged tuh George Thompson. After mah ma died ah stayed wid de Wommacks, a while. Aftuh dat mah pa taken me home. Pa's name wuz Jesse Flueur. Ah worked lak er slave. Ah cut wood, sawed logs, picked 400 pounds uv cotton evah day. Ah speck ah married de first time ah wuz about fo'teen years ole. Ah been mahried three times. All mah husband's is daid. Ole man England and old man Cullens run business places and ole man Wooley. His name wuz reason Wooley. De Woolies got cemetery uv dey own right dar near de Cobb place. No body is buried in dar but de fambly uv Wooleys. Ole man Allen Hale. He run er store dar too. He is yet livin right dar. He is real ole. De ole Warren Mitchell place whar ah use tuh live is Guvment land. Warren Mitchell, he homesteaded the place. We lived dar and made good crops. De purtiest dar wuz around, but now hit's growed up. Don lived dar and made good crops. De purtiest dar wuz around. Dar is whah all mah chillun wuz bo'n. Ah use tuh take mah baby an walk tuh El Dorado to sevice. Ah use tuh come tuh El Dorado wid a woman by de name of Sue Foster. Nothin but woods when dey laid de railroad heah. Dey built dem widh hosses and axes. Ah saw em when dey whoop de hosses and oxen till dey fall out working dem when dey laid dat steel. Ah wuz at de first burying uv de fust pussen buried in Caledonia graveyard. Huh name wuz Joe Ann Polk. We set up wid huh all night and sing and pray. An when we got nearly tuh de church de bells started tolling and de folks started tuh singin.

When evah any body died dey ring bells tuh let ya know some body wuz daid. Ah wuz born on Christmas day, an ah had two chilluns born on Christmas Day. Dey wuz twins and one uv em had two teeth and his hair hung down on her shoulders when hit wuz born but hit did not live but er week.

Arbery, Katie
Age: 80
815 W. Thirteenth

Pine Bluff, Arkansas
Interviewer: Mrs. Bernice Bowden
[M:8: pt. 1: 64–67]

"I am eighty years old. My name 'fore I was a Arbery was Baxter. My mother was a Baxter. Born in Union County.

"My mother's first people was Baxter and my grandmother was a Baxter and they just went by that name; she never did change her name.

"The boss man—that was what they called our master—his name was Paul McCall. He was married twice. His oldest son was Jim McCall. He was in the War. Yes ma'am, the Civil War.

"Paul McCall raised me up with his chillun and I never did call him master, just called him pappy, and Jim McCall, I called him brother Jim. Just raised us all up there in the yard. My grandmother was the cook.

"There wasn't no fightin' in Union County but I 'member when the Yankees was goin' through and singin'

'The Union forever, hurrah, boys, hurrah
We'll rally 'round the flag, boys,
Shouting the battle cry of freedom.'

(She sang this—ed.)
And I 'member this one good:

'Old buckwheat cakes and good strong butter
To make your lips go flip, flip, flutter,
Look away, look away, look away, Dixie land.'

"Pappy used to play that on his fiddle and have us chillun tryin' to dance. Used to call us chillun and say, 'You little devils, come up here and dance' and have us marchin'.

"My cousin used to be a quill blower. Brother Jim would cut fishin' canes and plat 'em together—they called 'em a pack—five in a row, just like my fingers. Anybody that knowed how could sure make music on 'em. Tom Rollins, that was my baby uncle, he was a banjo picker.

"I can remember a heap a things that happened, but 'bout slavery, I didn't know one day from another. They treated us so nice that when they said freedom come, I thought I was always free.

"I heered my grandmother talk about sellin' 'em, but I was just a little kid and I didn't know what they was talkin' about. I heered 'em say, 'Did you know they sold Aunt Sally away from her baby?' I heered 'em talkin'. I know that much.

"After freedom, our folks stayed right on Paul McCall's place. My grandmother cooked for the McCalls till I was eight or nine years old, then she cooked for the McCrays—they was all relatives—till I was twenty-one. Then I married.

"Paul McCall first married in the Baxter family and then he married into the McCray family. I lived on the McCall place till I was grown. They all come from Alabama. Yes'm, they come befo' the war was.

"Chillun in dem days paid attention. People raised chillun in dem days. Folks just feeds 'em now and lets 'em grow up.

"I looks at the young race now and they is as wise as rabbits.

"I never went to school but three months, but I never will forget that old blue back McGuffey's. Sam Porter was our teacher and I was scared of him. I was so scared I couldn't learn nothin'.

"As far as I can remember I have been treated nice everywhere I been. Ain't none of the white folks ever mistreated me.

"Lord, we had plenty to eat in slavery days—and freedom days too.

"One time when my mother was cookin' for Colonel Morgan and my eldest brother was workin' some land, my mother always sent me over with a bucket of milk for him. So one day she say, 'Snooky, come carry your brother's milk and hurry so he can have it for dinner.' I was goin' across a field; that was a awful deer country. I had on a red dress and was goin' on with my milk when I saw a old buck lookin' at me. All at once he went 'whu-u-u', and then the whole drove come up. There was mosely trees (I think she must have meant mimosa—ed.) in the field and I run and climbed up in one of 'em. A mosely tree grows crooked; I don't care how straight you put it in the ground, it's goin' to grow crooked. So I climb up in the mosely tree and begin to yell. My brother heard me and come 'cause he knowed what was up. He used to say, 'Now, Snipe, when you come 'cross that mosely field, don't you wear that old red dress 'cause they'll get you down and tear that dress off you.' I liked the dress 'cause he had give it to me. I had set the milk down at the foot of the tree and it's a wonder they didn't knock it over, but when my brother heard me yell he come a runnin' with a gun and shot one of the deer. I got some of the venison and he give some to Colonel Morgan, his boss man. Colonel Morgan had fought in the war.

"The reason I can't tell you no more is, since I got old my mind goes this and that a way.

"But I can tell you all the doctors that doctored on me. They give me up to die once. I had the chills from the first of one January to the next. We had Dr. Chester and Dr. McCray and Dr. Lewis—his name was Perry—and Dr. Green and Dr. Smead. Took quinine till I couldn't hear, and finally Dr. Green said,

"'We'll just quit givin' her medicine, looks like she's goin' to die anyway.' And then Dr. Lewis fed me for three weeks steady on okra soup cooked with chicken. Just give me the broth. Then I commenced gettin' better and here I am.

"But I can't work like I used to. When I was young I could work right along with the man but I can't do it now. I wish I could 'cause they's a heap a things I'd like that my chillun and grandchilllun can't get for me.

"Well, good-bye, come back again sometime."

Armstrong, Cora
Age: 75 or 80?
Junction City, Arkansas
Interviewer: Pernella Anderson
[M:8: pt. 1: 75]

"I was born in the Junction city community and belonged to the Cooks. I was ten years old at surrender. Mother and father had 12 children and we lived in a one room log cabin and cooked on a fireplace and oven. Mos and Miss Cook did not allow ma and pa to whip me. When ever I do something and I knew I was going to get a whipping I would make it to old Miss. She would keep me from getting that whipping. I was a devilish boy. I would do everything in the world I could think of just for devilment. Old mos was sure good to his slaves. I never went to school a day in my life. Old Miss would carry me to church sometimes when it was hot so we could fan for her. We used palmeter fan leaves for fans. We ate pretty good in slavery time, but we did not have all of this late stuff. Some of our dishes was possum stew, vegetables, persimmon pie and tato bread. Ma did not allow us to sit around grown folks. When they were talking she always made us get under the bed. Our bed was made from pine poles. We children slept on pallets on the floor. The way slaves married in slavery time they jumped over the broom and when they separated they jumped backward over the broom. Times were better in slavery time to my notion than they are now because they did not go hungry, neither necked. They ate common and wore one kind of clothes."

A duck, a bullfrog and a skunk went to a circus. The duck and the bullfrog got in, why didn't the skunk get in?

(Answer). The duck had a bill, the bullfrog had a greenback, but the skunk had nothing but a scent.

If your father's sister is not your aunt what kin is she to you? (your mother).

What is the difference between a four quart measure and a side saddle?

(Answer). They both hold a gallon. (a gal on)

Benford, Bob
Age: 79
209 N. Maple Street
Pine Bluff, Arkansas
Interviewer: Mrs. Bernice Bowden
[M:8: pt. 1: 146–48]

"Slavery-time folks? Here's one of em. Near as I can get at it, I'se seventy-nine. I was born in Alabama. My white folks said I come from Perry County, Alabama, but I come here to this Arkansas country when I was small.

"My old master was Jim Ad Benford. He was good to us. I'm goin' to tell you we was better off then than now. Yes ma'am, they treated us right. We didn't have to worry bout payin' the doctor and had plenty to eat.

"I recollect the shoemaker come and measured my feet and directly he'd bring me old red russet shoes. I thought they was the prettiest things I ever saw in my life.

"Old mistress would say, 'Come on here, you little niggers' and she'd sprinkle sugar on the meat block and we'd just lick sugar.

"I remember the soldiers good, had on blue suits with brass buttons.

"I'se big enough to ride old master's hoss to water. He'd say, 'Now Bob, don't you run that hoss' but when I got out of sight, I was bound to run that hoss a little.

"I didn't have to work, just stayed in the house with my mammy. She was a seamstress. I'm tellin' you the truth now. I can tell it at night as well as daytime.

"We lived in Union County. Old master had a lot of hands. Old mistress' name was Miss Sallie Benford. She just as good as she could be. She'd come out to the quarters to see how we was gettin' along. I'd be so glad when Christmas come. We'd have hog killin' and I'd get the bladders and blow em up to make noise—you know. Yes, lady, we'd have a time.

"I recollect when Marse Jim broke up and went to Texas. Stayed there bout a year and come back.

"When the war was over I recollect they said we was free but I didn't know what that meant. I was always free.

After freedom mammy stayed there on the place and worked on the shares. I don't know nothin' bout my father. They said he was a white man.

"I remember I was out in the field with mammy and had a old mule. I punched him with a stick and he come back with them hoofs and kicked me right in the jaw—knocked me dead. Lord, lady, I had to eat mush till I don't like mush today. That was old Mose—he was a saddle mule.

"Me? I ain't been to school a day in my life. If I had a chance to go I didn't know it. I had to help mammy work. I recollect one time when she was sick I got into a fight and she cried and said, 'That's the way you does my child' and I know she died next week.

"After that I worked here and there. I remember the first man I worked for was Kinch McKinney of El Dorado.

"I remember when I was just learnin' to plow, old mule knew five hundred times more than I did. He was graduated and he learnt me.

"I made fifty-seven crops in my lifetime. Me and Hance Chapman—he was my witness when I married—we made four bales that year. That was in 1879. His father got two bales and Hance and me got two. I made money every year. Yes ma'am, I have made some money in my day. When I moved from Louisiana to Arkansas I sold one hundred eighty acres of land and three hundred head of hogs. I come up here cause my chillun was here and my wife wanted to come here. You know how people will stroll when they get grown. Lost everything I had. Bought a little farm here and they wouldn't let me raise but two acres of cotton the last year I farmed and I couldn't make my payments with that. Made me plow up some of the prettiest cotton I ever saw and I never got a cent for it.

"Lady, nobody don't know how old people is treated nowdays. But I'm livin' and I thank the Lord. I'm so glad the Lord sent you here, lady. I been once a man and twice a child. You know when you're tellin' the truth, you can tell it all the time.

"Klu Klux? The Lord have mercy! In '74 and '75 saw em but never was bothered by a white man in my life. Never been arrested and never had a lawsuit in my life. I can go down here and talk to these officers any time.

"Yes ma'am, I used to vote. Never had no trouble. I don't know what ticket I voted. We just voted for the man we wanted. Used to have colored men on the grand jury—half and half—and then got down to one and then knocked em all out.

I never done no public work in my life but when you said farmin' you hit me then.

"Nother thing I never done. I bought two counterpins once in my life on the stallments and ain't never bought nothin' since that way. Yes ma'am, I got a bait of that stallment buying. That's been forty years ago.

"I know one time when I was livin' in Louisiana, we had a teacher named

Arvin Nichols. He taught there seventeen years and one time he passed some white ladies and tipped his hat and went on and fore sundown they had him arrested. Some of the white men who knew him went to court and said what had he done, and they cleared him right away. That was in the '80's in Marion, Louisiana, in Union Parish."

Burkes, Norman
Age: 73
2305 West Eleventh Street
Pine Bluff, Arkansas
Interviewer: Bernice Bowden
[M:8: pt. 1: 336–37]

"I didn't quite make slavery. Me and freedom came here together.

"I was born in Union County, Arkansas. My mother was born in Virginia and my father was an Alabamian.

"I've heered 'em say how they done in slavery times. Whupped 'em and worked 'em and didn't feed 'em much. Said they'd average about three pounds of meat a week and a peck of meal, a half gallon o' molasses. That was allowed the hands for a week. No sugar and no coffee. And they'd issue flour on Saturday so they could have Sunday morning biscuits.

"My father was sold to Virginia and he and my mother was married there and they moved with their white people here to Arkansas.

"They called their owner old Master. Yes'm, I can remember him. Many times as he whipped me I ought to remember him. I never will forget that old man. They claimed he was pretty good to 'em. He didn't whup 'em much, I don't think.

"If my mother was livin' she could tell you everything about Virginia. She was one hundred and two when she died. My folks is long livers.

"My oldest brother was sold in Virginia and shipped down into Texas about ten years before I was born and I ain't never seen him.

"They sold wives from their husbands and children from their parents and they couldn't help it. Just like this war business. Come and draft 'em and they couldn't help it.

"I think the way things is now, they're goin to build up another war."

Extra Comment
I was interviewing this man on the front porch and at this point, he got up and went into the house, so the interview was ended as far as he was concerned.

Culp, Zenia
Age: 80+
El Dorado, Arkansas
Interviewer: Mrs. Carol Graham
[M:8: pt. 2: 67–69]

"Yes'm, my name is Zenia, Zenia Culp 'tis now since I married. My old master's name was Billy Newton. Him and three more brothers come here and settled in this county years ago and Master Billy settled this farm. I was born and raised here and ain't never lived nowheres else. I used to be nurse girl and lived up at the big house. You know up there where Mr. John Dunbar's widow lives now. And the family buryin groun' is jus' a little south of the house where you sees them trees and tomb stones out in the middle of the field.

"Master Billy's folks was so good to me and I sure thought a heap of young Master Billy. Believe I told you I was the nurse girl. Well, young Master Billy was my special care. And he was a live one too. I sure had a time keepin' up wid that young rascal. I would get him ready for bed every night. In summer time he went barefoot like all little chaps does and course I would wash his foots before I put him to bed. That little fellow would be so sleepy sometime that he would say: 'Don't wash em, Zenia, jes' wet em.' Oh, he was a sight, young Master Billy was.

"Does you know Miss Pearl? She live there in El Dorado. She is young master's widow. Miss Pearl comes out to see me sometime and we talks lots bout young Master Billy.

"Yas'm, I'se always lived here where I was born. Never moved way from de old plantation. Course things is changed lots since the days when old Master Billy was livin'. When he went off to the war he took most of the men black folks and the womens stayed home to take care of mistress and the chillun.

"My husban' been dead a long, long time and I live here wid my son. His wife is gone from home dis evenin'. So I thought I'd come out and pick off some peanuts jes' to git out in the sunshine awhile. That's my son out there makin' sorghum. My daughter-in-law is so good to me. She treats me like I was a baby.

"You asks me to tell you something bout slave days, and how we done our work then. Well, as I tell you, my job was nurse girl and all I had to do was to keep up wid young Master Billy and that wasn't no work tall, that was just fun. But while I'd be followin' roun' after him I'd see how the others would be doin' things.

"When they gathered sweet potatoes they would dig a pit and line it with straw and put the tatoes in it then cover them with straw and build a coop over it. This would keep the potatoes from rotting. The Irish potatoes they would spread out in the sand under the house and the onions they would han[g] up in the fence to keep them from rotting.

"In old Master Newton's day they didn' have ice boxes and they would put the milk and butter and eggs in buckets and let em down in the well to keep em cool.

"Master's niggers lived in log houses down at de quarters but they was fed out of the big house. I members they had a long table to eat off and kept hit scoured so nice and clean with sand and ashes and they scoured the floors like that too and it made em so purty and white. They made their mops out of shucks. I always eat in the nursery with young Master Billy.

"They had big old fireplaces in Master's house and I never seen a stove till after the war.

"I member bein' down at the quarters one time and one of the women had the sideache and they put poultices on her made out of shucks and hot ashes and that sho'ly did ease the pain.

"The pickaninnies had a time playin'. Seein' these peanuts minds me that they used to bust the ends and put them on their ears for ear rings. Course Master Billy had to try it too, then let out a howl cause they pinched.

"Lan', but them was good old days when Master Billy was alive."

Johnson, Millie
Age: ?
El Dorado, Arkansas
Interviewer: Pernella M. Anderson
[M:9: pt. 4: 124–25]

"I was born in Caledonia, Arkansas, but I don't know when. I just can't tell you nothing hardly about when I was a child because my mind goes and comes. I was a slave and my white folks were good to me. They let me play and have a good time just like their children did.

"After I got grown I run around terrible. My husband quit me a long time ago. The white folks let me have my way. They said I was mean and if my husband fooled with me, told me to shoot him. I am going back home to Caledonia when I get a chance. My sister's boy brought me up here; Mack Ford is his name.

"A long time ago—I don't know how long it's been—I came out of the back door something hung their teeth in my ankle. I hollered and looked down and it was a big old rattlesnake. I cried to my sister to get him off of me. She was scared, so all I knew to do was run, jump and holler. I ran about—oh, I don't know how far—with the snake hanging to my ankle. The snake would not let me go, and it wasn't but one thing for me to do and that was stop and pull the snake off of me. I stopped and began pulling. I pulled and pulled and pulled and pulled. The snake would not let me go. I began pulling again. After awhile I got it off. When I pulled the snake away the snake brought his mouth full of my meat. You talk about hurting, that like to have killed me. That place stayed sore for twenty years before it healed up. After it had been healed a couple years I then scratched the place on a bob wire that inflamed it. That has been about 25 or 30 years ago and it's been sore ever since. Lord, I sure have been suffering too. As soon as it gets well I am going back to Caledonia. I am praying for God to let me live to get back home. Mack Ford is the cause of me being up here.

"I was born in slavery time way before the War. My name is Millie Johnson but they call me Bill."

Norris, Charlie
Age: 81
122 Miller Street
Pine Bluff, Arkansas
Interviewer: Mrs. Bernice Bowden
[M:10: pt. 5: 219–20]

"Born in slavery times? That's me, I reckon. I was born October 1, 1857 in Arkansas in Union County. Tom Murphy was old master's name.

"Yes ma'am, I remember the first regiment left Arkansas—went to Virginia. I member our white folks had us packin' grub out in the woods cause they was spectin' the Yankees.

"I member when the first regiments started out. The music boat come to the landin' and played 'Yankee Doodle.' They carried all us chillun out there.

"After they fit they just come by from daylight till dark to eat. They was death on bread. My mother and Susan Murphy, that was the old lady herself, cooked bread for me.

"I stayed with the Murphys—round on the plantation amongst em for five or six years after freedom. Andrew Norris, my father's old master, was the first sheriff of Ouachita County.

"My mother belonged to the Murphys and my father belonged to the Norrises and after freedom they never did go back together.

"My mother told me that Susan Murphy would suckle me when my mother was out workin' and then my mother would suckle her daughter.

"I was raised up in the house you might say till I was a big nigger. Had plenty to eat. That's one thing they did do. I lived right amongst a settlement of what they called free niggers cause they was treated so well.

"Sometimes Susan Murphy got after me and whipped me and old Marse Tom would tell me to run and not let her whip me. You see, I was worth $1,500 to him and he thought a lot of us black kids.

"Old man Tom Murphy raised me up to a big nigger and never did whip me but twice and that was cause I got drunk on tobacco and turned out his horse.

"Yes ma'am, I voted till bout two or three years ago. Oh Lawd, the colored used to hold office down in the country. I've voted for white and black.

"Some of the colored folks better off free and some not. That's what *I* think but they don't."

Page, Annie
Age: 86
412 ½ Pullen Street
Pine Bluff, Arkansas
Interviewer: Mrs. Bernice Bowden
[M:10: pt. 5: 234–39]

"I was born in 1852, they tell me, on the fifteenth of March. I was workin' a good while 'fore surrender.

"Bill Jimmerson was my old master. He was a captain in Marmaduke's army. Come home on thirty days furlough once and he and Daniel Cammack got into some kind of a argument 'bout some whisky and Daniel Cammack stabbed him with a penknife. Stabbed him three times. He was black as tar when they brought him home. The blood had done settled. Oh Lawd, that was a time.

"My eyes been goin' blind 'bout six years till I got so I can't excern (discern) anything.

"Old miss used to box me over the head mightily and the colored folks used to hit me over the head till seem like I could hear a bell for two or three days. Niggers ain't got no sense. Put 'em in authority and they gits so uppity.

"My brother brought me here and left me here with a colored woman named Rachael Rose. And oh Lawd, she was hard on me. Never had to do in slavery times what I had to do then.

"But the devil got her and all her chillun now I reckon. They tell me when death struck her, they asked if the Lawd called her, and they say she just turned over and over in the bed like a worm in hot ashes.

"Yes'm I 'member the war. I never knowed why they called it the Civil War though.

"I was born in Union County, Arkansas, 'bout a mile from Bear Creek, in 1852. That's what my old mistress tole me the morning we was sot free.

"My mistress was a Democrat. Old master was a captain in Marmaduke's army.

"I used to hope (help) spin the thread to make the soldiers' clothes. Old mistress card(ed) for me. Lucy Jimmerson—she the onliest mistress I ever had. She wanted to send us away to Texas but old master say it want no use. Cause if the Yankees won, they have to bring us back, so we didn't go.

"Did they *whip* us? Why I bet I can show you scars now. Old Miss whip me when she feel like fightin'. Her granddaughter, Mary Jane, tried to learn me my ABC's out of the old Blue Back Speller. We'd be out on the seesaw, but old Miss didn't know what we doin'. Law, she pull our hair. Directly she see us and say 'What you doin'? Bring that book here!'

"One day old master come home on a thirty-day furlough. He was awful hot-headed and he got into a argument with Daniel Cammack and old Daniel stobbed him right in the heart. Fore he die he say to bury him by the side of the road so he can see the niggers goin' to work.

"I never seen no Ku Klux but I heard of 'em 'rectly after the war.

"I'se blind. I jest can see enough to get around. The Welfare gives me eight dollars a month.

"My mother died soon after the war ended and after that I was jest knocked over the head. I went to Camblin and worked for Mrs. Peters. Then I runned away and married my first husband Mike Samson. I been married twice and had two children but they all dead now.

"Law, I jest scared of these young ones as I can be. I don't have no dealins with 'em."

Apparitions

"I told 'bout old master's death. Mama had done sent me out to feed the chickens soon of a morning.

"Here was the smokehouse and there was a turkey in a coop. And when I throwed it the feed I heard somethin' sounded just like you was draggin' a brush over leaves. It come around the corner of the smokehouse and look like a tall woman. It kept on goin' toward the house till it got to the hickory nut tree and still sound like draggin' a brush. When it got to the hickory nut tree it changed and look like a man. I looked and I said, 'It's old master.' And the next day he got killed. I run to the house and told mama, 'Look at that man.' She said, 'Shut your mouth, you don't see no man.' Old miss heard and said, 'Who do you s'pose it could be?' But mama wouldn't let me talk.

"But I know it was a sign that old master was goin' to die."

Superstitions

"I was born with a caul over my face. Old miss said it hung from the top of my head half way to my waist.

"She kept it and when I got big enough she said, 'Now that's your veil, you play with it.'

"But I lost it out in the orchard one day.

"They said it would keep you from seein' ha'nts."

Birthmarks

"William Jimmerson's wife had a daughter was born blind, and she said it was her husband's fault. She was delicate, you know, and one afternoon she was layin' down and I was sittin' there fannin' her with a peafowl fan. Her husband was layin' there too and I guess I must a nodded and let the fan drop down in his face. He jumped up and pressed his thumbs on my eyes till they was all bloodshot and when he let loose I fell down on the floor. Miss Phenie said, 'Oh, William, don't do that.' I can remember it just as well.

"My eyes like to went out and do you know, when her baby was born it was blind. It's eyes just looked like two balls of blood. It died though, just lived 'bout two weeks."

Sims, Fannie
Age: 78
El Dorado, Arkansas
Interviewers: Mrs. Carol Graham, Mrs. Mildred Thompson
[M:10: pt. 6: 159]

"How ole is ah? Ise about 78. Yes'm ah wuz live durin de wah. Mah old moster wuz Mistuh Jake Dumas we lived near de Ouachita rivuh bout five miles fum El Dorado landin. Ah membuhs dat we washed at de spring way, way frum de house. What dat yo say? Does ah know Ca'line. Ca'line, lawsy, me yes. Ca'line Washington we use tuh call huh, she wuz one uv Mr. Dumas niggers. We washed fuh de soldiers. Had tuh carry dey clo'es tuh dem aftuh dark. Me an Ca'line had tuh carry dem. We had tuh hide de horse tuh keep de soldiers fum gittin him. When we would take de horse tuh de plum orchard we would stay dah all day to dark wid "Blackie." Dat wuz de horse's name. Mah job mostly wuz tuh watch de chillun an feed mah mistress chickens.

Ah kin recollect when dey took us an started tuh Texas an got as fuh as El Dorado and found out dat us niggers wuz free. We went back and grandma's mistress's son took us home wid him fuh stretches and stretches. We lived on de ole Camden road.

In mah days ah've done plenty uv work but ah don' do nothing now but piece quilts. Dat's whut ah've been doing fuh mah white fokes since ah been heah. Ah jes finished piecing and quiltin two uv em. De Glove and de Begger. Mah husban' been dead 31 years dis pas' August. How ah counts is by dese twins ah raised. One uv em lives in dis heah place right heah. Ah aint much count now. Sometime mah laig gets so big ah jes had tuh sloop mah foot erlong."

Smith, Caroline
Age: ?
Route 1
El Dorado, Arkansas
Interviewer: Carol W. Graham
[M:10: pt. 6: 176–79]

"I first remembers living on the plantation of Mr. Jake Dumas near El Dorado Landing. You know it's Calion now. We lived up towards Camden and it was there that my ma and pa was married and buried. I was a big girl durin' the war. My job was to card and spin. And use to carry the children to school. When I would get to the school I would put the children off, git straddle and ride that horse home. When I would get there old mos would say Ca'line did you run him? I'd say naw sir. Then he'd say, 'Oh, Carryline put the horse in the lot and come out here. I'd say, 'Master I didn't run that horse' but didn't do no good. He sure would whip me. I'd get down and roll. I would stomp and he would do the same. I wondered how he could tell I'd run that horse. But course he could cause that horse had the thumps (heart beating rapidly).

"I remember seeing the soldiers come through during the war. They come by droves stealing horses, setting the cotton on fire and taking sumpin to eat, too.

"Yes, I does still member the songs we sung durin' the war but I've got the asthmy and ain't got much wind fur singin'.

"You want to know the reason,
You want to know the reason,

You want to know the reason, I'll tell you why,
We'll whip them Yankees, whole hog or die."

"Hooray, Hooray, Hooray for the Southern Girl.
Hooray for the homespun dress the Southern ladies wear.
My homespun dress is plain I know,
I glory in its name;
Hooray fo the homespun dress the Southern ladies wear."

"I've got the asthmy honey and jest caint sing no more.

"You asked 'bout my husband and chillun. I been married fo' times. My first man's name was Dick Hagler, the next Frank Bibby, the next Henry Harris and the last one was Tom Smith. That's where I get my name Ca'line Smith. I never did have but one daughter but she had sixteen chillun. She's daid now and mah granchillun is scattered.

"I got the asthmy and jes don' feel like talkin' no more. Long time ago when I was sick master always had a doctor to me now I have to hire one. And they always fed me good and clothed me but after I was free I would go round and work around to git a little sumpin to eat."

Tatum, Fannie
Age: 76
Junction City, Arkansas
Interviewer: Pernella M. Anderson
[M:10: pt. 6: 257–58]

"I was born on Wilmington Landing in 1862 on the Ouachita River and was carried away when I was two years old. My mother ran away and left my sister and me when we was three and five years old. I never saw her any more till I was eight and after I was eight years old I never saw her again in forty years. After my mama left me old Master Neal come here to El Dorado and had me bound to him until I was twenty-one. I stayed there till I was twenty-one. I slept by the jamb of the fireplace on a sack of straw and covered with saddle blankets. That was in the winter and snow was waist high. In summer I slept on naked floor and anywhere I laid down was my bed just like a dog.

"I wasn't allowed to eat at the table. I et on the edge of the porch with the dogs with my fingers. I worked around the house and washed until I was nine and then I started to plowing. At ten I started splitting rails. My task was two hundred rails a day. If I didn't cut them I got a beating. I did not know what a coat was. I wore two pieces, a lowel underskirt and a lowel dress, bachelor brogans and sacks and rags wrapped around my legs for stockings. That was in winter. Summer I went barefooted and wore one piece. My sun hat was a rag tied on my head.

"I did not know anything about Sunday School nor church. The children would try to teach me my ABC's but master would not let them. Never visited any colored people. If I see a colored person coming I run from them. They said they might steal me. After I got grown they let me go to a colored party and they whipped me for going. Tried to make me tell whether or not a boy come home with me but I did not tell it; one come with me though. That was the first time I got out. Of course they sent one of the boys along with me but he would not tell on me.

"I never slept in a bed until I was twenty-two years old. Never was with any colored people until I was grown. My play was with white children. My father was a white man. He was my ma's old master and they was Neals. They kept my hair cut off like a boy's all the time. I never wore a stocking until I was twenty-two and my hair did not grow out and get combed until I was twenty-two. My old master and mistress would have been mean to me but I was so smart they did not get a chance. The only thing I was treated like a dog.

"I live in Junction City but am here visiting my daughter."

Thomas, Mandy
Age: 78
13th and Pearl Streets
Pine Bluff, Arkansas
Interviewer: Mrs. Bernice Bowden
[M:10: pt. 6: 296]

"I know my sister told me I was five when my mama was freed. I was born down below El Dorado. Andrew Jaggers was my mother's old master.

"I just remember the soldiers goin' past. I think they was Yankees. They never stopped as I knows of.

"I've seed my young missis whip my mother.

"My papa belonged to the Agees. After I got up good sized, they told me 'bout my papa. He went with his white folks to Texas and we never did see him after we got up good size. So mama took a drove of us and went to work for some more white folks.

"I was good and grown when I married and I been workin' hard ever since. I was out pickin' huckleberries trying to get some money to buy baby clothes when my first girl was born. Yes ma'am."

Williams, Charley
Age: 80
El Dorado, Arkansas
Interviewer: Mrs. Carol Graham
[M:11: pt. 7: 150–51]

Mawnin' Missy. Yo say wha Aint Fanny Whoolah live? She live right down de road dar in dat fust house. Yas'm. Dat wha she live. Yo say whut mah name? Mah name is Charley. Yas'm, Charley Williams. Did ah live in slavery time? Yas'm sho' did. Mah marster wuz Dr. Reed Williams and he live at New London (SE part of Union County) or ah speck ah bettuh say near New London caise he live on de Mere-Saline Road, de way de soldiers went and come. Marster died befo' de Civil Wah. Does ah membah hit? Yas'm ah say ah does. Ah wuz bo'n in 1856. Mah old mutha died befo' de wah too. Huh name wuz Charity. Mah young marster went tuh de wah an come back. He fit at Vicksburg an his name wuz Bennie Williams. But he daid now tho. Dere was a hep uv dem white William Chillun. Dere wuz Miss Narcissi an she am a livin now at Stong. Den dere's Mr. Charley. Ah wuz named fuh him. He am a livin now too. Den dere is Mr. Raco Williams. He am a livin at Strong too. Dere wuz Miss Annie, Miss Martha Jane and Miss Madie. Dey is all daid. When young marster would come by home or any uv de udder soldiers us little niggers would steal de many balls (bullets or shot) fum dey saddul bags and play wid em. Ah nevah did see so many soldiers in mah life. Hit looked tuh me like dey wuz enough uv em to reach clear cross de United States. An ah nevah saw de like uv cows as they dad. Dey wuz nuff uv em to rech clar to Camden.

Is ah evah been mahried and does ah have any chillun? Yes'm. Yas'm. Ah's been mahried three times. Me an mah fust wife had seven chillun. When we had six chillun me an mah wife moved tuh Kansas. We had only been der 23 days when mah wife birthed a chile and her an de chile both died. Dat left me wid Carey Dee, Lizzie, Arthur, Richmond, Ollie and Lillie to bring back home. Ah mahried agin an me an dat wife had one chile name Robert. Me an mah third wife has three: Joe Verna, Lula Mae an Johnnie B.

Is dey hents? Ah've hearn tell uv em but nevah have seed no hants. One uv mah friens whut lived on the Hammonds place at Hillsboro could see em. His name wuz Elliott. One time me an Elliott wuz drivin along an Elliott said: "Charley, somebody got hole uv mah horse." Sho nuff dat horse led right off inter de woods an comminced to buckin so Elliott and his hoss both saw de haint but ah couldn' see hit. Yo know some people jes caint see em.

Yas'm right up dere is wha Aint Fannie live. Yas'm. Goodday Missy.

Williams, Columbus
Age: 98
Box 12, Route 2
Stevens, Arkansas
Interviewer: Samuel S. Taylor
[M:11: pt. 7: 154–58]

"I was born in Union County, Arkansas, in 1841, in Mount Holly.

"My mother was named Clora Tookes. My father's name is Jordan Tookes. Bishop Tookes is supposed to be a distant relative of ours. I don't know my mother and father's folks. My mother and father were both born in Georgia. They had eight children. All of them are dead now but me. I am the only one left.

"Old Ben Heard was my master. He come from Mississippi, and brought my mother and father with him. They were in Mississippi as well as in Georgia, but they were born in Georgia. Ben Heard was a right mean man. They was all mean 'long about then. Heard whipped his slaves a lot. Sometimes he would say they wouldn't obey. Sometimes he would say they sassed him. Sometimes he would say they wouldn't work. He would tie them and stake them out and whip them with a leather whip of some kind. He would put five hundred licks on them before he would quit. He would buy the whip he whipped them with out of the store. After he whipped them, they would put their rags on and go on about their business. There wouldn't be no such thing as medical attention. What did he care. He would whip the women the same as he would the men.

"Strip 'em to their waist and let their rags hang down from their hips and tie them down and lash them till the blood ran all down over their clothes. Yes sir, he'd whip the women the same as he would the men.

"Some of the slaves ran away, but they would catch them and bring them back, you know. Put the dogs after them. The dogs would just run them up and bay them just like a coon or 'possum. Sometimes the white people would make the dogs bite them. You see, when the dogs would run up on them, they would sometimes fight them, till the white people got there and then the white folks would make the dogs bite them and make them quit fighting the dogs.

"One man run off and stayed twelve months once. He come back then, and they didn't do nothin' to him. 'Fraid he'd run off again, I guess.

"We didn't have no church nor nothing. No Sunday-schools, no nothin'. Worked from Monday morning till Saturday night. On Sunday we didn't do nothin' but set right down there on that big plantation. Couldn't go nowhere. Wouldn't let us go nowhere without a pass. They had the paterollers out all the time. If they caught you out without a pass, they would give you twenty-five licks. If you outrun them and got home, on your master's plantation, you saved yourself the whipping.

"The black people never had no amusement. They would have an old fiddle—something like that. That was all the music I ever seen. Sometimes they would ring up and play 'round in the yard. I don't remember the games. Sing some kind of old reel song. I don't hardly remember the words of any of them songs.

"Wouldn't allow none of them to have no books nor read nor nothin'. Nothin' like that. They had corn huskin's in Mississippi and Georgia, but not in Arkansas. Didn't have no quiltin's. Women might quilt some at night. Didn't have nothin' to make no quilts out of.

"The very first work I did was to nurse babies. After that when I got a little bigger they carried me to the field—choppin' cotton. Then I went to picking cotton. Next thing—pullin' fodder. Then they took me from that and put me to plowin', clearin' land, splittin' rails. I believe that is about all I did. You worked from the time you could see till the time you couldn't see. You worked from before sunrise till after dark. When that horn blows, you better git out of that house, 'cause the overseer is comin' down the line, and he ain't comin' with nothin' in his hand.

"They weighed the rations out to the slaves. They would give you so many pounds of meat to each working person in the family. The children didn't count; they didn't git none. That would have to last till next Sunday. They would give them three pounds of meat to each workin' person, I think. They would give 'em a little meal too. That is all they'd give 'em. The slaves had to cook for theirselves after they come home from the field. They didn't get no flour nor no sugar nor no coffee, nothin' like that.

"They would give the babies a little milk and corn bread or a little molasses and bread when they didn't have the milk. Some old person who didn't have to go to the field would give them somethin' to eat so that they would be out of the way when the folks come out of the field.

"The slave lived in old log houses—one room, one door, one window, one everything. There were plenty windows though. There were windows all around the house. They had cracks that let in more air than the windows would. They had plank floors. Didn't have no furniture. The bed would have two legs and would have a hole bored in the side of the house where the side rail would run through and the two legs would be out from the wall. Didn't have no springs and they made out with anything they could git for a mattress. Master wouldn't furnish them nothin' of that kind.

"The jayhawkers were white folks. They didn't bother we all much. That was after the surrender. They go 'round here and there and git after white folks what they thought had some money and jerk them 'round. They were jus' common men and soldiers.

"I was not in the army in the War. I was right down here in Union County then. I don't know just when they freed me but it was after the War was over. The old white man call us up to the house and told us now we was free as he was; that if we wanted to stay with him it was all right, if we didn't and wanted to go away anywheres, we could have the privilege to do it.

"Marriage wasn't like now. You would court a woman and jus' go on and marry. No license, no nothing. Sometimes you would take up with a woman and go on with her. Didn't have no ceremony at all. I have heard of them stepping over a broom but I never saw it. Far as I saw there was no ceremony at all.

"When the slaves were freed they expected to get forty acres and a mule. I never did hear of anybody gettin' it.

"Right after the War, I worked on a farm with Ben Heard. I stayed with him about three years, then I moved off with some other white folks. I worked on shares. First I worked for half and he furnished a team. Then I worked on third and fourth and furnished my own team. I gave the owner a third of the corn and a fourth of the cotton and kept the rest. I kept that up several years. They cheated us out of our part. If they furnished anything, they would sure git it back. Had everything so high you know. I have farmed all my life. Farmed till I got so old I couldn't. I never did own my own farm. I just continued to rent.

"I never had any trouble about voting. I voted whenever I wanted to. I reckon it was bout three years after the War when I began to vote.

"I never went to school. One of the white boys slipped and learned me a little about readin' in slave time. Right after freedom come, I was a grown man; so I had to work. I married about four or five years after the War. I was just married once. My wife is not living now. She's gone. She's been dead for about twelve years.

"I belong to the A. M. E. Church and my membership is in the New Home Church out in the country in Ouachita County."

Washington County

[Blakely?] Aunt Adeline
Age: 89
101 Rock Street
Fayetteville, Arkansas
Interviewer: Mrs. Zillah Cross Peel
[M:8: pt. 1: 11–16]

"I was born a slave about 1848, in Hickmon County, Tennessee," said Aunt Adeline, who lives as care taker in a house at 101 Rock Street, Fayetteville, Arkansas, which is owned by the Blakely-Hudgens estate.

Aunt Adeline has been a slave and a servant in five generations of the Parks family. Her mother, Liza, with a group of five Negroes, was sold into slavery to John P. A. Parks, in Tennessee, about 1840.

"When my mother's master came to Arkansas about 1849, looking for a country residence, he bought what was known as the old Kidd place on the Old Wire Road, which was one of the Stage Coach stops. I was about one year old when we came. We had a big house and many times passengers would stay several days and wait for the next stage to come by. It was then that I earned my first money. I must have been about six or seven years old. One of Mr. Parks' daughters was about one and a half years older than I was. We had a play house back of the fireplace chimney. We didn't have many toys; maybe a doll made of a corn cob, with a dress made from scraps and a head made from a roll of scraps. We were playing church. Miss Fannie was the preacher and I was the audience. We were singing "Jesus my all to Heaven is gone." When we were half way through with our song we discovered that the passengers from the stage coach had stopped to listen. We were so frightened at our audience that we both ran. But we were coaxed to come back for a dime and sing our song over. I remember that Miss Fannie used a big leaf for a book.

"I had always been told from the time I was a small child that I was a Negro of African stock. That it was no disgrace to be a Negro and had it not been for the white folks who brought us over here from Africa as slaves, we would never have been here and would have been much better off.

"We colored folks were not allowed to be taught to read or write. It was against the law. My masters's folks always treated me well. I had good clothes.

Sometimes I was whipped for things I should not have done just as the white children were.

"When a young girl was married her parents would always give her a slave. I was given by my master to his daughter, Miss Elizabeth, who married Mr. Blakely. I was just five years old. She moved into a new home at Fayetteville and I was taken along but she soon sent me back home to my master telling him that I was too little and not enough help to her. So I went back to the Parks home and stayed until I was over seven years old. My master made a bill of sale for me to his daughter, in order to keep account of all settlements, so when he died and the estate settled each child would know how he stood. [This statement can be verified by the will made by John P. A. Parks, and filed in Probate Court in the clerk's office in Washington County.]

"I was about 15 years old when the Civil War ended and was still living with Mrs. Blakely and helped care for her little children. Her daughter, Miss Lenora, later married H. M. Hudgens, and I then went to live with her and cared for her children. When her daughter Miss Helen married Professor Wiggins, I took care of her little daughter, and this made five generations that I have cared for.

"During the Civil War, Mr. Parks took all his slaves and all of his fine stock, horses and cattle and went South to Louisiana following the Southern army for protection. Many slave owners left the county taking with them their slaves and followed the army.

"When the war was over, Mr. Parks was still in the South and gave to each one of his slaves who did not want to come back to Arkansas so much money. My uncle George came back with Mr. Parks and was given a good mountain farm of forty acres, which he put in cultivation and one of my uncle's descendents still lives on the place. My mother did not return to Arkansas but went on to Joplin, Missouri, and for more than fifty years, neither one of us knew where the other one was until one day a man from Fayetteville went into a restaurant in Joplin and ordered his breakfast, and my mother who was in there heard him say he lived in Fayetteville, Arkansas. He lived just below the Hudgens home and when my mother enquired about the family he told her I was still alive and was with the family. While neither of us could read nor write we corresponded through different people. But I never saw her after I was eleven years old. Later Mr. Hudgens went to Joplin to see if she was well taken care of. She owned her own little place and when she died there was enough money for her to be buried.

"Civil War days are vivid to me. The Courthouse which was then in the middle of the Square was burned one night by a crazy Confederate soldier. The old men in the town saved him and then put him in the county jail to keep him from burning other houses. Each family was to take food to him and they furnished bedding. The morning I was to take his breakfast, he had ripped open his feather bed and crawled inside to get warm. The room was so full of feathers when I got there that his food nearly choked him. I had carried him ham, hot biscuits and a pot of coffee.

"After the War many soldiers came to my mistress, Mrs. Blakely, trying to make her free me. I told them I was free but I did not want to go anywhere, that I wanted to stay in the only home that I had ever known. In a way that placed me in a wrong attitude. I was pointed out as different. Sometimes I was threatened for not leaving but I stayed on.

"I had always been well treated by my master's folks. While we lived at the old Kidd place, there was a church a few miles from our home. My uncle George was coachman and drove my master's family in great splendor in a fine barouche to church. After the war, when he went to his own place, Mr. Parks gave him the old carriage and bought a new one for the family.

"I can remember the days of slavery as happy ones. We always had an abundance of food. Old Aunt Martha cooked and there was always plenty prepared for all the white folks as well as the colored folks. There was a long table at the end of the big kitchen for the colored folks. The vegetables were all prepared of an evening by Aunt Martha with someone to help her.

"My mother seemed to have a gift of telling fortunes. She had a brass ring about the size of a dollar with a handwoven knotted string that she used. I remember that she told many of the young people in the neighborhood many strange things. They would come to her with their premonitions.

"Yes, we were afraid of the patyroles. All colored folks were. They said that any Negroes that were caught away from their master's premises without a permit would be whipped by the patyroles. They used to sing a song:

> 'Run nigger run,
> The patyroles
> Will get you.'

"Yes'm, the War separated lots of families. Mrs. Parks' son, John C. Parks, enlisted in Colonel W. H. Brooks' regiment at Fayetteville as third lieutenant. Mr. Jim Parks was killed at the Battle of Getysburg.

"I do remember it was my mistress, Mrs. Blakely, who kept the Masonic Building from being burned. The soldiers came to set it on fire. Mrs. Blakely knew that if it burned, our home would burn as it was just across the street. Mrs. Blakely had two small children who were very ill in upstairs rooms. She told the soldiers if they burned the Masonic Building that her house would burn and she would be unable to save her little children. They went away."

While Aunt Adeline is nearing ninety, she is still active, goes shopping and also tends to the many crepe myrtle bushes as well as many other flowers at the Hudgens place.

She attends to the renting of the apartment house, as caretaker, and is taken care of by members of the Blakely-Hudgens families.

Aunt Adeline talks "white folks language," as they say, and seldom associates with the colored people of the town.

Bean, Joe
Age: 89
Hulbert, Oklahoma
[S1:12: 46–51]

During the time they come to fighting in the Civil War I was about twelve year old; that make me about 89 year old now, and the year about 1849, when I was born on the Dick Bean plantation over at Lincoln, Arkansas, about 20-mile southwest of Fayetteville.

My father was name Joe Bean; mother was name Cosby Bean and when she died about 15-year back she was 112 year old. She was a Cherokee Indian slave; come here from Georgia when the Indians did, but I don't know her master's name, I mean the Indian master. Some time old Master Bean buy her, that's all I know about it.

Our old slave family was a big one, most of them is now dead, but I remember the names, all except two of the little children who died early, having no names. There was Anderson, Mary, Sarah, Cinda, Martha, Rochelle, and Christie; some of the girls still living.

The master was Dick Bean, the mistress was Nancy Bean; they both dead now, the master going first someday before the war closed, while his young son, Dick the Second, was fighting for the South. He come through the war safe enough and live to raise his own son, Dick the Third (I always calls him), who lets me live in this one-room log cabin on his farm, God Bless his soul!

The old master's house in Arkansas was a big six-room, two-story place of pine planks, with a porch all around the house. Not far from the big house was a rock building used for the looms; in there they made cloth and thread, and they make it for anybody what come there with cotton or wool. I helped throw the thread in the loom, and I get the dye stuff the walnut bark for black, the post oak bark that mix in with the copperas for yellow, the log-wood mix in with alum for the red-brown colors.

I remember the old slave cabins, all just alike, setting in a row, with a box-elder tree growing in the middle of the yard. The cabins was only one room, without windows, facing the south, with a fireplace in one end. Six of them cabins fill up the yard, near as I get to it now.

The flooring was rough plank, except around the fireplace where the stones reach out, and where we eat from the wooden dishes on the floor. Lots of good eats for the old master didn't hide out the vegetables and the meats, they always handy in the smokehouse and wide open for the slaves when they needs it. The beds was made of posts put together with wooden pegs, corded rope for the springs covered with cowhide first and then a homespun tick filled with grass straw. Cover that with a homespun quilt and you got the bed.

During the slave times Master Bean had two horses, a bay trotter and a brown single-footer, mighty fine travelers them riding horses. We ride on the squirrel hunts, me on the bay, master close behind on the brown, waiting for me to sight up a squirrel. Them was the best days of all.

But them days go when the fighting starts and when we starts to moving around. The first move was to Dardenelle (Arkansas), away over from Fort Smith close by the Arkansas River, on a place where lived the old master's married daughter, Eliza. That's where master died.

He stayed shut up in the house a long time 'fore he died. That worry me thought maybe he already dead. Worry me, too, because I always use to put on the master's shoes and tie 'em for him, and bring drinks of spring water to cool him after a long ride, and then I figures to find out is he living or not.

They won't let nobody in the room, just break me up because I was near crazy to be with him when he's sick and need me. So I go around the house and rolls me up a barrel to the window of his room, and there he was laying on the bed by the window and I knock on the glass so he'll turn and see me.

'Joe, Joe, come here!' I hear him like it was yesterday. 'Take a bucket to the spring and get Master Dick a fresh drink.'

They let me take the water to him, and I recollect that was about the last thing I get to do for good old Master Bean.

When he first get sick he was worried about the Federals coming and taking his money. He had gold and silver around the house, heaps of it. He stack it on the floor in long rows to count it before he sack it up getting ready to hide it from the soldiers or the stealing bands that rove around the country.

The money was buried by the master and an old slave man who was the most trusted one on the place. Folks heard about the money being buried and after master died some white man get hold of the old slave and try to make it tell where it was buried. The man heated an old ax and burn the old slave's feet, but he never told. Not until young Master Dick come back from the war.

Young master was full of grieving when he find his daddy dead and the money gone. The old slave ask him, "What you sorry so for, Master Dick?"

Master Dick just set there on the porch, face buried in his hands. 'Everything lost in the war,' the young master groaned. 'My daddy is gone, the money is all gone, don't know what me and mama will do.'

'Hush! Young Master Dick, I show where is the money hid. I show you that, but I can't bring back your old daddy; I can't bring back the old master.'

After freedom some of the slaves kept on with old mistress and young Dick, working for good wages.

Right after the war I come to Fort Gibson. Camped in a tent-house made of elm bark. A Creek Indian drifter moved out and we moved in. Lived about one-half mile from the garrison. Been around here ever since. Once I lived in Jesse James' cave at McBride Switch they calls it nowadays; another time I live on a patch of ground where folks say "Cherokee Bill" (Crawford Goldsby, hanged in 1896, by order of Judge Parker's court at Fort Smith), had a battle with officers on Fourteen-Mile Creek.

When I get to thinking about slave days always I remember of the slaves that run away. Master Bean had a white overseer, but he didn't allow for no whippings, 'cept maybe he cuff a young one around if he done something real mean or maybe sometimes he sell one for the same reason. Whippings, like some of them rich owners did, No! The old master's hide get all turned around if somebody hit a Negro. He'd let nobody chunk 'em around.

But the ones that run away, well, they get the dogs after 'em. Blood hounds they call 'em, and if a slave be gone two days say, the dogs was used to track, and the masters would say, 'If we don't catch them on this farm catch 'em on the next!'

One time I saw a slave whipped on another plantation. He was a new slave, what I mean, they had just bought him and the overseeer said the whipping was 'just to break him in!' First they beat him with a whip, then with a strap, after tieing him to a log. Peeled off his shirt and laid on with the whip, and then pour salt and pepper water over him so's his back would sting and burn.

I see them use blood-hounds a long time after the war. That's when the store safe was robbed at Melvin (Oklahoma), not far from where I live. Went to town when I heard about it, and they brought the dogs in to trail the robber. Them blood hounds look like fat cur dogs to me, but they starts out trailing and pretty quick they's barking and howling at a colored man's house.

Somebody yelled, 'We got him!' But when they all get to where the dogs are they found them all fighting over the pickings of the scrap bucket! And the robber is still free.

A black wool suit and a white poplin shirt, them's my wedding clothes. Got them from the store at Fort Gibson. I married Louisa Alberty; she was a free. Worked for Reverend Dunkin, she did, who was our preacher at the wedding. Married Mary Rogers the next time.

There was lots of children, can't remember all the names. Minnie, Linda, John, Jack, Tom, Potum, lots more than that, can't remember.

I belong to the colored Baptist church because I want a good resting place when I go; if they is such a place as Hell it don't seem like such a good resting place to me.

Holt, John A.
Age: 91
Joplin, Missouri
Interviewer: Bernard Hinkle
[S2:2 (MO): 196–98]

John A. Holt, ex-slave, and fighter of Civil War days, is still very much alive, up-to-date, and, while showing signs of his 91 years, is still mentally vigorous and alert.

Holt was born in slavery at Fayetteville, (Washington County,) Arkansas, October 16, 1847. At the time of his birth he was living with his mother at Polly Warmack's place, who owned his mother and him. John Holt, his father, was owned and lived with a family named Holt—hence his own name. His mother and father were legally united at the time, but after the War was over, they were remarried, according to a new law then put into effect regarding ex-slaves.

Life was very even and placid for John A. Holt, up until he was ten years of age, and then Mrs. Warmack, his owner, hired him out to neighboring farmers and planters, many of which were well-to-do land owners, while she, Mrs. Warmack, was not in very affluent circumstances.

Holt said: "I sure was worth m' weight in gold' those days. My slave mama use' to come over and collect five dollars in gold for my work, every month".

Mrs. Warmack's brother, one Carol Cleary was hung by the Union soldiers during the Civil War, but on that hangs an interesting tale, in which John A. Holt was an unwitting instrument.

One day, at the very beginning of the Civil War, John Holt and another Negro boy were cutting weed in a grove, near the edge of the farm, when they heard the thump, thump of many horses approaching, and presently, with a startled glance, the two badly frightened Negro boys found themselves face to face with the first contingent of Union soldiers, on their way south. It turned out to be a heavy vanguard of Union Cavalry, (which later fought at the "Battle of Cane Hill", Arkansas, southward from where Holt lived.)

Under threat of capturing all the Negro boys in the neighborhood and selling them to Cuba, to pay the war debt, the Union officers sternly questioned Holt and his companion concerning the disposition of all the older slaves, who seemed to have been spirited away—which they were. Holt said: "I was too young to know how to lie good, so I up and tells them fierce lookin' 'bluecoats' dat 'Marse Cleary' had done taken 'em all south fer pertection from dem."

Enlistment at that time was for only one year, so, one year later, when Carol Cleary, Mrs. Warmack's brother, returned from the South, the Union soldiers picked him up and hung him.

Holt tells an interesting reaction of the Union soldiers, prior to, and during the "Battle of Cane Hill", (Arkansas,) even in what, apparently, was a grave situation.

As John Holt put it: "This yer Union Calvary and Infantry was so many it took two days for them to get through our place headed for Cane Hill. After the first of the column reached Cane Hill and began fighting, (we still had hundreds on our place, drinking and eating and laughing their heads off every time they hear a boom, boom of cannon and the rattle of musketry.) They dumped every apple in our celler out on the ground and dem soldiers eat like hogs. Bee hives was turned over and men and dogs eat all our honey. Chickens heads went flying as they raided our flocks. Dey was sure a bunch of starved fighters".

Before the expiration of the Civil War, Holt, with a number of other boys, was made a member of the State Militia, and shipped to Fort Scott, Kansas.

He fought under Generals "Moonlight" and Blunt, at the "Battle of Fort Scott", in what is now known as "Price's Raid". Price, who was a Southern Confederate General, was badly defeated in this engagement. That was in 1864.

In later years, when the war was over, and the country at peace, John Holt, with his mother and father located in Joplin. For 26 years he was janitor at the old Central School, formerly where the Memorial Hall now stands. He also worked as janitor at the Lincoln School, up until his retirement several years ago.

Today he is living over the war again, but this time, peacefully. He now resides at 1109 Hill Street, with his daughter, Mrs. W. M. De Moss, who is 50 years old. His mother, Mrs. Holt "passed" some years ago, and his father, John Holt only recently passed on at the ripe old age of 103 years.

King, Susie
Age: 93
Cane Hill, Arkansas
Interviewer: Zillah Cross Peel
[M:9: pt. 4: 210–13]

Across the Town Branch, in what is dubbed "Tin-cup" lives one of the oldest ex-slaves in Washington county, "Aunt Susie" King, who was born at Cane Hill, Arkansas about 1844.

"Aunt Susie" doesn't know just how old she is, but she thinks she is over ninety, just how much she doesn't know. Perhaps the most accurate way to get near her age would be go to the county records where one can find the following bill of sale:

"State of Arkansas, County of Washington, for and in consideration of natural affection that I have for my daughter, Rebecca Rich living in the county aforesaid above mentioned, and I do hereby give and bequeath unto her one negro woman named Sally and her children namely Sam, and Fill, her lifetime thence to her children her lawful heirs forever and I do warrant and forever defend said negro girl and her children against all lawful claims whatsoever.

July, 1840	Tom Hinchea Barker.
Witness,	J. Funkhouser.
	Filed for record,
	Feb. 16, 1841.

When this bill of sale was read to "Aunt Susie" she said with great interest,

"Yes'm, yes'm that sure was my Ma and my two brothers, Sam and Fill, then come a 'nother brother, Allen, and then Jack and then I'm next then my baby sister Milly Jane. Yes'm we's come 'bout every two years.

"Yes'm, ole Missy was rich; she had lots of money, lots of lan'. Her girl, she jes' had one, married John Nunley, Mister Ab, he married Miss Ann Darnell, Mister Jack he married Miss Milly Holt, and Mister Calvin he married Miss Lacky Foster. Yes'm they lived all 'round 'bout us. Some at Rhea's Hill and some at Cane Hill," and to prove the keenness of this old slave's mind, as well as her accuracy, one need only to go to the county deed records where in 1849, Rebecca Rich deeded several 40 acres tracts of land to her sons, James, Calvin, William Jackson, and Absaolum. This same deed record gives the names of the wives of these sons just as "Aunt Susie" named them. However, Miss Lacky Foster was "Kelika Foster."

Then Aunt Susie started remembering:

"Yes'm, my mother's name was Sally. She'd belonged to Mister Tom H. Barker and he gived her to Miss Becky, his daughter. I think of them all lots of days. I know a heap of folks that some times I forgot. When the War came, we lived in a big log house. We had a loom room back of the kitchen. I had a good mother. She wove some. We all wove mos' all of the blankets and carpets and counterpanes and Old Missey she loved to sit down at the loom and weave some," with a gay chuckle Aunty Susie said, "then she'd let me weave an' Old Missey she'd say I takes her work and the loom away from her. I did love to weave, all them bright colores, blue and red and green and yellow. They made all the colors in the back yard in a big kettle, my mother, Sally did the colorin'".

"We had a heap of company. The preacher came a lot of times and when the War come Old Missey she say if we all go with her, she'd take us all to Texas. We's 'fraid of the Yankees; 'fraid they get us.

We went in wagons. Ole Missey in the carriage. We never took nothin' but a bed stead for Ole Missey. They was a great drove of we darkies. Part time we walked, part time we rode. We was on the road a long time. First place we stopped was Collins County, and stayed awhile I recollect. We had lots of horses too. Some white folks drove 'long and offered to take us away from Ole Missey but we wouldn't go. We didn't want to leave Ole Missey, she's good to us. Oh Lord, it would a nearly kilt her effen any body'd hit one of her darkies; I'd always stay in the house and took care of Ole Miss. She was pretty woman, had light hair. She was kinda punny tho, somethin' matter with her mos' all the time, headache or toothache or somethin'."

"Mister Rich went down to the river swimmin' one time I heard, and got drowned."

"Yes'm, they was good days fo' the War."

"Yes'm we stayed in Texas until Peace was made. We was then at Sherman, Texas. Peace didn't make no difference with us. We was glad to be free, and we com'd back to Arkansas with Ole Missey. We didn't want to live down there. Me and my man, Charlie King, was married after the War, and we went to live on Mister Jim Moores place. Ole Miss giv'd my ma a cow. I made my first money in Texas, workin' for a woman and she giv'd me five dollars."

"Yes'm after Peace the slaves all scattered 'bout."

"The colored folks today lak a whole heap bein' like they was fo' the War. They's good darkies, and some aint so good."

Me and my man had seven children all dead but two, Bob lives with me. I don't worry 'bout food. We ain't come no ways starvin'. I have all I want to eat. Bob he works for Missus Wade every mornin' tendin' to her flowers and afternoons works for him self. She owns this house, lets us live in it. She's good all right, good woman."

"I like flowers too, but ain't got no water, no more. Water's scarce. Someone turned off the hydrant."

"I belong to the Baptist church a long while."

"Do you know Gate-eye Fisher?" When I said "yes, I went down to talk to him last week," she said, "well, law me, Gate-eye ain't no fool. He's the best cook as ever struck a stove. He married my baby sister, Milly Jane's child. Harriet Lee Ann, she's my niece. She left him, said she'd never go back no more to him. She's somewhere over in Oklahoma."

"And did you see Doc Flowers? Yes'm, I was mos' a mother to him. One time my man and me heard a peckin' at the do'. We's eatin' supper. I went to the do' and there was Doc. He and his step-pa, Ole Uncle Ike, had a fight and Doc come to us and stayed 'bout three years. He started cryin'."

"Yes'm my Pa and Ma had belonged to Mister John Barker, before he giv'd my Ma to Miss Becky, my Pa was a leather worker. He could make shoes, and boots and slippers."

"Yes'm, Good bye. Come back again honey. Yes'm I'd like a little snuff—not the sweet kind. It makes my teeth feel better to have snuff. I ain't got much but snags, and snuff, a little mite helps them."

Smith, R. C.
Age: 96
Alderson, Oklahoma
Interviewer: Mrs. Jessie R. Ervin
8 December 1937
[OK: 397–405]

> One morning in May
> I heard a poor rebel say;
> "The federal's a home guard
> Dat called me from home...."

> I wish I was a merchant
> And I could write a fine hand,
> I'd write a love letter
> So she would understand.

I wish I had a drink of brandy
And a drink of wine,
To drink wid dat sweet gal
How I wish dat she was mine.

If I had a drink of brandy
No longer would I roam,
I'd drink it wid dat gal of mine
Dat wishes me back home.

I've heard the soldiers sing that song a heap of times. They sung it kind of lonesome like and I guess it sort of made them homesick to sing it. Us niggers learned to sing it and it is about the only one I can sing yet. I remembers the words to another one we used to sing but I've forgot the tune but the words go like this:

Old man, old man,
Your hair is getting gray,
I'd foller you ten thousand miles
To hear your banjo play.

I never was much at singing though. I guess my voice is just about wore out just like my body.

I've always had good health and I never had a doctor in my life. In the last three or four years I've had some pains from rheumatism. I think all our sickness is brought on by the kidneys and I made my own kidney medicine and allus stayed well.

I used to get a weed called hoarhound, it grows everywhere wild. I'd made a tea and drink it and it would cure the worst kind of kidney ailment. Peach tree leaves tea and sumac seed tea also were good kidney medicines. These were old Indian remedies.

My father was half Cherokee Indian. His father was bought by an Indian woman and she took him for her husband. She died and my grandfather, father and Auntie were bought by John Ross. He later bought up a lot of land claims from some Indian people named Tibets and he paid for the claims with slaves. My father was in this trade. Ross kept my grandfather till he died and he gave my auntie to one of his sisters. All of her offspring live up around Tahlequah now. My father played with Cornelius Boudinot when he was a child. Cherokee Bill was my second cousin.

My auntie hated being a slave. She had to take care of the babies on the farm while their mothers worked in the field. Sometimes she would get cranky and wouldn't speak to anybody for a week. This only made it harder for her but I guess she just couldn't help it.

My father was a big man, he weighed around 225 lbs. He had never been treated bad and it was purty hard for him to git used to being a slave. His master ordered him to be whupped and he wouldn't stand for it and he put up such a fight that they had him took to Fayetteville, Arkansas, and put in jail and held them there for sale. Didn't anybody want a big unruly ox of a nigger so he stayed in jail a long time.

Presley R. Smith was the jailer and he was kind to Pappy. They was two outlaws in jail at the same time Pappy was and one day he overheard them plotting to git out. They planned that when the jailer brought their meal to them that they would overpower him and take his keys and git out.

Sure enough when he come in that evening one of them knocked him down. No sooner than he done it my pappy waded in and took them by surprise and laid them both out. He kept them both from escaping and killing the jailer. Smith went right out and hunted up pappy's owner and give him $600 for him.

Pappy's owner was more than glad to see him as he considered him a bad old darky. Smith took him home and never from that day on did he have a bit of trouble with him. He never allowed his grown slaves to be whupped and when they went away from home he didn't write them no passes either. The patrollers didn't pay them no mind for they knowed Smith took care of his own niggers. We was all known as "Smith's free niggers."

My mother was give to Smith by his father when he married.

Our family didn't live in no quarters but we lived in one open room of the big house. The house was built in the shape of an "L." A big white house, three rooms across the front and three in the "L." We lived in the back one of the "L." The kitchen was away from the house but was joined to it by a plank walk. All around the house was big trees what we called "Heavenly trees" but the right name for them was Paradise trees. They made a heavy shade. Old Mistress had lots of purty flowers and they was a row of cedars from the gate to the house. The house was built in a rocky place and up above the house pappy built a stone wall and we had a garden on the level place along side of the wall. We called it the high place. There was enough level ground for a nice size garden. We also had a peach and apple orchard. We raised figs, too.

Master Smith always remembered about my father saving his life and he was good to him. Pappy learned the stone mason's trade and old Master let him hire out and he let him keep the money that he made.

Old Master's children went to school and they would come home and try to learn us everything they learned at school. I couldn't be still long enough to learn anything but my pappy and mammy both learned to read and write.

Old Master Smith was elected County Clerk and he held the office till the War broke out and for a while after. There wasn't much work for my pappy to do as he just looked after the garden and yard so old Master let him work at his trade as stone mason all over the country. Old Master was reasonably wealthy and very prominent. He owned a big farm but it wasn't all in cultivation. He had nine slaves besides our family and they worked the farm. Pappy took care of the yard, garden and barn and mammy done the cooking. Us children run errands, minded the flies off the table at meal-time and also minded them off Old Mistress when she took her nap. We also brought the cows or calves and as soon as we got big enough we helped mammy with the milking. None of us worked very hard except mother. I think back and I don't hardly remember ever seeing her setting down unless she was sewing or weaving. Poor thing, hard work was all she ever knowed.

My master refugeed me to Texas at the outbreak of the War. We went down in the winter and it was awful cold. We crossed the Indian Territory and the snow was two foot deep. We went out in west Texas on a ranch. The Kiowa and Comanche Indians give them a lot of trouble. They was always slipping into the country and stealing horses and cattle.

The owner of the ranch had a boy named Charley. He and I would ride, rope calves, and play around. We had good times together. His father would let us go with the boys sometimes when they went on round-ups.

One day the men started out to round up and brand the young stock and we wanted to go. Charley's father, for some reason, did not want us to go and he told us to stay at home. After they left he saddled his horse and started after them. He said that his father would let him stay with the outfit if he just caught up with them. I wouldn't go with him so he went without me. I can still see him as he turned and waved to me just before he rode out of sight. I couldn't help wishing that I could go with him but I dassent disobey the Master.

Nobody ever saw Charley again. They tracked his horse for several miles. That was easy as his horse had shoes on it. His horse was running and there was other tracks along with his that we supposed belong to a band of Kiowas or Cheyennes. They were hidden and the cowboys passed them but when Charley come by they surprised him and finally captured him. I'm sure they killed him for he would come back if he could have. I always wished I'd gone with him for they wouldn't bother a nigger but they sure had it in for white folks. I missed my friend so I could hardly stay on at the ranch. I never had no good times any more.

My Master went to Clarksville, Texas and bought a herd of cattle and I went over there and we took them to the Indian Territory around Webbers Falls in the Cherokee Nation and herded them there. I was there till the close of the war. My father and a lot more of the slaves of the neighbors around Fayetteville had slipped away and joined the northern army in Kansas. They belonged to the first and second Kansas regiment. They heard that if they would join up with the Yankees they would be set free so that's what they done.

Father died in Lawrence, Kansas at the close of the War. He and Mother never saw each other again after he enlisted. He died with pneumonia. Never got to enjoy his freedom after he fought so hard for it.

I was 17 or 18 years old when Abe Lincoln declared us free but I never got my freedom till August 4, 1866. Slaves in Texas never got their freedom till June 19, 1867 [sic].

We had an awful hard time after the War. My brother and I got a job in the Indian Territory as cowboys and we sent our money to mother when we could. She was an extra good cook and she managed to make a living for herself and my two sisters. Brother and I had a few head of stock that we sold and we bought her a house in Fayetteville and after that we got along purty well. We had a home to go to when we wanted to. I was a purty bad boy. I knowed a lot of outlaws. Knowed Belle Starr well. I never got mixed up in any of their shady dealings though. It's a wonder that I didn't though as there was plenty of it going on and I was a regular little dare-devil.

I was always so pert that it seemed like everybody wanted me to work for them. I never did have no trouble getting a job. I never had nobody that I ever worked for to turn me off.

There was an old man in Fayetteville, old Judge West, that we always sort of shunned. He and my father had a little trouble once and we supposed he would hold it agin us boys. My father's master took the job of putting a fence around the court house and grounds and he had my pappy out doing the job. Old Judge West come out and found fault with the way he was setting the posts. A nigger wasn't supposed to talk back but Pappy got back at the Judge. The old Judge got mad and said that he was going to have him whupped and he went to pappy's master and told him that he had to have him whupped publicly. Old Master wouldn't do it and for a while there was a sight of hard feelings over it.

One day after the surrender I met up with old Judge West. He asked me who my master was and I told him Presley R. Smith. He said, "Oh yes, you are one of Dave's boys." I told him that I was and he said, "He had a heap more sense than that master of his."

Jest before the War they had a heap of trouble with the Underground Railroaders. Nearly everybody lost one or two slaves. Old Judge West had a sight of vexation about that time. I remember he lost one of his men who got clean away to the north and he couldn't git him back. Another one decided he would try his hand at gitting away so he stole a horse and a suit of clothes and away he went. He got away to free territory and if the fool had had sense enough to a sold the horse they never would a done nothing about it but he strutted around with a fine horse and a fine broadcloth suit and his master told them that he'd stole the horse so they had to let him go back with his master. Judge West was purty hard on his slaves.

As I said I was a cousin to Cherokee Bill. He was a good feller when he was sober but he was hard to git along with when he was drinking. He always carried a pistol and he was a perfect shot so he was dangerous and everybody was scared to death of him. I could always handle him and git him to go home with me but I wasn't always with him.

Bill's trouble come about through ignorance. They was at a dance and several federal officers come there looking for a man. They finally got into a battle and one of the laws was killed. There was about thirty men in the battle and all was shooting to kill but Bill was known as a good shot and everybody said that ever time he shot somebody fell and they accused Bill of murder. He started scouting around first one place and then another. I still say they wouldn't a done nothing to him if he hadn't a shot that blacksmith. He went into town to have his horse shod and he didn't have the money to pay for it and the blacksmith wanted to hold the horse and Bill shot and killed him.

Bill's sweetheart lived in the neighborhood and he'd slip back once in a while to see her. Clint Scales, a colored deputy, said he would arrest him. Clint come to the girl's house and found Bill there. He never said anything to Bill about going to arrest him and they was setting there talking. Bill stooped over to get a coal of fire to light a cigarette and Clint hit him over the head with a fire stick and knocked him out and took him to jail in Fort Smith.

He might of got out of this if he hadn't shot the jailer at Fort Smith. After he had been in jail about a month his sister managed to slip a gun in to him. If he had waited till the jailer brought his supper to him and of taken the keys away from him he might of got away but he took the gun and tried to make the jailer open the door and let him out but the jailer wouldn't do it so he shot and killed him.

They hung Bill at Fort Smith and when they asked him if he had anything to say he said, "I didn't come out here to talk, I come out here to die." He was plucky to the last.

We had a lot of trouble gitting things settled after the War. I remember some excitement that we had in Arkansas over a governor's election. It caused what we called State War. I was about nineteen at the time and I was eager to enlist but they didn't need me. Baxter, a Democrat, and Brooks, Republican, was both running for governor. When the election was held there was so much fraud that you couldn't tell who was elected. Sides was drawn and they built up breastworks there on the State house grounds at Little Rock. They actually had war. The state house is right on the river and a steam boat, the Hallis, belonging to a man named Houston went to Fort Smith and come back with infantry rifles—these rifles shot a ball as big as the end of your finger and there was so many holes shot in the boat that it sunk and Houston was killed. Finally the United States militia was sent down and after about two months they settled it peaceably. Baxter was declared governor and Brooks was appointed postmaster.

I went back and forth from the Cherokee Nation to Fayetteville until my mother died. Then I married and settled there till I decided to go to Lehigh, Indian Territory and dig coal and I'd have a room full but I couldn't load one car. I was so dissatisfied that I decided to go down in the mountains by myself for a while. I went down into the McGee Mountains the other side of Atoka.

I am a prophet, yessum, the kind you read about in the Bible. I was born one. I can see and talk with hosts of people. AmHouf, a famous prophet in London, say that I was born to be a prophet but I had a poor chance. I wrote to AmHouf and kept up a correspondence with him till his death.

I wandered around in them mountains for days. I never seen a varmit, not even a wolf. One night I took a notion I'd go home. When I come to Boggy, just below Atoka, I started to walk across on a foot-log. Just as I started to step on it I heard somebody say, "Look out, you'll fall." I looked around and I couldn't see nobody. I started two or three times to cross and every time I'd hear them say, "Look out, you'll fall." I turned and went to the bridge about a quarter of a mile down the stream. I crossed and come back up to the foot-log. I could still hear people talking but I couldn't see nobody.

By this time I done got hungry so I went up to a house to try to buy something to eat. The man told me where there was a store and I went there and bought some sardines and crackers. The storekeeper told me if I could course my way through the wood that it would be a lot nearer. I went on about a mile and built a fire and camped for the night.

Next morning I started on and all of a sudden I heard a Wham. It sounded like somebody loading cross ties. Purty soon I seen about twenty-five or thirty people. One real old man and a woman in a wagon with wood on it. I walked on to meet them and the man hailed me with the Odd Fellows sign. The woman had on a gray coat and the man snatched it off her and put it on his shoulders and the woman disappeared. I walked up and tried to touch him but couldn't. Just then I realized that I had seen Father Abraham—Yessum, the one we read about in the Bible. I looked around and recognized my father and a lot more people. Some of them had just been buried but my father had been dead ever since the War. I didn't talk to them as they all disappeared.

When I got home I had a letter from AmHouf saying that he needed me. I answered his letter but another prophet answered me and told me AmHouf was dead.

I see things all the time. I'm in what they calls "firey trivets." I can foresee and foretell. Moses and the old prophets was in the firey trivets. I'm a natural born treasure hunter. I don't need no instruments to find treasure. I can walk over it at night and tell where it is located. I'm trying to raise one-hundred dollars right now to try to finance a trip for me on a treasure hunt. I know just where it is located but it will take a hundred dollars to git it out.

I ain't been able to do nothing for a month on account of the hosts that surround me. Their presence is so powerful over me that they weaken me.

Prayer and faith can overcome everything. Remember Jesus Christ was called Bellzebub but that didn't make it true.

Tuttle, Seabe
Age: 78
Richland, Arkansas
Interviewer: Zillah Cross Peel
[M:10: pt. 6: 369–71]

Seabe Tuttle, who was born in slavery in 1859, belonged to Jesse Middleton Tuttle of Richland, which was about seven miles east of Fayetteville.

"I was just a baby when the War was but I do recollect a lot of things that my ma told me about the War. Our folks all come from Tennessee. My mother was named Esther, she belonged to Old Man Tom Smith, who gave her to Miss Evaline, who was Mister Mid Tuttle's wife. The Tuttles and Smiths lived joining farms."

"You see, Mister Tuttle was a colonel in the Confederate army and when he went off with the army, he left all his slaves and stock in care of Mr. Lafe Boone. Miss Mollie and Miss Nannie, and Miss Jim and another daughter I disrecolect her name, all went in carriages and wagons down south following the Confederate army. They took my pa, Mark, and other servants, my mother's sister, Americus and Barbary. They told them they would bring them back home after the War. Then my mother and me and the other darkies, men and women and children, followed them with the cattle and horses and food. But we didn't get no further than Dardanelle when the Federals captured us and took us back to the Federal garrison at Ft. Smith, where they kept us six months. Yes'm they were good to us there. We would get our food at the com'sary. But one day my ma and my sister, Mandy, found a white man that said he would bring us back to Fayetteville. No'm, I disremember his name."

"We found us a cabin to live in here. Didn't have to pay rent then likes they do now. We lived here but after a while my mother died. They had two battles 'round here, the Battle of Prairie Grove and one was the Battle of Pea Ridge, after we comed back but no soldiers bothered us. I remember that back from where the Christian church is now, down to the Town Branch, there was a whole lot of Federal soldiers staying, they called it then Cato Branch, cause a man by the name of Cato owned all that land."

"Yes'm, I guess we had a purty good master and missus. We never did get treated much rough."

"After the War, Miss Evaline brought back all the colored people that she took with her, but my father. He got married down there and didn't come back for a long time. Then he did and died here. Two of Miss Evaline's daughters married down there. They didn't have no boys 'tall, just four girls."

"When Peace was made the slaves all scattered. We none was givin' nothin' for as I know. I worked on a farm for $13. a month and my board, for a man down at Oxford's Bend, then I went down to Van Buren where I worked as a porter in a hotel then I went to Morrilton and I married. We come back here and I worked all the time as a carpenter. I worked for Mister A. M. Byrnes. I helped build a lot of fine houses round here and I helped put a roof on the Main Bulding at the University."

"Yes'm, I own my home down by the school, I can't make much money these days. It kinda worries me. My folks all dead but three of my brothers children. One of these is blind. He lives on the old home my mother had. The county gives him a little food and a little money.

"Yes'm, my white folks were all good to us. Purty good to us.

"After Peace was made though, we all jes' scattered, somehow.

Woodruff County

Boone, J. F.
Age: 66
1502 Izard
Little Rock, Arkansas
Interviewer: Samuel S. Taylor
[M:8: pt. 1: 210–13]

"My father's name was Arthur Boone and my mother's name was Eliza Boone. I am goin' to tell you about my father. Now be sure you put down there that this is Arthur Boone's son. I am J. F. Boone, and I am goin' to tell you about my father, Arthur Boone.

"My father's old master was Henry Boone. My mother came from Virginia—north Virginia—and my father came from North Carolina. The Boones bought them. I have heard that my father, Arthur Boone, was bought by the Boones. They wasn't his first masters. I have heard my father say that it was more than a thousand dollars they paid for him.

"He said that they used to put up niggers on the block and auction them off. They auctioned off niggers accordin' to the breed of them. Like they auction off dogs and horses. The better the breed, the more they'd pay. My father was in the first-class rating as a good heathy Negro and those kind sold for good money. I have heard him say that niggers sometimes brought as high as five thousand dollars.

"My father don't know much about his first boss man. But the Boones were very good to them. They got biscuits once a week. The overseer was pretty cruel to them in a way. My father has seen them whipped till they couldn't stand up and then salt and things that hurt poured in their wounds. My father said that he seen that done; I don't know whether it was his boss man or the overseer that done it.

"My father said that they breeded good niggers—stud 'em like horses and cattle. Good healthy man and woman that would breed fast, they would keep stalled up. Wouldn't let them get out and work. Keep them to raise young niggers from. I don't know for certain that my father was used that way or not. I don't suppose he would have told me that, but he was a mighty fine man and sold for a lot of money. The slaves weren't to blame for that.

"My father said that in about two or three months after the War ended, his young master told them that they were free. They came home from the

War about that time. He told them that they could continue living on with them or that they could go to some one else if they wanted to 'cause they were free and there wasn't any more slavery.

"I was born after slavery. Peace was declared in 1865, wasn't it? When the War ended I don't know where my father was living, but I was bred and born in Woodruff near Augusta in Arkansas. All the Booneses were there when I knew anything about it. They owned hundreds and hundreds of acres of ground. I was born on old Captain Boone's farm.

"My father was always a farmer. He farmed till he died. They were supposed to give him a pension, but he never did get it. They wrote to us once or twice and asked for his number and things like that, but they never did do nothing. You see he fit in the Civil War. Wait a minute. We had his old gun for years. My oldest brother had that gun. He kept that gun and them old blue uniforms with big brass buttons. My old master had a horn he blowed to call the slaves with, and my brother had that too. He kept them things as particular as you would keep victuals.

"Yes, my father fit in the Civil War. I have seen his war clothes as many times as you have hairs on your head I reckon. He had his old sword and all. They had a hard battle down in Mississippi once he told me. Our house got burnt up and we lost his honorable discharge. But he was legally discharged. But he didn't git nothin' for it, and we didn't neither.

"My father was whipped by the pateroles several times. They run him and whipped him. My daddy slipped out many a time. But they never caught him when he slipped out. They never whipped him for slippin' out. That was during the time he was a slave. The slaves wasn't allowed to go from one master to another without a pass. My father said that sometimes, his young master would play a joke on him. My father couldn't read. His young master would give him a pass and the pass would say, 'Whip Arthur Boone's — and pass him out. When he comes back, whip his — again and pass him back.' His young master called hisself playin' a joke on him. They wouldn't hit him more than half a dozen licks, but they would make him take his pants down and they would give them to him jus' where the pass said. They wouldn't hurt him much. It was more devilment than anything else. He would say, 'Whut you hittin' me for when I got a pass?' and they would say, 'Yes, you got a pass, but it says whip your —.' And they would show it to him, and then they would say, 'You'll git the res' when you come back.' My father couldn't read nothin' else, but that's one word he learnt to read right well.

"My father was quite a young man in his day. He died in 1891. He was just fifty-six years old. I'm older now than he was when he died. My occupation when I was well was janitor. I have been sick now for three years and ain't done nothin' in all that time. If it wasn't for my wife, I don't know whut I would do.

"I was born in 1872, on December the eighth, and I am sixty-six years old now. That is, I will be if the Lord lets me live till December the eighth, this year.

"Now whose story are you saying this is? You say this is the story of Arthur Boone, father of J. F. Boone? Well, that's all right; but you better mention that J. F. Boone is Arthur Boone's son. I rent this house from Mr. Lindeman. He has the drug store right there. If anybody comes lookin' for me, I might be moved, but Mr. Lindeman will still be there."

Interviewer's Comment

If you have read this interview hastily and have missed the patroller joke on page three, turn back and read it now. The interviewer considers it the choicest thing in the story.

That and the story of an unpensioned Union veteran and the insistence on the word "son" seemed to me to set this story off as a little out of the ordinary.

Howell, Josephine
Age: 72
Brinkley, Arkansas
Interviewer: Irene Robertson
[M:9: pt. 3: 339–40]

"My mother was Rebecca Jones. She was born in Nashville, Tennessee. Grandma was a cook and a breeding woman. The Jones thought she was very valuable. They prized her high. She was the mother of twenty-one children. Mother was more than half Indian. She was bright color. The Jones wanted to keep her, thought she would be a fine cook and house woman and a fine breeder. She had such a terrible temper they sold her to McAlways, some of their relations close to Augusta, Arkansas.

"Mama said she was eight years old when Gabe McAlway come to Nashville, Tennessee and got her. He bought her. He was a young man and a saloon-keeper at Augusta, Arkansas. He put her out on the farm at his father's. She was a field hand. She was part African and a whole lot Indian. She was fractious and high tempered. The old man McAlway and the overseers would drop her clothes down in the field before all the hands and whoop her. Gabe never even slapped her. His aunt Mrs. Jones didn't want them to put her in the field. She wanted to keep her but couldn't she was so fractious, and she didn't know how bad old man treated her.

"When mother was sold she was brought from twenty brothers and her mother and never saw none of them no more. She left them at Wolf River. They took the boat. Wolf River is close to Memphis. They must have brought them that far but I don't know. This is what all she told me minua and minua time. Her own papa bought her when she was eight years old, Gabe McAlway. When she got to be a young maid he forced motherhood up on her. I was born before freedom. How old I am I don't know. Gabe McAlway was sort of a young bachelor. He got killed in the Civil War. He was a Scotch-Irishman. I never seen my father.

"Mother married then and had five children. She lived in the back yard of Mrs. Will Thompson. Dr. Goodridge stopped her from having children, she raved wild. She had such a bad fractious temper. She suckled both Mrs. Will Thompson's children, old man Nathan McGreggor's grandchildren. She lived in Mrs. Thompson's back yard but she slept in their house to help with the babies.

"Judge Milwee's wife and auntie, Mrs. Baxter, raised me from a baby (infant). Judge Milwee was in Brinkley but he moved to Little Rock. Them is my own dear white folks. Honey, I can't help but love them, they part of me. They raised me. They learned me how to do everything.

"My son live with me and I raising my little great-grandson. We can't throw him away. My baby's mother is way off in St. Louis. He is three years old.

"Mother never talked much about slavery other than I have told you. She said during of the War women split and sawed rails and laid fences all winter like men. Food got scarce. They sent milk to the soldiers. Meat was scarce. After she was free she went on like she had been living at John McAlway's. She said she didn't know how to start doing for herself.

"Some of our young generation is all right and some of them is too thoughtless. Times is too fast. Folks is shortening their days by fast living. Hurting their own bodies. Forty years ago folks lived like we ought to be living now."

Yell County

Hatchett, Matilda
Age: 99
424 W. Twenty-fifth Street
North Little Rock, Arkansas
Interviewer: Samuel S. Taylor
[M:9: pt. 3: 195–201]

"I was born right here in Arkansas about nine miles from Dardanelles (Dardanelle) in Sevier County. I think it's Sevier. No, it was Yell County. Yell County, that's it. You put the Dardanelles there and if they get that they'll get the Yell part. Can't miss Yell if you get Dardanelles.

"I wish I could get holt of some of my old white folks. Maybe you can find 'em for me. There's one big policeman here looks like them but I don't know whether he is or not. The first white owners that I knowed was Jackie George in South Carolina. That is where I heard them talkin' about him comin' from. I wasn't born there; I was born here. I wasn't born when he come from South Carolina. His wife was named Nealie. He was just like a ole shoe. Never whipped me but one time in my life.

"I'll tell you about it. This is what they whipped me for. Me and my brother, Sam, had to water the horses. I didn't have to go with Sam, but I was big enough to do that. We had one old horse named John—big old horse. I would have to git up on a ten-rail fence to git on him. One day I was leading ole John back and I got tired of walking. So when I come to a ten-rail fence, I got up on ole John. I got up on 'im backwards and I didn't have hold of no bridle nor nothin' because I was lookin' at his tail.

"The others got back there before they did. Ole master said to them, 'Where's Tilly?'

"They said to him, 'She's comin', leadin' ole John.'

"Atter a while they saw me comin', an' one of 'em said, 'There's Tillie now.'

"An' 'nother one, 'Man, she's sittin' on the horse backwards.' And old John was amblin' along nippin' the grass now an' then with his bridle draggin' and me sittin' up on his back facin' his tail and slippin' and slidin' with every step.

"Ole John was gentle. But they were scairt he would throw me off. Ole missis come out the gate and met him herself, 'cause she was 'fraid the others would 'cite him and make him throw me down. She gentled him and led him up to ole master. They was careful and gentle till they got me off that horse, and then ole master turned and lit into me and give me a brushin'.

"That's the only whippin' he ever give me. But that didn't do me no good. Leastwise, it didn't stop me from ridin' horses. I rode ole John ever chance I could git. But I didn't ride him backwards no more.

Dresses

"We used to wear homespun dresses. I have spun a many a yard and wove it. Did you ever see a loom? I used to have a wheel, and my children tore it up some way or 'nother. I still have the cards. We done our own knittin' and spun our own thread and knitted our socks and stockings.

Houses

"The white folks lived in pretty good houses and we did too. They lived in big log houses. The white folks' houses had piazzas between the rooms. Thad Haney didn't build them houses. His daddy, Tim Haney, built 'em. The Haneys come in by Tim bein' Thad's father. Thad married Jackie George's daughter—Louisa George. George was her daddy and Haney was her husband.

"There were four rooms besides the piazza. On one side, there was a big room built out of lumber. On the other side, there was a big room that a doctor lived in. There was a great big kitchen west of the piazza. The kitchen was about fifteen by fifteen. I know it was that large because we'd all eat at the same time. The old man, Tim, owned about thirty niggers. After he died they were all divided out among the boys. Every boy took his part of the land and his part of the niggers. But I wasn't at his house then. I was livin' with ole Jackie George. The white folks hadn't moved together then.

"But I went to old Tim Haney's funeral. The old white woman fainted and they rubbed her with camphor and stuff and had her layin' out there. I wasn't old enough to cry over him and wouldn't anyhow because I didn't care nothin' much about him. But I would have cried for my ole master though, because I really loved him.

Soldiers

"I saw the soldiers when they come through our place. The first start of us noticin' them was this. I was always up to the white folks' house. Thad was goin' back to the Rebel army. Ole master tole my dad to go git 'im a hat. He'd got 'im one and was ridin' back with Thad's hat on top of his'n. Before he could git back, here come a man jus' a ridin'.

"Thad was eatin'. He look out, and then he throwed his head back and said, 'Them's the Federals.'

"Thad finished his breakfast and then he ran on out and got with the Federals. He didn't join 'em. He jus' fooled 'em. The bridge was half a mile from our house and the Yankee army hadn't near finished crossing it when the head of it reached us.

"While they were at the house, pa came ridin' up with the two hats on his head. They took the hats and threw pa's on the ground and tried Thad's on. They took the mare but they give it back.

"Them folks stood 'round there all day. Killed hogs and cooked them. Killed cows and cooked them. Took all kinds of sugar and preserves and things like that. Tore all the feathers out of the mattress looking for money. Then they put old miss (Nealie Haney) and her daughter (Louisa Haney) in the kitchen to cookin'.

"Ma got scairt and went to bed. Dreckly the lieutenant come on down there and said, 'Auntie, get up from there. We ain't a goin' to do you no hurt. We're after helpin' you. We are freein' you. Aunt Dinah, you can do as you please now. You're free.'

. "She was free!

"They stayed 'round there all night cooking and eatin' and carryin' on. They sent some of the meat in there to us colored folks.

"Next mornin' they all dropped off goin' down to take Dardanelles. You could hear the cannons roarin' next day. They was all night gettin' away. They went on and took Dardanelles. Had all them white folks runnin' and hidin'.

"The Secesh wouldn't go far. They would just hide. One night there'd be a gang of Secesh, and the next one, there'd come along a gang of Yankees. Pa was 'fraid of both of 'em. Secesh said they'd kill 'im if he left his white folks. Yankees said they'd kill 'im if he didn't leave 'em. He would hide out in the cotton patch and keep we children out there with him. Ole mis' made him carry us.

"We was freed and went to a place that was full of people. We had to stay in a church with about twenty other people and two of the babies died there on account of the exposure. Two of my aunts died, too, on account of exposure then.

"The soldiers didn't take anything that night but food. They left all the horses. What they took was what they could eat. But they couldn't catch the turkeys. The lieutenant stayed around all the time to make the soldiers behave themselves. The meals he made my old mis' and her daughter cook was for the officers.

"Yes Lawd! I have been here so long I ain't forgot nothin'. I can remember things way back. I can remember things happening when I was four years old. Things that happen now I can't remember so well. But I can remember things that happened way back yonder.

Schooling

"I learnt to read a little after peace was declared. A ole lady, Aunt Sarah Nunly, learnt us how to spell and then after that we went to school. I went to school three weeks. I never went to school much.

"Didn't git no chance to learn nothin' in slavery. Sometimes the children would teach the darkies 'round the house their ABC's. I've heard of folks teachin' their slaves to read the Bible. They didn't teach us to read nothin. I've heard of it, but I've never seen it, that some folks would cut off the first finger of a nigger that could write.

Father's Children Freed before Emancipation

"My father had some children that were set free. They lived down on the river bottom. Their ole master was named ole Crow. He died and sot his niggers free. He had four slaves. He had five. If any of you know Philo Pointer, his father was one of 'em. They set him free. His daughter—Crow's daughter—wanted the niggers and they would break the ole man's will. They furnished them a wagon and set them free. They came by my father's place and he killed his hog and fed them and they put the rest of it in the wagon and went on to the free state. I've got an old piece of a dish them boys give my mama. It's done broke up to a piece now, but I saves that.

"Patsy Crow was the name of the girl that was freed, and one of the boys was named Joe Crow, and the others I don't know what it was. I guess it was Jim. Their old master had left a will givin' them the wagon and team because he knew it wouldn't be possible for them to stay there after he died. He said he didn't want his niggers to be under anybody after he died. Wills was wills in them days. His daughter wanted them niggers, but they didn't give them to her. They sot them free and sont them off.

Wants to See Her People

"I nursed three children for Thad Haney and Lousia, his wife. Them girls' names was: the oldest was Julia; the next one was named Emma; and the youngest one was named Virginia. If I can find them and see them again, I'll be so happy. I jus' want to meet them one more time—some of them—all of them if they're livin'; but I know they can't all be living.

"Matilda Haney was my name then, and I nursed Thad's children in slavery time.

Age

"I think I'm between ninety-seven and ninety-eight years old. They had an old-age contest in Reverend Smith's time. They had Reverend Coffee and another man here since Reverend Smith. The pastor we have now is Yates. Our church is Lee Chapel A. M. E. Church. The contest was in 1935 I think and the people all agreed that I was the oldest colored woman in North Little Rock. They said I was ninety-six years old then. That would make me about ninety-eight years old now. But I saw my children afterwards and they said I was a year older. I used to have my age in the Family Bible and my husband's too, but it got burnt up. Accordin' to them I oughta be about ninety-nine or a hundred.

Occupation

"My folks didn't raise no cotton. They raised about two bales a year. Didn't have nobody to raise it. Thirty slaves were not enough for that. And they didn't care nothin' about it nohow. They had forty-six acres of land in wheat and lots in corn and potatoes. They raised cows, hogs, horses, turkeys, chickens, and everything else. Even had peafowls. The geese used to run me 'round many a day.

"They ran a cotton gin and my father managed it. That was his job all the time before the War.

"After the War, my father farmed. He worked on shares. They never cheated him that he knew about. If they did, he didn't know it. He owned his horses and cows."

Appendix: Interviewers and Their Informants

Allen, Willie
  Claridy
Anderson, Pernella M.
  Ames, Armstrong, Johnson (Willie), Tatum
Angermiller, Mrs. Florence
  Johnson (Harry)
Ball, Mrs. V. M.
  Cummins
Bowden, Mrs. Bernice
  Arbery, Benford, Benson, Burkes, Coleman (Betty), Davis
  (Charlie), Dockery, Hardridge, Harris, Hart, Haskell, Haynes, Hill,
  Hinton, Jones (Cyntha), Jones (John), Jones (Nannie), Mann,
  McClendon, Meeks, Mitchell, Moore, Norris, Osbrook, Page,
  Parker (Fannie), Perry, Rassberry, Rhone, Ricks, Sexton, Stanford,
  Thomas (Mandy), Thomas (Tanner), Tillman, Tucker, Warrior,
  Washington, Williams (J. B.), Word, Young (John)
Cowan, Effie
  Densen, Simpson
Darsey, Barbara
  Kinsey
Davis, Mrs. Ada
  Pollard
Dulaney, Ethel C.
  Newton (George)
Edwards, Mrs. Blanche
  Waddell
Ervin, Mrs. Jessie R.
  Smith (R. C.), Strayhorn

Ervin, William V.
    Overton
Foote, E. Jean
    Williams (Belle)
Garrison, Ethel Wolfe
    Barber, Harshaw, Kye, Ray, Ross, Starr, Thompson (Victoria),
    Wagoner
Gauthier, Sheldon F.
    Buttler, Douglas, Young (Louis)
Graham, Mrs. Carol
    Culp, Sims, Smith (Caroline), Williams (Charley)
Hagg, Beulah Sherwood
    Blackwell, Stephens, White (Julia)
Hampton, Alex
    Jameson, Winn
Hatcher, Letha K.
    Williams (Horatio)
Hinkle, Bernard
    Holt
Hudgins, Mary D.
    Baker, Fergusson, Golden, Logan, Parker (Judy)
Lackey, Robert Vinson
    Rowe
LaCotts, Mrs. Annie L.
    Miller (Matilda), Payne
Liberato, Mary E.
    Winston
Livingston, L. P.
    Williams (Hulda)
Lucy, Thomas Elmore
    Little, Russell, Scott
McKinney, Watt
    Davis (Jeff), Gill, Turner, Wilborn
Menn, Alfred E.
    Coleman (Betty R.), Elgin, Thomas (Rebecca)
Miles, J. Tom
    Allen
Miller, Sallie C.
    Lee, Myhand, Newton (Pete), Rye

Peel, Mrs. Zillah Cross
>Aunt Adeline, King, Tuttle

Robertson, Irene
>Allinson, Braddox, Brown (Peter), Burgess, Charleston, Chase, Cotton, Darrow, Davis (Rosetta), Finley, Howell, Hudgens, Keaton, Lambert, Martin, Miller (Nathan), Myers, Roberts, Scroggins, Stiggers, Taylor (Lula), Vaden, Van Buren, Wells, Wesmoland, White (Lucy)

Sample, Velma
>Brown (Casie)

Smith, William E.
>Bates

Taylor, R. S.
>Baltimore

Taylor, Samuel S.
>Anderson, Badgett, Bailey, Bertrand, Blake, Boone, Briles, Brown (Betty), Crane, Dortch, Dothrum, Hatchett, Jeffries, Johnson (Ella), Jones (Evelyn), Junell, Kerns, Lucas, Pattillo, Peters, Robinson, Shelton, Sloan, Smith (J. L.), Stewart, Taylor (Anthony), Thomas (Omelia), Thompson (Ellen), Weathers, White (Julia), Williams (Columbus)

Unknown
>Bean, Bond, Brown (Betty), Green, Osborne, Quinn, Rains

White, Grace E.
>Chambers

Index: Alphabetical by Name of Informant

Name (County)

Allen, Hannah (Randolph), 352
Allison, Lucindy (Cross), 71
Ames, Josephine (Union), 358
Anderson, R. B. (Pulaski), 314
Arbery, Katie (Union), 358
Armstrong, Cora (Union), 361

Badgett, J. S. (Dallas), 90
Bailey, Jeff (Drew), 113
Baker, James (Hot Spring), 156
Baltimore, William (Jefferson), 181
Barber, Mollie (Phillips), 260
Bates, John (Pulaski), 315
Bean, Joe (Washington), 381
Benford, Bob (Union), 362
Benson, George (Jefferson), 184
Bertrand, James (Jefferson), 185
Blackwell, Boston (Jefferson), 186
Blake, Henry (Pulaski), 320
[Blakely] Aunt Adeline (Washington), 378
Bond, Scott (Cross), 72
Boone, J. F. (Woodruff), 397
Braddox, George (Prairie), 304
Briles, Frank (Arkansas—General), 1
Brown, Betty (Greene), 128
Brown, Casie Jones (Greene), 131
Brown, Peter (Phillips), 262
Brown, William (Cross), 86
Burgess, Jeff (Monroe), 243

General Index